*Images of English
Puritanism*

Images of English Puritanism

A Collection of Contemporary Sources 1589–1646

Edited, with an Introduction and

Prefatory Notes, by

Lawrence A. Sasek

Louisiana State University Press

Baton Rouge and

London

98 97 96 95 94 93 92 91 90 89   5 4 3 2 1

First Printing

Designer: Barbara Werden

Typeface: Linotron Garamond No. 3

Typesetter: G & S Typesetters, Inc.

Printer: Thomson-Shore, Inc.

Binder: John H. Dekker & Sons, Inc.

Library of Congress Cataloging-in-Publication Data

Images of English puritanism : a collection of contemporary sources,
1589–1646 / edited, with an introduction and prefatory notes, by
Lawrence A. Sasek.

p.   cm.

Includes index.

ISBN 0-8071-1528-2 (alk. paper)

1. Puritans—England—History—16th century—Sources.
2. Puritans—England—History—17th century—Sources. 3. Puritans—
England—Controversial literature—History—17th century—Sources.
4. England—Church history—16th century—Sources. 5. England—
Church history—17th century—Sources. I. Sasek, Lawrence A.

BX9331.I53 1989

285'.9'0942—dc19   89-30160
                                                                CIP

For Gloria

Maria Marry, sir, sometimes he is a kind of Puritan.

Sir Andrew Oh, if I thought that, I'd beat him like a dog!

Sir Toby What, for being a Puritan? Thy exquisite reason, dear knight?

Sir Andrew I have no exquisite reason for't, but I have reason good enough.

Maria The devil a Puritan that he is, or anything constantly, but a timepleaser; . . .

WILLIAM SHAKESPEARE
Twelfth Night

The painting of a *Puritane* is so hard and difficult, as that the joynt skill of *Apelles, Pyrgoteles, Praxiteles,* and of al the cunning Painters in Saint *Chrysostoms* time, will scarse reach this object.

OLIVER ORMEROD
The Picture of a Puritane

If the confused misapplication of this foule word Puritan be not reformed in England, and that with speed, we can expect nothing but a suddaine universall downfall of all goodnesse whatsoever.

HENRY PARKER
A Discourse Concerning Puritans

Contents

Contents

Part II   *Negative Portrayals of Puritanism*

Contents

Part III   *A Focal Document*

Preface

and

Acknowledgments

THIS project stems from my study and teaching of English literature of the Renaissance. In working with John Milton, especially, I found myself reading in some studies of his puritanism and in others denials, often vehement, that he was in any valid sense a puritan. It seemed to me desirable to find some texts that would help to clarify and place in context a definition of puritanism, or failing that, to point out the complexity of the subject. It occurred to me that a collection of passages and tracts, on the models of Stuart E. Prall (ed.), *The English Revolution* (London, 1968); Everett H. Emerson, *English Puritanism from John Hooper to John Milton* (Durham, N.C., 1968); H. C. Porter, *Puritanism in Tudor England* (Columbia, S.C., 1971); and Leonard J. Trinterud (ed.), *Elizabethan Puritanism* (New York, 1971), might prove generally useful to students of the period. The collection by Alan Heimert and Andrew Delbanco, *The Puritans in America* (Cambridge, Mass., 1985), appeared when my editorial work was nearly finished but provided encouragement. To these scholars I owe much for information about the puritans and for the models of scholarship they exemplified. Of course, my collection is more narrowly focused than theirs.

I must thank also the staffs of the Houghton Library of Harvard University, the library of the British Museum (the British Library), the Huntington Library, and the Louisiana State University Library for having preserved and made available early seventeenth-century texts—so many of which seemed in their own time ephemeral in nature—as well as for the courtesy and help these people extended me in my efforts to find works relevant to my project.

Of the tracts and excerpts printed here, I have used as a basis the copies in the Houghton Library of Harvard University for numbers 1, 3, 5–11, and 15–26. To the British Library I owe thanks for numbers 2, 4, 12–14, 27, and 28. Number 29 has been taken from a copy in the Hill Memorial Library at Louisiana State University. In addition, the texts of numbers 1, 2, 3, 6, 15, 17, 19, 22, 23, and 26 have been checked against the copies in the Huntington Library.

Also, I must acknowledge a considerable debt to the anonymous reviewers who read my text for the Louisiana State University Press for their thoughtful criticism and suggestions. And finally, I want to thank the numerous scholars whose research in puritanism has proved invaluable to all students of the culture of the early seventeenth century in England. Some of them are named in the Introduction and notes; I regret that limitations of time and space do not allow me to give due credit to all.

Images of English

Puritanism

Introduction

THE terms *puritan* and *puritanism* pose great and possibly unique difficulties for modern scholarship. No other terms, at least none designating literary, social, and generally cultural movements of the past, are at the same time so widely used, so necessary, and so hard to define to the satisfaction of anyone, even of the scholars most interested in the movement the terms designate. Christopher Hill has called the terms, as generally used, "an admirable refuge from clarity of thought."[1] Harry Grant Plum has noted, almost wistfully, that "it would be a great service to the general reader if scholars could find a definition to which all would adhere."[2] Nearly everyone agrees that there were puritans and that there was a puritan movement in England between 1560 and at least 1640, but just who were puritans and who were not, or what tenets or practices were central to the movement, seems impossible to determine with any precision.

One specific exception to the problem of definition only complicates the general difficulties in the long run. General agreement seems to exist

1   Christopher Hill, *Society and Puritanism in Pre-Revolutionary England* (2d ed.; New York, 1967), 13. Hill's first chapter has been widely influential. David Zaret, in *The Heavenly Contract: Ideology and Organization in Pre-Revolutionary Puritanism* (Chicago, 1985), refers to Hill's discussion and affirms that he follows Hill's "widely accepted definition of Puritans: those who sought a more evangelical and Protestant style of worship than that offered by the Church of England but who rejected outright separation from the church before the Civil War"; see p. 19. Margot Heinemann, in *Puritanism and Theatre: Thomas Middleton and Opposition Drama Under the Early Stuarts* (Cambridge, 1980), uses a fairly broad definition, as is indicated in a subsection heading, "Parliamentary Puritanism as a Broad Movement" (pp. 22–26), and as befits her subject. Heinemann also acknowledges a debt to Christopher Hill in dealing with the problem of definition; see p. 22n12.

2   Harry Grant Plum, *Restoration Puritanism: A Study of the Growth of English Liberty* (Chapel Hill, N.C., 1943), 3.

concerning New England puritanism. As Basil Hall has aptly said, puritanism "suffered an Atlantic sea-change" when the Pilgrims came to America.[3] A small and relatively homogeneous group, the American puritans were isolated geographically and developed a distinct culture. American literary history, for instance, takes cognizance of puritan poetry, whereas in England puritan verse has not achieved recognition, either for literary merit or as a distinct poetic mode.[4] American puritanism, then, can simply be defined as the religion and culture of the dominant group among the New England settlers and this group's descendants for a few generations. But if this definition arrived at inductively by study of this compact group is applied to the cultural scene in England, it begins to fray at the edges and melt away in its center. The American puritans were Calvinists in theology, and so were the English puritans, but so likewise were most of the opponents of English puritanism during all but the last years of the movement. The American puritans were not presbyterians, whereas at one time most of the vocal English puritans were, and the presbyterian church organization always had a strong following among them. The term *puritan* is useful in studies of America well into the eighteenth century, whereas in studies of England it becomes more often a retrospective than a contemporary designation after the early 1640s. The most that can be achieved from such comparisons, it seems, is a negative result: the conviction that the American puritans should be studied separately and perhaps ignored in any attempts to define English puritanism.

The terms *puritan* and *puritanism* differ in another, and interesting, way from most designations of political, social, religious, and cultural movements; they are now generally honorific when applied retrospectively and dyslogistic when applied currently. Very few persons will boast, or have ever boasted, of being puritans, yet many take pride in having descended from the puritans or in being of the stock of the puritans. In other words, a person who will not confess that he is a puritan may at the same time assert proudly that his grandfather was one. In New England there are Puritan restaurants, Puritan hotels, and Puritan manufacturing labels—patriotic nostalgia is commercially viable. But even there, and much more so elsewhere, *puritan* as a personal, current designation is equated with *pu-*

3 Basil Hall, "Puritanism: The Problem of Definition," *Studies in Church History,* II (1965), 294.
4 See for example, Robert Daly, *God's Altar: The World and the Flesh in Puritan Poetry* (Berkeley, 1978).

ritanical, an adjective operative in the moral, not the religious, realm and used to condemn someone who seems to oppose all pleasure not only for himself but also, and most vehemently, for others. *Puritan* connotes ostentatious virtue, rigor, and self-righteousness, with a strong suspicion of hypocrisy. In short, the term carries the unfavorable connotations it had when it entered the language and during the time when it was frequently applied to contemporaries.

The word *puritan,* though derived from *pure,* entered the English vocabulary as a term of denunciation. The first appearance recorded in the *Oxford English Dictionary* is a work by John Stow with the date 1567 (1564 would be more likely). Stow refers, with some historical inaccuracy, to "congregations of the Anabaptists in London, who called themselves Puritans." Since Anabaptists were considered perhaps the most dangerous of contemporary heretics, with a creed and way of life disruptive of the social and political order, Stow's reference gives a wholly unfavorable meaning to the word. *Puritanism* had a no more auspicious arrival; the earliest *OED* entry is dated 1572, when Gabriel Harvey equated it with "precisianism" while denying that he felt any sympathy for it. These first connotations have survived throughout history; they are entirely consistent with Samuel Johnson's definition of the puritan as "a sectary pretending to eminent purity of religion" and with pejorative uses of the term today.

Anglican, now frequently used as the antithesis of *puritan* in historical studies, provides an instructive contrast. The word itself goes back to the Middle Ages as a synonym for *English* and was therefore honorific. In its present religious meaning, *Anglican* first appears in the *OED* in a citation from Edmund Burke with the date 1797; *Anglicanism* dates only from 1846. The original meaning of *Anglican* has fallen out of use, and today, as throughout their history as religious terms, *Anglican* and *Anglicanism* have relatively clear denotations. Also, their present religious meanings can be read back into the past, causing no confusion. Finally, their connotations are relatively neutral; we can describe another as an Anglican or a non-Anglican with equal insouciance.

By contrast, *puritan* must bear a heavy load of connotations upon its very shaky, ill-constructed denotative foundations. Generally the connotations were unfavorable during the sixteenth and seventeenth centuries. In the eighteenth and early nineteenth centuries, a sort of balance was reached, and Samuel Johnson's caustic definition had to contend with Daniel Neal's eulogistic *History of the Puritans; or Protestant Nonconformists,* published beginning in 1732 and reprinted several times in the ensuing hundred years. During the nineteenth century, veneration of the early puritans grew. For example, J. R. Green's *Short History of the English People* (1874) presented to the general public in the later nineteenth and early twentieth centuries an equation of puritanism with most of what was valued in English life and culture. For Green and for many others, the puritans were the source of moral goodness and religious piety both in the past and for the present. Twentieth-century scholars have thus inherited the term *puritan* with its most favorable connotations, as well as with its widest and most vague definition.

In his essay "Puritanism: The Problem of Definition," Basil Hall focuses upon the writings of A. S. P. Woodhouse, G. M. Trevelyan, and Christopher Hill, concluding his examination of their handling of puritanism with a quotation from G. Kitson Clark: "Though Puritanism plays a very important part in the development of the English heritage it is extremely difficult to give a precise meaning to the word itself. . . . It is applied to a very large number of different people and it is difficult to find a common denominator." Looking at the "historiography" of the movement, Hall finds that "the word Puritan suffers from inflation" and that "it ceases to define" because of the range and variety of religious and political beliefs it has come to include. Furthermore, he sees no ultimate solution to the "problem of definition," noting that words, unlike currency, cannot be deflated. Yet he thinks it worthwhile to make scholars aware that the word carried a more limited meaning among those who applied it contemporaneously—that if its application to American colonists did not make the effort hopeless, it could be limited to "reluctant and imperfectly conforming Anglicans." Hall concludes by suggesting a more precise study of the theology of the movement and also of puritan concern with casuistry.[5]

A somewhat different, but ultimately not contradictory, approach is taken by Charles and Katherine George. Like Hall, they find the word

---

5 Hall, "Puritanism: The Problem of Definition," 283–96. Clark is quoted on p. 286; see G. Kitson Clark, *The English Inheritance* (London, 1950), 103. J. T. Cliffe, in *The Puritan Gentry: The Great Puritan Families of Early Stuart England* (London, 1984), recounts the problem of definition (pp. 4–6) and generally uses a broad definition; he cites both Christopher Hill and Charles and Katherine George (p. 241). John Morgan, in *Godly Learning: Puritan Attitudes Towards Reason, Learning, and Education, 1560–1640* (Cambridge, 1986), gives an entire chapter to exploring the complexities of Hall's "Problem of Definition" (pp. 9–22); Morgan excludes the separatists from his working definition, noting that "most historians now seem willing to omit the separatists from any definition of 'puritan'"; see p. 10.

puritan essentially meaningless as now used, but they argue more strongly than Hall that contemporary use was also imprecise. They can make no "list of 'puritans' on any doctrinal basis," and they note that they "have discovered no other set of adequately-defining elements." They consider it necessary to write of puritans but warn their readers that they will be using two meanings, one for each of two different groups: early clergymen and modern scholars.[6] As clearly as from Hall's study, there emerges from their discussion the conviction that the word *puritan* is regrettably imprecise but nonetheless unavoidable and perhaps indispensable.

In view of the problem of definition and the arguments that modern scholars should be aware of *puritan* and *puritanism* as terms once applied to contemporaries, as well as be aware of the fact that contemporary usage differed from modern usage, it seems worthwhile to present to those interested in Elizabethan and early seventeenth-century England a collection of documents from that time that deal at some length with definitions, especially documents written by those to whom the terms were applied. Even if the various defenses and explanations do not perfectly clarify or establish a neatly circumscribed meaning, they should at least enlighten by showing the various ways in which the terms were used and the various contexts in which they appeared. By way of further introduction, it seems useful to look at a few explicit modern definitions and to formulate a few generalizations concerning sixteenth- and early seventeenth-century definitions.

The problem of definition faces everyone writing about the history or culture of England between 1560 and 1640. The words *puritan* and *puritanism* appear frequently in works of the time and are solidly entrenched in modern scholarship. Inevitably the modern scholar finds himself writing about puritans with an uneasy feeling that his understanding of his key terms will not coincide with the interpretations given them by his audience, that his readers may be led to think of persons and ideas not relevant to his intentions. Many scholars try to solve the problem by stipulating a definition, and inevitably many thereby run into other difficulties. As may be expected, the stipulated definition given at the beginning of a work does

6 Charles H. George and Katherine George, *The Protestant Mind of the English Reformation, 1570–1640* (Princeton, 1961), 7–8.

not always prove to be identical with the working definition that emerges, explicitly or implicitly, at the end. We may legitimately argue that perfection, or even exactness, must not be sought in such matters of terminology; that to seek it is to court pedantry; and that enough has been achieved if a definition provides a starting point for an informative study, as it generally does. Unfortunately readers often carry a definition that has served well in one study into others where it fits poorly. At the least, the reader must be warned of the limits, the tentativeness, or the function of any definition.

Examining stipulative definitions in detail would require an extensive survey of modern scholarship dealing with the period 1560 to 1640, and the value of the results would not be proportionate to the space consumed by summaries. But it should be useful to identify some interesting and meaningful short definitions, to distinguish among them according to focus and broadness of scope, and to note some of the various criteria used to separate puritans from nonpuritans. It may be objected that to take definitions out of context is to misrepresent the author's intentions. However, a clearly stated definition has a vitality that must be reckoned with, that resists qualification.

In any study of puritanism, Christopher Hill deserves prominent mention. He has taken the problem of definition very seriously, devoting to it the entire first chapter of his *Society and Puritanism in Pre-Revolutionary England.* Using numerous citations from contemporary uses of the term, Hill limits *puritanism* to "a core of doctrine about religion and Church government, aiming at purifying the Church from inside." As a starting point he leaves out the separatists, or, as they were often called, sectaries. He then relates the puritan religious movement to political and social ideas, in a sense extrapolating it into nonreligious areas and broadening it considerably. Basil Hall's strictures on this sort of practice have obvious merit; however, the idea of a puritan has provided Hill with a starting point, from which he points out and explains many of the popular social and political movements that, but for his works, might have received less than their due consideration from modern scholars.[7]

For the other eminent scholars who pioneered the more recent analytic study of puritanism, the term *puritanism* is generally comprehensive. M. M. Knappen's authoritative study of Tudor puritanism gives a clear example of the term's possible inclusiveness. In his words, "The term

7 Hill, *Society and Puritanism in Pre-Revolutionary England,* 28.

'Puritan' is used in this book to designate the outlook of those English Protestants who actively favored a reformation beyond that which the crown was willing to countenance and who yet stopped short of Anabaptism. It therefore includes both Presbyterians and Independents, Separatists and Non-Separatists. It also includes a number of Anglicans who accepted the episcopal system, but who nevertheless desired to model it and English church life in general on the Continental Reformed pattern." Knappen has limited his concern to the religious situation before 1603. Even broader definitions appear in studies concerned with later times. William Haller's very influential study *The Rise of Puritanism,* while ranging far beyond the sixteenth century, has included under the term such widely diverse figures as Thomas Cartwright, John Milton, John Bunyan, and Daniel Defoe. Although he begins with an equation of Calvinism and puritanism while tracing the origins of the movement, he rejects narrow definitions of either term.[8]

Similarly and more recently, H. C. Porter, in his introduction to *Puritanism in Tudor England,* seems to identify puritanism with dissent and therefore includes in his collection of puritan writings both the separatists and "the puritan wing within the church of England." A different, but equally broad, definition seems to inform Stuart E. Prall's collection of puritan documents; dealing with a later period than Porter's, Prall identifies as puritans the religious revolutionaries—the opponents of the ruling powers in church and state just before, during, and just after the revolution that overthrew the monarchy and dispossessed the bishops.[9] In each instance, a definition serves the author well, but at the same time its referential value is limited to the work in which it appears.

A sensitive awareness of the problems entailed by a broad stipulative definition appears in Leonard J. Trinterud's introduction to a collection of Elizabethan documents. According to Trinterud, puritanism "defined as simply as possible . . . was the Protestant form of dissatisfaction with the required official religion of England under Elizabeth." Taking the mid-1570s as his focal point, Trinterud proceeds to classify puritans into "the original anti-vestment party, the passive-resistance party and the

8   M. M. Knappen, *Tudor Puritanism: A Chapter in the History of Idealism* (Chicago, 1939), viii. Knappen essentially repeats the definition on p. 489, there giving credit to Trevelyan. William Haller, *The Rise of Puritanism* (New York, 1938), 8–9.

9   H. C. Porter, *Puritanism in Tudor England* (Columbia, S.C., 1971), 9; Stuart E. Prall (ed.), *The Puritan Revolution: A Documentary History* (London, 1968), ix–xxii.

Presbyterian party"; but he grants that the categories are not discrete and that changes in circumstances, political or personal, could cause a given person to move from one category to another.[10] It is interesting that a scholar has felt the need first to isolate a limited period of time—a part of one decade—to arrive at a sound definition and then to add other terms in order to achieve precision. If we try to extend Trinterud's definition to cover all eighty years of the movement, we must not simply add other names to Elizabeth's but also develop a large number of other subordinate categories.

The distinction between modern and contemporary uses of the term is faced by John R. Knott, Jr., who includes William Winstanley, John Milton, Richard Baxter, and John Bunyan in one coherent study. Knott takes puritanism to be "a movement embracing many kinds of reforming instincts and practices." He explicitly distinguishes this "modern practice" from the contemporary use of the term "to identify those who attempted to reform the established church from within" and to exclude all separatists.[11]

By basing his study on specific individuals, Knott has used an approach followed by many scholars and explicitly recommended by Patrick Collinson, who has stated that puritanism must be defined by looking at puritans—that is, defined inductively. We may select a number of sixteenth- and seventeenth-century figures who are generally called puritans and, from a study of each of their actions and works, determine what principles they hold in common. Although Charles and Katherine George have argued the impossibility of finding any defining element, Collinson, in his earlier work, implicitly meets their objection, stressing the subleties of distinctions and noting that the differences between the puritans and their opponents "were differences of degree, of theological temperature so to speak, rather than of fundamental principle." He quotes Percival Wilburn (1581): "The hotter sort of protestants are called puritans." Collinson finds the term *puritan* "elusive and intangible," but unlike many scholars, he sees the same difficulty in the term *Anglican*. Then, in his recent biography of Edmund Grindal, Collinson adduces something more nearly approaching fundamental defining principles. He considers Martin Bucer a forerunner of the puritans because of "the prominence in his theology of the doctrine of election, his exalted conception of the ministry, his sense of reformation as an ongoing process of ceaseless edification, his concern with abuses, the

10   Leonard J. Trinterud (ed.), *Elizabethan Puritanism* (New York, 1971), 9–15.
11   John R. Knott, Jr., *The Sword of the Spirit: Puritan Responses to the Bible* (Chicago, 1980), 2.

8

high moral tone of his utterances" and finds these characteristics displayed by Grindal, who thus merits the designation *puritan*. At the same time, Collinson notes that the term *precisian* would not apply to Bucer or Grindal.[12] A distinction between precisians and puritans was not unknown in the sixteenth century; however, the two terms were much more often than not regarded as synonymous, and Collinson's observation shows his awareness of the discrepancies between modern and contemporary terminology.

Another attempt to find a defining emphasis is made by Paul S. Seaver, who calls attention to the almost protean nature of the movement. He sees an ongoing puritan movement but notes that it lies beneath the shifting grounds of argument—from the question of vestments to presbyterianism in church government, to Sabbatarianism, to Arminianism in theology, with its attendant ritual. Beneath the opposition to the surplice, to the bishops, and to Arminius's doctrine of grace, Seaver finds the "essentials of the Puritan platform. . . . sacraments rightly administered, discipline out of the Word, and liberty to preach."[13]

Using the inductive approach but concerned mainly with the political activity of puritans, John Dykstra Eusden selects ten figures who he feels had the puritan spirit and finds their puritanism grounded in "theology and belief and the attendant pattern of life." But he clearly explains the difficulty of separating many of them from the establishment Anglicans.[14]

12　Patrick Collinson, *The Elizabethan Puritan Movement* (Berkeley, 1967), 13, 26–27, 471. Of course, Collinson has a full understanding of the problem of terminology; see Patrick Collinson, "A Comment: Concerning the Name Puritan," *Journal of Ecclesiastical History*, XXXI (1980), 483–88, and Patrick Collinson, *English Puritanism* (London, 1983), especially pp. 7–11. Patrick Collinson, *Archbishop Grindal, 1519–1583: The Struggle for a Reformed Church* (Berkeley, 1979), 54.

13　Paul S. Seaver, *The Puritan Lectureships: The Politics of Religious Dissent, 1560–1662* (Stanford, 1970), 4. More recently, Seaver, in his detailed analysis of the writings of the London artisan Nehemiah Wallington, notes that "'Puritan' was a pejorative term that Wallington normally used only when quoting those hostile to the godly who employed such expressions about them as 'puritans and rebels' or who called them 'by the names of puritans, schismatical, seditious, factious, trouble-states, traitors that speak against Caesar, with many slanders,'" and that "the term did not have for Wallington a sectarian meaning"; see Paul S. Seaver, *Wallington's World: A Puritan Artisan in Seventeenth-Century London* (Stanford, 1985), 143–44.

14　John Dykstra Eusden, *Puritans, Lawyers, and Politics in Early Seventeenth-Century England* (New Haven, 1958), 18. Eusden's ten representative figures and the categories into which he divides them include four noted preachers (John Preston, Richard Sibbes, William Gouge, and Thomas Gataker), two polemical writers (William Prynne and Thomas Scott), and four writers associated with the universities (Paul Baynes, William Bradshaw, Samuel Ward, and Richard Holdsworth); see pp. 9–10. More recently, Peter Lake, in *Moderate Puritans and the*

John F. Wilson, in contrast, finds it possible to distinguish individual puritans clearly enough but virtually impossible to construct a meaningful definition of puritanism from their works, not so much because of the diversity of the puritans themselves but because of the various approaches—social, political, or religious, for example—to the movement taken by scholars from the several disciplines concerned with it. Indeed, the differences in approaches may account partially for the disagreement concerning John Milton, since it is primarily the literary scholars who try to dissociate him from puritanism. But Wilson does not abandon the term; he argues that modern scholars focus on external relationships, which vary in importance according to the discipline and special interest of the scholar, and ignore the essential elements. He postulates that "the essential claim made by the puritans was that their faith rendered intelligible *all* their experience, even those aspects not manifestly religious." Wilson sees the end of an identifiable puritan movement in the 1640s, but even with this eminently sensible limitation in time, we might wonder if the essential element is not too broad and comprehensive to provide distinctions.[15]

Where a stipulative definition based on principles or attitudes can lead is seen in Hugh Martin's formulation of three foundation principles of puritanism: "(1) A belief in the reality and audibility of God's voice in the Bible and in the contemporaneous work of the Holy Spirit. (2) A conviction of the need to worship God in the Spirit of Holiness. (3) A keen sense of responsibility to God for oneself and for other men." That the principles were held by Richard Baxter and by puritans there is no doubt, and the statement has provided Martin with a basis for an informative study. But for the seeker of definitions, two familiar problems arise. First, for Baxter the term *puritan* was dyslogistic, less odious than *Anabaptist* only. He thought himself and his congregation "mere Catholics," men of no faction, even though he respected the men called—mistakenly, in his view—

Elizabethan Church (Cambridge, England, 1982), explains the difficulty of defining puritanism and uses the inductive (or, in his words, nominalistic) approach to solve the problem. Lake says that the concept of puritanism "should only emerge from a study of the activities of particular men, in particular contexts, acting and reacting to events over a period." Lake is fully aware that the choice of figures involves some prior assumptions about puritanism. His central figures, or moderate puritans, are Edward Dering, Thomas Cartwright, William Whitaker, William Bradshaw, and—most notably—Laurence Chaderton; see pp. 1–15, especially pp. 11, 14.

15 John F. Wilson, *Pulpit in Parliament: Puritanism During the English Civil Wars, 1640–1648* (Princeton, 1969), vii, 97.

puritans. Also, from a study of the writings of William Laud, we could argue that the same three principles were held by this archenemy of all nonconforming and reluctantly conforming clergymen.[16]

A somewhat different need to tailor a definition to, or derive a definition from, the special object of study is seen in three quite dissimilar works by Geoffrey F. Nuttall, Horton Davies, and Alan Simpson. Here the stipulative definition is clearly a functional definition. According to Nuttall, the term *puritan* may be limited to those who "stayed, often in some discomfort," within the church, and it may exclude separatists. But his examination of individual beliefs and a comparison of them with Roman Catholic and Laudian faiths apparently suggests to him that the separatists also may be called puritans. Nuttall then includes the separatists, because the resulting definition is better suited for his study, *The Holy Spirit in Puritan Faith and Experience;* if we consider beliefs concerning the working of the Holy Spirit, the difference between separatist and strongly anti-Catholic nonseparatist is not so great as the difference between both these on the one hand and the Laudians on the other. Davies also begins with a narrower use of the term *puritan* and then broadens it, though not to include all separatists. Puritans are "all those who longed for further reformation in England according to the Word of God." Strictly used, the name will include only those who remained entirely within the church, but it may be extended to "semi-separatists" such as John Robinson, the leading spirit in the pilgrimage to America. However, a study of the worship of all groups leads to the conclusion that except for the "radical difference in the attitude towards the State Church, Separatists and Puritans were largely in agreement." A study of puritan worship, then, leaves the separatists out of the fold only because of church affiliation and does not seem to touch fundamental beliefs. And for Alan Simpson, only a very broad—perhaps the broadest possible—definition will serve, for he includes both English and American puritans in his study. While noting all the possible groupings within and without the church, he establishes a general principle as applicable to those he plans to consider: "Puritans were elect spirits, segregated from the mass of mankind by an experience of conversion, fired by the sense that God was using them to revolutionize

16   Hugh Martin, *Puritanism and Richard Baxter* (London, 1954), 76; J. M. Lloyd Thomas (ed.), *The Autobiography of Richard Baxter* (London, 1931), 84, 154. See *A Summarie of Devotions Compiled and Used by Dr. William Laud* (Oxford, 1667).

human destiny, and committed to the execution of his Will." [17] Here a puritan is equated with a zealous religious reformer, and probably only so general an equation will serve Simpson's purpose.

Attempts to confine puritanism to a definite, recognizable theological system—invariably Calvinism—were once very common but now seldom appear. Yet Juliet Dusinberre, in the literary study *Shakespeare and the Nature of Women*, notes that "Puritanism was a movement within the Church of England for closer identification with the principles of the early Protestants, which meant, in effect, with Calvin." [18] Seeking the roots of Shakespeare's thought and attitudes, Dusinberre explores the attitude toward women of the early reformers, especially Martin Luther and John Calvin, and the extent to which this attitude was present in Shakespeare's milieu. The word *puritanism* provides a useful label for one aspect of Reformation thought and attitudes, and here, as in many other places, a definition is stipulated to allow the term to be used for convenience in a specialized context.

The search for a single distinguishing attitude or emphasis, not a doctrine, appears in some recent works. J. Sears McGee, in *The Godly Man in Stuart England: Anglicans, Puritans, and the Two Tables, 1620–1670,* studies differing emphases on various commandments of the Ten Commandments and arrives at a distinction between puritans and Anglicans, a distinction that may help in the classification of specific religious figures. Using the common seventeenth-century notion that Moses' first table (or tablet) contained the first four commandments (in protestant numbering), which deal with man's relationship with God, whereas the second table dealt with man's relationship with his fellows, McGee finds that the puritans tended to put relatively more stress on the first table and the Anglicans on the second. [19] The distinction is subtle and provides no easily applicable touchstone, since all religious writers emphasized the importance of both tables; however, McGee's argument is based inductively on a significant number of figures commonly classified as puritan or Anglican, and it is informative. In addition, he provides us with an enlightening study of early seventeenth-century expositions of the Ten Commandments.

17 Geoffrey F. Nuttall, *The Holy Spirit in Puritan Faith and Experience* (Oxford, 1947), 9; Horton Davies, *The Worship of the English Puritans* (Westminster, England, 1948), 11, 77; Alan Simpson, *Puritanism in Old and New England* (Chicago, 1955), 39.

18 Juliet Dusinberre, *Shakespeare and the Nature of Women* (New York, 1975), 3.

19 J. Sears McGee, *The Godly Man in Stuart England: Anglicans, Puritans, and the Two Tables, 1620–1670* (New Haven, 1976).

Yet another approach is to define the term *Anglican,* which poses fewer problems and by an informally dialectic process helps to define *puritanism.* For instance, John F. H. New begins by saying that "the word Anglican is used here to include those generally satisfied with the Church's doctrine, organization, and ceremonial." Logically, then, the puritans are those dissatisfied with the same matters, but further exclusion can be made. New accepts the independents, many of whom were not at war with Anglican doctrine, but he rejects the separatists. He then finds some basic religious attitudes as in a sense definitive of puritanism: "The sharp antinomy between man's abject predicament and God's immeasurable power gave Puritanism its distinctive character and lay at the center of Puritan motivation." Of course, the question of how many of these puritan principles were held also by Anglicans and separatists arises, and New, after detailing similarities and differences between the factions on the use of the sacraments, concludes that "between Laud and Perkins there was no essential difference; and yet there was a slight difference in emphasis." At first glance, a distinction between Anglican and puritan seems hardly necessary, but New sees the differences on sacraments and other matters as the outgrowth of "intangible, but vital, theological beliefs" that often stood in strong opposition.[20]

One conclusion that can be drawn from a sampling of modern definitions is that many—though by no means all—modern scholars tend to exclude from the designation *puritan* all the separatists—those who opposed the idea of an established church or at least made no attempt to reform the church, preferring to set up a system of worship outside it. The Brownists, the Anabaptists, the Family of Love—to name the sects most commonly mentioned—are then not puritans. The true puritans are members of the established Church of England who want to remain within it but to purify it by removing a few recent accretions and a great many practices residual of medieval Catholicism. This limitation of the definition of *puritan* can be illustrated by two modern scholars, one concerned with a sect and one concerned with puritanism in the church. Alastair Hamilton, in his study of the Family of Love, states explicitly, "When discussing the situation in England, I shall be using the word Puritan to denote the English Protestants who wanted to reform the English church in a manner more radical than that entailed by the Elizabethan settlement." The words

20 John F. H. New, *Anglican and Puritan: The Basis of Their Opposition, 1558–1640* (Stanford, 1964), 2, 19, 63, 111.

echo Everett H. Emerson, who concludes his introduction to a selection of puritan writings with the following statement: "Puritans had one thing in common, that which gives them their name—their desire to complete the purification of the church of England begun in Elizabeth's day." [21]

This limitation of the definition has noteworthy implications for current attitudes toward puritanism. The stress on the desire to purify and to reform accounts for both the zeal and the aggressiveness of the puritans, the traits that made them admirable to friends but obnoxious to opponents. Ultimately this definition tends to dispel some of the aura surrounding the term *puritanism* by implicitly denying its association with freedom of conscience. Most of the ardent reformers had a positive program for the church, however much they might differ among themselves, especially on details. Like such strict enforcers of conformity as Archbishops John Whitgift, Richard Bancroft, and William Laud, the reformers wanted set forms of worship, applicable to everyone. They did not seek only liberty to worship God as they saw fit, leaving others to be guided by their consciences; they sought the establishment of a correct, pure system of religion binding on everyone. It may be that tolerance of others' beliefs and practices flourishes best when surrounded by indifference to religion; in the sixteenth and seventeenth centuries, most people thought that religious beliefs, both their own and their neighbors', were of the utmost importance. At any rate, there was little religious tolerance in England until after the civil wars and the turbulence of the 1650s, when the conviction began to grow upon a reluctantly accepting leadership and public that in order to avoid bloodshed and civil disorder, people must put up with beliefs and practices differing from their ideal ones.

To find a belief in religious freedom among the characteristics of puritanism, we would need to include independents and separatists, and we would need to go beyond 1640. But to include under the term such diverse figures as Edmund Grindal, archbishop of Canterbury, who promoted reform from within the episcopal hierarchy; Thomas Cartwright, who wanted to abolish episcopacy; Henry Barrow, who wanted to set up his own congregation; and the members of the Family of Love, who were ready to conform to any set system of religious worship or church government, protestant or Catholic, and yet were rejected by all other groups—to include all these is to have a very loose, broad definition indeed. It would

21   Alastair Hamilton, *The Family of Love* (Cambridge, England, 1981), 3; Everett H. Emerson, *English Puritanism from John Hooper to John Milton* (Durham, N.C., 1968), 46.

seem, paradoxically, that the eulogistic quality of the term *puritan* intensifies in direct proportion to its inclusiveness and vagueness.

Contemporary definitions beckon at this point, because so many modern scholars argue that *puritan* had a narrower meaning in the sixteenth and early seventeenth centuries than it has today. These definitions often, but not always, provide some refuge from vagueness and broad inclusiveness, but they lead us to other problems, some of them familiar. A definition may be narrow, yet ambiguous. Two limited definitions, even though each is precise, may contradict each other. Our best hope is to discover recurring themes and some overall pattern or patterns of ideas.

The vexing question of whether separatists are part of the puritan movement is hard to resolve by examination of contemporary sources. Some separatists explicitly place themselves outside the movement. For instance, Henry Barrow, an extremist by the standards of his time, denounces with nearly equal vehemence both the supporters of the establishment and their opponents within the church. On the one hand he condemns "Pontificals, that in all things hold and jump with the time, and are ready to justify whatsoever is or shall be by public authority established." On the other hand he shows a dislike, more personal if not stronger, for the reformers within the church, whom he calls "preachers, which make shew as though they sought a sincere reformation of all things according to the gospel of Christ, and yet both execute a false ministry themselves, and they, together with all their hearers and followers, stand under that throne of Antichrist, the bishops their courts, and accomplices, and all those detestable enormities which they would have utterly removed and not reformed." Barrow notes further that "these are hereupon called Precisians, or Puritans, and now lately Martinists."[22] Clearly, Barrow has something in common with the reformers, and his anger stems partly from impatience and disappointment with them; but ultimately he places them in much the same camp as the conformists and stands opposed to both groups.

The opposite tendency—to place all reformers, whether inside or outside the church, in one group—can be seen in official documents. An act of

22 Henry Barrow, "A Plaine Refutation," in Leland H. Carlson (ed.), *The Writings of Henry Barrow, 1590–1591*, Elizabethan Nonconformist Texts, V (London, 1966), 244–45. Spelling has been modernized in quotations.

35 Elizabeth (in 1593, the thirty-fifth year of Elizabeth's reign) is entitled by Henry Gee and William John Hardy "The Act against Puritans" and seems to be directed against attempts to reform worship within the church as well as religious meetings outside the established framework. The act itself never uses the term *puritan;* its introductory words speak of "wicked and dangerous practices of seditious sectaries." [23] Another act of the same year does speak of recusants, who are thus given a legal designation; however, *puritan* apparently was too imprecise for official use, and the authorities did not make a clear distinction between protestant reformers from within and protestant opponents from without. A generation later a kind of official notice is taken of puritans, but without any clear definition. Apparently James I refused to sign a proclamation until all references to "popish scandalous books" were accompanied by the words "as also all seditious puritanical books and scandalous to our person and state, as have been lately vented by some puritanical spirits." [24] (The proclamation was printed on August 15, 1624.) The adjective *puritanical* here seems to have a very general meaning, and this proclamation, as well as other statements and actions, indicates that James I looked with relatively equal disfavor on all who opposed the establishment, regardless of their religious affiliation.

Some difference of opinion about the meaning of the term *puritan* is made evident by its use in the Marprelate tracts. Defending puritans against the bishops, Martin Marprelate admits that the puritans are displeased with him because of his indecorous style and his use of personal invective. Indeed, most reformers reject his appellation and condemn his pamphlets. Thomas Cartwright, whom Marprelate calls a puritan and treats with great respect, protests that the term should not be applied to him. Asking that he be judged by what he has written, not by the accusations of others, Cartwright pledges, "So shall I be sure to be eased of the slanderous surmise of my disloyalty to her majesty's estate, and to the commonwealth; likewise of my love to puritanism, and Church confusion: the contrary of both which, I do most earnestly protest, with this offer, that if either be proved against me, I will refuse no extremity to be practiced upon me." [25]

23   Henry Gee and William John Hardy (eds.), *Documents Illustrative of English Church History* (London, 1910), 492.

24   W. W. Greg (ed.), *A Companion to Arber* (Oxford, 1967), 67, 226–28; see also Stephen Foster, *Notes from the Caroline Underground* (Hamden, Conn., 1978), 21.

25   [John Penry (?)], *O Read over D. John Bridges, for It Is a Worthy Work* (N.p., 1588 [?]), 1; A. F. Scott Pearson, *Thomas Cartwright and Elizabethan Puritanism, 1535–1603* (Cambridge,

Exactly what Cartwright means by *puritanism* is not clear, apart from his linking it with disloyalty to the state and disorder in the church. A common defense of those so accused, however, is to apply the name to the medieval heretics known as the Cathari or Catharoi, whose most reprehensible error, in the eyes of nearly everyone, was their belief that they could live pure lives, avoiding sin. They figure in an interesting jingle, "An Answer to a Popish Rime," by Samuel Hieron, an authentic puritan in the eyes of modern scholars, who rejects Calvinism and sectarianism together with puritanism:

> We do not hang on Calvin's sleeve,
> Nor yet on Zwinglius we believe:
> And Puritans we do defy,
> If right the name you do apply.
> All giddy Sects among us crept,
> We wish out of our Church were swept:
> No name do we delight in more,
> Than that at Antioch given of yore.

It was at Antioch, of course, that the term *Christian* was first used, according to Acts, Chapter 11, verse 26, and an interesting fact of which Hieron may not be aware is that *Christian*, like *puritan*, was originally a term of disparagement. A marginal note to Hieron's verses names the Cathari, "who dreamed of a state of perfection in this life"; they apparently deserve the name *puritan* "rightly applied," as do some factions that try to wreak "havoc" in the church.[26] Hieron, though frequently in trouble with the establishment, is a puritan in the narrowest sense of the term, since he rejects both separatists and too-zealous reformers within the church.

Among others now generally called puritans, the influential and popular William Whately refers to the Cathari as a heretical sect "of old condemned under the name of Puritans, from a conceited and imaginary purity, or an absolute freedom from all sin, whereof they boasted." He has heard that they are "revived in some parts of this Land," and he seeks to dissociate himself from them and from the name *puritan* without, however, condemning all those called puritans: "But I beseech you (brethren) let there be

---

England, 1925), 440. On the use of the term *puritan* by Cartwright and Whitgift, see Donald Joseph McGinn, *The Admonition Controversy* (New Brunswick, N.J., 1949), 26–27, 370–72.
  26 *The Works of Mr. Sam. Hieron* (London, 1634–35), Pt. 1, p. 553.

none, no not one amongst you, that out of a malicious desire to scourge piety, so nicknamed, upon our sides, shall mock at Puritanism, upon occasion of this hand of God which he hath stretched out against us, whom the world hath pleased, but falsely, to term Puritans." [27] Among other writers, the quest for the true puritan went back in time to the heretics of the early church, such as the Novatians, who believed that men could achieve moral and spiritual purity in this life.

The Family of Love occupies an anomalous position in disputes about puritanism. Basil Hall comments that King James was "almost alone" in applying the term *puritan* to the sect. [28] Here the king showed some political shrewdness but also, perhaps, some ignorance of the beliefs of the various religious sects. With the clear political aim of placating many who had objected to his earlier attack on puritans, James limited his definition in a way that might be approved by most moderate reformers. His choice of the Family of Love would have made sense if he had been trying to capitalize upon general disapproval of the eccentric marital practices of the sect. Yet in so focusing, he attacked the one group that was least likely to cause him trouble; the Familists generally advocated adherence to the established church, whether protestant or Catholic, and conformity in matters of worship. James would have gained much the same political advantage, as well as more respect from later scholars, if he had simply attacked the Anabaptists.

In short, the defenders of the Elizabethan settlement used the term *puritan* because of its theological implications—its association with heresies that proclaimed, in one form or another and to varying degrees, the perfectibility of man. They sought by its use to associate the older heresies with both contemporary sectarians and the element within the church desiring further reform—at least the more zealous reforming element—and so to discredit all opponents of the establishment. This dyslogistic use of *puritan* continued throughout the period under study, but among the reforming element so stigmatized, the term *puritan* underwent some change. At first the zealous reformers sought to limit it to the old heresies; then to include under it some separatists; and finally, as its use persisted, to insist upon a distinction between their puritanism and that of the heretics. A few actually took pride in being puritans in the sense that they wanted to

27   William Whatley, *Gods Husbandry* (London, 1622), Pt. 2, p. 75; William Whately, *Sinne No More* (London, 1628), 23.
28   Hall, "Puritanism: The Problem of Definition," 285.

purify religious practices. As they did so, their opponents adopted other derogatory terms such as *seditious sectaries* or *schismatics,* and finally, during the civil war, *roundheads* became the derogatory term of choice, at least for a time. This use of other derogatory terms indicates that for many people *puritan* was gradually coming to mean an advocate of purity in doctrine or worship—in general, a purity of religion.

The notion of purity served to link, though tenuously and ambiguously, puritanism with Calvinism. It has been noted that Samuel Hieron disavowed Calvinism and that modern scholars generally agree that *Calvinism* and *puritanism* are not interchangeable terms. Most puritans were Calvinists; so for a long time were most Anglicans. However, Calvin was sometimes invoked in attempts to define. As late as 1676, Elisha Coles, a schoolmaster and lexicographer whose aim was to make difficult English words comprehensible to foreigners, defined *Puritans* simply as "The Nickname of Calvinists." Since his *English Dictionary* went through twelve editions between 1676 and 1732, at least a couple of generations had a simple, though misleading, definition. Coles may well be looking back to earlier times for his source of information; for example, Peter Heylyn, whose life spanned the first six decades of the seventeenth century and who engaged in controversy with many reformers, notes in his church history, under the year 1565, that "in this year it was that the Zwinglian or Calvinian faction began to be first known by the name of Puritans." Yet Calvinism seems to trouble Heylyn less than the implications of the name *puritan,* "which name had ever since been appropriate to them, because of their pretending to a greater purity in the service of God than was held forth unto them (as they gave it out) in the Common Prayer Book; and to a greater opposition to the rites and usages of the Church of Rome than was agreeable to the constitution of the Church of England." Calvin may be relevant largely because he discussed with the Marian exiles in Geneva and elsewhere the question of purity of worship. Finally Heylyn raises another of the most frequent objections to the puritans: "But this purity was accompanied with such irreverence, this opposition drew along with it so much licentiousness, as gave great scandal and offense to all sober men."[29]

It would be irrelevant, then, to object that both Cartwright and his opponent Whitgift were Calvinists (as Heylyn must have been aware); in

29 See McGinn, *The Admonition Controversy,* 10; Elisha Coles, *An English Dictionary* (London, 1676); Peter Heylyn, *Ecclesia Restaurata; or, The History of the Reformation of the Church of England,* ed. James Craigie Robertson (2 vols.; Cambridge, England, 1849), II, 421–22.

fact, if the Lambeth articles represent Whitgift's theological beliefs, the difference between his beliefs and Calvin's was tenuous indeed. But in the light of Heylyn's argument, it is important to note that during the sixteenth and seventeenth centuries in England—unlike America—to be a Calvinist meant one or more or all of several things: One could be simply, or to some degree, Calvinistic in theology; one could advocate the Presbyterian system of church government; one could advocate the mode of worship practiced in Geneva; one could support use of the Genevan prayer book; or one could merely agree with Calvin on any limited question of doctrine, worship, or church government. Conversely, disagreement with Calvin on any single point enabled a person to deny that he was a Calvinist. Hieron, though a Calvinist in theology, can protest that he does not "hang on Calvin's sleeve"; that is, he does not advocate the Genevan model of church government. Whitgift could have disavowed Calvinism vigorously enough, but he could have gained no political advantage by doing so.

Another distinction found in works of the sixteenth and seventeenth centuries resides between the words *puritan* and *protestant*. Henry Smith, the Elizabethan preacher celebrated for his eloquence, poses among a list of questions "which are as yet unanswered" the question "whether those which are called Protestants, or those whom we call Puritans, be of the purest religion, and most conformed to the primitive Church." But the distinction most often appears in a three-category classification of religious attitudes into puritan, protestant, and papist. Any one of the three may represent the norm against which the other two are evaluated and found wanting. In Oliver Ormerod's lengthy work against the puritans, the protestant is the true Christian, whereas the puritan is linked in belief and practice with first the continental Anabaptists and second the papists. In Thomas Scott's *Interpreter* (1622), the puritan becomes the true Christian, whereas the protestant is a formalist and a timeserver tinged with papistic doctrines, modes of worship, and political aims. The anonymous author of *A Short Declaration of the Lives and Doctrine of the Protestants and Puritans* (1615) uses the Roman Catholic as the ideal and condemns the protestant by association with the puritan, who stands for opposition to good order in church and state. In each use the favored term represents not a middle way—an ideal lying between two extremes—but the one right way opposed to two wrong ways that have much in common. In some ways the puritan in all these classifications occupies a position of special concern not accorded to either protestant or papist, largely because of his zeal. In a jingle attributed to Peter Heylyn, the puritans emerge as the main obstacle to religious concord, having an influence out of proportion to their number:

> A learned prelate of this land,
> Thinking to make religion stand
> With equal poise on either side,
> A mixture of them thus he tried:
> An ounce of Protestant he singleth,
> And then a dram of Papist mingleth,
> With a scruple of the Puritan,
> And boiled them [all] in his brain-pan;
> But when he thought it would digest,
> The scruple troubled all the rest.[30]

Distinctions between puritans and protestants were obliterated finally by Daniel Neal, for whom puritans are protestant nonconformists, as indicated by the title of his history (*The History of the Puritans; or, Protestant Nonconformists*). Strictly speaking, Neal's definitions are retrospective, not contemporary, but in his time the problems of religious tolerance, of liberty of conscience, and of dissent from an establishment were not fully resolved. Interestingly, Neal, though stressing puritan concern with religious liberty, in an inconspicuous qualification lends support to Heylyn's objections. Neal admits that the puritans had a shortcoming, that he fears lest "their zeal for their platform of discipline would . . . have betrayed them into the imposition of it upon others, if it had been established by law."[31] The conditional statement seems a bit puzzling in light of our knowledge of the church history of the 1640s and of such strictures as John Milton's poem "On the New Forcers of Conscience under the Long Parliament." However, Neal does not include supporters of a rigid presbyterian establishment among the true puritans. He starts with nonconformity and applies the name *puritanism* to it. Viewing his subjects retrospectively as part of a movement toward tolerance of dissent, he designates as puritans many who would have rejected the name and excludes many to whom it was applied by contemporaries.

---

30 *Three Sermons Made by Master Henry Smith* (London, 1604), 55; Heylyn, *Ecclesia Restaurata*, I, cvii.

31 Daniel Neal, *The History of the Puritans; or, Protestant Nonconformists* (5 vols.; London, 1822), I, 467.

The attempt to equate puritanism with protestant nonconformity really begins with Thomas Fuller, with whose observations this commentary on contemporary definitions logically ends. Also writing retrospectively, but having lived through the years of bitter controversy, Fuller, whose broad sympathies and tolerant spirit enabled him to defend and praise such diverse figures as Thomas Cartwright and Richard Bancroft, pleads for the banishment of the term *puritan* from the language because of the dissension it promotes. Reporting on the year 1564, he takes up "The Original of Puritans. The Homonomy of the Term." Fuller's argument presents clearly the contemporary problem of definition and connotation:

The *English bishops,* conceiving themselves empowered by their *Canons,* began to show their authority in urging the *Clergy* of their *Dioceses* to subscribe to the *Liturgy, Ceremonies,* and *Discipline* of the *Church;* and such as refused the same were branded with the odious name of *Puritans.*

A name which in this nation first began in this year, and the grief had not been great, if it had ended the same. The *Philosopher* banisheth the term (which is *polysæmon*) that is subject to several senses, out of the *Predicaments,* as affording too much *Covert* for cavil by the latitude thereof. On the same account could I wish that the word *Puritan* were banished common discourse, because so various in the acceptions thereof. We need not speak of the ancient *Cathari,* or *Primitive Puritans,* sufficiently known by their *Heretical opinions. Puritan* was here taken for the *Opposers* of the *Hierarchy* and *Church-service,* as resenting of *Superstition.* But *profane mouths* quickly improved this Nickname, therewith on every occasion to abuse pious people, some of them so far from opposing the *Liturgy,* that they endeavored (according to the instructions thereof in the *preparative* to the *Confession*) *to accompany the Minister with a* PURE *heart,* and labored (as it is in the *Absolution*) *for a life* PURE *and holy.* We will therefore decline the word to prevent exceptions, which if casually slipping from our pen, the Reader knoweth that only *Non-conformists* are thereby intended.[32]

---

32 Thomas Fuller, *The Church-History of Britain: From the Birth of Jesus Christ Until the Year M. DC. XLVIII* (London, 1655), IX, 76. At present, the term *nonconformist* appears to be used chiefly by scholars who find a definable, coherent dissenting tradition leading from the Elizabethan period through the Restoration; for a notable example, see Richard L. Greaves, *Saints and Rebels: Seven Nonconformists in Stuart England* (Macon, Ga., 1985), 1–7.

Yet Fuller, as he predicted, is constrained to speak of puritans himself. When writing of the protests of the Family of Love to King James, he notes that they were trying "to separate themselves from the *Puritans.*" Of course, James himself had applied the name to the Family of Love, and Fuller is here doing little more than quoting, though in context the repetition indicates a kind of acceptance. Again, when Fuller laments that the Archbishop of Spalato enlarged the meaning of the term *puritans* to include "Anti-Arminians," whereas it had been "only taken to denote such, as *dissented* from the Hierarchy in *Discipline,* and *Church-Government,*" he seems to approve its use with some denotations. Finally, in discussing the Gunpowder Plot, Fuller has perforce to note that the plotters had intended to blame the "most innocent *Puritans.*"[33] The word *nonconformist* would lack the necessary pejorative force and historical applicability. Fuller's experience adumbrates the problems of modern scholars; for him, as well as for scholars today, the word *puritan* seems to be inescapable, and what remains is to be fully aware of its possible meanings and implications.

One difficulty with the contemporary definition of puritan stems from the fact that puritanism was not a definable party, either religious or political. A puritan was almost always a monarchist, not distinctly more or less so than an Anglican; even the question of secular authority in religious affairs brought about no distinct, cohesive movement. There was at times a clear program for change in church government—a sort of presbyterian party—but to limit the designation *puritan* to this group is to make it redundant and to narrow down meaningful use to one of many controversies. Contemporaries, like modern scholars, sense a religious temper—one that had an impact on social and political, as well as religious, history—and a temper is notoriously hard to define.

Another difficulty with contemporary definitions is that the term *puritan* appears almost exclusively in controversial writings, where, naturally enough, denotations are noted only in passing, and connotations are fully exploited. Possibly this fact in itself would create no insurmountable problem if the controversy focused on one issue and were limited to one brief period (though, as we have seen, Trinterud felt the need to distinguish three types of puritans even when he focused on the middle years of one decade). From 1564, when the term appeared, until the 1640s, when it came to be used as a designation of people of the past, the focal points of religious and political controversies moved from one topic to another. A

33   Fuller, *The Church-History of Britain,* X, 33, 34, 99–100.

lucid and factual account of the points at issue at various times is provided by Everett Emerson in his introduction to a collection of puritan writings. From the matter of vestments (a question of religious worship), interest shifted to church government (the question of episcopacy and presbyterianism), then to various religious practices, and finally to both church government and theology, as the established church became Arminian in doctrine.[34]

While the points of contention were shifting, the approaches to reform also changed. As Emerson summarizes, "The history of Puritanism during the eighty years from 1560 to 1640 consists largely of efforts to change the settlement of 1559, efforts made through every available channel."[35] Not only was the 1559 settlement broad in scope—it intended to encompass all religious matters—but also various channels were tried from time to time as they seemed available. At some times Parliament seemed to offer the best prospect; at other times, the queen; later, the king; and frequently, various noblemen. Under Grindal, briefly, the church hierarchy could be approached. Finally in 1640, Parliament became the wide channel for sweeping changes—changes that brought a host of more clearly definable parties into the religious and political arena and made the term *puritan* applicable only to the past.

From the foregoing survey, some tentative conclusions are possible—conclusions to be tested by their applicability to the selections that follow. First, *puritan* was and is primarily a religious term; in any context it refers to people who are defined, however vaguely, by their religious beliefs and practice (chiefly their practice). In the eyes of some there may be a puritan political grouping; many will see a puritan morality or a puritan social ethic. But the word is used in historical studies of an age when no aspect of life could be separated from religion, when religion determined or took precedence over political affiliation and guided, more or less imperfectly, moral and social behavior.

Second, in the absence of highly refined theological studies such as those suggested by Basil Hall, we cannot define the puritans as adherents of a particular theological system. Calvinism and respect for the Bible charac-

34   Emerson, *English Puritanism from John Hooper to John Milton,* 3–46.
35   *Ibid.,* 10.

terize the puritans but do not distinguish them from nonpuritans in any precise or even useful manner; for example, in the Admonition controversy, the conforming Whitgift showed no less knowledge of, or respect for, the Bible than did the puritan Cartwright, and theology was not an issue. Moreover, few of the people called puritans were systematic theologians; generally their fundamental theological beliefs were only implicit in their writings and actions. We must therefore focus on religious practices, which are, after all, what most of the disputes were about. It was the fact that some people objected to certain vestments, aspects of the liturgy, ways of behaving on Sunday, ways of conducting a church service, and ways of governing a church that led to their being called puritans and eventually to a few accepting the name. And it is in religious practices that we can find concrete, definite proposals for reform, proposals that might help distinguish puritans from others.

Because the writings that try to define are controversial and because the issues changed from time to time, where can we find a starting point for attempts at definition? Here another conclusion presents itself: Perhaps the Millenary Petition of 1603 deserves careful study, partly because of its concreteness and partly because of the moderate tone in which its requests are presented (Fuller called it a "calm, and still, but deep Petition").[36] Readings in histories of puritanism suggest that this petition has not been given due attention. The proposals found there make a good starting place from which to work both outward, by exploring social and political implications, as well as inward, by searching out the theological beliefs on which the items in the petition rested. As a touchstone of puritanism it might turn out to be particularly useful in that many of its proposed reforms are tangible and specific. For instance, in the church service it called for the elimination of the sign of the cross in baptism, of the ring in marriage, of bowing at the name of Jesus, of the practice of confirmation, and of the wearing of the surplice by ministers. In the conduct of the clergy it stressed the importance of a preaching ministry and condemned nonresidency. Other proposals were less specific but still clearly defined. Also, the proposals date from the midpoint of the puritan movement but look back to the settlement of 1559, and their durability is attested by the appearance of all except the question of the ring in marriage in the Root and Branch Petition of 1640. If at first glance the procedure seems to be reductive and to rest on externals only, we need only search out the rationale for each item

36   Fuller, *The Church-History of Britain*, X, 23.

to find ourselves involved in complexities of theological reasoning. We also are at the heart of the controversy about the need for, and the proper scope of, reformation itself—the controversy about the distance a person should travel away from the old faith and toward primitive Christianity.

One example can be given here. It has been noted that puritans insisted on a biblical foundation for the conduct of all religious activity, but so did many of their opponents. The objections to bowing at the name of Jesus may distinguish puritans from some opponents, yet a biblical text of undisputed canonicity at the time says explicitly that "at the name of Jesus every knee should bow" (Philippians, Chapter 2, verse 10). The puritans, then, were not simple literalists in the use of the Bible. In fact, their objection was based on two principles, one theological and one exegetical, which here converged: first, that a substantive difference existed between the name *Jesus* and the name *Christ,* a difference between the humanity and the divinity of the Savior; and second, that all parts of sacred scripture merit equal reverence.[37] Buttressing these principles was the suspicion of all practices of the Roman Catholic church. Here a concrete proposal regarding a fine point of religious worship proves to be a thread in a large, carefully knit fabric, a fabric that perhaps we can assess and visualize in its totality if we can determine why each concrete proposal was advanced.

To formulate an interesting and possibly fruitful hypothesis, we can identify every writer whose attitudes conform strictly to the Millenary Petition proposals as a true puritan. We can even draw a series of concentric and intersecting circles with the Millenary Petition at its core. To place any religious figure in his true relationship to puritanism, we can draw another circle representing his attitudes. If the circle coincides with the petition, he is simply a puritan. If it includes the Millenary Petition circle, he is still a puritan, though more radical than most. If it intersects the core circle, the extent of his puritanism is determined by the amount of common ground. We thus achieve a well-marked, limited definition with a very large and complex halo; but at least we have a distinct point of reference, and our basic, true puritans can focus our study of the movement.

The Millenary Petition serves as a starting point better than any other document because of its clarity, conciseness, breadth, moderate tone, and balance. Documents such as the earlier admonitions to Parliament and the

---

37   See Boyd M. Berry, *Process of Speech: Puritan Religious Writing and Paradise Lost* (Baltimore, 1976), 23–60; the first section is titled "Bowing at the Name of Jesus." John R. Knott, Jr., focuses on puritan regard for the Bible in *The Sword of the Spirit,* 13–41.

Theses Martinianae, or the later Root and Branch Petition, are much more contentious and somewhat less well balanced in that they devote proportionately much more space to attacks on bishops than do the separate writings of most reformers. The fact that the Millenary Petition was drafted on behalf of a thousand people, as its name indicates, suggests widespread support, even though the number of actual signers cannot be determined. Fuller gives the number 750, but he may be thinking of a Lincolnshire petition. Of course, the Root and Branch Petition had a much larger subscription, but it was drafted amid turmoil, when people are likely to take sides without necessarily agreeing with the whole platform of the party they have joined. By contrast, the Millenary Petition was patently intended as a judicious, pacific, and helpful work, addressed to a new regime with which the signers were eager to establish a rapport and whose help, or at least sympathy, they were trying to enlist.[38]

Of course, the value of the Millenary Petiton as a starting point for a definition of puritanism must remain, for the time being, speculative. For one thing, it nowhere uses the term *puritan,* nor did contemporaries specifically identify it with puritanism. It needs to be compared with documents in which some attempt at definition appears explicitly and in which contemporary terminology is illustrated.

38   See Stuart Barton Babbage, *Puritanism and Richard Bancroft* (London, 1962), 43–55.

Note on Editorial

Procedure

THE following collection of documents seeks to provide a better understanding of how the terms *puritan* and *puritanism* were used in the late sixteenth and early seventeenth centuries—with what denotations and connotations, and in what contexts—by the writers who now figure in studies of puritanism. When possible, entire works have been reprinted, and casual references that provide no reasoned context for the terms used have been excluded. Excerpts have been given when a section of a long work is self-contained or when it provides especially meaningful information. The documents are somewhat weighted, in volume, toward favorable use of the term, largely because defenses of a stigmatized group tend to be more thoughtful and judicious than attacks upon it. Adversely critical statements serve mainly to help define by contrast, and to illumine, the charges against which the puritans were defending themselves. That the works chosen are for the most part controversial and popular is determined not by editorial choice but by the nature of the problem; the terms appeared not in scholarly treatises but in works for a general public. That most of the works date from the seventeenth century is also a matter of constraint, for it is only then that extensive favorable treatments of puritanism, using that name, can be found.

In all texts, except in titles and proper nouns, spelling has been regularized to facilitate reading. Archaic and even obsolete words that can be found in a modern dictionary (apart from the *Oxford English Dictionary*) have generally been retained. Italic type has been retained where used for emphasis or for foreign terms but has been changed to roman type, with quotation marks inserted, where used repeatedly for quotations; here practice is consistent within a document but may vary from one document to another. Capitalization has been retained, no matter how eccentric it seems. Punctuation has been changed rarely, and then only to provide some consistency within a work. In modern textual theory, of course, italicization, punctuation, and capitalization, no less than spelling, are accidentals subject to the vagaries of typesetters and so may call for regularization with equal voice. However, the object here has been to present the text as nearly as possible with the meaning it had for its contemporary readers; of the accidentals, spelling alone does not affect content. The others impart emphasis and sometimes even determine the meaning of statements. Even a brief glance at some nineteenth-century reprints of Renaissance texts will discourage tampering with the originals, except for spelling. Finally, a few obvious misprints have been corrected silently; there seems no point in reproducing *whole* when *whose* is clearly intended, or *duty* when only *duly* makes sense. Generally the editorial practice tries to follow that of Stuart E. Prall in *The Puritan Revolution*.

Each text is preceded by a transcription of its original title page or, if an excerpt, of the title page of the work from which it was taken. Some epigraphs have been excluded in the transcription. To avoid what would be extensive repetition, explanatory footnotes have been dispensed with. In their place a Glossary of names and terms with minimal biographical data or brief definitions has been provided.

Part I
*Sympathetic Descriptions
of Puritanism*

1

[John Penry (?)]

Hay Any Worke for Cooper

1589

(Excerpt)

JOHN PENRY (1559–1593), a native of Wales, received a B.A. degree at Cambridge and an M.A. degree at Oxford. Although he preached at both Oxford and Cambridge, he never took orders. His first concern was religious reform in Wales, but he soon extended his interest to all of England, particularly to abolishing episcopacy throughout the realm. His writings were judged heretical in 1587 by the Court of High Commission, and thereafter Penry operated secretly. Although it remains impossible to prove beyond a shadow of a doubt exactly what he wrote, it is clear enough that he was the guiding spirit in the Marprelate attacks on the bishops; it was he who arranged for printings published under the name Martin Marprelate and for changing the locations of the secret press. For a time Penry moved to Scotland, where his views were received favorably. When he returned to England, he was quickly recognized, arrested, tried, and hanged. The charges leading to his conviction were based on purported oral comments and on manuscripts, not on the published Marprelate works. For a detailed study of Penry's works, see Donald J. McGinn, *John Penry and the Marprelate Controversy* (New Brunswick, N.J., 1966). In addition, an extensive annotated bibliography of this and other controversies of the time can be found in

Peter Milward's *Religious Controversies of the Elizabethan Age* (Lincoln, Neb., 1977).

Although the Elizabethan church settlement of 1559 evoked both protests and defenses from its inception, the controversy entered upon by Penry may be said to reach its early maturity in print with *An Admonition to the Parliament* (1572), by John Field and Thomas Wilcox. *A Second Admonition to the Parliament,* probably by Thomas Cartwright, followed in the same year and initiated a series of exchanges between Cartwright and that staunch defender of Anglican orthodoxy John Whitgift. Several other writers made their contributions, some anonymously, in rational arguments concerning ecclesiastical discipline. Among them was William Fulke, whose *Briefe and Plaine Declaration* (1584), defending those who sought further reformation, called forth a massive fourteen-hundred-page argument for the establishment by John Bridges, doctor of divinity and dean of Salisbury, in *A Defence of the Government Established in the Church of Englande for Ecclesiasticall Matters* (1587); Bridges's work led directly to the Marprelate controversy.

The first two works published under the pseudonym Martin Marprelate appeared a few months apart, in October 1588 and January 1589, and bore lengthy titles beginning with identical words: *Oh Read over D. John Bridges, for It Is a Worthy Work.* For convenience, the two are distinguished by words appearing near the ends of the title pages: "The Epistle" (the first work) and "The Epitome." Both dealt with familiar points of contention. From the beginning of Elizabeth's reign, many clergymen had objected to parts of the Book of Common Prayer, to the wording of some of the articles of religion, to the use of some vestments, and to various religious practices. Because it was the task of the bishops to enforce conformity, their strictness and even the legitimacy of their jurisdiction over the clergymen and laymen became focal points of discussion. Marprelate, reacting to Bridges's very strong defense of the church establishment and possibly as well to the length and erudition of his work, brought a new tone, style, and vocabulary to the old arguments. Although earlier controversialists had been vigorous enough in denouncing their opponents' arguments and had not entirely refrained from personal attacks, often impugning the motives of their opponents, Marprelate abandoned the usual restraints governing personal invective and in vehement, colloquial, and often vulgar language criticized the personal lives as well as the ideas of the bishops and their defenders. The liveliness of his style gained him an audience, but the tone was perceived as scurrilous even by those whom he defended, so his defense of puritans caused some—Cartwright, for example—to dissociate themselves from the name *puritan* as well as from Marprelate tracts.

The first two Marprelate tracts were answered in a very moderate tone by Thomas Cooper, bishop of Winchester, in *An Admonition to the People of England* (1589), signed T. C. Thereupon Marprelate promptly shifted the focus of his attack from Bridges to Cooper. Although some doubt existed about the identity of T. C., the bishop of Winchester became a likely target because of his readiness to enforce conformity; moreover, his name lent itself readily to the play of Marprelate's wit. The title *Hay* [Have Ye] *Any Worke for Cooper,* a common London street cry of the barrel makers, serves both to denigrate the person and to provide material for insulting images.

The extract here reprinted is the mocking dedicatory "Epistle to the Terrible Priests." It provides a good example of the Marprelate style in a short, self-contained discussion. Although it mentions puritans by name only in connection with one relatively minor issue, the compensation of the ministers, it makes very clear Marprelate's sympathy with those called puritans. The fact that it defends puritans, together with the style in which it is written, serves to explain both why the name *puritan* became odious to the conforming Anglicans and why many of the dissenting clergy hurried to explain that they were not puritans and had no sympathy for Martin Marprelate.

Hay any worke for Cooper:

Or a briefe pistle directed by Waye of an hublication to the reverende Byshopps counselling them if they will needs be barrelled up for feare of smelling in the nostrels of her Majestie and the State that they would use the advise of reverend Martin for the providing of their Cooper. Because the reverend *T. C.* (by which misticall letters is understood eyther the bounsing Parson of *Eastmeane,* or Tom Coakes his Chapaline) to bee an unskilfull and a deceytfull tubtrimmer. Wherein worthy Martin quits himselfe like a man I warrant you in the modest defence of his selfe and his learned Pistles and makes the Coopers hoopes to flye off and the Bishops Tubs to leake out of all crye. Penned and compiled by Martin the Metropolitane. Printed in Europe not farre from some of the Bounsing Priestes.

[John Penry (?), 1589. Excerpt: prefatory "Epistle to the terrible Priests."]

A man of Worship to the men of Worship that is Martin Marprelate gentleman Primate and Metropolitan of all the Martins wheresoever. To the John of all the sir Johns and to the rest of the terrible priests: saith have among you once again my clergy masters.

O Brethren, there is such a deal of love grown of late I perceive, between you and me, that although I would be negligent in sending my Pistles unto you: yet I see you cannot forget me. I thought you to be very kind when you sent your Pursuivants about the country to seek for me. But now that you yourselves have taken the pains to write, this is out of all cry. Why it passes to think what loving and careful brethren I have, who although I cannot be gotten, to tell them where I am, because I love not the air of the Clink or Gatehouse in this cold time of Winter, and by reason of my business in Pistlemaking, will notwithstanding make it known unto the world, that they have a month's mind towards me. Now truly brethren, I find you kind, why ye do not know what a pleasure you have done me. My worship's books were unknown to many, before you allowed *T. C.* to admonish the people of England to take heed, that if they loved you, they would make much of their prelates, and the chief of the clergy. Now many seek after my books, more than ever they did. Again, some knew not that our brother John of Fulham, was so good unto the porter of his gate, as to make the poor blind honest soul, to be a dumb minister. Many did not know, either that Amen, is as much as by my faith, and so that our Savior Christ ever sware by his faith: or that bowling and eating of the Sabbath, are of the same nature: that Bishops may as lawfully make blind guides, as David might eat of the shew bread: or that father Thomas tubtrimmer of Winchester, good old student, is a master of Arts of 45. years standing. Many I say, were ignorant of these things, and many other pretty toys, until you wrote this pretty book. Besides whatsoever you overpass in my writings, and did not gainsay, that I hope will be judged to be true. And so John a Bridges his treason out of the 448. page of his book, you grant to be true. Yourselves you deny not to be petty popes, the Bishop of St. David's in Wales, you deny not to have two wives, with an hundred other things which you do not gainsay: so that the reader may judge that I am true of my word, and use not to lie like Bishops. And this hath greatly commended my worship's good dealing. But in your confutation of my book, you have shewed reverend Martin to be truepenny indeed: for you have confirmed, rather than confuted him. So that brethren, the pleasure which you have done unto me, is out of all scotch and notch. And should not I again be as ready to pleasure you? Nay, then I should be as ungrateful towards my good brethren, as John of Cant. is to Thomas Cartwright. The which John, although he hath been greatly favored by the said Thomas, in that Thomas hath now these many years let him alone and said nothing unto him, for not answering his books, yet is not ashamed to make a secret comparison, between himself and Thomas Cartwright. As who say, John of Lambehith, were as learned as Thomas Cartwright. What say you old dean John a Bridges, have not you shewed yourself thankful unto her Majesty, in overthrowing her supremacy in the 448. page of your book. I will lay on load on your skincoat for this year anon.

And I will have my pennyworths of all of you brethren ere I have done with you, for this pains which your *T. C.* hath taken with me. This is the puritans' craft, in procuring me to be confuted I know: I'll be even with them too. A crafty whoreson's brethren Bishops did you think, because the puritans' *T. C.* did set John of Cant. at a *nonplus,* and gave him the overthrow, that therefore your *T. C.* alias Thomas Cooper bishop of Winchester, or Thomas Cooke his Chaplain, could set me at a *nonplus.* Simple fellows, methinks he should not.

I guess your *T. C.* to be Thomas Cooper (but I do not peremptorily affirm it) because the modest old student of 52. year standing, setteth Winchester after Lincoln and Rochester in the contents of his book, which blasphemy, would not have been tolerated by them that saw and allowed the book, unless mistress Cooper's husband had been the author of it.

Secondly, because this *T. C.* the author of this book is a bishop, and therefore Thomas Cooper, he is a Bishop, because he reckoneth himself charged amongst others, with those crimes whereof none are accused but bishops alone, pag. 101. lin. 26. Ha old Martin yet I see thou hast it in thee, thou wilt enter into the bowels of the cause in hand I perceive. Nay if you will commend me, I will give you more reasons yet. The style and the phrase is very like her husband's, that was sometimes wont to write unto doctor Day of Welles. You see I can do it indeed. Again, none would be so grosshead as to gather, because my reverence telleth Dean John, that he shall have twenty fists about his ears more than his own (whereby I meant indeed, that many would write against him, by reason of his bomination learning, which otherwise never meant to take pen in hand) that I threatened him with blows, and to deal by stafford law: Whereas that was far from my meaning, and could by no means be gathered out of my words, but only by him that pronounced *Eulojin* for *Enlogeni* in the pulpit: and by him whom a papist made to believe, that the Greek word *Enlogeni,* that is to give thanks, signifieth to make a cross in the forehead: py hy hy hy. I cannot but laugh, py hy hy hy. I cannot but laugh, to think that an old soaking student in this learned age, is not ashamed to be so impudent as to presume to deal with a papist, when he hath no grue in his pocket. But I promise you Sir, it is no shame to be a L. bishop if a man could, though he were as unlearned as John of Glocester or William of Liechfeld. And I tell you true, our brother Westchester, had as live play twenty nobles in a night, at Priemeero on the cards, as trouble himself with any pulpit labor, and yet he thinks himself to be a sufficient bishop. What a bishop such a card player? A bishop play 20. nobles in a night? Why a round three pence serveth the turn to make good sport 3. or 4. nights amongst honest neighbors. And take heed of it brother Westchester: it is an unlawful game if you will believe me. For, in winter it is no matter to take a little sport, for an odd cast braces of 20. nobles when the weather is foul, that men cannot go abroad to bowls, or to shoot? What would you have men take no recreation? Yea but it is an old said saw, enough is as good as a feast. And recreations must not be made a trade and an occupation, ka master Martin Marprelate. I tell you true brother mine, though I have as good a gift in pistle making, as you have at priemeero, and far more delight than you can have at your cards, for the love I bear to my brethren, yet I dare not use this sport, but as a recreation, not making any trade thereof. And cards I tell you though they be without horns, yet they are parlous beasts. Be they lawful or unlawful take heed of them for all that. For you cannot use them but you must needs say your brother *T. C.* his Amen, that is, swear by your faith, many a time in the night, well I will never stand argling the matter anymore with you. If you will leave your card playing so it is, if you will not, trust to it it will be the worse for you.

I must go simply and plainly to work with my brethren, that have published *T. C.* Whosoever have published that book, they have so hooped the bishops' tubs, that they have made them to smell far more odious than ever they did, even in the nostrils of all men. The book is of 252. pages. The drift thereof is, to confute certain printed and published libels. You bestow not full 50. pages in the answer of anything that ever was published in print. The rest are bestowed to maintain the belly, and to confute: what think you? Even the slanderous inventions of your own brains for the most part. As that it is not lawful for her Majesty to allot any lands unto the maintenance of the minister, or the minister to live upon lands for this purpose allotted unto him, but is to content himself with a small pension, and so small, as he have nothing to leave for his wife and children after him (for whom he is not to be careful, but to rest on god's providence) and is to require no more but food and raiment, that in poverty he might be answerable unto our Savior Christ and his apostles. In the confutation of these points, and the scriptures corruptly applied to prove them, there is bestowed above 100. pages of this book, that is, from the 149. unto the end. Well *T. C.* whosoever thou art, and whosoever Martin is, neither thou, nor any man or woman in England shall know while you live, suspect and trouble as many as you will, and therefore save your money in seeking for him, for it may be he is nearer you than you are ware of. But whosoever thou art I say, thou shewest thyself to be a most notorious wicked slanderer, in fathering these things upon those whom they call puritans, which never any enjoying common sense would affirm. And bring me him, or set down his name and his reasons that holdeth any of the former points confuted in thy book, and I will prove him to be utterly bereaved of his wits, and his confuter to be either stark mad, or a stark enemy to all religion, yea to her Majesty and the state, of this kingdom. No no, *T. C.* puritans hold no such points. It were well for bishops, that their adversaries were thus sottish. They might then justly incense her Majesty and the state against them, if they were of this mind. These objections, in the confutation whereof, thou hast bestowed so much time, are so far from having any puritan to be their author, as whosoever readeth the book, were he as blockheaded as Thomas of Winchester himself, he may easily know them to be objections only invented by the author of the book himself. For although he be an impudent wretch, yet dareth he not set them down, as writings of any other: for then he would have described the author and the book by some audient.

The puritans indeed, hold it unlawful for a minister to have such temporal revenues, as whereby ten ministers might be well maintained, unless the said revenues come unto him by inheritance.

They hold it also unlawful, for any state to bestow the livings of many ministers upon one alone, especially when there is such want of ministers' livings.

They hold it unlawful for any minister to be Lord over his brethren. And they hold it unlawful for any state to tolerate such under their government. Because it is unlawful for states, to tolerate men in those places whereinto the word hath forbidden them to enter.

They affirm that our Savior Christ, hath forbidden all ministers to be Lords, Luke. 22. 25. And the Apostle Peter, sheweth them to be none of God's ministers, which are Lords over God's heritage, as you Bishops are, and would be accounted. These things *T. C.* you should have confuted, and not troubled yourself, to execute the fruits of your own brains, as an enemy to the state. And in these points, I do challenge you *T. C.* and you Dean John, and you John Whitgift, and you doctor Cousins, and you doctor Capcase (Copcoat I think your name be) and as many else, as have or dare write in the defense of the established church government. If you cannot confute my former assertions, you do but in vain think to maintain yourselves by slanders, in fathering upon the puritans, the offsprings of your own blockheads. And assure yourselves, I will so besoop you if you cannot defend yourselves in these points, as all the world shall cry shame upon you, you think prettily to escape the point of your Antichristian callings, by giving out that puritans hold it unlawful for her majesty to leave any lands for the use of the ministers' maintenance. I cannot but commend you, for I promise you, you can shift off an heinous accusation very prettily.

A true man bringeth unanswerable witnesses against a robber by the highway side, and desireth the judge, that the law may proceed against him. Oh no my Lord saith the thief, in any case let not me be dealt with. For these mine accusers have given out, that you are a drunkard or they have committed treason against the state: therefore I pray you believe my slander against them, that they may be executed: so when I come to my trial, I shall be sure to have no accusers. A very pretty way to escape, if a man could tell how to bring the matter about. Now brethren bishops, your manner of dealing, is even the very same. The puritans say truly, that all Lord bishops are petty Antichrists, and therefore that the magistrates ought to thrust you out of the commonwealth. Now of all loves say the bishops, let not our places be called in question, but rather credit our slanders against the puritans, whereby, if men would believe us when we lie, we would bear the world in hand, that these our accusers are Malcontents and sottish men, holding it unlawful for the magistrate to allot any lands for the minister's portion, and unlawful for the minister to provide for his family. And therefore you must not give ear to the accusations of any such men against us. And so we shall be sure to be acquitted. But brethren do you think to be thus cleared? Why the puritans hold no such points as you lay to their charge. Though they did, as they do not, yet that were no sufficient reason, why you being petty popes, should be maintained in a christian commonwealth. Answer the reasons that I brought against you: otherwise, Come off you bishops, leave your thousands, and content yourselves with your hundreds, saith John of London. So that you do plainly see, that your Cooper *T. C.* is but a deceitful workman, and if you commit the hooping of your bishoprics unto him, they will so leak in a short space, as they shall be able to keep never a Lord bishop in them. And this may serve for an answer unto the latter part of your book, by way of an Interim, until more work for Cooper be published.

2

[Job Throckmorton (?)]

A Dialogue. Wherein Is Plainly Laide Open,
the Tyrannicall Dealing of L. Bishopps Against
Gods Children, 1589

JOB THROCKMORTON (1545– 1601) was educated at Oxford, where he received a B.A. degree in 1566. He served in Parliament twice, the last time in 1587. His religious views led him to associate with, and to support, John Penry and other radical reformers, but at a trial in 1591 Throckmorton was acquitted of complicity with them. In 1593 he denied under oath any knowledge of the authorship of the Marprelate tracts, yet Leland H. Carlson, in *Master Marprelate, Gentleman* (San Marino, Calif., 1981, pp. 158–71), convincingly argues Throckmorton's authorship of *A Dialogue. Wherein Is Plainly Laide Open, the Tyrannicall Dealing of L. Bishopps Against Gods Children.*

The *Dialogue* provides a good summary of the Marprelate attacks on the bishops. Its participants, unlike most of the characters in polemical dialogues of the time, emerge as distinct personalities, and one, Jack of Both Sides, even provides a dramatic reversal at the conclusion. The work was first published in 1589 and reprinted, as were several Marprelate tracts, during the contentions of the early 1640s.

For a polemical work, the *Dialogue* shows unusual concern for literary, especially dramatic, effects. Its setting is not described, but the road to London on which the verbal exchanges take place appears no less real than Chaucer's road to Canterbury. Care has been taken to foreshadow the appearance of two of the characters; at the opening, Jack of Both Sides and Puritan speak, indicating that they approach their journey's end, having started out from Orléans and La Rochelle, respectively. In due course they comment on another person who will soon overtake them, and after they discuss the religious problems of England for a brief time, Idol Minister appears. In the three-way dialogue that ensues, Jack and Puritan reinforce each other's cogent arguments, whereas the minister appears as an embodiment of Puritan's description of the conforming clergy as lazy, servile, and uneducated. The designation Idol Minister is a significant pun: He is both idle and an idolater. The last character, Papist, also receives an introduction before he enters the scene and speaks in character. A surprise ending is provided by Jack of Both Sides, who has chastised the minister as severely as has Puritan but now reveals to Papist that he is in fact a popish sympathizer and has agreed with Puritan only to encourage statements that will make Puritan all the more subject to punishment by the ecclesiastical authorities.

Puritan's statements, together with those in which Jack speaks in agreement with, and encouragement of, him, serve as the author's norm and give a widely comprehensive, favorable picture of a puritan as seen by the Marprelate group and their sympathizers. Puritan bases his argument on Scripture; in fact, all the significant biblical quotations (except for three used by Jack in an early speech) appear in Puritan's discourse. He strongly advocates a preaching ministry and a church on the congregational model, with pastors, elders, doctors, and deacons. He sees episcopacy as an evil, with no foundation in the Scripture or the early church. Like Martin Marprelate, he condemns the bishops for their personal conduct, arrogance, luxurious living, lack of charity, and dishonesty in dealing with clergymen and laymen. The question of church government so dominates the work that of the religious practices disliked by the ardent reformers, Puritan mentions only baptizing by women. Although supporting his ecclesiastical arguments only by Scripture, he indicates his approval of the Nicene, Athanasian, and Apostles' creeds. Throughout the work he speaks to the minister with vehemence, condemning him in remarkably blunt terms.

Most of the indictments handed out by Puritan and Jack focus on specific bishops and their defenders, most notably on John Aylmer, bishop of London; John Whitgift, archbishop of Canterbury; and Thomas Cooper, bishop of Winchester. Jack of Both Sides presents a wealth of specific detail. Aylmer is condemned for swearing, bowling, parsimony, lack of charity, and accumulation of personal wealth. Cooper's learning is impugned; his scholarly work is held to be largely plagiarized. Whitgift is severely criticized for his conduct in office, notably his enforcement of conformity, his appointment of unqualified people to important positions in the church, and his persecution of nonconformists. In addition, one significant moral charge is brought against him: his deceit in promising and then withholding preferments. However, his learning is denigrated only to the extent that he is compared unfavorably with Thomas Cartwright.

Numerous other ecclesiastical figures are cited for moral shortcomings, often with vividly told incidents adduced as evidence. Most notorious appears to be Marmaduke Middleton, bishop of Saint David's, who is accused of bigamy. Nicholas Bond, vice-chancellor of Oxford, is said to be fond of dancing. Martin Culpepper, warden of New College at Oxford, is said to prefer hunting to attending sermons. Others are cited for lack of religious zeal and doctrinal inadequacies: Papistic inclinations, or at least a readiness to abandon reformation for personal gain, are charged against Andrew Perne, Richard Bancroft, and John Sprint, as well as John Bullingham, bishop of Gloucester; Gabriel Goodman, dean of Westminster; and John Bridges, dean of Salisbury.

Favorable citations are given to Martin Marprelate, who provides the source of many accusations against the bishops; to Thomas Cartwright, for his learning as well as his religious orientation; and to Theodore Beza and John Calvin. Idol Minister's linking of puritans with La Rochelle, Geneva, and Scotland can be taken as approval of religious practices in those places. The queen appears to be above criticism; in fact, we are told that she would have proceeded against many ecclesiastical authorities, and perhaps against episcopacy, had not Whitgift pleaded for them. Characteristically, both reformers and defenders of the establishment during this period defer to the civil magistrate.

Some juxtapositions appearing here will become familiar to the reader of puritan and antipuritan works. To Puritan, Papist is closely akin to the conforming Anglican and more readily tolerated by the bishops than is Puritan. The relationship of the Book of Common Prayer to the ritual of the Roman Catholic church is mentioned briefly but explicitly. To the minister, the puritans, Martin Marprelate, and the Brownists—that is, the separatists—appear nearly identical, and Puritan does not dispute kinship with the others. Yet from the author's point of view, the people designated as "Gods Children" in the title of the dialogue are those called puritans.

A Dialogue.

Wherein is plainly laide open, the tyrannicall dealing of L. Bishopps against Gods children: with certaine points of doctrine, wherein they approove themselves (according to *D. Bridges* his judgement) to be truely the Bishops of the *Divell*. A Dialogue wherein is plainely laid open tyrannicall dealing of Lord Bb. against Gods children.

[Job Throckmorton (?), 1589.]

The speakers are these, *Puritan. Papist. Jack of both sides. Idol minister.*

Puritan   You are well overtaken sir, do you travel far this way I pray you?

Jack   Towards London sir.

Puritan   I shall willingly bear you company if it please you?

Jack   With all my heart, I shall be very glad of yours.

Puritan   From whence came you this way?

Jack   I come out of France.

Puritan   Out of what part of France came you I pray you? I came from *Rochell* myself, which is a part of France.

Jack   Is it so, but I came not near that place.

Puritan   Out of what part of France came you then?

Jack   I came from *Orleans.*

Puritan   I pray you what news from thence, is there any likelihood of peace there?

Jack   Yes surely, there is some hope of peace, for where the King's powers come, they do commonly yield presently.

Puritan   It is a good hearing.

Jack   What is he that comes after us so fast?

Puritan   He seems to be some preacher or dumb minister, it may be he goes our way, if he do I hope we shall have his company whereby we may pass away the time in some good conference, and also hear what news there is at home here in England.

Jack   I am content Sir, for I shall be glad to hear some good news, methinks I have been very long absent from hence.

Puritan   Very well, we will go the softlier that he may overtake us: but by
the way, I pray you, if you come from *Orleans,* there they have the mass,
for they are of the league: and then I suppose you have been partaker of
their Idolatry?

Jack   No I assure you, I detest all Idolatry, even from my heart.

Puritan   If you do so, I am very glad of it, but I pray you let me hear if you
can give me some proof out of the word of God, for the confirmation of
this your protestation against Idolatry?

Jack   I am well content to give you a taste thereof, whereby it shall appear
that I am far from it: For so dearly as I tender the salvation of mine own
soul, so careful am I to shun and fly from all Idolatry. For it is written
Deut. 6: 13. "Thou shalt worship the Lord thy God, and him only shalt
thou serve": And the Apostle Paul to the Corinth. 1. Epist. cap. 10. verse
14. commandeth us to "Fly from Idolatry," for Idolatry is sin, and "the
wages of sin is death," etc.

Puritan   It is well applied, and somewhat to the purpose, I am very glad
if it be done in singleness of heart: For methinks you could not possibly
be in that place but you must be forced to be present at their Idolatrous
Mass.

Jack   I was never present at it in my life, I thank God: but the Papists stick
not to say that our service book in english is (a great part of it) but a mere
translation of the mass book.

Puritan   Indeed it is true, that some part of our book of common prayer
(as they say) is a mere translation out of the mass book, but yet there is
no such blasphemy and Idolatry tolerated in it, as is daily in the mass:
although it greatly derogate from the word, and is full of great and
grievous corruptions: But I pray you how long were you in *Orleans* Sir?

Jack   I was there about a fortnight.

Puritan   No longer?

Jack   No Sir.

Puritan   Here comes the minister now, we will hear what news he can
tell us, he seems to be but an Idol shepherd: we shall have some good
conference with him I hope, to pass away the time?

Minist.   You are well overtaken gentlemen, which way travel you, I pray
you?

Puritan   Towards London, and if it please God.

Minist.   I shall be glad of your company and if it please you?

Puritan   We also shall be glad of yours Sir.

Jack   I pray you Mr. Vicar or parson, (for so you seem to be) what good news is there here at home, in England, for we have been both of us in France, and we would gladly hear some good news?

Minist.   Indeed I am a poor Vicar: truly we have no great good news here Sir: for our Church is so sore pestered with sects and schisms, that the reverend fathers, (and especially my Lord's grace of Cant.) are so sore troubled with them, that they have no leisure to recreate themselves for those fellows, they are so bold and malapert, that they prefer petitions to her majesty, the Lords of the council, yea and in print to the high court of parliament.

Puritan   Why sir, what be they that do this, what do you call them, are they papists?

Minist.   No they are worse than papists, for they are fantastical *puritans* and *Brownists,* and I cannot tell what.

Puritan   What be the points they hold, that are so schismatical, and erroneous?

Minist.   Forsooth they would have no Lord Bishops but every Minister to be of equal authority one with another, and so make a confusion in the whole state, for they have set down a new platform of (Discipline forsooth, as they call it) they cannot tell what themselves.

Puritan   I will tell you my opinion, of Lord Bishops it is but an human constitution, and not warrantable by the word, but utterly forbidden:

Minist.   Oh I perceive you are one of these fantastical *puritans* or *Brownists:* I pray you out of what place of France came you?

Puritan   I came from *Rochel.*

Minist.   I thought from *Rochel, Geneva* or *Scotland,* you seem to be a bird of one of those nests.

Puritan   Sir whatsoever I am, I do not doubt but to be able to prove by the word what I have said, and namely, the unlawfulness of Lord Bishops.

Minist.   Sir that point hath been handled by your betters, and manifestly confuted by my Lord's grace, in his writings against *Cartwright.*

Puritan   Indeed he that will be blind, cannot see it, but he that looks in both their works, with a single eye cannot but confess M. *Cartwright* to have confuted him by unanswerable evidences: or else why would he not have answered M. *Cartwright's* works, now a dozen years extant and more.

Minist.   As you of the fantastical crew think, but he hath done it, and that so sufficiently already, that there needs no more answers, and again his grace is now otherwise troubled with matters of state, that he cannot

46

intend it, or if he could, yet it is not for him so to abase himself, in regard of his high calling which he is now placed in.

Puritan As though the cause of God were to be neglected in respect of his high place, if he were lawfully called thereunto, as he doth very unlawfully usurp the same: contrary to the law of God: for is it possible he can be the true minister of God, and a temporal magistrate that is, to serve God and Mammon too. As the Apostle saith, "Let him that hath an office attend upon his office," and not offices.

Minist. Why how dare you presume to say so? Were not Lord Bishops established by her Majesty and consent of the whole Parliament?

Puritan I grant they were, but the Lord hath said contrary, in the commandment he gave to his ministers Luke 22. saying, "The kings of the gentiles reign over them, and they that bear rule over them are called gracious Lords, but ye shall not be so, but let the greatest among you be as the least, and the chiefest as him that serveth," and 1 Pet. 5. "Feed the flock of God which dependeth upon you, caring for it, not by constraint, but willingly, not for filthy lucre, but of ready mind: Not as though ye were Lords over God's heritage, but that ye may be ensamples to the flock." And in the first session of parliament, holden in the first year of her Majesty's reign, there was never a Lord Bishop in the land.

Minist. If you will have no Lord Bishops how should the Church be governed then?

Puritan According as our Savior Christ hath commanded, and as the holy Ghost hath set it down, viz. by pastors, Doctors, Elders, and deacons, Rom. 12. Ephes. 4. 1. Cor. 12.

Minist. You are very full of scripture, as though we have not the same offices in effect, though not in the same titles: as for example, have we not Parsons for Doctors, Vicars for Pastors, Churchwardens for Elders, and Sidemen for Deacons to distribute to the poor.

Puritan And what for Archbishops, and Lord Bishops?

Jack I will tell you for him, Archbishops for Popes, and Lord Bishops for Cardinals. Ha, ha, M. Vicar, I see you are a good Churchman, do not you use the pulpit sometimes?

Minist. No indeed sir, but I read the Homilies sometimes, and the Queen's Injunctions, and do my duty as other ministers do.

Puritan Methought so, by that fit comparison that you have made.

Jack And have you no more but one benefice neither, and yet do all that?

Minist. Yes indeed, I say service at two more, but I have little profit by them, marry the best is, they are somewhat near, for they are all three within four miles together.

Puritan   And how can you serve them all upon the Sabbath day?

Minist.   Some of them are but small, and I can make quick dispatch with them betimes, and take my Mare and ride to the other: and can make an end of all by ten of the clock, and spend an hour with good fellows at home before dinner too.

Puritan   And Master Vicar, do you think herein, that you discharge your duty to God, and those congregations, over whom you have taken this charge?

Minist.   Why sir, I discharge my duty better than those that take upon them four or five.

Puritan   Why? is there any that takes upon them the charge of so many?

Minist.   Yea a hundred in England.

Puritan   Well I will tell you, the fearful judgments of God hangs over our heads, and cannot be long deferred, but fall upon the whole land (whereto such dumb idols as you are, is committed the charge of souls) and to yourselves eternal destruction of body and soul: wherefore Mr. Vicar, as you tender your own salvation, leave this your unlawful calling of the ministry, and betake you to some occupation, or husbandry.

Minist.   I care not what any of you spiteful Puritans say, so long as I can have the favor of my Lord Bishop.

Jack   I pray you Mr. Vicar let me spur a question unto you, if I may be so bold? where do you serve?

Minist.   I serve in Middlesex Sir.

Jack   Who made you minister?

Minist.   My good Lord of London.

Puritan   Like enough, he hath made a great many of blind guides in his time besides you, for he made the Porter of his gate, minister of Paddington, being blind.

Jack   O monstrous, is this true, did he so indeed?

Puritan   It is most true, for the Bishop of Winchester hath recorded it in a book of his set forth in print.

Jack   Why, what will our Bishops grow to in time if they be suffered? for methinks this is a fearful thing, to make such ministers, as can neither see nor speak, for it is like if he were his porter, (no doubt of it) he had not the gift of teaching?

Puritan   Very true, but because he could do him no longer service, he was so good to him, to provide for the poor blind man that he might live.

Jack   Sure I think when they come once to be Lords, they clean forget God and all godliness, for I have heard that there was some good things in him before he was Bishop of London, for he wrote a book called the *Harborow of faithful subjects,* against Bishops: wherein he saith, "Come down ye Bishops with your thousands, and betake you to your hundreds, let your fare be Priestlike and not Princelike," etc.

Puritan   Indeed he wrote such a book, and the same words that you repeat, I have read in the same: but alas, when he was at the best, he was but a corrupt man, and the best things in it, savor but of earth: for there is many things handled in it very immodestly, and unchristianly: but one thing especially he sets down there, which himself practiceth clean contrary: where he speaks of the ability that should be in every minister of the word, that "he should know his quarter strokes, to be able to convince the adversary," etc.

Minist.   Why? will you have none Ministers but such as can preach? I can tell you, that the twentieth minister in the land cannot preach?

Puritan   The more the worse, for you and the rest how many soever there be stand without repentance in a most damnable state, for you are most notorious murderers of souls, in taking upon you so high a calling, and being so far unfit for it: so many as perish for want of teaching, in your charge, their blood the Lord will require at your hands:

Minist.   The Bishop knew my ability before he made me minister.

Puritan   Well, he stands in the state of damnation as you do, and thus much I say unto you, and to all Idol Ministers, and to him, and all usurping Archbishops and Lord Bishops, leave your unlawful callings into which you have intruded yourselves, and with speed repent, and humble yourselves before the Majesty of God, confessing your horrible and grievous sins with *Peter's* tears, in that you are the cause, yea and also the very murderers of so many souls, as perish in your charges: knowing that the Lord will in that great and terrible day, require their blood at your hands.

Jack   O Lord, my heart quaketh to hear of so great and grievous sins as are in our Bishops, and in the whole ministry: but our Bishops are the cause of all.

Puritan   I will tell you Sir, I am persuaded in my very conscience, that the Lord hath given many of our Bishops over into a reprobate sense, for they do willfully oppose themselves against the Lord his known truth, yea and *persecute* it, (and I suppose them to be in the state of the sin against the holy Ghost) for they have manifested in their published writings, yea and pressed forth by authority, such horrible blasphemous, heretical, yea damnable doctrines, which my very heart trembleth to repeat, in sort as they have set them down: which if those (whom they falsely call Puritans) should set down or hold the like errors and dangerous points, I warrant you they should soon be cut off from the face of the earth, and right well they were worthy.

Jack   Now Sir I pray you let me hear some of the points they hold, and that are so dangerous as you say, that I may be able to justify it to our dumb dog's teeth, at Austin's gate in London when I come home.

Puritan   First you shall understand, the Bishop of London hath published in print, and that in an Epistle or preface before *Barnardeus de loques* book of the Church, published in english, that the Puritans may as well deny the son of God to be consubstantial with God the father, as they may deny the superiority of Archbishops and Lord Bishops, flat contrary to the saying of our Savior Christ, Luke 22.

Jack   O monstrous and blasphemous wretch, that to maintain his fleshly pleasure, will make such an odious comparison.

Puritan   Nay, what say you to a Bishop that hath two wives and both now living? Do you not think it is a thing tolerable in a christian commonwealth, where the Gospel is professed?

Jack   No indeed do I not, I hope our magistrates will not suffer such a Bishop to live, it were monstrous among common Infidels, much more intolerable, that a Bishop in such a land as ours is, where the Gospel is truly taught: But I pray you is there any such now living?

Puritan   Yes indeed is there, and the Bishop of Saint Davids in Wales is the man, he is now living and both his wives, and yet still remains a Bishop.

Jack   Is it possible that a Bishop should commit such an horrible act as this, how far are our Bishops from obeying the commandment of the Apostle Peter: who saith, "Feed the flock, and be ensamples to the flock": what ensample is this? And doth not the same God which saith, "Thou shalt do no murder," which is death by our laws, doth he not also say, "Thou shalt not commit adultery": And yet a Bishop to have two wives at once, and live in a Church professing the sincerity of the Gospel: What say you to this Master Vicar, is not our Church well governed think you?

Minist.   If it be true, it is (I must needs confess) a horrible thing and worthy of death, but I do not believe it.

Puritan   It is very true, for the cause was brought before the high commissioners at Lambeth, and how it is smothered up among the

Bishops, and the rest of the commissioners, I know not yet, but I could tell you the whole conclusion if I were at London but half an hour.

Jack Why the suffering of this, and other like villainies, to be committed in our nation, are causes to stir up the Lord to wrath, against the whole land, whereby he may speedily bring his judgments upon us, yea even to our utter destruction.

Minist. It is so if it be true? but I will not believe it.

Puritan Well for the truth of the matter, I refer you to the high commissioners, where it is recorded, with his wives names, viz. Elizabeth Gigge and Alice Prime.

Minist. Indeed I have heard of the like before, that you puritans have put forth a book in print under the name of *Martin Marprelate,* wherein many such things are mentioned:

Puritan There is nothing set down in it, but there is good proof of the same, and the Bishop of Winchester, who took upon him to confute it, hath confirmed it for the most part, and that he denies is most true.

Jack What did he undertake to confute it? Alas he is altogether unlearned, (for I have heard of him in Oxford, and the papists say, they can make him believe the moon is made of green cheese) marry to get him a name (forsooth) being a correcter with a Printer in Fleet street in London, who printed a Dictionary called *Sir Thomas Eliot's* dictionary, *Cooper* translated a piece of *Robert Stephanus* his *Thesaurus* and joined it to the same with a few phrases, and so bereaved the famous Knight of his labor, and calls it by the name of *Cooper's Dictionary:* how say you Master Vicar, was not this a knavish trick tell me?

Minist. I say you deal very unreverently with my Lord: for I can say nothing to the matter else, for I know it not to be true?

Puritan What say you to this then master Vicar did you never hear of your Lord Bishop of London, who made the Dyers in Thames street who were robbed, by thieves that stole their cloth, and brought it within his liberties, which when the poor dyers hearing where their cloth was, and coming to the Bishop to demand their own goods, he said: if they would hang the thieves, he would then tell them more, which the dyers did, and at their deaths, confessed that to be the dyers cloth which the Bishop had, but the poor men were never the nearer for their cloth, nor cannot get it or any part of it to this day: and this is confessed to be true, by the bishop of Winchester in his answer to *Martin Marprelate,* published in print by authority: wherein he saith, it is the Bishop of London's own, by the laws

51

of the land, because it was taken within his liberties, marry he speaks nothing of the law of God, according to conscience, in keeping of thief-stolen goods from their right owners, for conscience is fled from them (it seems) so soon as they are gotten to be Lord Bishops once.

Minist.　Yes Sir I know there is such a book named *Martin Marprelate,* a most vile and slanderous libel but I do not think my Lord of Winchester doth approve anything that is set down there in any of those books, for they have put forth three or four books under that title.

Jack　Why Master Vicar, how do they get their books printed?

Minist.　Tush they do well enough for that, there is a seditious fellow one *Walde-grave,* who commonly prints all such books, (I know him well enough) he did keep a shop at the sign of the Crane in Paul's Churchyard: at which time he had his press and letters taken away from him, and destroyed for the same cause, by my Lord's grace of Canterbury, and now he works in corners up and down the country like a vagabond.

Puritan　With a seared conscience, did the Bishops that violence to him, in regard both of the cause, and also for the great charge he hath of wife and six small children, and now to bereave his Poor family of him, whose labors was their only comfort and maintenance.

Jack　Master Vicar how long was it since *Walde-grave's* goods were destroyed, I have heard of him before now, but I know him not?

Minist.　Tush you know him will enough I am sure, it is since his goods were destroyed about Easter was a twelvemonth.

Jack　And hath he been all this time absent from his family?

Minist.　Aye Sir, and if he had been there, he would easily have been had, for he hath been watcht well enough for that?

Puritan　I will tell you Sir how they deal with him, when they have any suspicion that he is at home, although he durst never come home, they stick not in the dead time of the night, to break down the main walls of his house, and enter in with constables and pursuivants, and this is a common thing with them.

Jack　I am persuaded, the Bishops had been better to have given him freely 2. hundred pounds towards the setting up of a new printing house for himself, than to have destroyed his as they have done:

Minist.　I think so, for it may be he would have followed his calling some other way, than to be employed in those things?

Jack　Yonder comes a man plodding apace after us whatsoever he be?

Minist.　It may be our company will increase, and so we shall go the more cheerful, for it begins to be late, and it is dangerous going hereabouts late, I can tell you?

Puritan   It may be he is one of your coat Master Vicar?

Minist.   I cannot tell, but if he be, he shall be welcome to me.

Jack   Surely he comes apace, whatsoever he be?

Minist.   It may be he would be glad of company?

Jack   Well let us go on and continue our talk?

Puritan   Master Vicar I think be weary of our communication, if you be let us know?

Minist.   No by my faith Sir not I, say what you will a God's name?

Puritan   Fie, Master Vicar, will you swear? I think you learned that of your Lord Bishop of London, for he useth it often, when he is at bowls.

Jack   What will Bishops swear?

Puritan   Swear Sir, Aye that they will, and defend it too, when they have done? For in the first Book of Martin, there is mention made of the Bishop of London's swearing, when he is at bowls: And the Bishop of Winchester in answering the same, saith thus, in page 62. of his book, "That our Savior Christ usually sware by his faith in his sermon, for he said Amen, Amen, which is as much to say" (saith he) "as by my faith, by my faith?"

Jack   Why is that a Bishop of God, that will swear thus?

Minist.   So, I have heard my Lord's grace of Canterbury swear by his faith an hundred times, yea and by God too sometimes, and what he doth, I take it as a good precedent for such as I am to follow?

Puritan   I'll tell you Master Vicar, I am of doctor *Bridges* his mind of our Bishops: for (saith he) page 339, 340. "That all our Lord Bishops in England, are the Bishops of the Devil": And I am sure of it by these two marks, viz. "by their tyrannical dealing against Gods Children," and "by their wicked and unconscionable lives, that they are not of God?"

Jack   I pray you hath Doctor Bridges written any book that is published to this effect?

Puritan   Yes indeed, and the Bishop of Canterbury hath confirmed it by his authorizing of the same, and also by his continual practice against God's children?

Jack   But I pray you Sir, how wickedly hath he wrested the Scripture, in saying our Savior Christ continually sware in his sermons, when he said Amen, Amen?

Puritan   Why the Bishop of Winchester is most impudent in all his actions, for he very blasphemously in his sermon, preached at *Mary Overies* at

London, said that "a man might as well find fault with the holy Scripture, as with our corrupt Common book of prayer?"

Jack Out upon him blasphemous wretch, he is certainly the Bishop of the Devil, as Doctor *Bridges* saith.

Puritan Will you hear some more of his Divinity?

Jack O Yes I pray you Sir? And yet my heart trembleth to hear of such odious blasphemies as these.

Puritan He saith in the 49. page of his book against Martin Marprelate: "That the Creed of the Apostles, Athanasius, and the Nicene, etc. contain in them many palpable lies." Now tell me your opinion of this, is it not sound and substantial doctrine I pray you tell me?

Jack Doctrine yea indeed, this may truly be said to be the doctrine of Devils. Why whither will our Bishops run in time trow you, if the Magistrate suffer them?

Puritan I well tell you, even to their father the Devil: For they have at no time taken in hand to write in defense of their hierarchy, but it hath made their eyes so to dazzle, that they run into most dangerous and damnable errors, (as in this book of the Bishops will be proved near 500. errors) yea in correcting and controlling the mighty word of God, and also have interlaced their writings with such contrariety of matter, as one part of their own books may serve to confute the other, with infinite absurdities: yea and by your leave too, even flat treason?

Jack Many good men did never judge the bishop of Winchester, to be but an hypocrite?

Puritan He is a most bitter man to all those that fear God, and have to deal with him, for he may well be compared to a horse with a galled back that hath been so rubbed, that he winces, frets, and chafes, so, that he is ready to throw himself to utter destruction, with purpose to hurt him that rubbed him: Even so, this Bishop takes to himself so much liberty in abusing and profaning the holy word of God, (against those that write in the Lord's cause, against their unlawful callings) and that I fear me, to the endangering both of body and soul.

Jack I have heard that when he was at Lincoln he dealt not so hardly with the ministers as now he doth, and that often in his Sermons at Northampton he would confess, that the Discipline was used and practiced in the Primitive Church, a long time after the Apostles.

Puritan It is very true, and yet he saith in his Book against *Martin,* that the holy Discipline is a platform devised he knows not by whom: And in another place of the same book he confesses that it was practiced by the Apostles, and long time after in the Primitive Church, and upon the words where he saith "it is not denied," there is pasted, at the commandment of the Bishop of Canterbury, "It is not yet proved," so that there is some Jar, between themselves, although these two are most conversant together, and join in one to persecute sincere and faithful preachers of the word, and others of the Lord's children.

Jack   I had thought they would not have dissented one from another of them?

Puritan   Why sir in the 49. page of the same book the Bishop of Winchester saith, the Bishop of Canterbury "is a giddy head, and to be bridled," because he authorized Doctor *Whitaker* his readings against *Bellarmina*, wherein the *Apocrypha* is defaced: And M. Doctor *Some* one of their affinity now, and a nonresident, he calls the Archbishop of Canterbury "An absurd Heretic," because he holds baptism administered by women, to be the seal of God's covenant: page 3. of his book against *Master Penry*, and many like things I could cite to you, of their dissenting one from another.

Jack   How like you of these things Master Vicar, be not these good fathers of the Church, think you?

Minist.   I like never a whit the worse of them for your words, for I know they are but slanders?

Puritan   Master Vicar, you I know like well of them, although the proofs that their adversaries do bring be never so manifest and plain against them, because you are in the same state, or worse (and may be) in that you do unlawfully usurp your place, and having no fit gifts to discharge your duty in any measure: Remember what the Apostle saith, 1. Corinth. 6: 19. "Woe is to me if I preach not the Gospel," this is rightly pronounced upon you, and all such Idols as you are?

Minist.   If I read sermons and homilies, is it not as much as if I preached: for Master Doctor *Bridges* saith, that "reading is preaching?"

Puritan   The Lord hath promised no such blessing unto reading as preaching, for the word preached is the only ordinary means to salvation: But I pray you for your comfort, hear what the prophet *Jeremy* saith to you, in the 48. Chap. "Cursed be that man, that doth the work of the Lord negligently," and Malac. 2: 7. saith, "the priest's lips should preserve knowledge, and they should seek the law at his mouth," but how can you shun this curse Master Vicar? I pray God humble your heart that you may acknowledge your sin, and crave pardon at his hands, and leave the ministry, lest the Lord with a strong hand throw you out to your everlasting woe.

Jack   Master Vicar he gives you good counsel, it were good for you to follow it, if you do not, it will be the worse for you?

Minist.   Well Sir it is no matter, there be as wise as he will give me other counsel?

Jack   Why I see Master Vicar is obstinate, he will not be persuaded by you?

Puritan   Even as he will, I speak my conscience to him, he may choose if he will follow it or no?

Jack   I marvel what good hospitality the Bishop of London keeps, I have heard that he is very covetous?

Minist.   Indeed he doth keep a good house?

Jack   What doth not the dogs run away out of his house with whole shoulders. I think a man may as soon break his neck, as break his fast at his *house?*

Puritan   Surely I can say thus much by report of one that was his Chaplain, whose name is *Haiward* Vicar of Saint *Martins, by Charing cross,* that oftentimes when he dined at his Palace in London, he hath made his servants, to take the fragments and carry them to *Fulham,* but if there be any dainty morsel left, he will wrap it up in his handkerchief, and carry it in his bosom for fear lest his men should beguile him.

Jack   O Master Vicar, you have a most bountiful Lord: he is so liberal, that he will not suffer the scraps to be bestowed upon the poor, but to be kept for his servants' supper?

Minist.   It is false, for I have often seen alms given at his gates, when he hath lain at London:

Puritan   I'll tell you what I have heard him say at Paul's Cross myself upon a time, following his text very well: (you must think) he burst me out with a great exclamation of himself, in that he was poor and had no money, protesting what charges he had been at, "and that Paul's Church can bear me witness": (saith he) "that I have no money." And shortly after some of his own servants being there present, and heard him, (belike thought to make their good Lord a liar) very shortly after, robbed him, of certain hundred of pounds, for which offense, he was so good unto his men, as to hang them up three or four in number, (although he had the most part of his money again) and some of the parties executed, protested to their knowledge, he had much more money at usury, and that his servants lived only upon bribes.

Jack   A Bishop a liar and a usurer, nay surely M. Vicar, if your Lord have those two faults, it cannot be but he hath more, so that for mine own part, I think him verily to be the Bishop of the Devil.

Puritan   Nay Sir I can give you proof for the same more, that he is surely the Bishop of the Devil, for *Martin Marprelate* hath set down a pretty thing in his *Epistle to the terrible priests,* that the Bishop of *London* when he throws his bowl, (as he useth it commonly upon the sabbath day) he runs after it, and if it be too hard, he cries, "rub, rub, rub," and saith "the Devil go with thee," *when he goeth himself with it:* So that by those words, he nameth himself the Bishop of the Devil: but by his practice of tyrannical dealing against the Lord's faithful ministers, not only calleth, but proveth himself to be the Bishop of the Devil.

Jack   Ha, ha Master Vicar, you see your Lord Bishop is a Devil by his own confession: so indeed, you are not the Lord's Minister, but the Minister of the Devil, as your Lord Bishop is the Bishop of the Devil.

Minist.   You use your speeches at pleasure of my Lord, it may be you will not so easily answer them when you are called thereunto?

Jack   Yes Master Vicar I warrant you? Send a pursuivant when you will for us, and we will answer it, if we cannot make our parts good enough, we will send the women of *Hampsteed* to him?

Minist.   What mean you by that?

Jack   If you will needs have me, I will tell you, you shall understand Master Vicar, that your good Lord, at his first coming to be the Devil's Lord at *London,* began to play *Rex,* (as he hath lately done at *Fulham,* in cutting down the trees, there, to the great impoverishing of the town) to cut down the woods at *Hampsteed* and needs he would do it, and began prettily well with it, the townsmen became suitors to him that he would not, they could not persuade him, for he was Lord of it, he said: Well seeing the men could do no good with him, the women took the matter in hand, and as the Devil's men came, (that is your Lord's) to cut down their woods, the women fell aswadling of them, so that they durst come no more to cut down any trees there. Thus you see the women overcame the Devil, and so feared him, that thereby they preserved their woods. For by very nature, these Devil's Bishops are given to destroy both Church and commonwealth? But if we be not good enough for them, we will entreat the women of *Hampsteed* to take the matter in hand.

Minist.   Well I doubt not but you will for all this lustiness, kiss the Clink or gatehouse for this gear, for my Lord's grace shall know of it, if my Lord do not?

Jack   Why Vicar of the Devil, let the whole convocation house of Devils know of it and you will, for they dare not, no not *Beelzebub* of Canterbury the chief of the Devils, come to disputation, thereby to approve their Callings to be lawful, and other points in controversy against the discipline of

God, as they have been often challenged, and offered by the puritans, even to adventure their lives against their Bishoprics, and yet they durst not. And I pray you tell me; if they were not the Bishops of the Devil indeed, would they refuse this offer?

Minist. Why the puritans have been often disputed with?

Puritan Where? In the Bishop's closet? For they are ashamed to have it tried before any Magistrate, Let them if they dare procure a free disputation, whereby every man may freely speak, and be indifferently heard, and if the Bishops and all their partakers be not overthrown, I will lose my life for it?

Minist. Have they not been already by public writing, and otherwise, but especially by my Lord's grace, his works against *Cartwright,* sufficiently confuted I pray you?

Puritan No indeed, but I will tell you what a nobleman professing the Gospel said, he demanded of the old Lord *Henry* Howard (the Earl of *Arundel's* uncle now living, being a professed papist) what he thought of *Whitgift's* answer to *Cartwright,* who answered, "There was no comparison to be made between them, for *Whitgift*" (saith he) "is not worthy to carry Cartwright's books after him for learning": Mark here the opinion of a papist, you know a deadly adversary to *Master Cartwright:* and yet the ambitious wretch will not stick now he is an Archbishop, to call those that are able to teach him (and which were in the Gospel before him) boys, and revile them far beyond all christian modesty: and again, if a man apply any new writer his opinion of the reformed Churches, in defense of the Lord's truth, as *Master Calvin, Beza* or others, he will not also stick to brag and tell him, that he is able to teach *Calvin* and *Beza,* or any of them all: but the wretch nor his associates, dares not dispute with *Master Cartwright, Calvin,* or *Beza's* inferiors.

Jack Tush, so, he sits now upon his cogging stool, which may truly be called the chair of pestilence, little may he do if he cannot brag, Crake, and face it out: for the truth is, he wrote against the Discipline, for no other end, but to get a Bishopric, for he never wrote since he hath caught one I warrant you: And the pied faced fool Doctor *Bridges* imitating him, hoping to leap like as he hath done, but it will not be?

Puritan O you are greatly deceived, Dr. *Bridges* hath utterly renounced the Bishops as I have heard, for that the Archbishop hath broken his faith with him?

Jack How comes that to pass I pray you?

Puritan I will tell you, at the beginning of the last parliament, there were

Bishops to be stalled, and his grace had promised him very confidently, that he would not only speak for him, also assure him of a Bishopric? Upon which the aspiring wretch did only rely, otherwise it may be he would have bribed some courtier to have dealt for him, as he did for his Deanery: But her Majesty lying at *Richmond,* and master Doctor repairing thither, upon the green afore *Richmond* house, met with Master *Thornby* the Master of the *Savoy,* who told him that he heard he was a suitor for the Bishopric of such a place: Master Doctor *Bridges* answered and said, it was true, he had the grant of it at his grace his hands: saith master *Thornby* I had a promise of it too: but it is certain that his Grace hath got it for another man, and he hath finished it, and all is past, I can assure you of it: With that the Doctor was in his mad mood, and said, "hath he served me so, why then I will say, and may speak it truly, there is no faith in a Bishop. Have I wrote in their defense, and have gotten the ignomy, shame, and reproach of it by public writing, and now to be thus vilely dealt with: I will tell you master *Thornby,* I do protest, and always will affirm it: That it is better to have one inch of policy, than all the Divinity in the world." If master *Thornby* will deny this to be true, there be both godly and worshipful will justify it to his face.

Jack   Nay it is like enough that the Bishop of Canterbury hath served him so, it is not the first like prank he hath played, for it is his manner, he will promise much and perform nothing: but persecute God's ministers, and glory in himself: For if any godly minister, or any other that fear God, come before him, he will offer them the oath, either to accuse themselves, or their christian brethren, or both, yea though no body be able to charge them with any offense: and if they will not swear, then to the Clink, Gatehouse or white Lion they go roundly, and when suit is made unto him for their liberty: Then except they will enter into bonds to perform this, or do that: why he will say they shall lie till they rot, with other bitter words. And he was wont to use these words often, and had a great pride in speaking them (I cannot tell whether he hath left them now or no,) "As long as the Queen and I live, it shall be this or that." Judge you of this man, whether he hath an humble spirit, or an aspiring mind, to join himself with his dread Sovereign the Queen's majesty. He were best to remember his predecessor *Cardinal Wolsey,* betimes, lest he have the same end *Cardinal Wolsey* had.

Minist.   I hope for these your taunting speeches to see you trounct, if I meet you handsomely in place where?

Jack   Why Vicar of the Devil, (I think you to be one of the Vicars of Hell, that *Martin* speaks of) it is no marvel, though you take the Bishops of the Devil's part. For *Winchester* when he went his visitations last, told your companions the dumb dogs, that if his grace of Canterbury, and himself had not kneeled before her Majesty for you, you had been all of you thrust out of the ministry?

Puritan   Oh wicked act, it had been better that neither of them had had a joint to bow, than to work such a villainy to God's Church.

Jack   Herein they used great policy (you must think) for if we had a learned Ministry once, they know their Kingdom would soon fall to the ground. Therefore they take order for that. For they will suspend and thrust all those out of the Ministry, that have gifts fit for that high calling: and keep none in, except nonresidents, such as gape after Bishoprics, or dumb Idol ministers?

Papist   You are well overtaken my masters? Which way travel you I pray?

Jack   Towards London Sir.

Papist   What good news is here abroad do you hear any?

Puritan   I know none good, for the land is sore troubled with these treacherous *Papists,* and filthy *Atheists:* and our church pestered with the Bishops of the Devil, non-residents, Popish priests, and dumb dogs, that there is no place, nor being for a faithful minister of the word: for if there be any in any charge, the Bishops have their *John Avales,* to fetch them up before them, and then if they will not subscribe, out of the ministry he goes roundly?

Papist   It was never merry world since there was so many puritans, and such running to Sermons as there is now.

Jack   Why? Do not you love to hear Sermons?

Papist   No, I care for none of these precise fellows, I will not come at any of their Sermons.

Jack   I smell you already, I perceive you are a Papist.

Papist   Whatsoever I be, you may be sure I am no puritan, for a Papist, is always better than a puritan, and more friends he shall find, both at home and abroad. And I have heard my Lord's grace of *Canterbury,* and the Bishop of *Winchester,* speak it with mine own ears.

Minist.   I can say thus much myself, my Lord's grace is not so much troubled with papists as with puritans?

Jack   And I can say thus much too, the papists have more favor of his grace a great deal, than the Puritans?

Papist   My Lord's grace you know, had a good master, and one that kept him far enough from this preciseness, I warrant you?

Jack   Who was his master I pray you?

Papist   Marry Master Doctor *Pearne* Sir.

Jack   What Doctor *Pearne?* why he is the notablest turncoat in all this land, there is none comparable to him? Why every boy hath him in his mouth, for it is made a proverb, both of old and young, that if one have a coat or cloak that is turned, they say it is *Pearnd.*

Puritan   And do you think the Bishop of Canterbury will be as good a turner, as his Master Doctor *Pearne* is?

Jack   Nay, he will exceed his Master, I am persuaded?

Puritan   Methinks there should be others as expert, and likely to make as good workmen in that art, as his grace or his master Doctor *Pearne* himself is?

Jack   Who should they be?

Puritan   What say you to *John* of *Glocester,* Doctor *Kennolde,* Doctor *Bancroft,* Doctor *Goodman,* the Abbot that now is of *Westminster,* Doctor *Sprent* of *Bristow,* and Master Doctor *Bridges* Dean of *Sarum.*

Jack   Yea and I may say to you, all the Bishops of the Devil and Nonresidents, are likely to say pretty well to the matter too?

Puritan   I had forgotten one that I should have nominated too, that is Doctor *Culpepper* of *Oxford,* who hath the name to be a notable hunter?

Jack   What Doctor *Culpepper,* I'll tell you there is many good things in him that way, but I will tell you one or two notes of his single gifts. For he is an Archdeacon, and going in his Visitation, not far from *Oxford:* It is an ordinary thing with them, to have a Sermon before they keep court, and always the court is kept in the Church? The Preacher somewhat troubling him, (in telling the spiritual fathers their duties) did sometimes nod at the preacher so as he did perceive him, to the end he should make an end of his Sermon: The Preacher nonwithstanding went forward with his text, which troubled Master Doctor sore. Then he fell a beckoning to the preacher, the preacher would not see his signs, although the audience greatly marveled at him, then Master Doctor (being sore galled you must think,) spake to him and bad him come down: the preacher thought it not long (though Master Doctor were weary to hear his duty told him in so plain a manner) and seeing he could use no means to get him out of the pulpit, called the crier to him, and bad him cry, "Hoyes," and so he did. Then went he very reverently about his business, and left the preacher in the pulpit: Now tell me I pray you, whether he had more mind to hear the word preached, or to be with his kennel of hounds.

Puritan   Is this Doctor *Culpepper* of *Oxford* I pray you?

Jack   Aye marry is it Sir, it is the same man, and very well known to love a hound, a hawk, and etc.

Puritan   I pray you can tell me, I have heard that Dr. *Bond* is made master of *Magdalens* in *Oxford,* contrary to the statutes of the University: Whereas one Master *Smith* was first elected, according to the orders of the house before him, he being one that stands for reformation in our corrupt Church government. Therefore as I have heard, the Bishops of Canterbury and *Winchester,* to prevent him, labored to her Majesty, that she would give commandment, that the house should accept of Doctor *Bond* in his stead, which by the Bishops' great labor, it was accomplished.

Jack   It is very true Sir, I can assure you of that, and he may well be called the *Bond* of iniquity for any goodness is in him, he looks I can tell you to be a Lord Bishop of the Devil shortly, besides he is a good dancer: I have heard how he ere now, hath come to a house in *Oxford,* (it shall be nameless,) where certain women of the town, were ready to go dance, (it may be a match made of him beforehand) comes me in the same house very pleasantly to them: saying, you are well met, and makes him ready for them: First put off his Cap, saying lie thou there Cap, then his tippet, lie thou there tippet, then his gown, lie thou there gown: and last of all his book (saith he) lie thou there Divinity and all: Then about the house he goes with the women: now tell me I pray you, if he do not draw in the *bond* of iniquity or no?

Puritan   Surely I see that no good men are left almost in any place, where they may be a help to increase or comfort those that fear God. For the Bishops have laid so many plots, that they have prevented all means whatsoever. Is not this a Devilish policy of the Bishop of Canterbury, to place such heads in the university: That none shall proceed, or be preferred but such as will subscribe. Well though the admonition which the Archbishop of *York* gave him in a letter before his death, do not work that effect in him, which the Bishop wisht: Yet our hope is, that the Lord will soon bring him to the same end, at the which, he may with the same Bishop confess his sin, in usurping that unlawful calling he is now in: that is a Pope or Pastor of pastors, with all other his injurious and tyrannical dealing with God's ministers and other his children. For of all the Bishops that ever were in that place, I mean in the See of *Canterbury* did never so much hurt unto the church of God, as he hath done since his coming. No Bishop that ever had such an aspiring and ambitious a mind as he, no not *Cardinal Wolsey:* none so proud as he, no not *Stephen Gardiner* of *Winchester:* none so tyrannical as he, no not *Bonner.*

Jack   How say you Master Vicar, were it not a good thing if all Bishops, and such Idol shepherds as you are were a dying, then you would be in better minds than all the days of your life before?

Minist.   You say your pleasure, but I care not what you say, that's the best of it.

Papist   Master Vicar the Gentlemen are disposed to move your patience, therefore you must bear with them.

Jack   Master Parson thinks I am in good earnest, but he is deceived, for I assure you I do nothing but to see what this puritan will say: and the puritan thinks I am one of his fraternity.

Papist   But are you not so indeed?

Jack   No truly, I came from *Orleans,* where I heard Mass everyday: see see how hard the Vicar and he are in talk, let them alone we will go on.

Papist   I can hardly believe that you heard Mass at *Orleans?*

Jack   If I had not been present at the Mass, I should have been taken for a *Hugonot,* and so I should hardly have escaped with my life.

Papist   I am the gladder of your company.

Jack   And I of yours, for I perceive you are a Catholic.

Papist   Yea indeed, and I will not deny it: look, I think the puritan and the Vicar will go by the ears?

Jack   He shall do the vicar no wrong for all my speeches to him: and he will be ruled by me, we will have him before my Lord's grace, for we will give him the slip, when we come in the City, and one of us will fetch a pursuivant and the other two shall dog him.

Papist   Content sir, if you please, let it be so?

Jack   How now my masters can you not agree?

Minist.   I will deal well enough with him, if he durst stand to his words.

Puritan   I will justify anything that I have spoken, if not let me lose my life, but to conclude, it is late, and because we must depart, I will tell you one thing, and I would wish you to make use of it, and hear what the Prophet *Esay* saith cap. 59. verse 10. "Their watchmen are all blind, they have no knowledge, they are all dumb dogs they cannot bark, they lie and sleep, and delight in sleeping. And these greedy dogs can never have enough, all these shepherds cannot understand," And Zacharie 11: 17. "O Idol shepherd that leaveth the flock, the sword shall be upon his arm, and upon his right eye: his arm shall be clean dried up, and his right eye shall be utterly darkened." And so fare ye well.

3

Josias Nichols

The Plea of the Innocent, 1602

(Excerpts)

JOSIAS NICHOLS (*ca.* 1555–1639) was educated at Oxford, where he received his B.A. degree in 1574. For a time he served as pastor in Kent and in his area became a leader of ministers demanding further reformation. John Whitgift suspended him from his position but shortly afterward restored him to it. *The Plea of the Innocent* was apparently called forth by the perceptible decline of Elizabeth and represents an attempt by Nichols to gain a sympathetic hearing from the new monarch, but in 1603, under James I, Nichols again lost his position. The work offended both the establishment and the separatists; it was attacked by William Covell in a possibly official answer. Nichols also wrote a work describing the principles of Christianity and another against Roman Catholicism.

The Plea of the Innocent is a comprehensive, detailed statement of the position of the dissenting ministers at the end of Elizabeth's reign. Nichols includes strictures against most of the religious practices attacked by one or another of the ardent reformers. Notably he opposes the reading of the Apocrypha in the service; he objects to the use of the sign of the cross in baptism; and he sees in the prescribed matrimonial service an unwarranted sacramental tone. Although he argues for peace and unity within the church and speaks deferentially of the authorities, he cannot accept the Anglican view that things indifferent can be established by authority, because for him no things are indifferent. For instance, if the apocryphal writings are not the revealed word of God, the minister must not read them during the service. Whatever is prescribed or firmly grounded in the Bible must be done, and whatever has no biblical warrant must be avoided.

Like many other reformers, Nichols finds no justification for the ecclesiastical ranks and offices of the Anglican church. In his second chapter he quotes the Nineteenth Article of the Church of England, which defines the "visible church of Christ" as "a congregation of faithful men in which the pure word of God is preached." The Bible allows elders or presbyters and pastors, but the offices of deans, archdeacons, and archprelates are human inventions, and Nichols sees no warrant for the office of deacon as the church defines it. Because preaching is the main function of a minister, nonresidency and the holding of more than one office should be outlawed. In principle Nichols is antiprelatical, but his personality, his own experiences, and his aim distance his work from the common type of antiprelatical tract. He has words of appreciation for Whitgift, and he denounces the attacks on bishops by Martin Marprelate. In his fifth chapter Nichols argues that no essential differences exist between the church hierarchy and the nonconforming ministers. His beliefs may not differ from those of Penry and Throckmorton, but his posture and his emphasis do. The book reflects a personality essentially uncompromising in its adherence to fairly radical reformist beliefs but very deferential to authority. At times Nichols seems to be trying to balance his rigorous opposition to Anglican ceremonies with obsequious, even fulsome, praise of the queen. Whatever ill feelings he nurses are directed against the extreme radicals and, especially, the Roman Catholics, whom he castigates in three of his eleven chapters.

Frequently Nichols tries to portray the dissenting ministers as the moderate party within the church. *Puritan* is a term of obloquy in his view, but the true puritans, who really deserve the name, are the ancient heretics who believed in various ways that man can attain purity or holiness in this life; with these Nichols has no sympathy. He also rejects some defenders of puritans, such as the Marprelate authors, because of the tone of their writings, their attacks on the state, and their lack of moderation. He criticizes the hierarchy of the Church of England, more often implicitly than explicitly, for maintaining positions too close to the church of Rome. Nichols appears to see his position as a mean between the extremes of Marprelate and the separatists on one side and the Roman Catholics on the other. Much of his argument calls on the conforming Anglicans to move nearer this center, away from pre-Reformation ceremonies and ecclesiastical discipline.

Of all governmental acts, Nichols seems to dislike most the act of 1571, which enforced subscription to the established religion as a requisite for ordination. One of its main points—recognition of the authority of the queen—Nichols, like nearly everyone else, finds unobjectionable. But he finds it impossible to attest that the Book of Common Prayer and the Articles of Religion have nothing in them contrary to the word of God, because he finds in both, and especially in the prayer book, many traditional postbiblical ceremonies, as well as many reflections and survivals of the pre-Reformation church—in general, much that is not warranted by the Bible.

The excerpts here reprinted include the dedicatory epistle to the bishops and ministers of the church; chapter 1, defining the term *puritan;* and chapter 7, further defining the term by arguing against attempts of the conforming clergy to link the puritans with the papists. These selections explain most clearly the basic positions that in Nichols's view led to false charges of puritanism. Among the sections of the book omitted here, chapters 2, 3, 4, 5, and 6 try to demonstrate the loyalty of the nonconformists to the state and to a truly reformed Church of England; chapters 8 and 9 continue the attack on the Roman church begun in chapter 7; and chapter 10 argues against subscription, nonresidency, and a nonpreaching ministry. Finally chapter 11 closes Nichols's work with a strong plea for tolerance of the nonconformists.

The Plea of the Innocent:
Wherein is averred; That the Ministers & people falslie termed Puritanes, are injriouslie slaundered for enemies or troublers of the State. Published for the common good of the Church and common wealth of this Realme of England As a Countermure Against all Sycophantising Papists, Statising Priestes, Neutralising Atheistes, and Satanising scorners of all godlinesse, trueth and honestie. *Written:* by *Josias Nichols,* a faithfull Minister of the Ghospell of Christ: and an humble seruant, of the English Church. 1602.

[Excerpts: dedicatory epistle, sigs. B–B5v; pp. 1–13, 148–54.]

To all the Reverend Fathers, the Bishops of this land, and to all the godly learned Ministers of Jesus Christ, and to all the true and faithful favorers of the holy faith and religion, now publicly professed and maintained in England: JOSIAS NICHOLS the least of the least of all God's Saints, wisheth all grace peace and joy in believing.

"A Good name (saith Solomon) is to be chosen above great riches, and loving favor is above silver, and above gold." Which then is most excellent, when it is found in the fear of God, and our light shineth to the glory and praise of God. But the name of a Minister is yet of more regard, by whose standing and falling many are drawn, and the reproach of such men reacheth nearest to the heavens, and God is most dishonored by their dishonor: for he hath said, "I will be sanctified in them that come near me: and before all the people I will be glorified." Howbeit, the Gospel proclaimeth all them blessed, who for Christ's sake are reviled, and against whom, men do falsely say all manner of evil. For wicked men and infidels speak evil of them, which run not with them to the same excess of riot: and beastly men will utter lewd words, against those things they know not. Hereof it cometh, that many men fall away, being not able to bear the reproach: yet he which believeth as he speaketh, and knoweth what he believeth: he suffereth as a Christian, and is not ashamed, but glorifieth God in this behalf. Notwithstanding when a brother shall reproach his brother, and one christian ill another, and the house of God shall be divided: then is it most dangerous. For there will the enemy of mankind, cast in many burning firebrands and heap on much dry wood, that we might be all consumed one of another. And such (my most reverend and beloved brethren) hath been our case and condition: because we have desired and sought after the good proceeding and perfection of our Church, in the service and worship of Christ, and withholden our hands from doing and allowing of some things, in our judgment, hurtful to the same, and contrariant to the gospel of truth: We have suffered and endured much reproach and contempt which we have patiently borne, and with great silence, for divers years sustained that on our part, the sacred word of righteousness, might not be ill spoken of, and as much as in us lieth, we might cut off all occasions to the common adversary, to prevail against the holy Church of Christ, which is among us. But now it seemeth to me, that notwithstanding all this, the state of things is worse than ever before: and I cannot tell whether our connivance in suffering all evil speeches against us, hath done the Church harm. For now the papist begin to comfort themselves, yea they challenge unto them the name of honest and true men and good subjects: and by the reproachful name of puritan, all godly protestants are most cunningly depraved. To have been called precisian, puritan hotheaded, proud, contentious, schismatics and troublers of the Church, we have borne it patiently (God knowing our innocency) and could yet bear it more, so as by our suffering of contempt, the Church of England, might receive honor, and God's people rejoice under good guiding pastors. But when it is grown so far, that we are called and accounted worse than papists, enemies to the state, worse than seminary priests, like Jesuits, subverters of the commonwealth and enemies to her Majesty's most royal crown and dignity (for whose safety we do continually and instantly pray) and that this is so far grown, that the traitorous priests do brag of extraordinary favor, and under the name of puritans most fraudulently and with most gross and palpable lying and slandering traduce all Christian churches so that we verily think that if such things go forward, they will in a short time cause a most woeful overthrow of the whole state and of the Christian Church among us: we cannot now forbear any longer, but that we must needs show unto all the world our innocency: that the wrong which by ill and false report hath been done unto us, through our negligence and want of honest defense, be not made a strong forge, and a close mighty engine, to destroy all the happy and godly proceedings of her Majesty, turning upside down the joyful flourishing of the Christian religion and Gospel. And we cannot now heal this sore by any private doing; for it is spread abroad so universal, and men's minds are so universally possessed therewith, that we have no way to do good but to come into the open theater of the world to plead for ourselves and to make manifest the uprightness of our cause, against all these most false, unjust and slanderous imputations. Let me therefore entreat you all (Reverend Fathers and Brethren) in godly charity to receive this our most just apology and with Christian equity to consider of it, and with heavenly wisdom weighing the estate of the Church, and the present necessity, take every thing in that meaning as it is written. And I do not doubt, but although the known and professed enemy of all goodness the Popish faction, (which now these three and forty years have used all cunning treachery and treasonable platforms, to bereave her Majesty (whom God almighty preserve still among us of this present light and life of this world, and all this Realm by that means, of the heavenly light and life of the world to come) though I say, these vowed enemies of the Gospel and of this land, do fret, chafe and fume; yet shall not you my dear brethren, neither any honest Christian and faithful subject, have any just cause, to mislike this manner of writing: but rather (through the hand of my God upon me) find and think it necessary at this time to be published to all Christian people of this English nation. For I do herein declare and show, what hath been our cause and manner of proceeding, and that as plainly without concealment, and as faithfully, without partiality to ourselves, as I may boldly avouch everything, to any man's conscience, which will be content with truth and all the truth: and secondly how agreeing all our cause and doings from time to time, hath been to the present estate, and her Majesty's proceedings in the Gospel: Thirdly in clearing our cause and doings of the greatest accusations and imputations, I make it plain how unequal and unjust, the comparison is, between us and the Papist: and lastly I do a little touch, some other things necessarily appertaining to the premises. Now it may be that herein I shall not satisfy all men: peradventure I shall offend some of the reverend Bishops and some other learned Prelates standing for conformity: and it may be I shall not perfectly answer the expectation of the godly Ministers, who desire reformation, or of some other wise and learned Christians. Herein doubtless I have cause to suspect mine own insufficiency. For who can tell how to walk perfectly with the Lord and yet avoid all occasions of offense, where both the parties have been at so hot war, and where there are men of so many contrary judgments and affections? much less a man of so little helps and small gifts as I have. How be it I crave the patience and charitable taking of this my writing of them both; and I hope they will accept my good will. For in an especial love toward both parties I have taken this in hand: and have set God before mine eyes before them both, that so near as I could and as far as I know and am able, I utter that which is right in his sight, not seeking to please any man of either side: but endeavoring to do a work pleasing to God, and good for his Church, I might minister occasion of profit to them both. Knowing, that now is the time that either side should cast off the love of themselves, and turning their eyes from the sweet reflex of their own praise, join in one heart against the common enemies, for the peace, increase, perfection and honor of the church of God in this land. Which my good and honest meaning, if I have not so fully accomplished as I desire, I humble myself unto God, and travail herein under his mercy: and I am ready, upon good demonstration of my fault, to make amends and to satisfy either party. But if there be any of the reverend Fathers, or of the learned Prelates (which God forbid) that be proud, froward or malicious, and will stand stiff upon their conceived purpose, seeking themselves and their own things, and not the glory of God, and the things which are Christ's: I esteem them no further than they deserve; I pray God amend them, and turn their hearts. So on the other side, if there be any man who seemeth to like of reformation, who yet being an hypocrite and false hearted, hath any hidden poison in him (for it is no rare thing to have a Judas among twelve, and false creeping brethren, who would bring the church into bondage, and make a prey of the same) as I know none such, so I do renounce them in this Apology, and all other whatsoever, that do not love her Majesty with all their heart, and are not true and upright favorers of the Gospel, as it is taught in England by public authority, or have in him any treacherous or wicked purpose against the same, any manner of way. And I pray God to make them to be known: yea if any man be guilty in his conscience of any evil, let him be ashamed, and let him bide himself and seek the shifts of wicked men in darkness.

But for us, our cause is just before God, and we have done no hurt to her Majesty, and we know and believe, that when the appointed time of God shall come, and his counsel hath sufficiently tried us: he will bring forth our righteousness as the light, and our judgment as the noonday. Therefore I think it my duty without all fear, to open to all the world, what manner of trespassers we are, and to commend to the conscience of all wise, learned, and godly christians (when they shall thoroughly understand and rightly weigh everything as it is) the righteousness of our cause, and the uprightness of our meaning. O God and heavenly Father, thou of all flesh and searcher of the heart and reins, send forth thy light and thy truth, judge thou the cause of thy servants, and take it into thine own hands: And cause thy people to return and discern between the righteous and the wicked, between him that serveth God and him that serveth him not. And let thy gracious countenance shine always upon this land and upon thine anointed handmaid our Sovereign Queen Elizabeth: defend, protect and guide her, establish thy covenant of peace with her and this English nation forever, even the sure mercies of David. For thy holy son's sake Jesus Christ. Amen. *At Eastwell in Kent this 4. of June. 1602.*

> Cap. 1. Wherein is showed, 1. That they be not puritans in deed who now in England are so called: 2 That name is very fit and proper for all papists. 3 What are the causes that some of her Majesty's most faithful and obedient subjects are termed puritans. 4 The true state of their cause.

We read in the story of the primitive Church of divers sorts of heretics, who for their opinions of their own pureness, contrary to the truth of holy scripture, might very well be called puritans. As namely such as very proudly and odiously (as Saint *Augustine* writeth) called themselves *Cathari*, (which may well, out of the original word, be translated by the name of Puritan) for their purity or cleanness: and these he saith followed *Novatus*, and were therefore called *Novatians*. The *Pelagians* also were Puritans, holding (as he saith) that the life of a just man in this world, hath no sin at all, and that of them the Church is made up in this mortal life, that it might be altogether without spot or wrinkle: Of this latter sort were the *Donatists*. There were also Puritans called *Jovinianists*, affirming that a man cannot sin after he hath received the lavacre of regeneration. *Ebion* also and divers others, thought so well of themselves, that they clave to the law, as the Pharisees, looking to be justified by their works and not by faith only. All these and many others having opinion of their own purity, and despising others, might justly and truly be called *Puritans*. But such ministers and other good christian men and women, who in this Land, under her Majesty's most happy reign (whom God continue in safety with the longest liver) have embraced the gospel, and by it abandoned all these and all other heresies and falsehoods, and endeavor to follow the same gospel, with all their souls, and in simplicity and humbleness of mind, have been desirous that themselves should draw nearer and nearer unto God, and that the church of England (as it is very well, and very much reformed out of popish idolatry and superstition) might more and more grow forward unto such perfection, as in this frail life might be attained: be very uncharitably and unjustly called by that odious and heretical name of puritan. For if we would search all England from the tenth year of her Majesty's most gracious reign (about which time this wicked slander did first begin) unto this present time: there cannot be brought forth anyone, out of those, who faithfully and in the fear of God have sought reformation (howsoever for that cause they have been and are untruly so called) that ever did arrogate any such thing to themselves, as to be thought purer than other men: but always they have acknowledged themselves to be great and grievous sinners, as well as other men: accounting their own righteousness to be as a stained cloth: and rejoicing of no other pureness, but that which is by the blood of Christ, when for his sake our sins are forgiven, and through faith in him our souls are purified, and his righteousness imputed unto us, by the free mercy and grace of God. Therefore except we would call black, white: and bitter sweet, there is no reason in the world to call any such by the odious name of puritans.

    2   But the Papists indeed being the true followers and scholars of the *Cathari, Novatus, Pelagius,* and of the *Ebionites, Donatists* and of all suchlike

puritan heretics, may justly and very fitly be called puritans. For they hold that in their regenerate men after Baptism, there is nothing that may be said to have the reason of sin, and that they are able to fulfill all the commandments of God: and they affirm that they have an inherent righteousness which they keep as a pure and immaculate robe, to the obtaining of salvation: and that they are righteous, justified, and deserve salvation by their works: that they have among them devout and holy men, (whom they call religious) Monks, Friars, Nuns, Jesuits and Seminaries, who in their religious order live (as they say) a seraphical and angelical life, and being virgins, void of all secular affairs, as pure and chaste votaries, in contemplation serving God day and night, are able to merit not only for themselves, but also for others: and of the superabundance of their works of Supererogation they may communicate to others, and the Pope may by indulgence, apply their merits for the relief of others out of purgatory, and suchlike. These undoubtedly may and are properly to be called puritans, because they indeed arrogate unto themselves purity and holiness, and despise all others: which the true children of God (though thus belied and slandered) dare not in any case to do; but contrarily they cry out with the Psalmist unto God: "Enter not into judgment." And with the Publican: "Have mercy upon me a sinner."

3   But the cause original and order, whereby these reproachful terms were given to good Christians, I find to be this: In the beginning of her Majesty's most happy reign (whom I humbly pray our God to prolong as long as sun and moon endure) the Gospel being published, and Preachers ordained to teach the people: Many people within a while feeling some taste of the heavenly comfort, began to delight in hearing of Sermons, singing of Psalms, in reading and godly talk of holy Scriptures which they were taught. And therewithal did somewhat refrain profane and unprofitable customs, and sometime they admonished their neighbors, if they did swear, and pray them to go with them to the Sermon. The greater sort of the people, being old barrels which could hold no new wine, addicted partly to popery and partly to licentiousness, having many of them no other God, but their belly, would deride and scoff at them, and called them holy brethren and holy sistern: saying, "He is one of the pure and unspotted brethren." Divers Ministers also entering upon that weighty charge, when they (being learned) came to the practice of the communion book, found themselves troubled in some things, and some certain ceremonies were a scruple unto them. And as it is said in the preface of the said book, it was not thought fit at the first to take away all those things, which seemed to be superstitious, but to take the middle way to abandon some and to retain some: So by this occasion the Papists and other people not well affected to

religion and godliness, after a while began to find holes in the Ministers' coats, and devised divers ways of molestation and troubled them, not a little. They open their cause to the reverend Bishops of those times, and found great kindness at their hands at the first, and they were a good and comfortable shadow unto them for a season. But about the tenth year of her Majesty's reign, the papists as men which began to shake off the fear, wherewith the mighty God protecting and blessing her Majesty's most godly and Christian proceedings, had strocken them, the Papists (I say) began to come forth of their dens, and as it is well known to the state, practiced divers treacherous attempts; but among other, they preferred such grievous accusations against the godly and faithful Ministers; that then and from thenceforth, they were left naked, and a great storm fell upon them, and so it continued now and then sharper, and sometimes there was a calm, and men breathed and returned to the Lord's work. About anno 1571. (as I take it) Subscription was first enforced upon the ministry, for which cause in that time certain men wrote an admonition to the parliament, opening divers things worthy reformation. Whereupon arose great volumes of proving and defending, which are famously known to all men, that understand of these causes. But how flesh and blood did in these writings oversway the Christian moderation and mildness, which brethren should have been very careful of in contending for truth, by the hot pursuit of either side, I rejoice not to rehearse, and I am sorry as often as I think upon the lamentable effects and hurt of the Church in those times. Howbeit, our merciful God, whose unchangeable love, doth swallow up many of our infirmities and follies, granted unto us in the midst of these fiery contentions, a goodly space of quietness about the time that the reverend Father Master *Grindall* was Archbishop of Canterbury. In which time in all the south parts of England, there was great concord among the ministers, and they joined in great love and joy one with another in the Lord's work. So that in the space of 4. or 5. years (as I remember) there were infinite souls brought to the knowledge of Christ: and the people rejoiced for the consolation seeing and beholding how greatly they were bound to praise God, for her Majesty's most christian government, under whose most godly proceedings, they had sucked and tasted the sweet and undeceivable milk of God's truth, even the holy faith of God's elect, the doctrine of salvation. It was a golden time, full of godly fruit, great honor to the Gospel, great love and kind fellowship among all the Ministers, preaching the faith, and the people united in the true fear of God and cheerful reverence to her Majesty. But this life not affording constant prosperity to heavenly love and growth of godliness.

After the said Archbishop's decease, there came forth a new and fresh assault of Subscription, universally imposed, and again enforced upon all the Ministers in three articles.

First of the Queen's Majesty's Sovereign authority over all persons, etc. Second, that the book of common prayer and of ordaining Bishops, Priests and Deacons, contain in it nothing contrary to the word of God, etc. Third, to allow and approve all the articles of religion agreed upon by the Archbishops and Bishops, etc. 1562. and to believe all therein contained to be agreeable to God. When in the visitations and public meetings the Ministers were called to subscribe: they offered very freely and willingly to subscribe to the first article of her Majesty's most lawful authority. And for the other two they refused to do any further, than by law they were bound, and namely according to the statute made for that purpose Anno 13. Hereupon many in divers Shires were suspended from the execution of their Ministry, and some deprived. And great division arose in the Church, the one suing for reformation and to be eased of such burdens, and the other urging very straitly the former things, and punishing such as would not be conformable. Then came there forth a new cloud of writing and men's affections waxing hot and drawing to the worse, it was a very common name to all these Ministers to be called puritans: As men which made conscience of many things, which the reverend Fathers, and many learned men affirmed to be lawful.

In all this time there was much preaching in the Universities, about non-residents and unpreaching ministers: and there should you see a plain division, one sort called youths, and the other sort which took not such liberty, were called precisians. And this is grown both in the University and in the country town and city, that whoso feareth an oath, or is an ordinary resorter to sermons, earnest against excess, riot, popery, or any disorder, they are called in the university precisians, and in other places puritans.

4   And thus as faithfully as I can, I have showed how this name came up, and whereupon honest and godly men have been and are called puritans or precisians: here it followeth to be considered out these things, what is their offense, and the state of their cause: which may be referred to four heads: 1 scruple in the use of certain ceremonies: 2 scruple in subscribing beyond the statute: 3 seeking for reformation of some ceremonies and of some part of the ecclesiastical discipline. 4 the people do hear sermons, talk of the scriptures, sing Psalms together in private houses, etc. Now whether for these causes they be justly called puritans and troublers of the state, etc. it remaineth to be examined and discussed. For the plain opening whereof, I will first show such honest reasons as make for their lawful excuse, proving manifestly that they are

to be holden as good and faithful subjects, honest christians, and godly ministers. Secondly I will open the vanity of the principal imputations which are urged against them; and thirdly, propound some other such considerations as are necessarily annexed to both.

Cap. 7. Wherein is proved, that the Ministers seeking reformation, falsely called puritans, are not in any sort to be compared to papists in evil: much less to be equalized with traitorous seminary priests or Jesuits. 1. by their contradictory doctrine. 2. by their contrary acts and doings.

One part of the sufferings of our blessed Savior Jesus Christ, was this, that he "was counted with the transgressors," and therefore: as Saint Mark saith, "He was crucified between two thieves." We are not then to think it strange to be matched, with Anabaptists, Donatists, Papists, rebels, and I cannot tell what: "For the servant is not greater than the master." And I hope that if we suffer with him in righteousness, we shall rejoice with him in glory. Let us then examine this calumniation. If we be like or worse than papists in evil to the Church of England: it is either in our doctrine or in our doings. First I will prove not in our doctrine, and that by two arguments; the former is this: we hold, believe and teach all the articles of the Christian faith according to the holy Scriptures, even as the church of England doth; a thing so apparent as the sun at noondays. And the papists are herein directly contrary, to the faith and doctrine of the church of England and to the word of God approving the same. Therefore if sound doctrine and faith, be the chief mark to know a good man, and that the doctrine and faith of England be good and true: and that the doctrine of the papists, be naught, wicked and abominable: then are we, who follow the good and true doctrine of the Church of England, not to be compared to the papists in evil, who are deadly enemies to the same. Secondly that part of our doctrine, wherein we seem to differ from the reverend Fathers of our Church; being such (as is before declared) as agreeth to the principal canon of our Church in general, and in particulars with the usage of the Apostles, and with the laws, injunctions, canons and apologetical writings of our Church: against all which, the papists most constantly do war and cavil: therefore in this also we be not to be compared unto them. My latter argument touching our doctrine, is concerning the civil Magistrate. We the ministers aforesaid, desiring the abolishing of all popish remnants, do hold, believe and confess, that all obedience is to be performed to the civil Magistrate although they were evil and infidels, as the Scripture teacheth. And that no Bishop, Priest or Minister can deprive a King or discharge the subjects of the oath of allegiance. And that our Queen *Elizabeth* (God bless her) is supreme governor over all persons, born in her dominions, whether they be ecclesiastical or civil; and that no foreign potentate, as namely the Pope of *Rome,* hath any jurisdiction within her dominions and countries, but is a wicked usurper over Kings and Princes. But all Papists, if they be true catholics (as they term themselves) and namely all Priests, Secular, Seminary and Jesuit, do hold clean contradictory, even manifest treason and rebellion against the civil power ordained of God. Therefore there is no comparison to be made in regard of doctrine, between us and the papists. And that you may perceive, that this concerneth all Protestants, as well as the Ministers falsely called puritans: do but consider these words of *Bristow:* "Of catholics thoroughly discharged of their fealty, yet for common humanity, for their accustomed use, for their continual, and (as it were) natural institution, the Prince is better obeyed and served, than of Protestants, which in heart are in a manner all puritans." Note here (that I may use Master D. *Fulke's* words) that "papists profess themselves to be subjects, of courtesy and not of duty, of custom and not of conscience, of natural institution, and not of the law of God. O Lord and Savior, send her Majesty few such subjects and servants." Now this courteous or rather currish obedience is expounded, what it is, by that beastly bull of *Pius* the fifth, against our noble Sovereign, with the faculty granted to *Campion* and *Persons,* by which the Pope licenseth the papists to dissemble their obedience until public execution of that Bull may be had: that is, to be privy traitors, till with hope of success, they may be open rebels.

2   Now for our doings, what it hath been, ever since our troubles, we need not to be ashamed to confess: and we refer ourselves to all men. If we have committed any indignity against her Majesty's person, Crown, or Sovereignty, or had intelligence with any of her enemies, or gone about to draw away the people from their obedience, or any suchlike. But we have done (in the knowledge of all men) altogether clean contrary, both by word and deed, in our preaching openly, and exhortations and example privately. And in our troubles we have willingly and patiently submitted ourselves to the punishments which have been inflicted upon us: only craving favor and ease, so far as agreeth to holy scripture and the peace of the Church. And in all that we have gone about, we have labored for the good, for the beauty and perfection of our Church: that it might increase and flourish more and more, to the glory of God, and to the honor and comfort of her Majesty. These men the papists have done clean

contrary, especially since the 10. year of her Majesty's happy reign: never being without one cruel treason or another; sometime by desperate bloody murderers: sometime by open rebellion, foreign invasion and procuring of Bulls from Rome: sometime by Priests, sometime by Jesuits, and sometime by other means, as is plainly set forth in the book called the Execution of justice, in the writings of Sir Francis Hastings, Doctor *Sutlief,* D. *Fulke,* and divers others. The things on both sides are so notoriously known, that I need not here to repeat them in particular. I pray God, that for our sins, he do not give us over to blindness, that in such palpable and manifest experience of the traitorous hearts of papists, we suffer not ourselves to be taken by their wily flatteries, and forsaking our trusty and faithful friends, we yield ourselves to the bloody slaughter of enemies.

4

[William Bradshaw]

English Puritanisme, 1605

W ILLIAM BRADSHAW (1571– 1618) took his B.A. and M.A. degrees at Emmanuel College in Cambridge; later he became a fellow of Sidney Sussex College at the same university and took orders. Although ecclesiastical preferment eluded him because of his religious views, several times he received permission to preach and gained a reputation for his sermons. Among his friends and admirers he counted Laurence Chaderton, of Emmanuel College; Thomas Cartwright; Thomas Gataker, who wrote his biography; William Ames, who translated his *English Puritanisme* into Latin; and Bishop Joseph Hall. The paradoxes in Bradshaw's career are explored by Peter Lake in *Moderate Puritans and the Elizabethan Church* (Cambridge, England, 1982, pp. 262–78); the relevant chapter is significantly titled "William Bradshaw: Moderation in Extremity."

Bradshaw's writings include several treatises against ceremonies—one denouncing the use of the cross in baptism—which in themselves would earn him the title *puritan.* His defense of puritanism remains a lucid, authoritative description of congregational church government. But while opposing a hierarchical national church, Bradshaw preached submission to civil authority and nonresistance to any ecclesiastical authority established by the government. His ideal apparently was a church composed of autonomous congregations but subject to the king. This deference to the crown, together with his genial personality, enabled Bradshaw to live a relatively peaceful life in the midst of the controversies of the day.

English Puritanisme was published anonymously in Holland in 1605. In 1610 William Ames published a Latin translation with some additions, and he long received credit for authorship of the English work. In 1640 and again in 1641, Bradshaw's treatise was reprinted with substantive, but minor, additions and deletions and with numerous typographical errors.

Bradshaw's treatise begins with the uncompromising thesis statement that all religious practice must be grounded on the word of God as written in the Bible. The word is "of absolute perfection"; therefore, nothing can be permitted in worship or discipline that lacks warrant in the Bible, and nothing enjoined there can be omitted. Traditional practices, developed over long periods of time, must be condemned as human inventions. Apparently no matters are indifferent; whatever the Bible does not prescribe, it prohibits by implication. Words such as *idolatry* and *superstition* clearly impugn the medieval church and the survival of Roman Catholic practices in the Anglican church. Bradshaw's only readily perceptible departure from his thesis concerns congregational singing: He permits the people to say no more than "amen" in prayers conducted by the minister, but he argues that singing, "by the very ordinance and instinct of nature," requires a chorus of voices. Whether he perceived that an appeal to the laws of nature might lead to the use of other arts, even sartorial, in the service remains unclear. And despite his insistence on biblical sanction, in developing his congregational theory Bradshaw does not cite biblical texts. His mode of discourse is declarative, not argumentative. A very neat organization, with chapters and subheadings, produces a useful handbook for the church.

Except by implication, the treatise has nothing to say of theology and little about vestments or the administration of the sacraments, all leading concerns of the opponents of the ecclesiastical establishment. Bradshaw concerns himself almost exclusively with church government and ecclesiastical discipline. The relationship of ecclesiastical to civil authority is defined and then refined by the use of examples and analogies. Although Bradshaw attacks no individuals by name, his dislike of the organization and practices of the established church and its leaders becomes very clear as he develops his congregational model. Behind all of his most vehemently stated proposals lies the unspoken assumption that the episcopal system must be abolished.

For Bradshaw the individual congregation is the true visible church, which governs itself and is subject only to civil authority. The pastor serves as its head, but mainly because he exercises the primary function of a minister by preaching; and his preaching must be grounded solely upon Scripture. Lest the minister become a petty tyrant, the congregation must choose elders who share in the ministry and who are chosen for the soundness of their religion without regard to their social status. Although this precept justifies the use of "preaching cobblers" and the menial tradesmen so often satirized by adherents of the establishment, Bradshaw's model provides for traditional scholarship by the rule that a "doctor"—that is, someone with formal learning in religion—has an important place in the congregation, his main function being instruction of the ignorant. In fact, the preeminence of the pastor is mentioned not so much to exalt his importance—though as the skilled preacher he has a dominant role—as to argue that no higher ecclesiastical authority may be permitted. There can be no archdeacons, bishops, or archbishops, and finally no pope.

Rules governing censure are clearly based on the nonconformists' dissatisfaction with the establishment. Bradshaw condemns all investigation into the beliefs and religious and moral conduct of church members. He specifically mentions the ex officio oath. This witness oath, which allows an ecclesiastical or civil officer ex officio—that is, by virtue of his office—to interrogate persons under oath concerning their beliefs and actions, had a long history but had fallen into disuse until John Whitgift revived it, with a list of specific topics for questioning, in 1583. It became anathema to the dissenters. In Bradshaw's scheme only public impiety or immorality, such as forces itself on the attention of the congregation, may be dealt with. Moreover, Bradshaw's dislike of what he considered the arrogance of the ecclesiastical authorities shows itself in his harsh description of the treatment meted out to suspected dissenters by bishops and their officers and in his instructions that the offender must be approached with courtesy and exhorted to repentance. On the obdurate no public humiliation—no wearing of a white sheet, for example—can be inflicted. The congregation's gravest sanction is to expel the sinner; and if he takes the initiative and leaves, the congregation has no power over him.

The relationship of church and state remains somewhat hazy, though its importance is stressed, and careful attempts are made to define it. One point is absolutely clear: An ecclesiastical officer cannot hold civil office, and hence he cannot inflict civil or criminal penalties, such as fines or imprisonment. Less clear, and even somewhat ambiguous, is the power of the civil authority over the church. On the one hand, only the civil authority can punish the church officers of a congregation, higher ecclesiastical authorities having been proscribed. On the other hand, a civil official, even the king, remains subordinate in religious matters to the congregation to which he belongs; he is subject to censure like any other member, though he must be approached with all the ceremony due to his position in the state. Implicit in Bradshaw's argument may be the concept of a monarch who can rule with only one restriction on his power: the authority to set up an episcopal form of church government or otherwise to limit the congregation's self-rule. In spite of Bradshaw's deference to the king, the scheme of church government could not but offend a monarch who believed, as did James I, "no bishop, no king."

English Puritanisme Containeing the maine opinions of the rigidest sort of those that are called Puritanes in the Realme of England. Printed *1605.*
[William Bradshaw.]

To the Indifferent Reader.

It cannot be unknown unto them that know anything that those Christians in this Realm which are called by the odious and vile name of Puritans, are accused by the Prelates to the King's Majesty and the State to maintain many absurd, erroneous, Schismatical, and Heretical opinions, Concerning Religion, Church Government and the Civil Magistracy. Which hath moved me to collect (as near as I could) the chiefest of them, and to send them naked to the view of all men that they may see what is the worst that the worst of them hold. It is not my part to prove and justify them, Those that accuse and condemn them must in all reason and equity prove their accusation, or else bear the name of unchristian slanderers. I am not ignorant that they lay other opinions (yea some clean contradictory to these) to the charge of these men, the falsehood whereof we shall (It is to be doubted) have more and more occasion to detect. In the meantime all Enemies of Divine Truth shall find, That to obscure the same with Calumniations and untruths, is but to hide a fire with laying dry straw or tow upon it. But thou mayest herein observe, what a terrible Popedom and Primacy these rigid Presbyterians desire. And with what painted bugbears and Scarecrows, the Prelates go about to fright the States of this Kingdom withal. Who will no doubt one day see, how their wisdoms are abused. *Farewell.*

ENGLISH PURITANISM

CHAP. I

Concerning Religion or the worship of God in general.

IMPRIMIS, *They hold and maintain* that the word of God contained in the writings of the Prophets and Apostles, is of absolute perfection, given by Christ the head of the Church, to be unto the same, the sole Canon and rule of all matters of *Religion,* and the worship and service of God whatsoever. And that whatsoever done in the same service and worship cannot be justified by the said word, is unlawful. And therefore that it is a sin, to force any Christian to do any act of religion or divine service, that cannot evidently be warranted by the same.

2   *They hold* that all Ecclesiastical actions invented and devised by man, are utterly to be excluded out of the exercises of religion? Especially such actions as are famous and notorious mysteries of an Idolatrous Religion, and in doing whereof, the true religion is conformed (whether in whole or in part) to Idolatry and superstition.

3   *They hold* that all outward means instituted and set apart to express and set forth the Inward worship of God, are parts of divine worship and that not only all moral actions but all typical rites and figures ordained to shadow forth in the solemn worship and service of God, any spiritual or religious act or habit in the mind of man, are special parts of the same, and therefore that every such act ought evidently to be prescribed by the word of God, or else ought not to be done? it being a sin to perform any other worship to God, whether External or Internal, Moral or Ceremonial, in whole or in part, than that which God himself requires in his word.

4   *They hold it* to be gross superstition, for any mortal man to institute and ordain as parts of divine worship, any mystical rite and Ceremony of Religion whatsoever, and to mingle the same with the divine rites and mysteries of God's Ordinance. But they hold it to be high presumption to institute and bring into divine worship such Rites and Ceremonies of Religion, as are acknowledged to be no parts of divine worship at all, but only of civil worship and honor: For they that shall require to have performed unto themselves a ceremonial obedience, service and worship, consisting in rites of Religion to be done at that very instant that God is solemnly served and worshiped? and even in the same worship make both themselves and God also an Idol. So that they judge it a far more fearful sin to add unto, and to use in the worship and

service of God or any Part thereof such mystical rites and Ceremonies as they esteem to be no parts or parcels of God's worship at all: than such as in a vain and ignorant superstition, they imagine and conceive to be parts thereof.

5   *They hold* that every act or action appropriated and set apart to divine service and worship, whether *moral* or *ceremonial*, real or typical? ought to bring special honor unto God and therefore that every such act ought to be apparently commanded in the word of God, either expressly, or by necessary consequent.

6   *They hold* that all actions whether Moral or Ceremonial appropriated to Religious or Spiritual Persons, Functions, or actions, either are or ought to be Religious and spiritual. And therefore either are or ought to be instituted immediately by God, who alone is the author and Institutor of all Religious and Spiritual actions, and things: whether Internal or External, Moral or Ceremonial.

CHAP. 2.
Concerning the Church.

1   *They hold and maintain* that every Company, Congregation or Assembly of men, ordinarily joining together in true worship of God, is a true *visible church* of Christ; and that the same title is improperly attributed to any other Convocations, Synods, Societies, combinations, or assemblies whatsoever.

2   *They hold* that all such churches or Congregations, communicating after that manner together, in divine worship, are in all Ecclesiastical matters equal, and of the same power and authority, and that by the word and will of God they ought to have the same spiritual privileges, prerogatives, officers, administrations, orders, and Forms of divine worship.

3   *They hold* that Christ Jesus hath not subjected any Church or Congregation of his, to any other superior Ecclesiastical Jurisdiction, than unto that which is within itself. So that if a whole Church or Congregation shall err, in any matters of faith or religion, no other Churches or Spiritual Church officers have (by any warrant from the word of God) power to censure, punish, or control the same: but are only to counsel and advise the same, and so to leave their Souls to the immediate Judgment of Christ, and their bodies to the sword and power of the Civil Magistrate, who alone upon Earth hath power to punish a whole Church or Congregation.

4   *They hold* that every established Church or Congregation ought to have

her own spiritual officers and ministers, resident with her, and those such, as are enjoined by Christ in the new Testament and no other.

5 *They hold* that every established Church ought (as a special prerogative wherewith she is endowed by Christ) to have power and liberty to elect and choose their own Spiritual and Ecclesiastical Officers, and that it is a greater wrong to have any such forced upon them against their wills, than if they should force upon men wives, or upon women husbands, against their will and liking.

6 *They hold* that if in this choice any particular Churches shall err, that none upon Earth but the Civil Magistrate hath power to control or correct them for it, And that though it be not lawful for him to take away this power from them, Yet when they or any of them, shall apparently abuse the same, he stands bound by the Law of God, and by virtue of his Office (grounded upon the same,) to punish them severely for it, and to force them under Civil mulcts to make better choice.

7 *They hold* that the Ecclesiastical Officers and Ministers of one Church, ought not to bear any Ecclesiastical office in another, but ought to be tied unto that Congregation of which they are members, and by which they are elected into Office, And they are not, (without just cause, and such as may be approved by the Congregation) to forsake their callings, wherein if the Congregation shall be perverse, and will not hearken to reason, They are then to crave the assistance and help of the Civil Magistrate, who alone hath power, and who ought by his Civil sword, and authority, procure to all Members of the Church, whether Governors or others, freedom from all manifest injuries and wrongs.

8 *They hold* that the Congregation having once made choice of their Spiritual Officers unto whom they commit the Regiment of their Souls, they ought not (without just cause and that which is apparently warrantable by the word of God) to discharge, deprive, or depose them. But ought to live in all Canonical obedience and subjection unto them agreeable to the word of God. And if by permission of the Civil Magistrate, they shall by other Ecclesiastical officers, be suspended or deprived, for any cause in their apprehension good and justifiable by the word of God, then they hold it the bounden duty of the Congregation to be continual suppliants to God: and humble suitors unto Civil authority for the restoration of them, unto their administrations, which if it cannot be obtained, yet this much honor they are to give unto them, as to acknowledge them to the death, their Spiritual Guides and Governors, though they be rigorously deprived of their Ministry and service.

9   *They hold* that though one Church is not to differ from another in any Spiritual, Ecclesiastical, or Religious matters whatsoever, but are to be equal and alike. Yet that they may differ and one excel another in outward Civil circumstances, of place, time, Person etc. So that although they hold that those Congregations of which Kings and Nobles make themselves members, ought to have the same Ecclesiastical Officers, Ministry, worship, Sacraments, Ceremonies: and form of divine worship, that the basest Congregation in the country hath. And no other. Yet they hold also: That as their Persons in Civil respects excel, So in the exercises of religion in civil matters they may excel other assemblies. Their Chapels, and Seats may be gorgeously set forth with rich Arras and Tapestry, Their Fonts may be of Silver. Their Communion Tables of Ivory and if they will covered with gold. The Cup out of which they drink the Sacramental blood of Chirst may be of beaten gold set about with Diamonds. Their Ministers may be clothed in silk and velvet, so themselves will maintain them in that manner, otherwise, they think it absurd and against common reason, that other base and inferior Congregations must by Ecclesiastical Tithes, and Oblations maintain, the silken and velvet suits and Lordly retinue of the Ministers and Ecclesiastical Officers of Princes and Nobles.

10   *They hold* that the Laws, Orders, and Ecclesiastical Jurisdiction of the visible Churches of Christ, if they be lawful and warrantable by the word of God, are no ways repugnant to any civil State whatsoever, whether Monarchical, Aristocratical, or Democratical, but do tend to the further establishing and advancing, of the rights and prerogatives of all and every of them. And they renounce and abhor from their souls all such Ecclesiastical Jurisdiction or Policy, that is any way repugnant and derogatory to any of them, especially to the Monarchical State, which they acknowledge to be the best kind of civil Government for this Kingdom.

11   *They hold* and believe that the equality in Ecclesiastical Jurisdiction and authority, of Churches and Church Ministers, is no more derogatory and repugnant to the State and glory of a Monarch, than the Parity or equality, of Schoolmasters, of several Schools, Captains of several Camps, Shepherds of several flocks of Sheep, or Masters of several Families. Yea they hold the clean contrary, that Inequality of Churches and Church Officers in Ecclesiastical Jurisdiction and authority, was that principally that advanced Antichrist unto his throne, and brought the Kings and Princes of the Earth unto such vassalage under him, and that the civil authority and glory of Secular Princes and States

hath ever decayed, and withered, the more that the Ecclesiastical Officers of the Church have been advanced and lifted up in authority, beyond the limits and confines that Christ in his word hath prescribed unto them.

CHAP. 3.

Concerning the Ministers of the word.

1   *They hold* that the Pastors of particular Congregations are, or ought to be the highest Spiritual Officers in the Church, over whom, (by any Divine Ordinance) there is no superior Pastor but only Jesus Christ; And that they are led by the spirit of Antichrist, that arrogate or take upon themselves to be Pastors of Pastors.

2   *They hold,* that there are not by any divine Institution in the word, any ordinary National, Provincial, or Diocesan Pastors or Ministers under which the Pastors of particular Congregations are to be subject, as Inferior Officers. And that if there were any such, that then the word of God would have set them down more distinctly and precisely than any of the rest: For the higher place that one occupieth in the Church, of the more necessity he is unto the Church: Of the more necessity he is to the Church, the more carefully would Christ (the head of the church) have been in pointing him out, and distinguishing him from other. Hence, in the old Testament, the High Priest, his Title, Office, Function, and special Administration and Jurisdiction is more particularly and precisely set down than the Office of any of the Inferior Priests and Levites. Also in the New Testament, The Office of a Pastor is more distinctly, and more precisely set down, than of a Doctor or any other inferior church Officer; So that a man may as well call into question the whole New Testament, as doubt whether there ought to be a Pastor in every congregation, or doubt of his proper Office and function. And if by God's ordinance there should be an ordinary Ecclesiastical Officer above the Pastors of particular congregations, then Christ out of all question would with that special care and cost have set it forth: by Titles, prerogatives, peculiar Offices, Functions, and gifts. That the Churches and people of God, should have reason rather to doubt of any office or Jurisdiction, than of the peculiar office or Jurisdiction of the Primates, Metropolitans, Archbishops, and Prelates of the world.

3   *They hold* that if there were a Supreme National Ecclesiastical Minister or Pastor, that should be the Prince of many thousand Pastors: that then also Christ (as he did in the Jewish Church) would have appointed a solemn National or provincial Liturgy or worship, unto which at some times of the

86

year, the whole body of the People should ascend, and that unto the Metropolitan City as unto a Jerusalem, and that he would (as he did in the Jewish Church) more precisely and particularly have set down the manner of solemnization thereof, than of his parochial worship forasmuch therefore as they cannot read in the new Testament of any higher or more solemn worship, than of that which is to be performed in a particular Congregation they cannot be persuaded that God hath appointed any higher Ministers of his service and worship under the new Testament, than the elect ministers of particular Congregations.

4   *They hold* that the High Priest of the Jews, was typically and in a figure the supreme head of the whole Catholic Church, which though it were visible only in the Province and Nation of Jewry, Yet those of other Nations and Countries (as appears, by the History of Acts, Even though they were Ethiopians,) were under this High Priest, And acknowledged homage unto him. So that he was not a Provincial Metropolitan, but in very deed, an Oecumenical and universal Bishop of the whole world. And therefore they hold, (this being the best ground in the word, for Metropolitan and Provincial Pastors or Bishops,) that the Pope of Rome who alone maketh claim unto, and is in possession of the like universal Supremacy: hath more warrant in the word of God, to the same, than any Metropolitan, or Diocesan (not dependent upon him) hath or can have. So that they hold, that by the word of God, either there must be no Metropolitans and Diocesans, or else there must be a Pope.

5   *They hold* That no Pastor ought to exercise or accept of any Civil public Jurisdiction and authority, but ought to be wholly employed in spiritual Offices and duties to that Congregation over which he is set. And that those Civil Magistrates weaken their own Supremacy that shall suffer any Ecclesiastical Pastor to exercise any civil Jurisdiction within their Realms, Dominions, or Seigniories.

6   *They hold* that the highest and supreme office and authority of the Pastor, is to preach the gospel solemnly and publicly to the Congregation, by interpreting the written word of God, and applying the same by exhortation and reproof unto them. They hold that this was the greatest work that Christ and his Apostles did, and that whosoever is thought worthy and fit to exercise this authority, cannot be thought unfit and unworthy to exercise any other spiritual or Ecclesiastical authority whatsoever.

7   *They hold* that the Pastor or Minister of the word, is not to teach any Doctrine unto the church, grounded upon his own Judgment or opinion, or upon the Judgment or opinion of any or all the men in the world. But only that

truth, that he is able to demonstrate and prove evidently, and apparently, by the word of God soundly interpreted, and that the people are not bound to believe any doctrine of Religion or Divinity whatsoever, upon any ground whatsoever, except it be apparently justified by the word, or by necessary consequent deduced from the same.

8   *They hold* that in interpreting the Scriptures, and opening the sense of them, he ought to follow those rules only that are followed in finding out the meaning of other writings, to wit, by weighing the propriety of the tongue wherein they are written, by weighing the Circumstance of the place, by comparing one place with another, and by considering what is properly spoken, and what tropically or figuratively. And they hold it unlawful for the Pastor to obtrude upon his people a sense of any part of the divine word, for which he hath no other ground but the bare testimonies of men, and that it is better for the people to be content to be ignorant of the meaning of such difficult places, than to hang their Faith in any matter in this case upon the bare Testimony of man.

9   *They hold* that the people of God ought not to acknowledge any such for their Pastors as are not able by preaching, to interpret and apply the word of God unto them in manner and form aforesaid. And therefore that no ignorant and sole reading Priests are to be reputed the ministers of Jesus Christ, who sendeth none into his ministry and service, but such as he adorneth in some measure with spiritual gifts. And they cannot be persuaded that the faculty of reading in one's Mother tongue the scriptures etc. which any ordinary Turk or Infidel hath, can be called in any congruity of speech a ministerial gift of Christ.

10   *They hold* that in the assembly of the Church, the Pastor only is to be the mouth of the Congregation to God in prayer, and that the people are only to testify their assent by the word *Amen*. And that it is a Babylonian confusion, for the Pastor to say one piece of a prayer and the people with mingled voices to say another, except in singing, which by the very ordinance and instinct of nature, is more delightful, and effectual, the more voices there are joined and mingled together in harmony and consent.

11   *They hold* that the Church hath no authority to impose upon her Pastors or any other of her officers, any other ministerial duties, Offices, Functions, Actions, or ceremonies, either in Divine worship or out of the same than what Christ himself in the scriptures hath imposed upon them, or what they might lawfully impose upon Christ himself, if he were in person upon the Earth, and did exercise a ministerial Office in some Church.

1 2   *They hold* that it is as great an injury to force a congregation or Church to maintain as their pastor, with tithes and such like donations, that person that either is not able to instruct them, or that refuseth in his own person ordinarily to do it, as to force a man to maintain one for his wife, that either is not a woman, or that refuseth in her own person to do the duties of a wife unto him?

1 3   *They hold* that by God's Ordinance there should be also in every church a Doctor whose special office should be to instruct by way of Catechizing the Ignorant of the Congregation (and that particularly) in the main grounds and principles of Religion.

CHAP. 4

Concerning the Elders.

1   For as much as through the malice of Satan, there are and will be in the best Churches many disorders and Scandals committed, that redound to the reproach of the gospel and are a stumbling block to many both without and within the church, and sith they judge it repugnant to the word of God, that any Minister should be a Sole Ruler and as it were a Pope so much as in one Parish, (much more that he should be one over a whole Diocese, Province or Nation) they hold that by God's Ordinance the Congregation should make choice of other officers, as Assistants unto the Ministers in the spiritual regiment of the Congregation who are by Office jointly with the Ministers of the word to be as Monitors and Overseers of the manners and Conversation of all the Congregation, and one of another: that so everyone may be more wary of their ways, and that the Pastors and Doctors may better attend to prayer and Doctrine, and by their means may be made better acquainted with the estate of the People, when others' Eyes besides their own shall wake, and watch over them.

2   *They hold* that such only are to be chosen to this Office, as are the Gravest, Honestest, Discreetest, best grounded in Religion, and the Ancientest Professors thereof in the Congregation, such as the whole Congregation do approve of and respect, for their wisdom, Holiness, and Honesty, and such also (If it be possible) as are of civil note and respect in the world, and able (without any burden to the Church) to maintain themselves, either by their Lands, or any other honest Civil Trade of life. Neither do they think it so much disgrace to the policy of the Church, that Tradesmen and artificers, (endowed with such qualities as are above specified) should be admitted to be Overseers of the

Church as it is that persons both Ignorant of Religion and all good letters, and in all respects for person, quality, and state, as base and vile, as the basest in the Congregation, should be admitted to be Pastors and Teachers of a congregation. And if it be apparent that God (who always blesseth his own Ordinances) doth often even in the Eyes of Kings and Nobles, make Honorable the Ministers and Pastors of his Churches upon which he hath bestowed spiritual Gifts and graces though for Birth, Education, Presence, Outward State, and maintenance they be most base and contemptible, so he will as well in the Eyes of all holy men, make this office, which is many degrees inferior to the other, precious, and Honorable, even for the Divine calling and ordinance sake.

CHAP. 5.

Concerning the Censures of the Church.

1   *They hold* that the spiritual keys of the Church are by Christ, committed to the aforesaid spiritual Officers and Governors, and unto none other: which keys they hold that they are not to be put to this use, to lock up the Crowns, Swords or Scepters, of Princes and civil States, or the civil Rights, prerogatives, and immunities, of civil subjects in the things of this Life, or to use them as picklocks to open withal, men's Treasuries and Coffers, or as keys of Prisons, to shut up the bodies of men; for they think that such a power and authority Ecclesiastical is fit only for the Antichrist of Rome and the consecrated Governors of his Synagogues, who having no word of God which is the sword of the spirit, to defend his and their usurped Jurisdiction, over the Christian world, doth unlawfully usurp the lawful civil sword and power of the Monarchs and Princes of the Earth, thereby forcing men to subject themselves to his spiritual vassalage and service and abusing thereby the spiritual Keys and jurisdiction of the church.

2   *They hold* that by virtue of these Keys, they are not to make any curious Inquisitions into the secret or hidden vices or crimes of men, extorting from them a confession of those faults that are concealed from themselves and others: or to proceed to molest any man upon secret suggestions, private suspicion, or uncertain fame, or for such crimes as are in question whether they be crimes or no; But they are to proceed, only against evident and apparent crimes, such as are either granted to be such of all civil honest men: or of all true Christians, or at least such, as they are able, by evidence of the word of God, to convince to be sins, to the conscience of the offender; As also such as

have been either publicly committed, or having been committed in secret, are by some good means brought to light, and which the delinquent denying, they are able by honest, and sufficient testimony to prove against him.

3   *They hold* that when he that hath committed a scandalous crime cometh before them and is convinced of the same, they ought not (after the manner of our ecclesiastical Courts) scorn, deride, taunt, and revile him, with odious and contumelious speeches, Eye him with big and stern looks, procure proctors to make Personal invectives against him, make him dance attendance from Court day to Court day, and from term to term, frowning at him in presence, and laughing at him behind his back: but they are (though he be never so obstinate and perverse) to use him brotherly, not giving the least personal reproaches, or threats, (but laying open unto him the nature of his sin by the light of God's word) are only by denouncing the judgments of God against him, to terrify him, and so to move him to repentance.

4   *They hold* that if the party offending be their civil Superior, that then they are to use even throughout the whole carriage of their censure, all civil compliments, Offices, and Reverence due unto him, That they are not to presume to convent him before them, but are themselves to go in all civil and humble manner unto him, to stand bare before him, to bow unto him, to give him all civil Titles belonging unto him; And if he be a King and Supreme Ruler, they are to kneel down before him, and in the humblest manner to Censure his faults; So that he may see apparently that they are not carried with the least spice of malice against his Person, but only with zeal of the health and Salvation of his soul.

5   *They hold* that the Ecclesiastical Officers laying to the charge of any man any Error, heresy, or false opinion whatsoever do stand bound themselves, first to prove that he holdeth such an error or heresy, and secondly to prove directly unto him that it is an error by the word of God and that it deserveth such a censure, before they do proceed against him.

6   *They hold* that the Governors of the Church ought with all patience and quietness, hear what every offender can possibly say for himself, either for qualification, defense, apology or Justification of any supposed Crime or error whatsoever; and they ought not to proceed to censure the grossest offense that is, until the offender have said as much for himself in his defense as he possibly is able. And they hold it an evident Character of a corrupt Ecclesiastical Government, where the parties convented may not have full liberty to speak for themselves, considering that the more liberty is granted to speak in a bad

cause, (especially before those that are in authority and of judgment,) the more the iniquity of it will appear, and the more the Justice of their sentence will shine.

7 *They hold* that the oath *ex officio,* whereby Popish and English Ecclesiastical governors, either upon some secret informations, or suggestions, or private suspicions, go about to bind men's consciences, to accuse themselves and their friends, of such crimes or imputations as cannot by any direct course of Law be proved against them, and whereby they are drawn to be instruments of many heavy crosses upon themselves and their friends, and that often for those Actions that they are persuaded in their consciences are good and holy. (I say) that they hold that such an oath (on the urger's part) is most damnable and Tyrannous, against the very Law of Nature, devised by Antichrist, through the inspiration of the Devil, That by means thereof the professors and practicers of the true Religion, might either in their weakness by perjury damn their own souls, or be drawn to reveal to the Enemies of Christianity, those secret religious acts and deeds, that being (in the persuasion of their consciences) for the advancement of the Gospel, will be a means of heavy sentences of condemnation against themselves and their dearest friends.

8 *They hold* that Ecclesiastical Officers have no power to proceed in Censure against any crime of any Person, after that he shall freely acknowledge the same, and profess his hearty penitency for it: And that they may not, for any crime whatsoever lay any bodily or pecuniary mulct upon them, or impose upon them any Ceremonial mark or Note of shame, such as is the white sheet or any such like: or take any fees for any cause whatsoever, but are to accept of as a sufficient satisfaction, A private submission and acknowledgment if the Crime be private, and a public, if the crime be public and notorious.

9 *They hold,* that if a member of the Church be obstinate, and show no signs and tokens of repentance of that crime, that they by evidence of scripture have convinced to be a crime, that then by their Ecclesiastical authority they are to deny unto him the Sacrament of the Supper. And if the suspension from it, will not humble him, then (though not without humbling themselves in prayer, fasting and great demonstration of sorrow for him) they are to denounce him to be as yet no member of the Kingdom of heaven, and of that Congregation, and so are to leave him to God and the King. And this is all the Ecclesiastical authority and jurisdiction that any spiritual Officers of the Church are to use against any man, for the greatest crime that can be committed.

10   *They hold,* that the Officers of the Church are not to proceed unto the extremest Censure against any man, without the free consent of the whole congregation itself.

11   *They hold* that the Minister, or any other particular Officer offending, is as subject to these Censures, as any other of the Congregation.

12   *They hold* that if any Member of the Congregation having committed a Scandalous sin shall of himself forsake the worship of God, and the Spiritual Communion with the Church, that then the Ecclesiastical Officers have no authority or jurisdiction over him, but only the Civil Magistrate, and those unto whom he oweth Civil subjection, as Parents, Masters, Landlords, etc.

CHAP. 6.
Concerning the Civil Magistrate.

1   *They hold* that the Civil Magistrate as he is a Civil Magistrate hath and ought to have Supreme power over all the Churches within his Dominions, in all causes whatsoever. And yet they hold that as he is a Christian he is a Member of some one particular Congregation, and ought to be as subject to the Spiritual Regiment thereof prescribed by Christ in his word, as the meanest subject in the Kingdom, and they hold that this Subjection is no more derogatory to his Supremacy, than the Subjection of his body in sickness to Physicians, can be said to be derogatory thereunto.

2   *They hold* that those Civil Magistrates are the greatest Enemies to their own Supremacy, that in whole or in part, communicate the virtue and power thereof, to any Ecclesiastical Officers. And that there cannot be imagined by the wit of man a more direct means to checkmate the same, than to make them Lords and Princes upon Earth, to invest them with Civil Jurisdiction and authority, and to conform the State and limits of their Jurisdiction to the State of Kings, and bounds of kingdoms.

3   *They hold* that there should be no Ecclesiastical officer in the church so high, but that he ought to be subject unto, and punishable by the meanest Civil Officer in a Kingdom, City, or Town, not only for common crimes, but even for the abuse of their Ecclesiastical offices, yea they hold that they ought to be more punishable than any other subject whatsoever, If they shall offend against either civil or ecclesiastical laws.

4   *They hold* that the Civil Magistrate is to punish with all severity the Ecclesiastical officers of churches, if they shall intrude upon the rights and

prerogatives of the Civil authority and Magistracy, and shall pass those bounds and limits that Christ hath prescribed unto them in his word.

5   *They hold* that the Pope is that Antichrist, and therefore that Antichrist because being but an Ecclesiastical Officer he doth in the height of the pride of his heart make claim unto and usurp the Supremacy of the Kings and Civil Rulers of the Earth. And they hold that all defenders of the Popish faith, all endeavors of reconcilement with that church, all plotters for toleration of the Popish religion, all countenancers and maintainers of Seminary Priests and professed Catholics, and all deniers that the Pope is that Antichrist: are secret enemies to the King's Supremacy.

6   *They hold* that all Archbishops, Bishops, Deans, Officials, etc. have their Offices and Functions only by will and pleasure of the King and civil States of this Realm, and they hold that whosoever holdeth that the King may not without sin remove these Offices out of the Church, and dispose of their Temporalities and maintenance according to his own pleasure, or that these Offices are *Jure divino,* and not only or merely *Jure humano:* That all such deny a principal part of the King's Supremacy.

7   *They hold:* that not one of these opinions can be proved to be contrary to the word of God, and that if they might have leave that they are able to answer all that hath been written against anyone of them.

FINIS

5

[Thomas Scott]

The Interpreter

1622

THOMAS SCOTT (*ca.* 1580–1626) received the B.D. degree from Peterhouse in Cambridge and served for a time as chaplain to King James. While rector of a church in Norwich, Scott wrote a satiric pamphlet directed against the projected marriage of Prince Charles to the infanta of Spain. Having offended the royal court, Scott went into exile but soon returned to serve as minister at Ipswich. Finally he became a preacher to English soldiers in Utrecht, Holland, where he was murdered by a probably insane soldier. His writings show a strong opposition to Roman Catholicism and a lively, well-informed interest in foreign affairs. The authorship of *The Interpreter,* which was published anonymously, is attributed to Scott in British Museum Ms. Additional 24942, and the work's contents and point of view are consistent with his political and religious beliefs.

At the beginning of his verse pamphlet, Scott recognizes a distinction between earlier and contemporary usages of the terms *puritan, protestant,* and *papist.* In former times, he notes briefly, a puritan was one who objected to some ceremonies of the Church of England and to its episcopal form of government; a protestant, one who embraced the ceremonies and episcopacy, but differed from the church of Rome on substantial doctrinal points; and a papist, one who thought the pope infallible. But Scott finds the new definitions quite different and elaborates two of them at some length.

Only the puritan receives favorable treatment. In political orientation, Scott's chief interest, the puritan serves the king loyally but not obsequiously, supports all efforts to keep the Palatinate protestant, supports French religious reformers, and chiefly mistrusts Spain. He stands ready to fight in all these causes. In 1624 Scott published a tract with the bellicose title *Certaine Reasons and Arguments of Policie, Why the King of England Should Hereafter Give over All Further Treatie, and Enter into War with the Spaniard.* *The Interpreter* reflects a similar attitude; in fact, a distrust of Spanish intentions, with resulting opposition to James's attempts to reach an accommodation with Spain, characterizes most of Scott's numerous tracts.

In his religious and moral attitudes and practices, Scott's puritan mirrors the ideal, religious citizen. He prays twice each day and hears two sermons on Sunday. He refuses to buy church offices, and if he holds one, he uses it solely for the benefit of the people, not for his own gain. In morals he avoids dissembling; he speaks the truth whatever his position and whatever the cost, most notably if he is a member of Parliament. He makes no reckless charges of treason against those who argue against governmental policy. He supports the cause of individual liberty, presumably in religious, as well as in civil, affairs.

Scott's protestant, by contrast, does not want to fight for the Palatinate or help the protestant forces in the Low Countries. He seeks rapprochement with Spain, stupidly unaware of Spanish designs against England. In religious practice he observes saints' days, makes a kind of idolatrous holiday of May Day with all its profane revelry, and does not criticize the church of Rome. Governed by personal ambition, he defers to secular authority, defies the king, flatters his superiors, and in general does whatever seems necessary to secure advancement to high office in church or state. Having no settled religious or moral principles, he changes his beliefs with changing times, as his superiors may dictate. The steadfast, loyal puritans suffer greatly at his hands, for he has no sense of justice. In short, he is a timeserver.

Scott treats the papist very briefly, noting only that he gives total obedience to the church of Rome and that the ruling forces in England consider him a loyal citizen. Throughout *The Interpreter* one basic opposition rests either on the surface of the argument or just below it: Criticism of the prevailing political and religious establishment is good, whereas acceptance is mindless and harmful. The work breathes dissent. Although particular issues, especially England's relationship with Spain, figure prominently, Scott most vehemently opposes the cast of mind that supports the status quo in the interests of personal advancement, and he sees this attitude everywhere within the church. Wholly convinced that the nonconformists are right, he cannot find any sincere, thoughtful convictions or worthy motives among the supporters of the establishment. To him the Church of England is an organization run by timeservers calling themselves protestants. In tone and attitude, *The Interpreter* resembles the works of many separatists, though Scott remained within the church.

The Interpreter Wherein three principall termes of State much mistaken by the vulgar are clearly unfolded. Anno 1622.
[Thomas Scott.]

*To such as understand not the
English tongue perfectly.*

That the unwise may learn to understand,
how certain words are used in our land,
And that they may write sense whilst they remain
in foreign parts, or shall return again
(for idioms, fashions, Manners, alter here,
as friendship and religion everywhere)
I have some elegancies for our tongue
observed, as they are used now, among
our ablest linguists, who mint for the Court
words, fit to be proclaimed; and do resort
where Lords and Ladies couple and converse
and trade lip learning both in prose, and verse.
and by these few the docible may see,
how rich our language is, religious we.
    Time was a Puritan was counted such
as held some ceremonies were too much
retained and urged: and would no Bishops grant
others to rule, who government did want.
    Time was a PROTESTANT was only taken
for such as had the Church of Rome forsaken

97

for her known falsehoods in the highest point
But would not for each toy, true peace disjoint.

    Time was, a PAPIST was a man who thought
Rome could not err, but all her canons ought
to be Canonical, and blindly led
he from the truth, for fear of error fled.

    But now these words, with divers others more
have other senses than they had before.
which plainly I do labor to relate,
As they are now accepted in our state.

A Puritan:
(So nicknamed: but indeed the sound Protestant.)

    A Puritan is such another thing
As says with all his heart, God save the King
And all his issue: and to make this good,
will freely spend his money and his blood.
And in his factious and fond mood, dare say
'tis madness for the Palsgrave thus to stay
And wait the loving leisure of kind Spain
who gets at first, only to give again
in courtesy; that faithless Heretics
may taste the faith and love of Catholics
And Hope too. for a Puritan is he
That doth not hope these Holy-days to see
And would a wasted Country on condition
Scorn to receive, although the High Commission
of England, Spain, and Rome would have it so:
false favors he'd not take from a true foe.
    A Puritan is he that rather had
Spend all to help the States, he is so mad
Than spend one hundred thousand pound a year
to guard the Spanish coasts from Pirates' fear,
The whilst the Catholic King might force combine
Both Holland, Beame, and Paltz to undermine,
And by his cross-curse-christian counterwork
To make Rome both for Antichrist and Turk

98

right Catholic. So th'empire first divided
By holy mother's pious plots, (who sided
the East, and West, that she might get between,
and sit aloft and govern like a Queen)
The *Turk* did great *Constantinople* gain
and may win *Rome* too, by the help of Spain.
    A Puritan is he that would not live
upon the sins of other men: nor give
money for office in the Church or State,
Though 'twere a Bishopric, he so doth hate
all Ceremonies of the Court and Church,
which do the coffer and the conscience lurch
of both the treasures. So that (covetous) he
would not have such as want both, better be.
    A Puritan is he that thinks, and says
he must account give of his works and ways,
And that whatsoever calling he assumes
it is for others' good. So he presumes
rashly to censure such as wisely can
by taking timely bribes of every man
enrich themselves, knowing to that sole end,
God and the King did them their honors send.
And that *Simplicity* hath only mounted
by virtue; but such fools they'll not be counted.
    A Puritan is he that twice a day
doth at the least to God devoutly pray:
And twice a Sabbath goes to Church to hear,
to pray, confess his sins, and praise God there
in open sight of all men; not content,
God knows his heart, except his knee be bent
That men and Angels likewise may discern,
he came to practice there, as well as learn,
And honor God with every outward part,
with knee, hand, tongue, as well as with the heart.
    A *Puritan* is he which grieves to think
Religion should in *France,* shipwreck and sink,
whilst we give aim: And that those men should sway
the kingdom there, who made the King away

The whilst all such as helped to crown the father
should by the Son be now proscribed the rather.
    A *Puritan* in unadvised zeal
Could wish that Huntsmen ruled the Commonweal,
And that the King's hounds were the only spies
for they would tell truth, as the other lies.
He wisheth beasts were men, as men resemble
beasts: for surely they would not dissemble,
But would tell where the fault lies, and hunt home
the subtle fox either to Spain or Rome.
    A *Puritan* is he that speaks his mind
in Parliament: not looking once behind
to others' danger, nor yet sideways leaning
to promised honor, his direct true meaning.
But for the laws and truth doth firmly stand
By which he knows Kings only do command,
And Tyrants otherwise. He crosseth not
this man because a Courtier, or a Scot,
Or that because a favorite, or so:
But if the State's friend, none can be his foe.
But if the State's foe, be he what he will
Illustrious, wise, great, learned, he counts him ill.
He neither sides with that man nor with this
but gives his voice just as the reason is
And yet if Policy would work a fraction
to cross religion by a foreign faction
pretending public good, he'll join with those
who dare speak truth, not only under the Rose
But though the white Rose and the Red do hear
and though the pricking Thistle too be there.
yea though the stars, the moon and sun look on
and cast through clouds oblique aspect upon
his clear and free intentions, he's as bold
and confident as the bright Marigold
That flatterer, that favorite of the sun
who doth the selfsame course observe and run
not caring though all flowers else wax sere,
so he the golden livery may wear.

But our free, generous, and noble spirit
Doth from his ancient English stock inherit
such native worth and liberty of mind,
as will omit no slavery of this kind,
yet he is ready to obey wheresoe're
he may not prejudice the truth by fear,
nor faintly seem to shrink, withdraw, give way
whilst other mushrumps do the state betray.
He'll not a Traitor be unto the King
nor to the Laws (for that's another thing
men dream not of: who think they no way can
be Traitors unto many for one man)
But his chief error is to think that none
Can be a Traitor till law calls him one.
And that the Law is what the state decrees
in Parliament: by which whilst that he sees
his Actions and intentions justified
He counts himself a Martyr glorified
If in this cause he suffers; and contemns
All dangers in his way. Nay he condemns
All such as Traitors be to Church and state,
who for the love of one all others hate,
And for particular ends, and private aims
forsake their Country and their conscience maims.
    His Character abridged if you would have,
    He's one that would a subject be, no slave.

A Protestant
(so will the Formalist be called.)

A Protestant is such another thing
As makes within his heart God of the King
And as if he did with his crown inherit
A never-erring, and infallible spirit,
Labors to blow him up by praise of wit
And by false flatteries cozen him of it.
    A *Protestant* is one that shakes the head
And pities much the *Palsgrave* was misled

to meddle with *Bohemia,* and incense
The Spanish wrath, 'gainst which there is no fence.
That his Revenues in the *Paltz* again
were well restored he wishes, so that Spain
would take the honors of that house, and give
Mentz his demands, letting the Palsgrave live:
for such a favor as his lands and life,
not one except the father of his wife,
That King of peace and love dares boldly crave.
But what is it he may despair to have
By means of th'English and the Scottish Saint
who at their pupils' suit doth still acquaint
The Spanish *Patron,* how the first of May
Philip and *Jacob* make one holy day:
what therefore's given to one, the other must
Be sharer in: for James is surnamed Just.

And for this year by holy church's count
The Calendar reformed hath singled out
These two most sacred saints to wait upon
Our Savior's feast of Resurrection,
which by the English Heathen computation
meets with May day amongst the Catholic nation,
And may be such a day as that for goodness,
which some called ill May day from people's woodness.
A day of feasting, and a day of pleasure,
A day of marriage and withal of Treasure,
A day of Catholic unity and love,
which may a kind of Resurrection move
in our State union, almost now forgot,
being buried both by th'English and the Scot.
Spain strikes betwixt, and like a Lord commands,
They join their Laws together as their lands.
And join they will, but in despite of Spain,
making his holy day of hope but vain.

A Protestant is he that fain would take
occasion from the East or West to shake
our League with the United Provinces,
to which end he hath many fair pretenses.

Our honor first for in the *Greenland* they
And the East Indies beat our ships away.
Our profit likewise, for in both those places
we do great loss sustain, beside disgraces:
And in the narrow Seas where we are masters,
They will presume to be our herring tasters.
But we should have white herrings wondrous plenty,
If they would give us two of every twenty:
Or stay our idle leisure, till that none
remained, for them or us, but all were gone.
And if they will not thus our humors serve,
That we (saith he) should leave them they deserve.
A herring cob we see will make him quarrel,
what would the man do, think you, for a barrel?
Well could I wish these things were all amended,
But greater business now is to be tended.
Our lives, religions, liberties and lands,
upon this nice and tickle quarrel stands,
And we must for a fitter time attend,
else Spain will soon this controversy end.
  A *Protestant* is he that by degrees
climbs every office, knows the proper fees,
they give and take, an entrance of the place,
and at what rate again they vent that grace,
knows in how many years a man may gather
enough to make himself a reverend father:
Or from the lowest civil step arise
To sit with honor in the starry skies:
for he hath gone that progress, step by step,
as snails creep up, where safely none can leap,
for snails do leave behind their silver slime
and gild the way for falling as they climb.
  A Protestant is he that with the stream
Still swims and wisely shuns every extreme,
Loves not in point of faith to be precise
but to believe as Kings do, counts it wise.
If Constantine the great will Christened be,
this will the white Robe wear as well as he,

And in the hallowed fountain plunge amain
his naked body, as if every stain
were now washed off, and his inflamed zeal
Thirsted these waters which soul's sin doth heal.
Again if Julian will renounce his faith,
this man will say just, as his Sovereign saith,
If he intend Religion to betray,
and yet will walk a close and covert way,
Corrupting men by office, honor, bounty,
you shall find this man will deserve a County,
By double dealing and by broking so
That none shall think him ere they find him too
Apostated; for no way so doth work
to make a man an *Atheist, Jew,* or *Turk*
as do Corrupted manners which lets in
a deluge of impiety and sin.
These backed by favor and preferment may
have power to make all error open way,
and every man will censure opposition
when gilden flattery kills without suspicion.
This poisoned vial then was poured in,
when first the Church got means to maintain sin,
and now the means withdrawn or misemployed
makes all Religion and all conscience void,
for man that hunts for honor, wealth, or fame,
will be as those be who dispose the same.
So that no readier way there can be found
to conquer us, than to corrupt the sound
by Bribes; the worst assault that can befall
to bodies politic, confounding all.
Gifts blind the wise. And though the Chequer be
open and empty, as erst full and free,
yet other bribes can work the same effect
that Mammon would: the favor and respect
of favorites, a nod or wink from Kings,
employment, office, grace, are able things.
　　　Besides the honored style of Viscount, Lord,
Earl, Marquess, Duke, can work at every word

strange alterations more than Circe's Cup
In such as can no otherways get up.
    Will he speak truth directly? make him then
a Dean, or Bishop, they are no such men,
The wolf hath seen them first, their throat is furred,
you shall not hear from them a factious word.
    Stands he for Law, and custom of the Land?
make him an officer, give him Command.
Command where he may gain, this will bewitch
Demosthenes, who labors to be rich.
    What is he bold and forward? send him out
on some embassage; or employ the stout
At sea or land some desperate voyage, where
they may be lost: then leave them helpless there,
undo them thus. Before they had too much
But being poor, they'll nothing dare to touch.
This ostracism will sure abate their pride,
And they shall give great thanks for it beside.
If he be poor, oppress him, shut him out
in forlorn banishment, where round about
the faithless world, he may his living seek,
Then no man after him will do the like.
If he be faint, check him, or do but chide,
he'll hold his tongue, and his tail closely hide.
Is he free-tongued? though serious and discreet,
Proclaim him silent: whip him through the street:
Thus whatsoe're is done, no bird shall dare
To warn the rest, till all be in the snare.
Is he a Rich man? then the Fleet and fine
will make him seem (although he be not) thine.
Briefly, whatsoe're he be, except alone
directly honest, (of which few or none
remain alive) a Statist ways can find:
By policy to work him to his mind.
And thus the commonwealth may conquered be,
The Church deflowered, beslaved our liberty
without all bloodshed, under the pretense
of peace, religion, love, and innocence.

A Protestant is an indifferent man,
that with all faiths, or none, hold quarter can:
So moderate and temperate his passion,
as he to all times can his conscience fashion.
He at the Chapel can a Bishop hear,
And then in Holborn a Religious Friar:
A Mass ne'er troubles him, more than a play,
All's one, he comes all one from both away.
    A Protestant no other fault can spy
In all Rome's beadroll of iniquity,
But that of late they do profess King killing,
which Catholic point to credit he's unwilling:
only because he gains by Kings far more,
than he can hope for by the Romish whore.
He saith this only doth the Pope proclaim
for *Antichrist,* because that *Greekish* name
doth signify *Against the Lord's anointed,*
As if it only 'gainst this doctrine pointed.
And therefore leaving this out of their Creed,
He in the rest with them is soon agreed.
And so the King's part may be safe from fear,
Let God himself for his own part take care.
    A Protestant is he that guards the ear
of sovereign Justice, so that truth to hear
he's not permitted; nor to know the danger
he stands in, 'twixt the subject and the stranger:
The plots which strangers have, grief of his own,
which may too late be prevented, known.
For though his foes be wily wolves and foxes,
his subjects shackled asses, yoked oxes,
yet time will show them not to be such daws,
As will look on whilst others change the Laws,
and Rob the State, Religion do deflower,
having their Prince imprisoned in their power,
As Princes have been prisoners to their own,
And so may ours too if the truth were known.
The liberty of will by strong affection
may be restrained, which is the worst subjection.

For then the understanding will not see,
But rusheth on whatsoe're the danger be.
A Protestant is he whose good intention
Deserves an English and a Spanish pension,
both for one service, and obtains it too
By winning Spain more than their arms could do
with long delays, and losing us and ours
what lost to get again we want both powers
And perhaps will.

     Others by treaties and disputes may gain
But we by blows, else old said saws be vain.
A Protestant is he that hath no eye
Beyond his private profit, but doth lie
In wait to be the first that may propound
what he foresees power plots. The solid ground
He ne'er examines, be it right or wrong,
All's one, since it doth to his part belong.
For to his part belongs to soothe and flatter
The greatest Man though in the foulest matter,
And him he holds a Rebel that dare say
No man against the Laws, we must obey.

     His Character abridged if you will have,
He's one that's no true subject, but a Slave.

A Papist.

A *Romanist* is such another thing
As would with all his heart murder the King,
That saith the house of *Austria* is appointed
To rule all Christians and for this anointed
by Christ's own vicar. And they Rebels are
who dare against this house make any war,
Invasive or defensive; Jesuits' wit
And Indian gold, do both attend on it,
And all Rome's Hierarchy do plot, pray, curse,
And spend the strength of body, soul, and purse
to this sole end, that every state beside
may be the vassals to the Austrian pride,

And so Rome may of both the Emperies
keep still the Civil and Religious keys.
    A Romanist is he that sows debate
'Twixt Prince and people, and 'twixt every state
where he remains: that he by the division
may work himself some profit in decision.
Or bring in *Rome* and *Spain* to make all friends,
Who having footing once have half their ends.
For as the Devil since first he got within
man's heart, keeps still thereby original sin,
So those wheresoe're once they interest gain
keep all; or such a party let remain
behind, assured to them as may procure
A relapse, when men think themselves secure.
Thus each disease, though cured, remains in part:
And thus the frail flesh oft betrays the heart.
Now for the rest, no Romish false opinion
Can make a Papist in the King's dominion.
Nor absence from the Church, for at this season
He is no Papist that commits not Treason.
Let him to Church resort, or be recusant,
All's one, he's counted a good Protestant.
Nay 'tis a question if *Guy Fawkes* were one,
But 'tis resolved that *Papist* he was none.
    His Character abridged if you will have,
    He is Spain's *subject* and *a Romish Slave.*

6

Robert Bolton

The Foure Last Things, 1633 (Excerpts)

and

Two Sermons, 1635 (Excerpt)

Rᴏʙᴇʀᴛ ʙᴏʟᴛᴏɴ (1572–1631), born of a middle-class Lancashire family, studied at Oxford, taking his M.A. degree in 1602 and becoming a fellow of Brasenose College. Learned in both Greek and Hebrew, he lectured on logic and natural philosophy; one of his lectures, delivered before King James, evoked the king's high praise. After some vacillation Bolton experienced a religious conversion, took the B.D. degree (in 1609), and became a clergyman. His devotional works, most of which were published posthumously, became very popular. By the time of his death his personal reputation was so great that his biography, written by his friend Edward Bagshawe, was published as a preface to his most famous work, *The Foure Last Things.*

Bolton's writings are not controversial. Although not thoroughly conforming to the religious practices of the Church of England, he remained in favor with the authorities. Quite possibly he would have been called a timeserver by more-zealous reformers had not his great reputation for piety, his learning, and the high standard of conduct he promoted exalted him above criticism. No one could take exception to his frequent strictures against gambling, profanity, sloth, pride, and in general all dishonest or immoral activity. Nonconformist ministers must have found very congenial his statement "If I see the power of grace soundly appear in a man's whole carriage and a constant partaking with GOD, good causes, and good men, he shall for my part, be ever right dear unto my heart, though he differ from me in some indifferent things" (see the second assize sermon that follows). At the same time, his aversion to Anabaptists, separatists, and in general to all promoters of disunity within the church undoubtedly appealed to the rigidly conforming Anglicans. Moreover, he generally avoided writing directly on ceremonies or church government, the most controversial topics of the day.

Mentions of the puritans appear only as obiter dicta in Bolton's works, but his comments on the term indicate that he was troubled by its use—or abuse, as he would have called it. In a relatively early work, *A Discourse About the State of True Happinesse* (1611), he objects that many who show "too fiery zeal against idleness, drunkenness, other shameful corruptions" are called puritans; in a marginal note he adds, "The world is come to that wretched pass, and height of profaneness, that even honesty and sanctification, is many times odiously branded by the nick name of Puritanism" (p. 132). In the sixth edition of the same work (1631), he speaks even more strongly: "I am persuaded there was never poor persecuted word, since malice against God first seized upon the damned angels; and the graces of Heaven dwelt in the heart of man; that passed through the mouths of all sorts of unregenerate men, with more distastefulness, and gnashing of teeth, than the name of Puritan doth at this day" (p. 193).

In the selections here reprinted, Bolton tries to arrive at a definition of *puritanism,* distinguishing two uses entirely separate and totally opposed in both denotation and connotation. He argues that if one accepts *puritanism* as a term of obloquy, it can be truly applied only to several distinct, identifiable groups: the Novatians and Donatists of antiquity, Anabaptists, separatists, those who seek to exculpate themselves from all particular sins, those who take pride in their moral character, those who think themselves justified by the observance of religious ceremonies, those afflicted with spiritual pride, and those who hold their own particular beliefs in fine points to be the only true test of holiness. That there existed and still exist men who can be called puritans in the fully opprobrious sense of the term Bolton admits readily enough, but briefly and in passing.

His main concern devolves upon the men called puritans because of beliefs and practices similar to his. In their defense he boldly adopts the term *puritan* but modifies it by calling them "Christ's puritans" or "Christ's Catharoi," daring even to use the Greek name of a particular heresy. He appears to be saying that if the name is to be applied to the strictly religious and moral, it should be taken in its root sense and be used to designate genuine purity. His true puritans then become scrupulously good and holy men who base their religion on Scripture and who make abundant use of sermons, either as preachers or as auditors. Bolton's rhetoric conveys the impression that these constitute the great majority of men called puritans in his time. He leaves the reader with the notion that the term, instead of being abandoned or applied strictly to the ancient Cathari and their contemporary emulators, should, as currently used, be considered a term of praise, not reproach. In other words, anyone called a puritan is most likely a truly good and scrupulously religious person.

M. Boltons Last and Learned Worke *of the* Foure Last Things, Death, Judgment, Hell, *and* Heaven. With an Assise Sermon, and Notes on Justice *Nicolls* his Funerall. *Together with the Life and Death of the Authour.* Published E. B. and reviewed, with Marginall Notes, and an Alphabeticall Table added thereunto. *London, Printed by* George Miller, *dwelling in the Black Friers.* 1633.

> A Sermon Preached At Lent Assises, *Anno Domini,* MDCXXX. At *Northampton,* before Sir Richard Hutton And Sir George Crooke, *His Majesties Iustices of Assise, &c.*
> {Excerpts: pp. 169, 244−47.}

> Text. 1.Cor. Chap. 1. Ver. 26. For Brethren, ye see your calling, how not many wise men after the flesh, not many mighty, not many noble are called.

And thus I have done with the reasons peculiar to every several sort of greatness: I now come to those which are common to them all.

1. All the great ones according to the flesh in any of these kinds: I say, ye are all as yet deadly enemies from the very heart-root to the profession and practice of the holy men, without which holiness we cannot see GOD: you cannot endure to be called puritans; much less to become such: and yet without purity, none shall ever see the face of GOD with comfort.

Mistake me not. I mean CHRIST's καθαροὶ CHRIST's puritans, and no other, *Mat.* 5.8. *Joh.* 13.11. and 15.3.

Secondly, I mean only such as *Bellarmine* intimates, when he calls King JAMES puritan: for, he so calls him, saith D. *Harkwit* against *Carrier,* because in the first book of his *Basilicon Doron,* he affirms, that the religion professed in *Scotland* was grounded upon the plain words of the Scripture: And again in his second book, that the reformation of Religion in *Scotland* was extraordinarily wrought by GOD. Gracious and holy speeches (as you see) with men of the world are puritanical. And if a man speak but holily, and name but reformation, Scripture, conscience, and such other words which sting their carnal hearts, it is enough to make a man a puritan.

Thirdly, I mean the very same, of whom Bishop *Downam* one of the greatest scholars of either Kingdom, speaks thus in his Sermon at Spittle, called *Abrahams Triall:* "And even in these times (saith he) the godly live amongst such a generation of men, as that if a man do but Labor to keep a good conscience in any measure, although he meddle not with matters of State, or Discipline, or Ceremonies, (as for example, if a Minister diligently Preach, or in his preaching seek to profit rather than to please, remembering the saying of the Apostle, *If I seek to please men, I am not the servant of* CHRIST, *Gal.* 1.10. Or if a private Christian make conscience of swearing, sanctifying the Sabbath, frequenting Sermons, or abstaining from the common corruptions of the time) he shall straightway be condemned for a Puritan, and consequently be less favored than either a carnal Gospeler, or a close Papist, etc."

Fourthly, I mean none but those whom the Communion Book intends in that passage of the prayer after Confession: "That the rest of our life hereafter may be pure and holy."

Now these come by their purity by preaching the Word. Now saith CHRIST, ye are καθαροὶ, clean by the Word which I have spoken unto you, *John* 15.3. The Word must first illighten, convince, and cast them down: so that out of sight of sin, and sense of divine wrath, being weary, sick, lost, wounded, bruised, broken-hearted, (these are Scripture phrases) and thereupon casting their eyes upon the amiableness, excellency, and sweetness of the LORD JESUS, and the All-sufficiency of his blood to cure them, resolve to sell all, to confess and forsake all their sins, not to leave an hoof behind: and then taking him offered by the hand of GOD'S free grace, as well for an Husband, Lord, and King, to love, serve, and obey him, as for a SAVIOR to free them from hell. They put on with the hand of faith the perfect purity of his imputed righteousness, attended ever with some measure of inherent purity, infused by the sanctifying Spirit, and after entering the good way, their lives are ever after pure and holy.

These are CHRIST'S καθαροὶ, and the Puritans I mean. And these men of purity some never mean to be: nay, they heartily hate the very image of JESUS CHRIST in them, they speak spitefully against them, *David* was not only the drunkards' song, but those also that sat in the gate spoke against him: they are your *music,* and matter of your mirth; "I am your music," saith the Church in the person of *Jeremy, Lam.* 3. They will many times call upon a roguish vagabond at your feasts to sing a song against them, whom they should rather set in the stocks; they are transported, and inwardly boil with far more indignation and heart-rising against their holiness, purity, precise walking, and all means that lead thereunto, though enjoined upon pain of never seeing the face of GOD in glory: than more simple, poorer, and meaner, men; and that's a reason they stick faster in the Devil's clutches than they, and that few of them are called, converted, and saved, according to my Text.

Secondly, ye that are thus the world's favorites, are very loath to become fools; and therefore in the meantime lie locked full fast in the Devil's bands, and cannot escape except ye be such. I speak a very displeasing thing to worldly-wise men, but they are the very words and wisdom of the Spirit of GOD, 1 *Cor.* 3.18. "Let no man deceive himself: if any man among you seemeth to be wise in this world, let him become a fool, that he may be wise."

Let no man deceive himself; such caveats as this are wont to be premised when men out of their carnal conceits are peremptory to the contrary, and would venture their salvation (as they say) that it is not so. See *Ephes.* 5.6. 1 *Cor.* 6.9. *Mat.* 5.2. And did not most of your hearts rise against these words of mine (you must become fools, or never be saved) until I brought Scripture?

Two sermons Preached at Northampton at Two Severall Assises There. The one in the time of the Shrevalty of Sir *Erasmus Dryden* Baronet. *Anno Domini,* 1621. The other in the time of the Shrevalty of Sir *Henry Robinson* Knight, *Anno Domini,* 1629. By *Robert Bolton* Bachelour in Divinity, Late Minister of *Broughton* in Northampton-shire, and sometimes Fellow of *Brasen-nose* College in Oxford. *Published by E. B.* London, Printed by George Miller dwelling in the Blacke-Fryers. 1635.

The Second Assise Sermon
[Excerpt: pp. 83–88.]

Prov. 29.2
When the righteous are in authority, the people rejoice: but when the wicked beareth rule, the people mourn.

But here before I enter upon the particulars, give me leave to prevent an exception, remove a scruple, which may perhaps arise already in some men's hearts, and so dull their attention, and blunt the impression of the ensuing points. What? may some say, here is nothing but JESUS CHRIST, pure preferment, holy truth, divine light, I know not how many kinds of righteousness, clear conscience, sad forethoughts of the last day, etc. All (for anything I see) tending wholly to Puritanism; I think he would have us all so righteous, that we should turn Puritans, etc.

Before I speak to the point, let me tell you, that I am right glad, that I have now in mine eye, such an honorable, noble, judicious, and understanding Auditory, who I know will do me right, were there now before me a number of drunkards, whoremasters, deboist swaggerers, scorners of Religion, sensual *Epicures,* Stigmatical scurrile jesters; O how would they take on, stamp, and play the Bedlams! how they would rage, rail, and cavil: though by the mercy of GOD, they should be no more able to overthrow by any sound reason what I say, than to remove the mightiest rock, when they are reeling drunk, either with wine or malice. Now upon this occasion let me acquaint you with the truth, about this unhappy imputation, ordinarily laid by Protestants at large upon the power of godliness. Nowadays, every boisterous *Nimrod,* impure drunkard, and self-guilty wretch, is ready with great rage to fly in the face of every professor, with the imputation of puritanism; if he doth but look towards Religion, labor to keep a good conscience in all things, he is presently a Puritan, and through this name, many times by a malicious equivocation, they strike at the very heart of grace, and power of godliness, at GOD'S best Servants, and the King's best subjects. For there is none of them all, but in their sense, with all their hearts, they would be the strictest Puritans in a Country upon their beds of death; I mean, that their consciences should be enlightened, and they not sealed up with the spirit of slumber, like drunken *Nabal,* for a day of vengeance. But let none here out of humor, malice, faction, or mistake, strain, and wrest, for I mean not,

First, the natural Puritan intimated. Prov. 30.12. "There is a generation," etc. You shall find many of these, especially among the common and ignorant people; charge them with sin in general, and they will confess, and yield: but descend to particulars, and you can fasten nothing upon them, they are true Justiciaries; press one of these with the first Commandment, and how he stands in his carriage towards it, oh he is infinitely free, he never served any

GOD, but one, etc. with the second, Images, I never worshipped any Images in my life, I defy them, etc. They are excellently laid out in their colors, and to the life, by that reverent man of GOD, Master *Dent* in his Plaine mans Pathway to heaven.

They are a kind of people who yet lie in the darkness of their natural ignorance, and dung of their own corruption, and yet with their own testimony, confirm themselves in a great opinion of their own integrity.

Secondly, I mean not the moral Puritan, who thinks himself as safe for salvation by the power of civil honesty, as if he were already a Saint in heaven; whereas it is clear. Heb. 12.14. without addition of holiness to civil honesty, and conscionable dealing with our Brethren, none shall ever see the LORD.

Thirdly, I mean not the superstitious Puritan, who out of a furious self-love to his own will-worship, and senseless doting upon old Popish customs, thinks himself to be the only holy devoid man, and all forward professors profane. You shall hear a knot of such fellows speak. *Esa.* 65.5. "Come not near to me, for I am holier than thou."

Fourthly, I mean not the Pharisaical Puritan, characterized to the life, *Luke* 18.11, 12. Who being passingly proud of the godly flourish of outside Christianity, thinks himself to be in the only true spiritual temper, and whatsoever is short of him, to be profaneness, and whatsoever to be above him to be preciseness.

Now these kinds are true Puritans indeed: for they think themselves to be the only men, and all others hypocrites; whereas poor souls, they were yet never acquainted with the great mystery of grace, but are mere strangers to that glorious work of conversion, pangs of the new birth, wrestling with inward corruptions, breaking their hearts, and pouring out their souls every day before GOD in secret, open-heartedness, and bountiful doles to distressed Christians, and the poor members of CHRIST, self-denial, heavenly-mindedness, walking with GOD, etc.

Fifthly, I mean not the true Catharists, pestilent heretics about the year of our LORD 253.

They were also called Novations, of *Novatus* their Author, but *Cathari,* from their opinions, and profession, who wickedly denied to the relapsed, reception into the Church upon the repentance, etc. and called themselves pure.

Sixthly, I mean not the African Donatists, about the year of our LORD 331. who were also called, *Circumcelliones, Circuitores, Parmeniani, Montanistae, Montenses.*

Seventhly, Not the furious Anabaptists, of our times, who are as like the ancient Donatists, as if they had spit them out of their mouth.

Eighthly, Not the giddy Separist.

Ninethly, Nor the unwarrantable Opinionist, *quam talis,* as ungroundedly disopinionated; I speak thus, because I am persuaded, good men may differ in things indifferent without prejudice of salvation, or just cause of breach of charity, or Disunion of affections. If I see the power of grace soundly appear in a man's whole carriage and a constant partaking with GOD, good causes, and good men, he shall for my part, be ever right dear unto my heart, though he differ from me in some indifferent things.

By Puritans, then I mean only such, as JESUS CHRIST his own mouth styleth so, *John* 13.10. and 15.3. The same word is used here, but in a more blessed sense, that *Eusebius* hath to describe equivocally, the cursed Sect of the Novations. You are all pure, or clean, saith CHRIST, by the word which I have spoken unto you; I mean then only CHRIST's καθαροὶ, whom the powerful work of the Word hath regenerated, and possessed with purity of heart, holiness of affections, and unspottedness of life, to whom he promiseth blessedness, *Matth.* 5.8. "Blessed are the pure in heart": And to whom alone his beloved Apostle promiseth the blessed vision of GOD in glory, 1 *John* 3.3. Now that the name of Puritans (which is, as you may conceive by that which hath been said, a very equivocal term) is put upon such as these in contempt, and reproach; is more than manifest by a thousand experiences, and by the testimony of a great Doctor at Saint *Paul's* Cross. And yet I dare say, the greatest opposites to these derided ways of purity, if he die not like drunken *Nabal,* would upon his bed of death, give ten thousand worlds, to have lived as one of them. And through the name of Puritan, by a malicious equivocation, they strike at the very heart of grace, and the power of godliness.

Secondly, I add, through the sides of this Nickname, they have labored to wound, and lay waste the truth of our blessed Religion, as pure as any since the Apostles' time, etc. Hear what I heard Doctor *Abbot's* Professor there complain of, at Oxford Act.

What Doctor *Hackwell* saith of *Carrier.* Thus those whom we call Papists, he calls temperate Protestants, and those whom we call Protestants, he calls State Puritans, Epist. Dedicator.

He concludes it by good consequent, that by *Carrier's* assertion, our greatest Bishops, our wisest Counselors, our gravest Judges, and our Sovereign himself, must be accounted the great masters of Schisms.

7

Martin Mar-Prelat [Pseud.]

The Description of a Puritan

1640

*T*he *Description of a Puritan* was ap-
pended to Job Throckmorton's *Dialogue Wherein Is Plainly Layd Open the
Tyrannicall Dealing of Lord Bishops Against Gods Children* when Throckmorton's work was reprinted in 1640 under the pseudonym Martin Mar-
Prelat. *The Description* was not written by any of the original Marprelate
group, of course. In tone and even in some details it anticipates John
Geree's more extensive character sketch of a puritan, though *The Description*
is written in the present tense, whereas Geree six years later writes of the
past. Mar-Prelat's catalog of actions and attitudes provides a very favorable,
concrete description of the demeanor of a puritan.

Most of the characteristics noted here are entirely familiar. The rejection
of some practices, such as the use of the ring in marriage and the administration of baptism by women, has survived from a much earlier period.
The objections to the ex officio ("self-accusing") oath, to nonresidency, and
to timeservers appeared perennially in writings against the religious establishment. But relatively new here is the objection to long hair; in fact, the
reference to a puritan's "round Head" suggests a date of composition very
close to the date of printing, for it was not until the 1640s that the term
roundhead came into use. In general, it came to be applied now to some,
now to all, of the parliamentary army; it was sometimes equated with
puritan and was sometimes distinguished from it. In contrast, the reference

to the Geneva Bible looks back in time, for this Bible had steadily lost popularity with Bible purchasers, having been superseded by the King James Version. Its last printing appeared in 1644, in Amsterdam, only four years after *The Description*. The puritan here shown, then, is basically an old-fashioned nonconformist, despite the reference to his hair; his rejection of earlier traditions has itself become traditional.

A Dialogue Wherein Is Plainly Layd Open the Tyrannicall Dealing of Lord Bishops against Gods Children. With Certaine Points of Doctrine, Wherein They Approve Themselves (according to Dr. Bridges his judgment) to be truely the Bishops of the Divell. Published by the worthy Gentleman, Dr. Martin Mar-Prelat, Doctor in all the Faculties, Primat and Metropolitan. Reprinted in the time of Parliament, Anno Dom. 1640.
[Excerpt: pp. 33–34.]

Here Follows the Description of a Puritan, (As They Are Now termed) by profane Papists and Atheists, etc.

> Long hath it vext our Learned age to scan,
>   who rightly might be termed a PURITAN.
> A PURITAN both Laic and Divine,
>   I will according to my skill define.
> A Puritan, is he, that when he Prays,
>   his Rolling Eyes up to the Heavens doth raise.
> A Puritan, is he, that cannot fare,
>   to deck his round Head with a Bonnet square.
> Whose Turkey robe, in his fair furred train
>   above his ankle, turneth up again:
> That at his Belt a buff clad Bible bears,
>   stampt with the true *Genevah* Characters;
> Whose thin beat Volume scorneth to admit,
>   the bastard monuments of Human Writ.
> Whose Hair, and Ruffs, dare not his Ears exceed:
>   that on high Saints' days wears his working Weed.
> That Crosses each doth hate, save on his pence,
>   and loathes the public Rope of Penitence.

That in his censure each alike gainsays,
Poets in Pulpits, Holy Writ in Plays.
Roods in the Windows, and the Marriage Ring:
the Churching, Veil, and Midwives' Christening.
A Puritan, is he, that listeth not to pray
'gainst Thunder, in the coldest Winter day.
A Puritan, is he, that quite denies
The help of Angels to a Benefice.
That cannot brook a Deputy, to serve
and feed himself, but let his people starve.
That loves alike an Organ in a Quire,
as th'Elephant delights a Swine to hear.
That never in his life did kneel before
the gate of a Cathedral Chancel door.
A Puritan, is he, that cannot Dine,
nor Sup, without a double Grace divine.
A Puritan, is he, that through the year,
two Lord's day Sermons doth either preach or hear.
A Puritan, is he, that will not lend,
a gainful Oath, to his distressed Friend.
A Puritan, is he, that for no meed
will serve the time, and great men's humors feed.
That doth the self-accusing Oath refuse:
that hates the Ale-house, and a Stage, and Stews.
A Puritan, is he, whose austere life,
will not admit a Mistress and a Wife.
That when his betters swears, doth bite the lip;
nor will be drunken for good fellowship.
That wisheth for the amendment of the best:
blames the least ill, and doth the worst detest.
Reader, if such be termed a Puritan,
God make me wise, and thee an honest man.

8

Sir Benjamin Rudyerd

The Speeches of Sir Benjamin Rudyer in the

High Court of Parliament

1641

(Excerpt)

S IR BENJAMIN RUDYERD
(1572– 1658) studied at Oxford and at the Inner Temple. His verses earned
him a reputation as a poet, as well as the friendship of Ben Jonson. Entering
Parliament in 1620, Rudyerd served for a time as a spokesman for the royal
court. With the approach of the civil war, he adopted the role of peacemaker, trying to mediate between the king and the parliamentary majority; he continued his conciliatory attempts throughout the era of the Long
Parliament. Thereafter he retired from political activity. His speeches in
Parliament, many of which were published, were praised by his contemporaries for their literary grace. The speech from which the excerpt is taken
was delivered in November 1640, according to a note in the copy in the
Thomason collection in the British Library.

Rudyerd opens with a protest against the charges leveled at the puritans.
In fact, he regards those maligned by that name as the truly religious men
and the truly loyal subjects of the king. Holding that religion constitutes
the really basic issue facing the Parliament, with civil questions deriving
from it, Rudyerd appeals to the members to recognize the conscientious

objections voiced by the reformers concerning ecclesiastical government and religious practices. His later works show him a believer in episcopacy, but here Rudyerd severely criticizes the ruling bishops of his time. Against them the so-called puritans stand for such laudable causes as the religious observance of Sunday, the importance of preaching, and the rejection of "antiquated ceremonies."

In the political realm the puritans support the Parliament, not against the king but against the king's evil advisers, including highly placed churchmen. Throughout his political career Rudyerd supported the monarchy, and in his speech he uses one common way of resolving the dilemma of the parliamentary royalists who eventually fought against Charles: He argues that the king will be best served by the elimination of many of his chosen officials. Nowhere does he criticize the king himself. And the puritan here drawn, a person loyal to both king and Parliament, cannot be accused of disloyalty to the state.

The Speeches of *Sir Benjamin Rudyer* in the high Court of *Parliament*. Printed for Thomas Walkly. 1641.

[Excerpt: first speech, pp. 1 – 10.]

The Speeches of Sir Benjamin Rudyer in the High Court of Parliament

Mr. SPEAKER,

We are here Assembled to do *God's* business and the King's, in which our own is included, as we are Christians, as we are Subjects. Let us first fear *God,* then shall we honor the King the more: for I am afraid, we have been the less prosperous in *Parliaments,* because we have preferred other matters before Him. Let Religion be our *Primum Quaerite,* for all things else, are but *Etcetera's* to it, yet we may have them too, sooner and surer, if we give *God* his Precedence.

We well know what disturbance hath been brought upon the Church, for vain pretty Trifles. How the whole Church, the whole Kingdom hath been troubled, where to place a Metaphor, an *Altar.* We have seen Ministers, their Wives, Children, and Families undone, against Law, against Conscience, against all Bowels of Compassion, about not dancing upon Sundays. What do this sort of men think will become of themselves, when the *Master of The House* shall come, and find them thus Beating their Fellow-Servants? These Inventions were but Sieves made of purpose, to winnow the best Men, and that's the Devil's occupation. They have a mind to worry Preaching, for I never yet heard of any, but diligent Preachers that were vexed with these and the like devices. They despise Prophesy, and as one said, They would fain be at something that were like the Mass, that will not bite. A muzzled Religion. They would evaporate and dispirit the power and vigor of Religion, by drawing it out into solemn, specious formalities, into obsolete, antiquated Ceremonies new furbished up. And this (belike) is the Good work in hand which D. *Heylin* hath so often celebrated in his bold Pamphlets. All their Acts, and actions are so full of mixtures, involutions and complications as nothing is clear, nothing sincere in any of their proceedings; Let them not say that these are the perverse suspicious malicious interpretations of some few factious Spirits amongst us, when a Romanist hath bragged and congratulated in Print, That the face of our Church begins to alter, the language of our Religion to change. And *Sancta Clara* hath published, That if a Synod were held, *non intermixiis Puritanis,* setting Puritans aside, our Articles and their Religion would soon be agreed. They have so brought it to pass, that under the Name of Puritans, all our Religion is branded, and under a few hard words against Jesuits, all Popery is countenanced.

Whosoever squares his actions by any rule; either Divine or Human, he is a Puritan. Whosoever would be governed by the King's Laws, he is a Puritan. He that will not do whatsoever other Men will have him do, he is a Puritan. Their Great work, their Masterpiece now is, To make all those of the Religion, to be the suspected party of the Kingdom.

Let us further reflect upon the ill effects these Courts have wrought, what by a defection from us, on the one side, a separation on the other. Some imagining whither we are tending, made haste to turn, or declare themselves Papists beforehand, thereby hoping to render themselves the more gracious, the more acceptable. A Great multitude of the King's Subjects, striving to hold communion with us; but seeing how far we were gone, and fearing how much further we would go, were forced to flee the Land, some into other inhabited Countries, very many into Savage Wildernesses, because the Land would not bear them. Do not they that cause these things cast a reproach upon the Government?

Mr. *Speaker,* let it be our principal care that these ways neither continue, nor return upon us. If we secure our Religion, we shall cut off and defeat many

Plots that are now on foot, by Them and Others. Believe it Sir, Religion hath been for a long time, and still is the great design upon this Kingdom. It is a known and a practiced principle, That they who would introduce another Religion into the Church, must first trouble and disorder the Government of the State, that so they may work their ends in a confusion which now lies at the door.

I come next Mr. *Speaker,* to the King's business more particularly, which indeed is the Kingdom's, for one hath no existence, no being without the other, their relation is so near; yet some have strongly and subtly labored a divorce, which hath been the very bane both of King and Kingdom.

When Foundations are shaken, it is high time to look to the Building. He hath no Heart, no Head, no Soul, that is not moved in his whole Man, to look upon the Distresses, the miseries of the Commonwealth, that is not forward in all that he is, and hath, to redress them in a right way.

The King likewise is reduced to great straits, wherein it were undutifulness beyond Inhumanity to take advantage for him: let us rather make it an advantage for him, to do him best service when he hath most need. Not to seek our own good, but in Him and with Him, else we shall commit the same crimes ourselves, which we must condemn in others.

His Majesty hath clearly and freely put himself into the hands of this *Parliament,* and I presume there is not a Man in this house but feels himself advanced in this high trust; but if he prosper no better in our hands than he hath done in theirs, who have hitherto had the handling of his affairs, we shall forever make ourselves unworthy of so gracious a confidence.

I have often thought and said that it must be some great extremity, that would recover and certify this State, and when that extremity did come, It would be a great hazard whether it might prove a remedy, or a ruin. We are now Mr. *Speaker* upon that vertical turning point, and therefore it is no time to palliate, to foment our own undoing.

Let us set upon the remedy, we must first know the Disease: But to discover the diseases of the State, is (according to some) to traduce the Government; yet others are of opinion, that this is the half way to the Cure.

His Majesty is wiser than they, that have advised him, and therefore he cannot but see and feel their subverting destructive Counsels, which speak louder than I can speak of them: for they ring a doleful, deadly knell over the whole Kingdom. His Majesty best knows who they are: for us, let the Matters bolt out the Men; their Actions discover them.

They are Men that talk largely of the King's service, have done none but their own, and that's too evident.

They speak highly of the King's power, but they have made it a miserable power, that produceth nothing but weakness, both to the King and Kingdom.

They have exhausted the King's revenue to the bottom, nay through the bottom, and beyond.

They have spent vast sums of money wastefully, fruitlessly, dangerously: So that more money without other Counsels, will be but a swift undoing.

They have always peremptorily pursued one obstinate pernicious course. First, they bring things to an extremity, then they make that extremity of their own making, the reason of their next action, seven times worse than the former, and there we are at this instant.

They have almost spoiled the best instituted Government in the world, for Sovereignty in a King, liberty to the Subject; the proportionable temper of both which, makes the happiest state for Power, for Riches, for duration.

They have unmannerly and slubberingly cast all their Projects, all their Machinations upon the King: which no wise or good Minister of state ever did, but would still take all harsh, distasteful things upon themselves, to clear, to sweeten their master.

They have not suffered his Majesty to appear unto his people, in his own native goodness. They have eclipsed him by their interposition, although gross condense bodies may obscure, and hinder the Sun from shining out, yet is he still the same in his own splendor. And when they are removed, all creatures under him are directed by his light, comforted by his beams: But they have framed a superstitious seeming maxim of State for their own turn; That if a King will suffer men to be torn from him, he shall never have any good service done him. When the plain truth is, that this is the surest way to preserve a King from having ill servants about him. And the Divine Truth likewise is, *Take away the wicked from the King, and his Throne shall be established.*

Mr. *Speaker,* Now we see what the sores are in general: and when more particulars shall appear; let us be very careful to draw out the cores of them; not to skin them over with a slight suppurating, festering cure, lest they break out again, into a greater mischief; consider of it, consult and speak your minds.

It hath heretofore been boasted, That the King should never call a *Parliament* till he had no need of his people; these were words of Division, and malignity. The King must always according to his occasions, have use of his Power, Hearts, Hands, Purses. The people will always have need of the King's Clemency, Justice, Protection. And this Reciprocation is the strongest, the sweetest union.

It hath been said too of late, That a *Parliament* will take away more from the King, than they will give him. It may well be said, That those things which will fall away of themselves, will enable the Subject to give him more than can be taken any way else. Projects and Monopolies are but leaking Conduit Pipes; the Exchequer itself at fullest, is but a Custom, and now a broken one; frequent *Parliaments* only are the Fountain: And I do not doubt, but in this *Parliament,* as we shall be free in our advices, so shall we be the more free of our purses, that his Majesty may experimentally find the real difference of better Counsels, the true solid grounds of raising and establishing his Greatness, never to be brought again (by *God's* blessing) to such dangerous, such desperate perplexities.

Mr. *Speaker,* I confess I have now gone in a way much against my Nature, and somewhat against my Custom heretofore used in this place. But the deplorable, dismal condition both of Church and State have so far wrought upon my judgment, as it hath convinced my disposition, yet am I not *Vir Sanguinum,* I love no Man's ruin; I thank *God,* I neither hate any man's person, nor envy any man's fortune, only I am zealous of a thorough Reformation in a time that exacts, that extorts it. Which I humbly beseech this House, may be done with as much lenity, as much moderation, as the public safety of the King and Kingdom can possibly admit.

9

[Henry Parker]

A Discourse Concerning Puritans

1641

Henry Parker (1604–1652), after receiving his B.A. and M.A. degrees at Oxford, studied law and was admitted to the bar at Lincoln's Inn. Thereafter he held several political offices, including that of secretary to the House of Commons, secretary to the company of merchants in Hamburg, and secretary to the army in Ireland. Before and during the early years of the civil war, he supported the presbyterians, but by 1649 he was an independent, siding with the army. A detailed study of his life and thought can be found in W. K. Jordan's *Men of Substance* (Chicago, 1942), where Parker is linked with Henry Robinson as a pioneering advocate of religious tolerance. *A Discourse Concerning Puritans,* published anonymously, has sometimes been attributed to John Ley, but in its style and its concern with the relationship of religious to secular power, it seems more characteristic of Parker. Furthermore, anonymous publication seems to have been one of Parker's habits.

A Discourse is perhaps the longest and most detailed defense of puritanism available from the period immediately before the civil war. Parker's justification of the Scottish position and frequent references to the war with Scotland as a continuing action, his support of Parliament, his deference to the king, and his opposition to the bishops suggest that the work was written in 1640, perhaps at the beginning of the Long Parliament. Another 1641 edition, advertised as much enlarged, contains few substantial changes but has an interesting preface in which Parker takes issue with Richard Hooker on many topics while at the same time praising Hooker's learning and skill in argumentation.

In the basic argument of *A Discourse*, Parker takes the name *puritan* as a dyslogistic appellation and condemns its indiscriminate, generally misguided, and very harmful use. The true puritan, appropriately so designated, is guilty of "fury, faction, and hypocrisy." But most commonly, antipuritans apply the name to "men of strict life, and precise opinions" who show "singularity in zeal and piety"; puritans are more loyal to the cause of reformation and, in politics, to the king than are their opponents. Addressing himself to all loyal, religious, and right-minded persons, Parker pleads for unity in the church and tolerance of nonconformists.

Parker's long essay, at first glance, seems to ramble casually from one topic to another, but actually it achieves coherence through the systematic distinctions the author makes between religious attitudes. He places the blame for disunity in the kingdom on antipuritans and subdivides them into several categories. First he leaves aside, as not relevant to his arguments, both those who are simply and quietly not puritans and the Roman Catholics (who are inevitably, because of their alien beliefs, hostile to puritans and whose denunciations do not lead to confusion in terminology). With those who are averse to some puritan tenets, Parker merely pleads for a toleration of differences and for respect for objections to "antiquity" in ceremonies and objections to episcopacy. He directs his most vehement argument against those who "hate and persecute good men" by calling them puritans. In this category his outstanding example seems to be Henry Leslie, bishop of Down in Ireland, a strong opponent of presbyterianism who attacked the puritans at some length in a sermon; Parker cites him frequently and at length. As examples of innocent victims of this kind of attack, Parker names John Bastwick, William Prynne, Henry Burton, Lord Say, and Lord Brook. John Calvin and Theodore Beza are also said to come under antipuritan strictures.

In current, reprehensible usage, Parker distinguishes four types of puritans: (1) puritans in church policy, or ecclesiastical puritans; (2) puritans in religion, or religious puritans; (3) puritans in the state, or political puritans; and (4) puritans in morality, or ethical puritans. Not all four categories receive equal treatment; the ecclesiastical puritan is given the most detailed and extensive attention, whereas at the other extreme the religious puritan is treated summarily and briefly. This disproportion reflects Parker's interest in church government and politics, his relative lack of interest in religious practices, and his concern with morality instead of doctrine. Of course, religious questions appear in discussions of each of the categories, since in Parker's age, and especially during the immediate time when he wrote A *Discourse,* no separation between secular and religious concerns was practical.

The defense of ecclesiastical puritans brings in some religious practices, such as auricular confession (which Parker especially dislikes) and ceremonies (to which he is relatively indifferent). The enforcement of conformity by the bishops reveals their arrogance, which perpetrates its greatest harm in their assumption of civil power. A long, fictional disquisition written by Parker (for the emperor Theodosius I against Ambrose, who forced him to do penance for a wartime massacre) eloquently presents the case for the supremacy of the monarch in state questions (a supremacy that Parker later qualifies when speaking of the relations of the king and the Parliament). The tendency of bishops to usurp authority in civil questions leads Parker to denounce episcopacy itself and, in a later section of his *Discourse,* to take the Scottish side in the English wars with Scotland; these were popularly called the Bishops' Wars by the antiprelatists, who saw the sole purpose of the English invasion of Scotland as the establishment of episcopal church government there. He even justifies the Scottish counter-invasion of England as a necessary defensive action. Oddly, Parker cites at length the definition of puritanism written by King James but ignores James's famous dictum "no bishop, no king"; he also dwells on the conciliatory statement of the preface to James's *Basilikon Doron* (1603). Perhaps he is also thinking of the fact that James accepted presbyterianism in Scotland, however unwillingly. Unexpectedly also, Constantine I here appears as a negative example: He gave too much power to bishops. But in A *Discourse* Parker does not argue for a presbyterian model of church government; he finds Calvin no less arrogant than bishops in assuming de facto political control of Geneva and in arguing the supremacy of the ministers over the civil magistrate. This work foreshadows Parker's alliance, later in his career, with the independents in their opposition to the presbyterians.

About religious puritans Parker notes merely that all opponents of the Roman church are called puritans by some. He does not develop the argument with specific examples. The political puritan he defines by similarly broad generalizations. All supporters of the Parliament and the Scots are called puritans. Here Parker gives his case for Scotland, including the interesting argument, which shows him an original political thinker, that the Scots must be right because they act unanimously; a whole nation would not fight against its best interests. Loyalty to the king stands as the most important issue, but only Anabaptists are truly disloyal; only they think it lawful to depose the king. The Scots and the English Parliament oppose the bad counselors, including the English bishops, who would give the king unlimited power, to his own harm. A king is truly served when Parliament asserts its own rights, thereby advising him and sharing the responsibility for his actions. In these arguments Parker has not yet developed his final antimonarchical theories.

In discussing the ethical puritan, Parker becomes most vehement. He charges that anyone who denounces immorality, even one who simply lives an austere moral life and does not take part in any controversy, may be called a puritan. The antipuritans subvert traditional goodness by seeing only hypocrisy in outwardly pious and moral behavior. Parker even suggests that Christ himself must have acted on many occasions in the manner denounced as puritan. Here more clearly than in his other arguments, Parker seems to ally himself with the so-called puritans and to give the term a eulogistic connotation. He finds it necessary to append a conclusion addressed to the reader in which, with considerable word play, he disclaims being a puritan but professes himself a friend to all except antipuritans. *A Discourse* remains an eloquent defense of many nonconformist attitudes and a clear testimony to the troublesome indefiniteness of the term *puritan* as used contemporaneously on the eve of the civil war.

A Discourse Concerning Puritans. A vindication of those, who unjustly suffer by the mistake, abuse, and misapplication of that Name. A Tract necessary and usefull for these Times. *Printed for* Robert Bostock, 1641.

[Henry Parker.]

A Discourse Concerning *Puritans*.

It is a common Maxim amongst Politicians, that a State is maintained by Accusations, but ruined by Calumnies: and therefore (says Marquis *Malvezzi*) happy shall the Subjects be of that wise Prince, which countenances Accusations, and checks Calumnies: for the suffering of Accusations to go less in repute, and Calumnies to get footing, hath been the increase of manslaughter, and the continuance of enmity in all ages. Many believe that nothing which is done would be known, if this means of dispersing privy calumnious speeches were not used, whereas little is known because it is used: For falsehood constantly affirmed for truth sometimes deceives, and when it does not, but is known to be falsehood, yet it forces to some suspension of judgment, and makes us yield some way even to that which we believe not. This is most apparent at this day in this Kingdom in the Case of Puritans, for did accusation and legal process take place, few crimes would be proved against Puritans, and did not malicious calumny prevail, as few men would be proved Puritans, whereas now nothing is so monstrous, which is not branded upon Puritans, and no man is so innocent as to escape that brand. So great also is the audacity of those which lacerate the fames of Puritans, and with so much confidence do they vent their obloquies, that they which know the falsity thereof, and easily perceive that the same aspersions are more truly due to the Authors and raisers of them, yet they are dazzled, and driven to some doubtful admittance thereof. Neither could this audacity be so prevalent amongst the vulgar, but that Scholars, and the greatest of the Clergy are now become the most injurious detesters and depravers of Puritans, having taken up in Pulpits and Presses, almost as vile and scurrilous a license of fiction and detraction, as is usual in Play-houses, Taverns, and Bordelloes. Some men divide generally all Protestants into Puritans, and Antipuritans, but I shall admit of subdivisions in both, for all men are not alike, which either affect or disaffect, either Puritans or Antipuritans. Antipuritans I shall thus divide. Some Antipuritans are so termed merely because they are no Puritans, but such I dislike not, for I myself am neither the one nor other, I neither merit the name of Puritan, neither do I hate them so as to profess myself an Antipuritan.

Others are accounted Antipuritans, because they are of the Romish Religion, and so profess themselves, but their enmity is but a due antipathy, and as a necessary consequence of their Religion, and such I take no notice of, I think Puritans expect no other from them. Others again there are which are very averse from some Puritanical Tenets, and hold Puritans in very many things erroneous, but yet they mean well themselves, and bear no hatred to the Persons of Puritans, they allow Puritans sound in the most and weightiest matters of faith, they hold dissent in disputable things no ground of malice, and they attribute no infallibility to themselves in those things wherein they dissent: from these men I am but little removed. The worst sort of Antipuritans, and they which ought only to be so called, are they which bitterly hate and persecute many good men under the name of Puritans, and many good things in those which are Puritans, whose antipathy is to men's persons, as well as opinions, and in opinions those which are sound, as well as those which are erroneous. These are the Antipuritans which I shall now strive to detect, whom I hold to be of great number and power in the State at this day, whom we may account the chiefest causers, and procurers of all those mischiefs and plagues which now incumber both Church and Commonwealth, and to be guilty of all those crimes, which falsely they charge upon Puritans, being therein like *Caesar's* enemies, which therefore only hated him, because they had deserved hatred from him. By such Antipuritans is all love to goodness: and zeal to the Protestant Religion, and all hatred of vice, and dislike of Popish Superstition, brought into contempt. For as they admit all true of Puritans which Papists object against Protestants, so they account all Protestants almost (besides their own faction) Puritans. By such is the Religion of the *Scots* made ridiculous; by such is the amity of the two Nations, and therein the Honour and safety of the King his Crown, and Progeny much endangered. By such is *Calvin,* and the Reformers of our Religion for harkening therein to *Calvin,* traduced, and another reformation attempted; by such is Antiquity preferred to obscure Scripture, Uniformity in Ceremonies to the disadvantage of unity in hearts; by such is the outside and walls of Religion trimmed and decored, whilst the soul thereof is neglected; or defaced; by such is the King's heart stolen from his Subjects, and the Subjects estranged from the King; by such is the Name of Royalty pretended whilst a Papal Hierarchy only is intended; by such is dissension nourished in the State, that they may fish in troubled waters; by such is truth in other men styled fiction, and fiction in themselves styled truth; by such are innovations preached and printed for necessary points, whilst necessary doctrines in other men are prohibited. In the power of such it now remains to teach and publish all things consonant to their own ends, and to quash and silence all gainsayers, and either to promote or detrude all Suitors for preferment at their discretion being absolutely possessed of Presses, Pulpits, and the ears of great men; by such are many good men reviled and oppressed for their constancy to the true Religion, whilst many factious, semipopish Dunces are unduly preferred everywhere for neutrality in Religion, or some worse innovation; by such are Puritans made as Sinks and Sewers to unload and discharge their own filth into, whilst their black railing tongues expume nothing against Puritans, but what is true of themselves. These things (if I am not deceived) will appear in this ensuing Discourse.

In all ages true Religion hath been odious amongst Heathens, and true devotion amongst Sensualists, Judaism appeared to Paynims mere Superstition: Christianity seemed to the Jews gross blasphemy: and now amongst Christians Protestantism is nothing else but Heresy: and amongst Protestants Zeal is misnamed Puritanism; But in this word Puritanism is a greater mystery of defamation than ever was before, it may well be called βάθος τῷ Σατάνῳ, it is a word of depravation, fit only for these times wherein the shine of the Gospel is at the brightest, and the malice of Satan at the highest. This word sprung up almost with the Reformation, no sooner had the woman brought forth, but the Serpent pursued her to devour her issue, and she being fled into the Wilderness, this stream of infamy was spewed forth after her to overtake her.

The Bishop of *Downe* in *Ireland,* in his Visitation speech 1638, endeavors to make it credited, that Puritans have increased since the Reformation by degrees, both in number and malice: but the contrary is most apparently true.

Dissent in Ecclesiastical Policy about Ceremonies and other smaller matters being not of the substance of Religion, first gave occasion to raise this reproachful word Puritan in the Church: but since that time men's minds being better satisfied, and peace being more firmly settled about those indifferent things, the more few Puritans remained, and the more moderately those few became inclined, the more furiously their enemies raged against them. *Bastwick, Prin,* and *Burton,* the only men which Law can take hold of, are Names now as horrid in the World as *Garnet, Faux, Ravilliack. Precisians* have now won the Scene from *Jesuits:* Poisoning of Emperors, massacring of Provinces, blowing up of Parliaments are all now grown into oblivion, and drowned in the stories of Ceremony-haters. Howsoever as amongst Antipuritans, so amongst Puritans (it must be confessed) there are some differences to be observed. Some Puritans think all Puritans alike to be loved, and all Antipuritans alike to be hated, but sure there is truer affinity in mind between some which are Puritans, and some which are not, than between some Puritans and others, or some of the contrary opinion and others. *Paul* unconverted equally opposes *Peter* as *Simon Magus* does, and in regard of this joint opposition, both are unanimous, but even in this opposition both have their opposite ends. *Magus* opposes maliciously for ambition and Lucre's sake, but *Paul* ignorantly seeking thereby the same God's Honor whom *Peter* serves in a truer way. Therefore in regard of the main end, there is more unity and consent between *Paul* the persecutor, and *Peter* the persecuted than betwixt *Paul* and *Magus,* though both persecutors of the same cause. The like is now visible in *England,* for every man which is an Antipuritan is not so for the same Reasons, some have more of malice, others are more ignorant, some are pestilent

Engineers, and through the sides of Puritans knowingly stab at Purity itself, others are but Engines misemployed, or by their own blind zeal misled, and these perhaps whilst they persecute God's children, imagine they do God a grateful service therein.

In *Samaria,* from an unkindly mixture of *Israelites* and *Syrians* a strange *heterogeneous* offspring different in Religion from both did arise; and the like is now in *England,* nay it may be said here (as it was in *Constantine's* day) there are almost as many Religions as Opinions and as many Opinions as Men. Papists have their differences, Protestants theirs, therefore needs there must be many more differences where Papists and Protestants live so confusedly blended together. For example's sake how many differences have we even about indifferent Ceremonies; and that merely amongst Protestants? Some men loathe Ceremonies out of antipathy to Popery, which too superstitiously extols them; others again admire them for Antiquity's sake, which before Popery innocently (yea, and perhaps profitably for those infant times of the Gospel) used them. These two sorts of men, though different, are not dangerous. Again some men are thought to disrelish Ceremonies out of stomach to that authority which commands them; but if there be any such, I think they are very few, and scarce visible to the eye of man. Others on the contrary give reverence to them for Popery's sake, which depends so much upon them; and I fear there are many such amongst us. Again, some men stand devoted to Ceremonies as they are the lightest things of the Law; like the Tithers of Mint and Annis in the Gospel, embracing them instead of weightier matters, and none are more unmerciful than these to scrupulous minded men. Others in the meanwhile account all things of the same moment, both great and small, pretending to spy some faults, and some truths on either side, and therefore they hold it indifferent to assent to either, or dissent from either in any point whatsoever. But the wisest sort conceive there may be errors on both sides, but not alike gross and pernicious, and therefore such eschew the wrong, and apply themselves to the right in either side, yet neither honor, nor despise either side alike. And these instances show that all men do not profess, or condemn Puritanism alike, or from the same ends, and yet in the Chaos of this Country, as things now stand,

> *Frigida cum calidis pugnant, humentia siccis,*
> *Mollia cum duris, sine pondere habentia pondus.*

I could wish therefore that all well meaning men would take notice of these things, and affect by reason, not passion; for since some good men are Pu-

133

ritans, and not all, and since some ill men are Puritans, and not all, this ought
not to be a rule of love and hatred in all cases alike. That which is most objected
to Puritans, is fury, faction, and hypocrisy: if I see these in a man reputed no
Puritan, yet to me He is a Puritan: and if I see not these in a man reputed a
Puritan, as to me He is no Puritan.

If *Gracchus* be invective against Sedition, I censure him by his actions, not
by his words, and if *Cato* be accused of mutiny, I censure him by himself, not
by his accusers, I condemn none merely because condemned by others; for it is
usual for the Wolf to sit on the bench and condemn the Lamb at bar, for that
which is most proper to the Wolf most unnatural to the Lamb, and yet this
proves the Wolf the more a Wolf, and the Lamb the more a Lamb. I cannot but
profess it, there is nothing more scandalizes me at this time, than to see
Puritans being so few in number, so despicable in condition, so harmless in
example, so blameless in opinion, yet sentenced and condemned in judgment,
as if they were the greatest Incendiaries, and the only Innovators in the
Christian World. Doctor *Heylyn* a violent pamphleteer against Puritans, calls
Burton the great *Dictator* of Puritans, and the Law hath passed upon him with
great severity, yet *Burton's* crime was that He wrote against *Altar-worship,* and
it was adjudged that his style was seditious. It is not manifest that his intention was seditious therein, and if it was so, it is manifest that He was most vain
and absurd therein as our State is now established, and as our King is generally
revered. They which pretend great danger to the King likely to ensue out of
such paper machinations as these, may have three mischievous ends therein.
First, that they may be thought the only solicitous men of the King's safety.
Secondly, that they may disparage the common people's loyalty. Thirdly, that
they may crush their adverse Puritanical party; but, it is thought, they which
pretend most danger hereby to the King: do least believe themselves and
therefore they do spin that disaffection and division out of the sufferings of
Burton, which his attempt could never have effected. Let us then a little farther
search into the mysterious abuse, and misapplication of this word Puritan.
Those whom we ordinarily call Puritans are men of strict life, and precise
opinions, which cannot be hated for anything but their singularity in zeal and
piety, and certainly the number of such men is too small, and their condition
too low, and dejected: but they which are the Devil's chief Artificers in abusing
this word when they please can so stretch, and extend the same that scarce any
civil honest Protestant which is hearty and true to his Religion can avoid the
aspersion of it, and when they list again, they can so shrink it into a narrow
sense, that it shall seem to be aimed at none but monstrous abominable

Heretics and Miscreants. Thus by its latitude it strikes generally, by its contraction it pierces deeply, by its confused application it deceives invisibly. Small scruples first entitle me to the name of Puritan, and then the Name of Puritan entitles me further to all mischief whatsoever.

The *Scots* rise up against *Episcopacy,* it is questioned by some, whether they so rise up, for the good of Religion, or for the overthrow of wholesome Discipline.

Answer is soon made, that Episcopacy cannot be unpleasing to any but Puritans, there is no opinion can smell sharper of Puritanism, than that of a Church parity, and of Puritans what good can be expected? but the Scots also desire redress in other grievances, and here their intention is again questioned. Answer is as soon made again. That the Scots being declared open Puritans, they must needs be enemies to Monarchical government, and that no redress can ever satisfy them, but such as shall debase royal dignity, and establish a popular rule amongst them. But some of the Scots in some actions do very much misdemean themselves, and here it is thought by some, that this ought not to redound to the prejudice, or blame of the whole Nation: but straight the Antipuritan steps in again with answer to the former purpose, that the same faction which makes them all Puritans, makes them all mutineers, and that there is no trust to be given, nor favor showed to any whose very religion is disobedience. Other the like examples may be instanced in. Parliaments of late in *England* have been jealous of religion, this laudable zeal made them at first come into contempt as Puritanical, and then the imputation of Puritanism made this laudable zeal contemptible; and so by degrees, as anything else might be charged upon Puritans, as disobedience, and disaffection to Monarchy, so nothing could be charged but proceeding from Puritanism. Some scrupulous opinions make *Say, Brooke,* Puritans, Puritanism infers them mutineers, mutiny makes all that they can do or say, all that they forbear to do, or say, it makes their very thoughts wicked and perverse. Thus we see what a confused imposture there is in this infamous term of Puritan: but we will yet further evidence by plain instance how broad the devil's net is in the vast application of this word, and how deep his pit is by its abominable sense, and the nature of its importance, that we may the better discover that net which entangles so many, and shun that pit which engulfs so sure. Puritans (as I said before) were at first Ecclesiastical only, so called because they did not like a pompous or ceremonious kind of discipline in the Church like unto the Romish: but now it is come about, that by a new enlargement of the name, the world is full of nothing else but Puritans, for besides the Puritan in Church policy, there are now added Puritans in religion, Puritans in State, and Puritans in morality. By this means whole Kingdoms are familiarly upbraided with this sin of Puritanism: As for example, All in *Scotland* which wish well to the Covenant, though some Papists, some Courtiers, and almost all the whole body without exception have now declared themselves for it, yet all these are manifest Puritans. So also in *England,* all the Commons in Parliament, and almost all the ancient impartial temporal Nobility, and all such as favor or relish the late proceedings of both the houses, which is the main body of the Realm, Papists, Prelates, and Courtiers excepted, nay, and it's likely all *Scotland,* and more than half *Ireland,* all these are Puritans. They which deprave this great Council of the Kingdom, suggest to the King that the major part is gulled and dored by the Puritan party; but this is only because they are ashamed to speak it out openly in gross terms, that all the major and better part in the Court of Parliament is Puritanical. But this suggestion is utterly false and impossible, for such as the major part in Parliament is, such are those that chose them and sent them thither, and such are those that now approve their actions there, and both in the elections of Parliament men, and in the consultations of Parliament affairs, the King's party is as wise, cautious, and vigilant (if not more) as the other party, and no subtlety could circumvent or cheat them out of their votes, if the Puritans were so small and inconsiderable a side, as now they make them. No man of what capacity soever can admit this, it is to all undeniable, that the blame of a parliament, is the blame of the whole Kingdom. But I return to my Ecclesiastical puritan. Though it be true that Ecclesiastical puritans are fewer now, than heretofore they have been, yet it is as true that Ecclesiastical puritanism is made a larger thing by far than it was, being now spread abroad like a net to ensnare the more, as our many late additions and innovations testify, which have crept into the Church (as may be feared) for the vexation and molestation of such men as were not disquieted with former ceremonies. It is generally suspected, that our prelates have aimed at two things in the novelties which they have lately induced into the Church; first, the suppression of those which are enemies to their pride, avarice, and ambition, by them termed puritans: secondly, their own further ease, promotion, and advantage. Both these ends seem to be leveled at in sanctifying the Altar, and unsanctifying the Lord's day in advancing auricular confession, and corporal penances, by external mortifications, and crying down lecturing, and preaching; for if we mark it, these new Doctrines do not only serve to terrify and scandalize tender consciences, and thereby to deprive, and silence many painful good Ministers, and to scare away into foreign Plantations, whole troops of Laymen, and to enwrap the rest in opposition; but each of these doctrines besides hath a further reach in it of benefit to the Clergy. The Communion Table hath lately gained a new Name, a new Nature, a new Posture, a new Worship that Emperors and Kings may be brought again to take notice how far the persons and offices of Priests excel in sanctity the persons and offices of Princes. *Theodosius* within one hundred years after Prelacy began to arrogate to itself was presently taught this lesson, for taking his seat in the Chancel according to the Eastern and ancient fashion, a Deacon was sent to him in great state to let him understand that none but men in holy Orders might presume to set their feet on that sacred ground. This was then the Bishops' Law, not the Emperor's, nor known in any other of his Dominions, but *Italy* only, but sure it was fit discretion, that much should be ascribed by Bishops to that place, from which they were to derive much, and which would be sure to repay their homage with so great an advantage of homage back again. Preaching is now also grown too burthensome, and the Lord's Day to Priests according to that sanctity which Puritans allow it, it requires too much praying, preaching, singing, which are not only to them tedious but also apt means to increase, and foment Puritanism amongst the people. Auricular Confession also is a godly device to bring the Laity into subjection, and to make the people bow before the power of the Keys, and it may aptly force the consciences of Kings themselves to fear the scourges of gowned men. Add lastly Mr. *Wats* his bodily mortification to Mr. *Sparrow's* confession, and then Laymen will soon be inured again to find out the fittest penances, especially *Præsbyteris, & aris advolvi,* and so in time their purses, their bodies, their consciences shall all be made sensible of the spiritual Scepter of Priests.

It's no great wonder then if our Court Divines, and their dependents do what they can to draw us nearer daily towards Popery, under shew of Antiquity, Uniformity, and Charity, for (without all doubt) of all Religions, Popery is the most beneficial to Priests, most tyrannous to Laymen. Neither is it strange that they pretend so much zeal to devotion to the King's Crown and Prerogative, as things now stand in *England,* as if none truly affected the same but themselves, for it's clear, that they cannot subject the people but by the King, nor the King without the people: and so long as they stand possessed of the King's good opinion, no man shall have power to confute them.

King *James* is a great instance for Antipuritans, and a great prop to the Episcopal Cause, it's alleged of him that He hated Puritans for their hatred to Episcopacy, and loved Episcopacy for its amity to Monarchy: His Aphorism was, *No Bishop, no King:* Let us therefore appeal from King *James* in their words to King *James* in his own. In his Preface before his *Basilicon Doron* his words are: The style of Puritans properly belongs to that vile Sect of the Anabaptists only called the Family of Love. Such were *Browne, Penry*. Howbeit there are others which participate too much with Anabaptists contemning civil Magistrates, etc. It is only this sort of men which I wish my son to punish in case they refuse to obey Law, and cease not to stir up Rebellion. But I protest upon mine Honor, I mean it not generally of all Preachers or others, which like better of the single form of Policy in our Church of *Scotland,* than of the many Ceremonies in the Church of *England,* which are persuaded that Bishops smell of a Papal supremacy, that Surplices, Caps, etc. are outward badges of popish errors. No, I am so far from being contentious in these indifferent things, that I do equally love and honor the learned and grave of either opinion. It can no ways become me to pronounce sentence so lightly in so old a controversy. Since we all agree in grounds, the bitterness of men in such questions doth but trouble the peace of the Church, and give advantage to Papists by our division. These were the golden words of that peaceful, just Prince upon his second thoughts: O that they were now duly pondered, and taken to pieces word for word! O that they were esteemed and understood in their own weight amongst us, that they might reconcile our present differences, and that the same peace which followed him to his glorious Urn, might still bless these our times! O how contrary are these mild words to the unnatural suggestions of Antipuritans! Such as daily accuse all good men for Precisians, and all precise men for Puritans, and all Puritans for the only Firebrands of the World, thus arming the King against his Subjects, and by consequence raising Subjects against the King: Puritans here are described both what they are, and what they are not, the King had been misinterpreted before, writing generally of Puritans, now to avoid all mistake, he expresses himself plainly and definitely. A Puritan positively in King *James* his sense, is He which imitates Anabaptists in rebellion, turbulence, and opposition to Law, and such are liable to Law; but negatively a Puritan in the acception of King *James* is not He which dislikes Episcopacy, or the Ceremonious Discipline of *England.* This King *James* protests upon his Honor, though to his great dishonor He be now often cited to the contrary. As for those which relish not Bishops and Ceremonies or the *English* Policy, He wishes them to be at peace only with those of the opposite opinion, He himself vowing equal love and honor to the grave, and learned of either side, and not taking upon him to be a Judge in so old, and difficult a controversy; He only like a sweet arbitrator persuades both parties to peace and amity. I wish our Bishops would now stand to this arbitration, I wish they would neither condemn the Scotch discipline, nor urge the English; I wish they would put difference between seditious and scrupulous Puritans, and not infer the one out of the other; I wish they would either disclaim King *James* as a manifest favorer of Puritans, or else imitate him in the same definition, and opinion of them. K. *James* further takes notice, that the reformation in *Scotland* was far more disorderly, than in *England, Denmark* etc. whilst the main affairs there were unduly carried by popular tumults, and by some fiery-spirited Ministers, which having gotten the guiding of the multitude, and finding the relish of government sweet, did fancy to themselves a democratic form of policy, wherein they were likely to be *Tribuni plebis.* That the Crown might be disencumbered of these usurping ringleaders, the King advises the Prince to entertain and advance godly, learned, and modest Ministers, promoting them to Bishoprics, but restraining them heedfully from pride, ambition, and avarice. These things then are hence observable. 1. *Scotland* differs from *England* in turbulent Ministers: Secondly, this is imputed to the iniquity of the times, not to Puritanism, as if by nature the Scots were more inclining to Puritanism than other Nations. Thirdly, notwithstanding that iniquity of those times, there was a number sufficient of worthy Ministers fit for preferment. Fourthly, King *James* erects Bishops' Sees in *Scotland* for peculiar reasons, and therefore He speaks not of *Denmark* etc. Lastly, notwithstanding that peculiar reason, He advises the Prince to be indifferently at war with both extremes alike, as well to repress Papal Bishops as to curb proud Puritans. For (says the King) the natural sicknesses which have ever troubled and been the decay of all Churches since the beginning changing the Candlestick from one to another, have been pride, ambition, and avarice: and these wrought the overthrow of the Romish Church in divers Countries. K. *James* knew well how apt Churchmen had ever been to abuse their power and pomp, what enemies they had been to our Savior, and what a tyranny they had created over all Christendom ever since *Constantine* almost, and therefore though He dislikes a democracy in the Church, (as He had reason) yet He so limits and circumscribes his Bishops both in power and honor, that they might be as sensible of their chains and fetters, as of their Miters and Crosiers. I wish K. *James* had particularly signified what bonds and bounds He thought fit to prefix to Episcopacy, to preserve it from corruption, and what his opinion was of a Prelacy so active in secular affairs as ours is now in *England,* and how it would have pleased him to see a Metropolitan amongst Protestants almost a rival to the French Cardinal. The world, in my opinion, hath little reason to dote upon a gowned empire, we have all smarted long enough under it, men of mean birth commonly bear preferment with little moderation, and their breeding having been soft and effeminate, in their malice and cruelty, they nearest of all approach to the nature of women: and by the advantage of learning they extend their power, and win upon others more than they ought. When the Church was at first under Heathen or Jewish Governors, which sought as enemies to ruin it, not as Fathers to protect it, they which were within could not live in peace and unity without some Political bonds, so at that time there was a necessity of some coercive power, within besides that which was without. The world is now unsatisfied what kind of power that was, whether Episcopal or Presbyterial, or what Episcopacy, or Presbytery was in those days. Yet methinks what government soever then was, it is not necessarily precedentary to us now. The Episcopal faction at this day takes advantage by the abuses of the Presbyterial, and the Presbyterial by the Episcopal, and most men think either the one power or the other necessary, and some more favor the Episcopal as K. *James,* some the Presbyterial as M. *Calvin;* but sure the Presbyterial is less offensive than the Episcopal, and yet neither the one nor other of necessity. Kings may grant *usuram quandam jurisdictionis* either to Bishops or Elders, but the jurisdiction itself is their own property, from which they ought not to depart, nor can without wrong to their charge committed to them. For the power which God gives the Prince, is not given for his use alone, but for the people's benefit, so that since He cannot let it fall to decay without making it insufficient for good and entire government which is mischievous to the people, he cannot justly lessen it at all. And it is manifest that except one supreme head be alone in all causes as well Ecclesiastical as civil, human nature must needs be destitute of those remedies which are necessary for its conservation, since power cannot be divided, but it must be diminished to him which suffers that division, and being diminished it proves insufficient. All confess some government necessary for men in holy Orders, to whom the power of the Keys belongs, but some account Princes but as mere temporal or Lay persons, and therefore conclude against their authority over sacred Ecclesiastical persons as incompetent, especially in cases merely ecclesiastical. For this cause spiritual Governors have ever been in the Church to whom some have attributed a divine right depending from none but God, and subordinate to none but God, but this hath been controverted by others, and no little debate and strife hath followed hereupon. But it seems to me, that princes do receive from God a spiritual unction, whereby not only their persons are dignified, and their hearts prepared and enlarged with divine graces fit for rule; but their functions also ennobled and sanctified above any other whatsoever, and higher advanced than the sense of Laic or Secular will bear. To Princes an assistance of counsel is requisite in spiritual as in civil affairs, but that, that Council ought to be composed only of persons Ecclesiastical, or that those persons ought to be invested with all those Ensigns of Honor and authority which our Bishops now claim as of divine right, seems not necessary. Clergymen are not always the most knowing in all Ecclesiastical cases, neither are they at all indifferent and impartial, in many which concern their own honor and profit, (as the world feels to its regret) therefore for jurisdiction they are not the most competent. But be they of what use soever, they may still remain subordinate, and at the Prince's election, and admitted of *ad consilium solum,* not *ad consensum:* and it had been happy for all Christians these many hundred years by-past if they had not been further hearkened to. The Sacerdotal function is not all disparaged by this subordination, for whether the order of Princes be more sacred than that of Bishops, or not, it is all one to Priests, for an obedience they owe, and must pay, be it to the one Order, or the other. Our Bishops at this day stand much upon their Divine right of Jurisdiction, and they prefer their style to the providence of God immediately, not to the grace of the King: and though in words they acknowledge a Supremacy of power to remain to the King; yet indeed I think they mean rather a priority of order. Whatsoever Supremacy they mean, if it be not such as makes them merely subordinate, and dependent, so that the King may limit, alter, or extinguish their jurisdiction, as far as He may to his civil Judges, they derogate much from his Kingly office.

Bishops for their claim of jurisdiction ought to prove, that they alone did exercise it over all in all causes from our Savior's days, till the entrance of Christian Princes: and that being cleared, they must further prove, that those times also are leading, and precedentary to ours. In both these their proofs are lame, especially in the latter; for neither is the power of the Keys the same thing as Jurisdiction, nor is jurisdiction now as it was in Apostles' days, nor is the State of the times now the same as then.

In those days either Christians were to implead one another before Infidel Magistrates whatsoever the case were, criminal or civil, spiritual or temporal, or else they were to erect some tribunal in the Church, or else they were to await no justice at all: and because some judicature within the Church was most fit, therefore Christ himself according to the exigence of those times, did endow his Church with a divine Oeconomy, which was partly miraculous, and of use then, but not now. The Spirit of God did then internally incite such and such men at such times to reside and preside in such and such places; and some of the Apostles at sometimes could judge by inspiration without proofs and allegations, and could execute sentence of death or other spiritual punishment upon secret hypocrites, not intrenching upon temporal authority, but in these times this discipline is useless, and therefore decayed. Whatsoever the offense then was, what injury or trespass soever betwixt brother and brother, the only remedy was *Dic Ecclesia,* and yet that precept serves as strong for temporal as spiritual trespasses, so that it cannot be enforced now to continue, unless we mean to drown all temporal authority. As for the extent also of spiritual power in those days I will only cite a learned Politician of the Popish religion: who admitting (it seemed) that the keys of heaven were given to Saint *Peter* alone, and his Successors, and not to all Bishops and Ministers whatsoever, thus proceeds. By the keys given to S. *Peter* many Holy Fathers mean, the one of knowledge, and the other of power, and that that power ought not to be understood universally, but only concerning the Kingdom of Heaven which is spiritual: for the Civil, Royal, and Temporal power is expressly forbidden him by Christ. Even so that also of knowledge, it is not to be understood of natural, politic, or moral things, but as Saint *Paul* saith, of Christ's mysteries only.

Wherefore in matters of faith Ecclesiastical authority may approve and Secular cannot condemn, but in matters of policy what all the Prelates in the world approve, temporal authority may condemn. It is a great wrong to pretend, because Christ hath given Saint *Peter* the cognizance and power of the Kingdom, and forbidden him the earthly, contrary to this precept to extend spiritual things to temporal. Saint *Augustine* often saith, *That Grace doth not destroy anything in Nature, but leaveth her all her own, adding moreover divine perfection.* The Temporality hath of its own nature, power, to forbid all things repugnant to public quietness and honesty; and Christ came not to take away this authority from Magistrates, He only adds power to his Ministers in matters of faith, not known by nature, but revelation. For aught we know, the power of opening or shutting Heaven, of binding and loosing sins was miraculous, and so but temporary: but admit it in this Catholic Writer's sense, yet we plainly see, it is no prejudice at all to limit Secular Princes thereby. The same learned Papist writes: That the Eastern and Western Churches continued in unity and charity for the space of nine hundred years after Christ, and this peace was easily kept, because the Supreme power was then in the Canons, to which all Churches acknowledged themselves equally subject. Ecclesiastical Discipline was then severely maintained in each Country by its own Prelates, not arbitrarily, but absolutely according to Canonical rigor, none of them intermedling in another government. No Pope of *Rome* did pretend to confer Benefices in other Bishops' Dioceses, or to get money out of others by way of

Dispensations and Bulls: but when *Rome* began to shake off all subjection to Canons, then notwithstanding any ancient order of the Fathers, Councils, or Apostles themselves, instead of her ancient Primacy she brought in an absolute Dominion, free from any Law or Canon and this made the division. Neither could any re-union be brought to pass within these 700 years, because this abuse which caused the Division is not remedied. Whilst the union held, Saint *Paul's* doctrine was jointly observed, that *Everyone should be subject to Princes, no man pretended to be free from punishment.* Nay, and after the division, the same opinion remained, that every Christian in temporal business is subject to the Prince. And nothing is more temporal than offense, because nothing is more contrary to the Spirit. Amongst the *Greeks* also it is still held that Bishops ought to judge what opinion is sound, what Heretical, but to punish those of hurtful opinions belongeth to the Secular.

The State of *Venice,* as well as other Catholic Kingdoms, walks between two extremes, between Protestants, which have no other aim but to diminish Ecclesiastical authority, and the Court of *Rome* which hath no other aim, but to increase it, and to make the Temporal her servant.

Those of the Court of *Rome,* making use of Religion for worldly ends and respects under a spiritual pretense, but with an ambitious end and desire of worldly wealth and honor would free themselves from obedience due to the Prince, and take away the love and reverence due by the people to draw it to themselves. To bring those things to pass, they have newly invented a doctrine that talks of nothing but Ecclesiastical greatness, liberty, immunity, and jurisdiction.

This doctrine was unheard of, till about the year 1300, then it began to be written scatteringly in some books, but till 1400, there were not written above two Books which treated of nothing else; after this such Writers increased a little, but after 1560, there were scarce any Books printed in *Italy,* but in diminution of Secular authority and exaltation of the Ecclesiastical. And now the people have scarce any other Books to read, nor have the Confessors any other doctrine, or need any other learning. Hence comes this perverse opinion, that Magistracy is a human invention, and to be obeyed for policy only, not for conscience: but that every intimation of Ecclesiastical persons is equivalent to a divine precept; there want not in *Italy* pious, learned men which hold the contrary, but they are not suffered to write, or print. Neither are foreign Books permitted, or ancient Authors left ungelded of all which serves for Temporal authority: as appears by a book printed 1607, called *Index Expurgatorius:* and *Clement* the Eighth in 1595, published a rule in his *Index,* that all Catholic Writers' Books since 1515, might be corrected, not only by expunging but also by interlining, and this hath been practiced though not publicly above seventy years. Thus we find the Court of *Rome's,* but not the Author's meaning, and finally, we are sure to have no book true. I have hitherto cited this egregious Politician, for these purposes.

First, That we may see how easy it is for Clergymen to wrest all authority out of the Temporality's hands, if Princes will be so easy to be hoodwinked, and deluded by them, and to resign their judgments to them in such cases as concern their profit, and advancement.

Secondly, That we may take notice how far the learnedst of Papists themselves do discover, and detect the errors and tyranny of the Court of *Rome,* and that mystical way of deceiving whereby all hope of remedy is cut off. I observe this also the rather because our Prelates in *England* at this day assume to themselves almost as vast and unquestionable a power of shifting and repressing all adverse disputes, and of authorizing and publishing all arguments whatsoever favoring their cause, as the Court of *Rome* does.

Thirdly, that I might produce the same Author against himself in those points wherein he taxes Protestants. We will yield that for the space of nine hundred years the See of *Rome* did not usurp over other Sees, but did acknowledge equal subjection to the Canons, and that the division and separation of the Eastern Churches happened, when *Rome* arrogated above Canons; but withal we must have it yielded to us, that those Canons had been composed only by Clergymen, and that in too much favor of Clergymen, and too much abridgment of Temporal Rights and Privileges, and that they did concern matters more than merely spiritual, and speculative, and things known by mere revelation. So that though one Prelate did not usurp over another, yet all Prelates had usurped over the Laity from the times of *Constantine* almost.

It is true, the Church had Bishops before in its times of persecution, but of what power or pomp? It is said of *Calvin,* that in regard of his sway in *Geneva,* he wanted nothing but the Name of Bishop; and it may be as truly said of the Bishops before *Constantine,* that they wanted all but the Name.

The power of Bishops before the installment of Christian Princes, was rather like that of Arbitrators than of Judges, and that held in all cases alike, Civil and Spiritual, but in case of disobedience they did not intrench so far upon the Lay power, as to inflict any pecuniary, or corporal punishment, but they did deny the Sacrament, and eject delinquents out of the Congregation, and this was then an abscission from Christ, being done *Clave non errante:* that is, whilst God did inspire (according to his promise) a miraculous power of binding and loosing infallibly.

The Priestly function was then an Office, not a Jurisdiction, of sacred dignity, not Power: but the Function of a Prince was ever sacred both for honor and power, for dignity and command. *Constantine* the Great was the first Prince which took upon him the care and protection of the Church, after that it had suffered contempt and poverty for 300 years: and now did even that authority and protection cease, and devolve into his hands, which the poor persecuted Bishops had but feebly managed before; but such was the extraordinary indulgence of this pious Emperor, as well to religious persons, as to Religion itself, that taking little notice what the Church had gained by him as its Head and Governor, He heaped up greater Titles and Honors upon Bishops, Archbishops, Patriarchs, and Popes, as if some other supreme Ruler more sacred and competent than himself were necessary. Nevertheless it is thought, that this was as poison poured into the Church, and not Balm, for from that very time Clergymen began to be more glorious, but less gracious, more rich outwardly, but more poor, and vile inwardly. Within a little space after *Constantine* there was just cause of complaint that excessive Honors had corrupted the Church, and that Religion had prospered better in former times, when it had wooden Chalices and golden Priests, than now, when it had golden Chalices, but wooden Priests. It is remarkable also, that soon after *Constantine* the temporal power being too much restrained, and abased, and the spiritual as much enlarged and exalted, the whole face of Christendom began to be embroiled with wars, and poisoned with heresies, so that the Historians of those times have almost nothing else to write of but the forcible investing and divesting by arms of such Bishops and Patriarchs, and of the oppositions of such and such Councils and Synods, and of the Appeals, Jars, Schisms, Excommunications, and Commotions of such, and such Priests, and Monks. Nay, such were the ill effects of those ages which were certainly more zealous than politic, that they cannot yet be wholly rectified, and purged in these our latter times, which are grown too too contrary, being more politic than zealous: Thus did the Church fare for 900 years till the *Roman* Bishops began to Empire above all, and then did the greatest part of the Clergy themselves, especially East from *Italy,* make their departure and separation. Neither did the Romish Vice-god after this great rent and division in the World hang his head for shame, or seek any reunion by letting fall his pompous, painted plumes, but audaciates himself rather to mount higher yet, and to detrude the Western Emperor quite out of the bounds of *Italy.* And in this, his industry fails him not, for after much bloodshed in many cruel conflicts He gains in *Italy* a Temporal, and in all *Europe* besides a spiritual Monarchy, making a triple Mitre shine as gloriously upon the seven-hilled City, as the

Diadem had done before. During his wars with the Emperor of *Germany,* He had other contestations also with *England,* and some other Potentates at some times, but all dismayed him not, only once He was heard to say, *It was time for him to compound with the Dragon, that he might crush the lesser Adders at his pleasure.* Yet after this even this Holy tyranny grows too insolent and insufferable, and so conspires its own dissolution, so that many Countries in the Northwest parts lying more remote from *Rome,* quite revolt from her Allegiance, and Protest against her. Amongst those other Countries also less distant, which still in words confess her Supremacy, her Reign is now but little more than precarious: *Venice* regards not Bulls and Anathemas, *France* disdains a younger brother's benediction, and *Spain* being honored with the title of the Pope's eldest Son, confesses him a Father, but employs him as a Chaplain, gives verbal, but reaps real honors by him.

Augustus having cashiered an unworthy Commander, gave him leave to say, that he had cashiered *Augustus:* and so the Pope's great sons shake off his yoke by degrees, but conceal it, and give him leave to do the like.

It is now very good policy in the Pope, not to pretend to Temporal things as they stand *in ordine,* or have relation to spiritual things, but rather to relinquish his right to spiritual things, as they stand in order to Temporal: it is eminent wisdom in him to forbear threatening, roaring, cursing, and sending his ridiculous Epigrams, out of his own Territories: as he was wont to do: Nay, his very last refuge of sending forth his poisoning and stabbing Ministers cannot remain in season much longer. But to return to our learned Statesman: as He justly taxes the Court of *Rome,* so He unjustly taxes Protestants of the contrary extreme, and this will appear out of his own words. For He grants, first, that the Secular Magistrates have nothing diminished of their authority by Christ's coming: and it is clear that Princes were absolute Governors of the Church before Christ both in Spiritual and Temporal cases.

In the next place He yields, that the power and knowledge of Clergymen called the power of the Keys, is no other but such as Christ infuses in mere supernatural things, known only by Faith and Revelation, not by any Physical, or Ethical Principles; but it is easily proved by us, that such power can extend to no proper jurisdiction at all in human affairs, but is a mere speculative notion, and such we deny not.

Thirdly, He yields that in Jurisdiction there be three things distinct.

First, matter of Law.

Secondly, matter of fact.

Thirdly, matter of execution: whereby retribution is made to every fact according to Law. The first of these, and that in Spiritual Cases alone being tryable by Clergymen only. Admit this and nothing follows, but that things merely Spiritual, are best known to Spiritual persons, there is no power here concluded. As for example, In case of Heresy, that I hold such an opinion, must appear by witnesses and proofs, and herein all kinds of witnesses besides Clergymen are competent.

Next, that this opinion is heretical, requires the judgment of Ecclesiastical persons, but it does not follow, if they be the fittest Judges herein, that they must be the supreme Judges herein, and not as well Dependent and Subordinate as our Civil Judges are in common actions. But in the last place, that such an heretical opinion so dangerous and pestilent to the Church and Commonwealth ought to be corrected or eradicated by such coercive force, and the raising of that force whereby it is to be punished is in the judgment, and in the power of the Supreme Magistrate, for two Magistrates cannot have a Supreme power of the same sword. Either the Secular must command the Ecclesiastical, or the Ecclesiastical must command the Secular, as to coercive power, or a worse confusion than either must needs follow.

So then, it is the Execution of Justice alone, which is essential to the Supreme Governor. Matter of Law requires a Counselor, matter of fact a witness, Matter of Execution alone intimates a Prince, and that Principality cannot be divided betwixt two persons of a several nature.

From hence then it appears plainly that no Catholic differing from the Court of *Rome* ascribes more to Clergymen, than this first point of adjudging according to the Law of God in things Divine; and this implies rather a dependent, than an independent condition in the Judge: and in this Protestants join with full consent. But all this while I find myself in a digression: my scope is not to prove that Protestants do attribute sufficient to Priests, it lies upon me to prove that they attribute too much to them, and herein I am to undertake not only the Episcopal, but the Presbyterial side also, not only Protestant Prelates, but even Master CALVIN that great Archprelate also.

Divines have much trumped the World hitherto in not setting forth the true bounds and limits of Ecclesiastical Jurisdiction, but if I mistake not, the first power (which they claim as most essential) they take to be the power of the Keys, though they define not certainly what this is, whether a Power, or Office; or to whom belonging, or of what extent, and continuance.

The second power which they insist upon, as next issuing out of the power of the Keys, is in Excommunication, Ordination of Ministers, Expositions of Scriptures, etc.

The third and more remote kind of causes wherein they challenge an Ecclesiastical power, is of such as concern Matrimony, Testaments, Heresies, Fasts, Tithes, and Immunities of Clergymen, etc. And further doubtless they would proceed, but that these savor so much of the Temporality, and discover their trumpery; but I have said, if in all these cases Clergymen are necessarily more knowing and impartial than all the else, there is necessity of their Counsel to declare matter of Law, but not of their Consent in applying coercive, and forcible remedies for the execution of Law. I have said also that Clergymen being as well Citizens of the Commonwealth as sons of the Church, and these Cases importing as well perturbance of the State as annoyance to the Church, that there can be but one Head which ought to have command over both, and in both. It is manifest also that many Cases are partly temporal, and partly spiritual, and that scarce any is so temporal, but that it relates in some order to spiritual things, or any so spiritual, but that it hath some relation to temporal things, so that the true subject of Ecclesiastical and civil justice cannot rightly be divided. Further, also it is as manifest that where any doubt, strife, or uncertainty may arise between one Jurisdiction, and another, neither acknowledging any supreme power of decision, no assured peace can continue, and by consequence no stability or permanent subsistence to either, is to be expected. It is natural therefore to be inferred, that either the Temporal or the Ecclesiastical Magistrate must be in all Cases absolutely predominant, and that since the Ecclesiastical ought not by Christ's own command, therefore the temporal ought, as hath been further proved by sundry arguments, and Scripture proofs alleged out of this famous Politician. So much of the temporal power, and its necessary Supremacy: my endeavor shall be now to maintain that no Ecclesiastical power is at all necessary in mere Ecclesiastical persons.

Master *Calvin* according to the Popish ground maintains, that spiritual jurisdiction differs from temporal, and is not incompatible but assistant thereto, because it proposes not the same ends, but several, which by several means may be the better compassed. But the spiritual Magistrate (as I conceive) can propose no other end than what the Secular ought to aim at, for either the Prince ought to have no care at all of the Honor of God, and the good of men, and that which is the prime mean of both, true Religion, or else his ends must be the same which the Prelate aims at, *viz.* to vindicate Religion by removing and correcting scandalous offenders. Secondly, to preserve the innocent from contagion by the separation of open offenders. Thirdly, to prevent further obduration, or to procure the amendment of such as have transgressed by wholesome chastisement.

This is beyond all controversy, as also that the Person and Power of a Prince, are as sacred to effect these ends, as the Prelates: and certainly, God did not so sanctify their persons and offices for any less end. And therefore in ancient times Holy Bishops did Preach and recommend nothing more to Princes than the care of Religion, though proud Prelates now arrogate this only to themselves, and though it be still apparent, that no offense is so spiritual, but that it is a civil evil, as well as a blemish to Religion: forsomuch as true Religion is the foundation of a State. And this could not be, neither were Princes answerable to God for the corruption of Religion, if God had not given them a supreme power, and that effectual to bring all offenders whatsoever to confession, satisfaction, and contrition or to expel them the congregation by themselves, or their surrogates.

Master *Calvin* instances in adultery and drunkenness etc. and says, that the temporal power punishes these by external force, and for public example's sake, as it concerns the State, but the Spiritual Judge punishes them without force internally for the amendment of the delinquent. He might as well have named swearing, lying, stealing, murdering, and all sins whatsoever, and so have made all men twice punishable, and the Ecclesiastical Court as full of business as the temporal, to the great vexation of the State, and danger of division, out of this false ground only that temporal power hath not competence for the amendment of offenders, or for the care of Religion, but only for the satisfaction of wronged parties, and the expedition of civil justice.

This is a way to erect *regnum in regno,* and to maintain such concurrent jurisdictions, as cannot possibly stand together; for all being subject to sin and offense, as well the Spiritual as temporal, either the one or other must go unquestioned, and this may produce division: or else both; and that will cause most certain confusion. Both sides here seem strangely puzzled, the rigidest of the Episcopal faction allow Princes a coercive power over Priests, and Prelates, where they perform not what their duty is in their functions or jurisdictions, and this power requires a higher power of summoning, arraigning, and legally trying them: and yet the moderatest of the Presbyterial faction would have Princes questionable, tryable and punishable by the Spirituality. This is a gross confusion, which will appear to be so more plainly in the sequel; when it is more fully cleared, that to Princes alone God has precisely committed *utramque tubam,* and *utramque tabulam* too, as our reverend *Andrews* says.

'Tis true, as *Calvin* alleges, Princes are sons of the Church, they are in it, not above it: the word intruding the Church universal, such as is both militant and triumphant; past, present, and future, for that hath no other head but

Christ: to that all Princes and Priests are equally sons: but take Church for such or such a National, Local Church, and then the Prince is head thereof, under Christ; and the Clergy are part of his charge, and under his protection. The same man also may in diverse respects be both father and son to the same man without confusion of relations. A King, a Bishop may hear the Word, and receive the Sacrament from an inferior Minister; a Subject may be natural Father to his Prince, and in this respect a filial subjection is due from the superior, and so a King may refer his own case to his Chancellor, yet this destroys not the greater, higher, and more general superiority in other things, at other times. And to me it seems that even in the exercise of the Keys, the Priest officiates under the Prince, as the Chancellor does in matters of Law, even when the King's own case lies in Judgment before him, and when perhaps he makes a decree against his own Master, and contrary to his own Master's private advertisement: and yet the King is not properly either Lawyer, or Theologue, though both are actuated, and organized as it were, by the soul-like commanding, overseeing, and overruling of his more sublime and divine power.

Herein the Priest also may learn a limitation from the Lawyer, for though the Judge be bound to pronounce right judgment against his own Master, yet this holds not in all cases alike; because of his limited condition, for in Criminal cases such as concern the safety of the King's own person, or the royal dignity of his calling, therein judgment must be utterly mute. And therefore it is a weak argument of Master *Calvin,* though it be his best; when he infers a necessity of an Ecclesiastical Judicature from hence, because else the Prince himself wanting punishment, should escape free: for the reason is the same in matters of Law; the King is not questionable, or responsible, for personal crimes, and yet this is held no political mischief. Besides if the Prince shall not go unquestioned, or undisciplined by the Spiritual, yet the supreme spiritual Magistrate must, and this is an equal, if not a greater mischief: for both cannot be equally liable to the judgment of each other. Neither is it to much purpose that the example of Bishop *Ambrose* so harshly, so unreverendly treating pious penitent *Theodosius,* is so confidently cited always by either faction Episcopal and Presbyterial; for though the name of *Ambrose* be great, yet I will crave leave to speak as an advocate against him in the name of the Emperor *Theodosius.*

Reverend Sir, you take upon you to be a judge over me, and to condemn me of a bloody Massacre committed unjustly at *Thessalonica,* and being so condemned, you proceed against me with your ghostly punishment, subjecting me to your Ecclesiastical severity: But I pray consider what mischiefs may follow hereupon; if Emperors may be punishable by Bishops, then common equity requires that Emperors have the benefit of a fair hearing and arraignment, or else were their condition more miserable than the condition of the meanest vassals: for as Princes' actions are more inscrutable, and their counsels more mystical; so also their ends are for the most part more liable to envy, and misinterpretation: It is not possible for you without due discussion, inquiry, and examination of impartial witnesses, perfectly to understand all the true circumstances, reasons, and grounds of this my fact; and without this understanding it is not possible for you to pronounce a just censure against me. It's necessary then that some Tribunal be prepared for you, and some Bar for me, that upright sentence may pass, and that justice may be done understandingly, and upon this it must needs follow that I am your mere Subject, and must lay down my Scepter to bow myself under your Crosier, till this difficulty be fully ended. Admit this also, and then you may use what procrastination you please in this intricate decision; or in the like manner question me of all other enormities, and scandalous deviations, which rumor, envy, or treason itself forges against me; and thus shall I have no leisure to judge other men, it will scarce be possible for me to acquit myself in judgment from other men: that power which God hath put into my hands for the protection of so many Myriads, will be utterly disabled by that higher power which is put into your hands over me. By the same reason also that I am to render an account to you in this place, I am to render the like to all your superiors, equals, or inferiors in other jurisdictions, of all sins whatsoever, whether real, or imputable, Ecclesiastical, or Civil, so that no end is like to be of my trials, purgations, or condemnations.

You will say, my crime is sensibly evident; if I would deny this, you could not prove it so; and if I would not confess this, you could not force me, for it was a political thing, and far off acted: and my mere confession can give to you no jurisdiction. But be my crime as manifest in itself as the disobedience of *Saul* was to *Samuel*, or as *David's* murder was to *Nathan*, or as *Solomon's* incontinence was to all the world, or as *Manasses* his Idolatry: yet why should I suffer more than they? What new coercive, vindictive authority have Priests gained over Princes by Christ's Gospel, which the Jewish Priests never used, claimed, or heard of? If Excommunication, etc. be now necessary, sure it was in use before Christ; and then we should have heard of some Kings Excommunicated, etc. by some Priests; for if the Temporal power had not of its own nature a competent force and habitude to restrain all things repugnant to public quietness, and honesty, a Spiritual power was necessary; and yet we read of none such. But if there was a sufficiency in the Temporal power, as in most manifestly apparent; then we cannot imagine that Christ came to take away any of this authority from Magistrates: but that power which he added, was rather an excellency of grace and virtue in matters of faith, and illumination.

It cannot be alleged by you, that that punishment is merely spiritual, and so no political evil: for as it puts other men into the condition of Publicans, Heathens, and worse, so it further yet degrades, disables, and oppresses Princes. How shall he be honored and obeyed as the Vice-gerent of God in all causes, whom the Laity sees ejected out of the Church, and expelled out of the Communion of the faithful, as a rotten contagious member? how shall he be held more sacred than a Priest, whom the sentence, interdiction, and the confounding blow of a Priest's spiritual execration, shall render so contemptible, miserable, and abominable in the eyes of the world?

Saint *Paul* being accused in matters of Doctrine, made his appeal to a wicked Heathen Emperor; and yet now a Christian godly Emperor being accused by any Churchman, no appeal is allowed, though in mere civil accusations. Saint *Peter's* Keys did either endure some new power not before known to the world, or not; if it did, then our Savior's Gospel came into the world to the detriment of civil government, which is contrary to Religion, and all reason: and if no new addition of power were imported, then *Tiberius* himself, though a Heathen, and Tyrant, remained as absolute as before; and yet in his time there was more necessity of an Ecclesiastical judicature, than is now. But you will say, if Princes be not subject to some chastisement, then some scandals must pass unremediable. Not so, for here God is the revenger, and strikes often, as he did *Uzziah;* but if not, yet either the Temporal or Spiritual Governor must pass unchastised, which is all one; for two Supremes cannot be, nor no entire government without some supremacy, nor no supremacy without immunity, and exemption from judgment.

The perpetual conflicts and contestations between Princes and Prelates, which are likely to ensue, will soon clear this; that either Princes must at last submit to the tribunals of Churchmen, and reign at their discretion; or else Churchmen must submit to them: for both tribunals cannot stand compatible. For my part, I excuse so grave a Father as you are, of ambition herein; and therefore I am the less cautious in submitting myself at this time: but I conceive this Doctrine may be the ground of dangerous consequences to others, and therefore I desire it may not from me pass into a precedent for the time to come.

Let not proud Prelates from this my voluntary humiliation, arrogate to themselves as if it had been due; or derogate thereby from the more sacred order of Princes: neither let Princes from this particular learn to yield to any Spiritual Monarchy whatsoever. My belief is, that the Prince is the Head, the Fountain, the Soul of all power whatsoever, Spiritual, or Temporal; wherein he ought not to endure at all any kind of rivality of Ecclesiastical persons, nor can admit of any diminution in any part of his jurisdiction, without offense to God, damage to his charge, and danger to himself. So much for *Theodosius,* and so much for that jurisdiction which is due to Prelates: I should now speak of the exercise thereof, as it is granted by the favor of Princes, but this is a very tender point.

It seems to some, that Princes ought not to encumber men in Sacred Orders, in any kind of judicature which is not purely Spiritual; nor that Prelates can accept of any Temporal employment whatsoever, without dishonor to their Orders, and neglect to their cure of Souls: and yet now none so greedy of such employment. A sacred place may not be put to secular uses, that's profane: but a sacred person may, that's honorable.

A Bishopric nowadays is but a Writ of ease, to dismiss from Preaching, and attending God's service; whereby the man is preferred from the Church to the Court, from the Altar to some Tribunal, from God's spiritual to the King's temporal affairs. In the High Commission, at the Council Table, in the Starchamber, and the Chequer, Churchmen are now more active than in their own Consistories, and yet their ambition further aims (as 'tis said) to the Chancery, Court of Requests, etc. which could not choose but redound to the scandal of Religion, the obstruction of Justice, and vexation of the Subject: if there were not learned and skillful men enough in Policy and Law to serve the King, unless Divinity were deprived of some of her followers, there were some seeming umbrage why the King might borrow of God; but when God's more holy office is neglected, that the King's meaner may be the worse administered, the world much gazes and wonders at it.

The functions of Divines are too sacred for any secular person to officiate and therefore it should seem their persons also ought to be too sacred for secular functions; for it seems preposterous, that it should be thought an honor to Priests to relinquish spiritual, and adhere to temporal employments. *Nic: Machiavel* did observe that Christian Religion had long since fallen to the ground had not the regular strictness of poor inferior Priests and Friars held, and propped up the reputation of it in the World, as much as the pride and luxury of the great Cardinals and Princelike Bishops, did strive to sink and demolish it. The same observation holds true amongst us Protestants at this day, for the more our Prelates enjoy, the more still they seek; and all our three Kingdoms are grown so sick of their pride, injustice, and pragmatical faction, that scarce any remedy but blood-letting can cure them. We find in Scripture the most high and holy Offices of Religion performed by Princes, even amongst, and above the greatest of Priests; but we scarce find any instance at all where Priests intermeddled with any State affairs, either above, or under Princes, and yet with us now the employing and entrusting of Clergymen in Temporal businesses, is held as politic as it was in times of Popery: although no time could ever justly boast of that use. But to pass over Temporal businesses, how violent have our Bishops been in their own Canons about Ceremonies, and indifferences? and what disturbance hath that violence produced? They strive as for the beauty and glory of Religion, to bring in the same forms of Liturgy, the same posture of the Communion Table, the same gesture at the Communion, etc. in all our three Dominions; as if uniformity were always beautiful: and yet we see, all men are created with several faces, voices, and complexions, without any deformity to the universe.

'Tis not external variety, but internal dissension, which spoils the harmony of Religion; and dissension is more nourished by the harshness of Pastors over their flocks, especially over the weak ones in scruples, than by permitting various Rites and Forms in the external worship of God. Certainly, liberty and variety in indifferences, and Ceremonies is more favored in Scripture, than any universal similitude, or rigorous force whatsoever, over the perplexed, anxious consciences of weak men. We see in *Scotland,* where there is no Ceremonies, they enjoy that uniformity without contention, which we aim at only, and seek to purchase with infinite debate, and persecution; and under their peace and unity, the Protestant Religion thrives, and Romish Superstition utterly ceases: whereas under our strife and disagreement, Religion and true Devotion is overrun and overgrown, like Corn choked with weeds. Nay, it is thought that if our Bishops had been more gentle-handed all this while towards such as disrelished Ceremonies for Popery's sake, and had rather pitied them as men of tender consciences, than persecuted and defamed them, as seditious Puritans, these differences had not lasted so long: for when the reformation was not yet fully perfected, the Puritans of those days were more fiery than now; but not being so odious in the Church, less combustion followed thereupon: whereas now they are so unmercifully treated, that no moderate compliance can serve the turn.

There seems now little remaining of Puritanism, but the breathless carcass of it, and yet till that too be interred and consumed, no truce can be admitted. The very sufferings of Puritans now are sufficiently quit, and imputed as the effects of their own malice, their punishment is argument enough for the desert of their punishment; the more they have borne, the more they must now bear; and the more they now bear, the more they shall hereafter. Fury is one of the main things objected to Puritans; but in truth, the World has not anything more furious than such as most pretend against them.

Hence it is, that the hatred of Puritans flows and descends from the highest of the Clergy to the lowest: and young Students in the University know it now their wisest course to study the defamation of Puritans, as the first and most necessary point of their learning and qualification, and as their surest path to promotion. And to make their detestation sure, and themselves irreconcilable, they must engage themselves by some notable service of novelty, quarreling with some point of Protestantism, or refining some point of Popery; they must tax Protestants as some ways injurious to Princes, or extol Papists as zealous observers of Antiquity. It must be maintained that Royalty cannot stand without the prop of Episcopacy, though it never yet found greater enemy; and that Puritanism only hinders the stretching of our Religion, or else Papists and we should soon agree. Those of vulgar wits which serve not for such strains, that they may be redeemed from suspicion of Puritanism, must do something factiously, or be vicious, or else their hopes of preferment are almost desperate.

Charity to Papists, conformity to Ancient Fathers, and decent uniformity amongst ourselves, are the specious colors wherewith they dress and deck all their pretenses; for want of Sectaries living in these days, they rake out of their tombs *Hacket, Copinger, Browne,* etc. to upbraid us, for want of opposites enow here in *England,* they calumniate the *Scots* to our dishonor; for want of true imputations, they forge any crimes how monstrous soever, and their most sure one is, that which is most undiscernible, hypocrisy. Nevertheless it must be believed that the Antipuritan disparages not our Ancestors in the reformation, but for love of antiquity; not tears in sunder the bonds of Religion, Nature, Policy betwixt two the most close-united Nations of the World, but out of love to unity: nor fills whole Kingdoms with blood, but out of love to Order. Such was sure *Diogenes* his humility, trampling upon *Plato's* Couches; such was *Nero's* uniformity, setting on fire the streets of *Rome:* Such was *Procrustes* his symmetry, cutting his guests according to his beds. And therefore it's thought *Puritans* are not so much hated for their opposition to Ceremonies, as Ceremonies are multiplied, and enforced for suppression of all zealous Christians, under the umbrage of *Puritans:* and that for the same purpose the enemies of Piety have blown those coals which they might have quenched.

The Bishop of *Downe* makes a very sharp speech to the *Puritans* in *Ireland,* as being very disobedient, and animated therein by the *Scotish* Covenanters; but his chiefest eloquence uttered against his own Countrymen the *Scots,* whom he paints forth as the chiefest Traitors, perjured Rebels, Heretics and Hypocrites in the World: nay, he denounceth them worse than Anabaptists, and such as have more than justified the *Powder-Traitors,* and all the rebellious practices of the *Jesuits.* Afterwards he adds also, That *Puritanism* is not the National sin of *Scotland* only, but that they of the same faction in *England* had been as deep in the same condemnation, but that they had not so much power. See here the lively portraiture of an *Antipuritan,* see a true *Boner* revived again, but in *Protestant* habit; and for ought I see, here are none exempted from this black venomous censure in all the King's Dominions, but those of the Popish and Episcopal Faction. It's not to be wondered at that the King thinks ill of his Subjects, or that *Burton* or *Prin* suffered worse than Traitors' merits: It's rather to be wondered at, that our streets do not run with blood daily, since this is the Gospel our Reverend Fathers of the Church preach. This speech was thought worthy to be dispersed in Print over all our Kingdoms in English; but since, because it redounds so much to the honor of the three Nations, and the repute of *Protestant Religion,* it's Translated into Latin, and Copies are Printed for all Christendom to take notice of. In this speech it's urged, that *Puritans* who began about 80 years since, have proceeded from bad to worse by six degrees; first they did dislike, then contemn Bishops; then they did disobey their jurisdiction; then separate themselves; then they fell into the Heresy of holding no difference between Bishop and Presbyter: lastly, they rebelled, and grew more immoderate than *Anabaptists.* And here Saint *Cyprian* is alleged, who says, That the contempt of Bishops is the beginning and ground of all Heresies and Schisms.

Here we see what *Puritans* are, the most cursed Miscreants on earth; next we see who *Puritans* are, all such as hold not with Episcopacy: that is in probability half *Ireland,* more than half *England,* all *Scotland,* and many other *Protestant* Countries. King *James* did put a difference betwixt such as disrelisht Bishops, and Ceremonies merely, and such as under that pretext fraudulently sought to perturb the State, and make a factious separation. But here the difference of all *Puritans* is gradual only, not substantial; for dislike of Bishops is the beginning of all *Heresy,* and must needs end in *Anabaptism* and rebellion.

How plainly does it here appear, that Episcopacy is the true *Helena* of all this war; and yet Saint *Cyprian* is to be understood of the Pastoral function, not of the Ecclesiastical jurisdiction of a Bishop, or else in his sense the *Genevans,* and the greatest part of *Protestants* are Heretics, and King *James* made a frivolous distinction. Such stuff as this had not misbeseemed a *Papist,* but it's very odd in a *Protestant* Bishop; except we consider him, as one who hath lookt back towards the *Onions* and *Fleshpots* of *Egypt,* and is enamored again upon those glorious titles and ensigns of Honor, and Pomp, which *Rome* confers upon her Courtiers. But to conclude this point, I wish Princes would not allow such Bishops to be carvers to themselves, and make them Judges in cases of their own interest: they are surely good spectacles for Princes in Theological deliberations, as Temporal Counselors are in State affairs; but miserable are those Princes whose eyes cannot see without such spectacles. If Religion did not prosper worse, if peace were not more violated, if persecution were not more common in countries where Bishops govern, than where they are expelled, we might suspect the *Scots,* as Heretical, and Rebellious by nature; for choosing all the plagues of war rather then Bishops: but when we see the contrary, we may as well listen to the *Scots* against Bishops, as to Bishops against the *Scots.* So much of the Ecclesiastical *Puritan,* next after whom sprung up the *Puritan* in Religion, of whom I shall speak very briefly.

There are many men amongst us now, which brook Bishops and Ceremonies well enough; and perhaps favorably interpret our late innovations: and yet these may be too grave to escape the name of *Puritans.* To be a *Protestant* may be allowed, but to dispute against *Papists,* smells of preciseness: to hold the *Pope* fallible is tolerated, but to hold him Antichrist is abominable *Puritanism:* to go to Church is fashionable, but to complain of the *Mass,* or to be grieved at the public countenance of *Popery,* whereby it entwines our Religion, and now drinks up that Sap which is scarce afforded to *Protestantism,* or at all to take notice how far some of our Divines are hereat conniving, if not cooperating, is a symptom of a deep infected *Puritan.*

He that is not moderate in Religion is a *Puritan,* and he that is not a *Cassandrian,* or of Father *Francis Syncler's* faith, is not moderate: he savors too much of *Calvin's* gross learning, exploded now by our finest wits. But I pass from this kind of *Puritan* to another, whom I shall call my Political *Puritan;* for the bounds of *Puritanism* are yet larger, and enclose men of other conditions.

Some there are yet which perhaps disfavor not at all either Ecclesiastical Policy, or moderate *Papists;* and yet nevertheless this is not sufficient to acquit them from the name of *Puritans,* if they ascribe anything to the Laws and Liberties of this Realm, or hold the Prerogative royal to be limitable by any

Law whatsoever. If they hold not against *Parliaments* and with *Ship-money,* they are injurious to Kings; and to be injurious to Kings, is *Proprium quarto modo* to a *Puritan.*

Our present civil, nay more than civil war with *Scotland,* and all the mischiefs thereon attending, the disaffection between the King and his Subjects, and all the mischiefs thereon attending the discontinuance of *Parliaments,* the proper remedies of all State maladies, and universal grievances, which is a mischief whereby all mischiefs become incurable, all are caused by the abusive mistaken and injurious misapplication of this word *Puritan.*

The *Scots* are Puritans, and therefore enemies to Monarchy, the English are Puritans, and therefore haters of Royal prerogative, both the Nations have been hitherto famous for their devout reverence, and obsequious zeal to their Princes; but now Puritanism has infected them, and perverted them to disloyalty. Thus is the King's heart alienated from his Subjects, and by consequence, the Subject's loyalty blunted towards him, to the incomparable, almost irreparable detriment of both: neither is this disaccord between the King and his best Subjects, more fatal and pernicious to the Commonwealth, than his accord with the Recusant faction. Papists have now gotten the repute of the best Subjects, and fittest for trust in places of eminent service; nay 'tis almost necessary that foreign Papists be brought in for the supporting of the endangered royalty: for though the Popish faction at Court be strong and active enough for matter of Counsel, yet for matter of force the Puritans in City and Country be too predominant.

The Bishop of *Downe* in his visitation speech lays all the calamities of Church and Commonwealth upon Nonconformists, and for proof thereof instances in the Covenanters, whom he charges of rebellion, charging withal that rebellion upon Puritanism. The first thing (says he) that made me out of love with that Religion, was their injurious dealing with Kings, which I observe both in their practice and doctrine. He taxes first their doctrine, because they deny the King's supremacy in causes Ecclesiastical, and allow Subjects to resist, nay and depose their King, if he be a Tyrant. Surely *Ahab* could say little for himself, if he could not lay his own crimes upon *Elijah;* but see here by what art of confusion all *Scots* are called Puritans and all Puritans rebels.

King *James* spoke not so confusedly as if Puritanism were a Religion; and all that disliked Bishops and Ceremonies were of that Religion; and all of that Religion were enemies to Kings. If a Bishop needed any proof, if his Ἀυτος ἔφη were not unquestionable, I would desire him to prove all Covenanters

Puritans, and all Puritans, deniers of the King's supremacy: or to instance in any Kings which have been deposed or murdered by Presbyterial authority. How far Bishops have encroached upon Kings, is known to all the world: Our Protestant Bishops lately have by Oath and Canon combined together to bind the King's hands though he be Supreme, that he shall not govern our Church but by Archbishops, Bishops, Archdeacons, etc. and yet these troublers of *Israel* have the face to tax *Elijah* of their own sin.

Presbytery indeed has heretofore passed her bounds, yet not of late, but Episcopacy has ever from *Constantine* claimed an independence of Divine right, till this instant. I conceive there are not in all the King's Dominions, three men, except Papists and Anabaptists, which hold it lawful to depose, or by any force to violate the persons of Kings, how ill soever. The *Scotch* Divines indeed maintain that a great body of men may defend themselves against the unjust Sword of misled Kings, because they cannot fly, or otherwise save themselves; and this they take now to be their own case; whereas our Court Divines in *England* hold, that in such case, we ought all to yield our throats without defense. This seems unnatural, and truth was never unnatural, but I forbear to dispute a point so horrid to man's imagination: The Bishop next instances in the rebellious practices of Puritans, and reckons up some facts in *Scotland* appointed by the Presbytery without King *James* his privity, and some other seditious Sermons, and actions whereby he was much annoyed. But what? did not King *James* know his own enemies, or how to blame them? did he condemn all *Scots* alike, or all Bishop-haters alike, or join the English in like condemnation? we know well enough, that King *James* called rebellious precisians Puritans, but he never called all Puritans rebellious precisians: He never used those terms as convertible, but declared his contrary meaning by a manifest difference taken between them. But the Bishop's main instance is in the present *Scotch* insurrection; this he calls a rebellion of Puritans, and far greater than the Powder-treason: For (says he,) that plot was but the act of a few discontented Gentlemen, but in this rebellion of the Puritans they have engaged a great part of the Kingdom, so that this may be said to be the common sin of that sect. What could have been raked out of Hell more slanderous to our Religion, more Apologetical for Popery.

The Powder-Traitors are here preferred before the whole sect of Puritans: The sin of the Powder-Traitors was, that they being but an inconsiderable party, sought the destruction of their King and his issue, and the flower of the Nobility, Gentry, Commonalty, and the extirpation of the true Religion, by a most diabolical bloody practice and conspiracy. And it ought not to be charged upon the mere actors, as a symptom of discontent, only we know how far the Romish Religion itself favors and gives ground to such damned feats, and how far it has owned some having proved prosperous, and justified the doing thereof in nature as impious, though perhaps in degree not so heinous as this. For take this as it was conspired, and questionless, since the crucifying of *Jesus Christ,* the light never discovered any treason more ugly, and horrible.

Now to outmatch this deed of darkness, the *Scotch* Nation by a strange general unanimity have armed themselves to oppose the ill government of Bishops, and other alterations in the service of God, and the administration of justice, and being invaded therefore by another Nation, have used force to defend their lives; and seeing that defense not safe in their own Country, they have since pursued it further by way of prevention in the Country of their Invaders. That is the greatest act of rebellion whereby the common peace and safety of a Kingdom is most disturbed and impeached; but by the common act of a whole Kingdom, that mischief cannot be effected, therefore the Bishop fails in his politics when he thinks that the *Major* part disturbing the *Minor,* is more traitorous, than the contrary. The unanimous act of a whole Kingdom ought to be presumed to be less injurious, and more wise than the act of any small inconsiderable party, for it hath scarce ever been seen that a whole Kingdom, or the majority thereof hath ever been treasonable to itself in procuring its own ruin.

Many States have perished by the machinations of a few ill affected, ill advised Counselors, (scarce ever any perished otherwise) but the total body and collection, has never been guilty of its own ruin: and if it were, such Treason could not be so great as that which is plotted by a few. Whilst the *Scots* contained themselves within their own territories, and were considered as a kingdom within themselves, as they were when the Bishop passed his censure, they were not rightly so censured: neither was he then privy to their intrusions, that they would infest our kingdom with the same combustion, and so prove a disturbance to the greater part of our British Monarchy, whereof they themselves are but a member of less bulk and value. Cursed therefore are those uncharitable exasperating censures, whereby the King is too far incensed, and by whose rash instigations the commotions themselves become the harder to be appeased.

Great insurrections are like great fires, wherein delay is mischievous, and small remedies rather turn to fuel, than extinguish: and violent counsel against an enraged multitude is like oil, or pitch cast into the flame. The wise politician proportions his remedy according to the mischief, if water will not prevail, he useth milk; if a little quantity will not suffice, he pours as the combustion itself requires. Unfortunate *Rehoboam* stands as a Seamark to warn all Princes how to shun this rock of violent counsel against a people violently enraged and aggrieved. Some men have interpreted the designs of the *Scots* to have been treasonable from the beginning, and wholly bent upon the spoil and havoc of the English Nation from their first stirring: Others have wholly justified their intentions and proceedings hitherto as defensive only, and enforced by necessity: both these, I conceive, are too rash and headlong in their guesses. In so great a body of men, there must needs be variety of opinions, and it's likely contrariety of affections; and therefore it behooves the King to be the more tender, moderate, and circumspect in his deliberations, as well for the one side as the other, especially since the *Scots* have not evidently and universally as yet declared themselves for the worse. We may at once be charitable in hoping the best, and wise withal in preventing the worst; nay, a charitable and sweet demeanor, if it be not too fond, may prove a great part of our prevention: doubtless *Rehoboam* himself, had he not been willfully devoted to young, rash, and violent Counselors, might have easily retained within his obedience many of his well-meaning Subjects, and reclaimed others of more moderation; and by that means have divided and dissipated the most obstinate, headstrong, and furious of all the rebellious party. Some Princes think themselves bound in Honor to do unwise things, and this was the error of *Rehoboam,* his aged Counselors advised him to that which was most politic, concluding that to be most honorable; but his *Genius* rather led him according to the advice of his young Gallants, to conclude that most politic which to his haughty stomach seemed most honorable: but what was the event? to avoid the scorn of young men, he incurred the scorn of old men; to avoid the unjust censure of fools, he incurred the just censure of wise men; to gain the honor of appearing stout, he purchased the dishonor of being rash; to show a contempt of danger, he made himself a prey to it; rather than to decline a blow by a gentle bowing of his body, he yielded himself to be inevitably oppressed by it.

At this time of revolt the *Israelites* were not so wicked, as their revolt after made them; it may be so with the *Scots,* they are yet *Protestants,* and perhaps may be retained so: and who can think of *Protestants,* that so great a body of them, can at one fall so desperately tumble into the depth of mischief, as to make Fasting, Praying, Oaths and Sacraments, mere instruments and trains to commit murder, theft, sacrilege, treason, and the most unnatural of all crying crimes? But to return to our own Nation, and what we suffer by our own Divines.

Manwaring's Doctrine is common at Court, and 'tis not long since a Bishop's Chaplain in Term-time, challenged a Judge of Treason, for delivering Law according to conscience. And this is now no prodigy, for Pulpits are not public enough to preach an unlimitable prerogative in; 'tis fit our learned Doctors should mount the Benches of Justice also, there to advance Logic instead of Law; for Law is grown injurious to Princes, and smells rank of *Puritanism.* Divines themselves will lose nothing to Princes, but all other men shall, that they may gain the more: and neither Lawyers nor Statesmen must direct them in anything, but both Lawyers and Statesmen must be directed by them in all things: but let us a little examine how the conditionate and absolute forms of government come within the circle of Theology. The *Israelites* were governed by Monarchs, but not all alike absolute. The Patriarchs were not so absolute as the Judges, nor the Judges as the Kings, nor the Kings as those Heathen Emperors, which at last made them tributary. The due of *Caesar,* and the due of *Solomon,* and the due of *Samuel,* and the due of *Jacob,* was not the same as to all points of State, or all degrees of Royalty, and yet the nation was the same, and the form of government still remained the same.

It should seem that God approved that degree of Sovereignty best, which was by himself settled in the person of *Moses;* for when that people afterwards desired a King, of a more awful and large prerogative, in imitation of other Nations, the thing displeased God. *Samuel* also wrote a book of this subject, showing the just conditions of Regal power; (the loss whereof is much to be lamented) for if it had been God's will that all Kings should be equally absolute in all respects, and free from all limitations and obligations alike, *Samuel* needed to have written little thereof; one word had determined all. But in Scripture, as it now remains, *Samuel's* book being not extant, our chiefest light and guide now is by example, not rule; and example we find very various.

The State and Sovereignty of the *Jewish* Kings in general, we find mild, and gracious; but much differing in particulars. *Solomon* was heavy over his Subjects, and under his Son they would not bear the like; yet *Solomon's* pressure was not upon the states of his Subjects by taxes, and impositions, for He made silver in *Jerusalem* as stones for plenty; nor did He vex their persons by Military hazards and services, for He was at peace with all the world: Neither did He any way let fall, or lessen their honor amongst other Nations; He made them rather a spectacle of glory and prosperity to the world. *Solomon's* harshness was only in employing so great multitudes for his own pompous attendance, and for the performance of such public works, and structures, as did tend to the Magnificence and beauty of the State. Besides, Scripture does not satisfy us, neither by rule, nor example, whether Kings ought to be successive always, or elective; or whether primogeniture of Males, or unigeniture of Daughters, ought to take place: many things are left so uncertain, that it is not always safe for Kings wholly to rely upon examples; and for the rule of obedience, it is general, and no more advantageous for free Monarchs, than conditionate Potentates; no more for supreme, than subordinate commanders.

The Law of Nature best determines, that all Princes being public Ministers for the common good, that their authority ought to be of sufficient latitude for that common good; and since Scripture is not expressed concerning that latitude, as to all people, the same not being to all alike necessary, the several Laws of several Countries best teach that certain latitude. I could wish therefore that Princes herein would not so much consult with Divines, as Lawyers; or rather with Parliaments, which are the Grand Courts and Councils of Kingdoms; for (as *Cotton* says) Every man in particular may deceive, and be deceived; but no man can deceive all, nor can all deceive one. Ancient times are not precedentary to ours by any necessity, for Laws are now more learned, exact, and particular; and Courts, and Tables of Justice, and Policy, are more wisely and methodically composed and elected, than they were; and therefore there needs not that vocal power, or indisputable force to remain in the breasts of Princes, as was of old.

The Courts of Parliament, and their unquestionable Acts, and Ordinances, and their infallible avisoes, are now in all well-governed Countries, the very Oracles of all Policy, and Law, they are the fountains of civil blood, spirits, and life; and the sovereign antidotes of public mischiefs. That Prince was never yet deceived which relied upon them, nor can He choose but be deceived, which thinks he can be assisted with any more wise or faithful advertisement, than that which is given him by his whole Realm united, and contracted in a less circumference. What end can all the flower of the Nobility, Gentry, and Commonalty of a Nation, being wise and religious, have in seducing their Sovereign, or in limiting that Sovereignty by which alone they are protected? Or what one party of particular men can better understand the true limits of sufficient Sovereignty, and the profit thereof; than this collective universality, whose rays like the Sun's, are everywhere dispersed; and yet whose body of light is here as in a refulgent Globe concentered?

Individuals may have many particular ends, severed from the Prince's or the State's, but Communities can aim at nothing but the common good; as the lesser fountains scatter their branching streams up and down in various meanders, whilst the Sea contains itself in an entire body, within its constant bounds. Individuals also have but their own particular set limits of perfection, and have judgments besides apt to be darkened by their own several interests and passions; whereas the common body enjoys a confluence of several perfections, and hath the less force from abroad to overcloud them. Of all men therefore it will most concern Princes to suspect them which are enemies to public assemblies, and to confide in them most, whose ends are not divided from the generality's; and as they tender their own happiness, to expect it chiefly from that generality, by which they are Kings, to which they are Gods, from which their very Diadems receive honor and sanctity, to which their very Royal Order imparts life, and breath, and necessary subsistence. I come now to my Ethical *Puritan*.

The name of *Puritan* must not rest here, for there may be some moderate, well inclined, facile men, whose education may be such that they are not much versed or insighted either in matters of Religion, or matters of State; they may be such as are no ways busy but in their own particular affairs, and yet it behooves, that these men too be brought in within the opprobrious compass of Puritanism. To the Religious, Ecclesiastical, Political Puritan, there must be joined also an Ethical Puritan.

This detested odious name of Puritan first began in the Church presently after the Reformation, but now it extends itself further, and gaining strength as it goes, it diffuses its poisonous ignominy further, and being not contented to Gangrene Religion, Ecclesiastical and Civil policy, it now threatens destruction to all morality also. The honest strict demeanor, and civil conversation which is so eminent in some men does so upbraid and convince the Antipuritan, that even honesty, strictness, and civility itself must become disgraceful, or else they which are contrary cannot remain in grace: But because it is too gross to deride virtue under the name of virtue; therefore other colors are invented, and so the same thing undergoes derision under another name. The zealous man is despised under the name of zealot, the Religious honest man has the vizard of an hypocrite and dissembler put upon him to make him odious.

Puritans by some are paralleled to Jesuits, Jesuits are called Popish Puritans, and Puritans, Protestant Jesuits; yet this is not indeed disparageable to them: For doubtless fiery zeal and rigor were not blamable in Jesuits, were not their very Religion false; as celerity and expedition in a Traveler is not in itself faulty, but commendable, though the Traveler being in a wrong path, it causes him to stray the further from his journey's end.

My Lord of *Downe* professes that the first thing which made him distaste the Religion of Puritans (besides their gross hypocrisy) was sedition: So gross hypocrisy, it seems, was the first. What is gross or visible hypocrisy to the Bishop, I know not, for I can see no windows or casements in men's breasts, neither do I think him indued with Saint *Peter's* prophetical spirit whereby to perceive and search into the reins, and hearts of hypocrites; but let him proceed. It is a plausible matter (says he) with the people to hear men in authority depraved, and to understand of any liberty and power appertaining to themselves. The profession also of extraordinary zeal, and as it were contempt of the world works with the multitude. When they see men go simply in the Streets, and bow down their heads like a Bull-rush, their inward parts burning with deceit, wringing their necks awry, shaking their heads as if they were in some present grief, lifting up the white of their eyes at the sight of some vanity, giving great groans, crying out against this sin and that sin in their superiors, under color of long prayers, devouring widows', and married wives' houses; when the multitude hears and sees such men, they are carried away with a great conceit of them, but if they should judge of these men by their fruits, not by outward appearance, they should find them to be very far from the true Religion. See here the froth of a scurrilous libeler, whereby it is concluded that he that is of severe life, and averse from the common vanities of the time, is an hypocrite: If these descriptions of outward austerity shall not only show what is an hypocrite, but point out also who is an hypocrite, our Savior himself will hardly escape this description; doubtless our Savior, and many of his devoutest followers did groan, shake their heads, and lift up their eyes at the sight of some public sins, and vanities, and did not spare to tax the vices of Superiors, and to preach too, and admonish the meaner sort of the people; yet who but an *Annas* or *Caiphas* will infer from hence that therefore their inward parts burn with deceit, and that their end is merely to carry away the multitude; such as judge only by outward appearance, and have not their senses exercised to discern betwixt good and evil? It is likely the High Priests and Pharisees did thus blaspheme in those days, and that the rather, because from their own feigned sanctity, they were the more apt to suspect the same in others: But what? must we needs follow them, or this Bishop in this? But to proceed with this Bishop, Saint *James* (says he) gives us a full description of true Religion.

Wisdom from above is first pure, then peaceable, gentle, and easy to be entreated, full of mercy and good fruits, without judging, and hypocrisy.

None of these properties will agree with the Religion of Puritans. It is not pure, for it allows Usury, Sacrilege, Disobedience, Rebellion, etc. It is not peaceable, for these men are the incendiaries of Christendom. It is not gentle, nor easy to be entreated, for they are more austere than *Cato,* and not to be moved by persuasion or command. It is not full of mercy and good fruits, for they are all for sacrifice, nothing for mercy; for the first Table, not the second; for faith, not charity; they pull down Churches, but build no Hospitals. It is not without judging, for they are known to be most rigid censurers. And he is an hypocrite which spies a mote in his brother's eyes, and not a beam in his own.

Here is a confused proof, that such Puritans are hypocrites, but no proof at all, that this man is such a Puritan. If my Lord *Say* be such a Puritan, this denotes him an hypocrite, but this does not prove that my Lord *Say* or *Brooke,* or *Dod,* or *Clever,* etc. or any the most famous Puritan living is guilty of Usury, Sacrilege, Rebellion, pulling down of Churches, setting the World on fire, or of renouncing the second Table and all works of justice and charity, or of censuring and condemning malignantly other men: If these things were true of particular men, calumny were needless; Accusation would better suppress them. And sure it is not out of favor that Law proceeds not, for malice has often enough showed her teeth, and would have bitten if she could, neither would she now calumniate if she could accuse.

The Bishop expects not to be believed, if he puzzle, and work some into doubt, it is sufficient: but since bitter censuring, and calumnious condemning of others is so infallible a sign of hypocrisy, how does the Bishop wipe this off from himself? Can Puritans speak worse of any, than he doth of Puritans? Sure they may well join with him upon this issue, that the greatest slanderer is the greatest hypocrite; and yet seek no further for slanders, than this very speech, wherein he so eagerly inveighs against slander; but if individuals cannot be thus convinced by the Bishop, how shall these signs and symptoms be applied to whole Sects, Religions, Kingdoms?

The most ordinary badge of *Puritans* is their more religious and conscionable conversation, than that which is seen in other men's: and why this should make them odious or suspected of hypocrisy amongst honest and charitable men, I could never yet learn. A seeming religious consists in doing actions outwardly good, and the goodness of those actions is apparent to man; but the false hypocritical end of them is only discerned by God: and therefore with what conscience can I condemn that good which is visible, for that evil which is not visible? *Say, Brooke, Dod, Clever, etc.* are known to me; yet no otherwise but as men singularly devout, and as all the Prophets, and Apostles would, if they were now living: and shall I conclude, because they seem so, therefore they are not so? I am so far from this, that my own conscience binds me to honor them, and that in those things, wherein I have not the grace to follow them. I have been a diligent inquirer into *Puritans,* and have exactly tried them three ways. First, in themselves; and so I find them zealous, at least seeming so outwardly, and distinguished principally from other men by their remarkable, and singular zeal to God and the Truth: and this to me is no ground of uncharitable censure. Secondly, in those, which in these times think and speak charitably of them; and they are so many in number, and of so good quality, that indeed to the Popish and Episcopal faction, all the Kingdom almost seems *Puritanical;* but for this I cannot think the worse of them. But thirdly, when I consider *Puritans,* and compare them with their common notorious adversaries, then their goodness seems most evident to me, as if it were legibly engraved in the open wickedness and scandal of their chief opposers. Nothing but Truth, Holiness, and Goodness, seems to me to be the cause, that Papists do so implacably abominate them: that our proud Hierarchists, Ambidexters, and Neuters in Religion, do so uncessantly pursue their subversion; that Court-flatterers, and time-serving Projectors, and the ravenous Caterpillars of the Realm, do so virulently prosecute them with defamations and contumelies; that Stage-poets, Minstrels, and the jesting Buffoons of the age, make them the principal subject of derision: lastly, that all the shameless rout of drunkards, lechers, and swearing ruffians; and the scum of the vulgar are so tickled with their reproach, and abuse. Certainly, nothing but an unappeasable antipathy could be the cause of all this, and no testimony of goodness can be more sure, unerring, and unanswerable than such antipathy.

Amongst wicked men there may be particular hatred, but not a general antipathy: One wicked man hates not another as wicked, but rather loves him therefore, or else the World did not observe a decorum in loving her own, and hating strangers. As there cannot be division in Satan's kingdom; so there cannot be communion or compatibility betwixt Christ's and Satan's Subjects. But 'tis a miserable thing to see how far this word *Puritan* in an Ethical sense dilates itself. Heretofore it was Puritanical to abstain from small sins; but now 'tis so to abstain from gross open sins. In the mouth of a drunkard, He is a *Puritan* which refuseth his cups; In the mouth of a swearer, he which fears an oath; In the mouth of a Libertine, He which makes any scruple of common sins; In the mouth of a rude Soldier, He which wisheth the *Scotch* war at an end without blood. It is sufficient that such men think themselves tacitly checked and affronted by the unblamable conversation of *Puritans.* Bishop *Lake* that good and godly man moved at the declining state of his time is said to have expressed his regret thus: We fear, saith he, a relapse into Popish error, and superstition; but my heart misgives me worse than so: Utter irreligion and Atheism, methinks, begins to prevail strangely amongst us: we are not so likely to lose the light of truth, as the heat of zeal; and what benefit is in Religion, where the name of it is honored, but the power of it is not at all seen? where God's will is truly understood, but his commands are wholly slighted? where men know like Christians, but live like Heathens? The soul of Religion is hearty devotion, and that grows daily more and more ridiculous amongst us; and yet Religion without the soul of it, is rather a curse than a blessing to us. No impiety is so heinous in an ignorant Sodomite, as want of piety is in a right instructed Israelite. In this wise I have heard that good Prelate did complain; and this makes me think, that he had in his complaint some respect to this word *Puritan,* than which, certainly the Devil hath not a more fatal engine whereby to confound Religion, and to subvert all true zeal, goodness, and devotion. Thus far it appears what a vast circumference this word *Puritan* has, and how by its large acception it is used to cast dirt in the face of all goodness, Theological, Civil, or Moral: so that scarce any moderate man can avoid its imputation. And thus it does mischief to men, not commonly noted for *Puritans,* but if a man be so noted, though perhaps irregularly, then it is farther otherwise abused: for all such a Man's evil shall be charged upon his *Puritanism,* and all his good defaced for his *Puritanism.* Such a man is condemned for murder, and adultery; and at his death gives strong assurances of unfeigned repentance, and contrition of heart. He was a *Christian,* a *Protestant,* a *Minister,* a *Puritan;* yet this crime is recorded and blown abroad, not for the shame of *Christians, Protestants, Ministers,* but of *Puritans.* And as for his attestation of deep humiliation, how excellent soever, the honor of them, if any be acknowledged, shall redound to the *Christian,* the *Protestant,* the *Minister,* to anything else except the *Puritan.*

Howsoever in the first place it ought to be observed, that an unclean stream does not always receive its uncleanness from the filth of the Fountain, but in the second place a pure stream necessarily infers a pure Source. 'Tis true, Trees are known by their fruits, and so are Men generally by their works; but this similitude holds not in all men, at all times: for good men sometimes commit foul sins, and bad men perform laudable services. *David* defiles *Uriah's* wife, and to conceal it from the world, makes drunk and murders *Uriah;* and together with him casts away the lives of many other faithful Soldiers: yet nothing moved at this his own misdoing, at the same time He sentences to death a Subject of his for damnifying a neighbor, to the value of a poor Lamb. What might *Joab,* and the other privy *Ministers* of these his foul deeds, censure all this while of this his externally professed sanctity, and purity, and strictness in point of justice to other men; or of his so great indignation against petty offenders? What might they judge of the root, from whence these fruits sprung? did they conclude these fruits good? or did they conceive that such fruits might grow upon a good stock? It's strange, that He which would be so rigid to a petty Felon, should himself find no remorse at his own murder and oppression, in spoiling so gallant a Commander, of his wife, of his sobriety, of his life, and to continue so long a time without regard either what himself had done, or what *Uriah* had suffered. But it's well, *David* lived in those times when the name of *Puritanism* was not invented to blast all goodness: had he lived amongst us, he had been accounted a *Puritan,* and being a *Puritan,* God might have forgiven him, but the world never would: but it seems the world was not then poisoned with the same base word, though I believe under some other nickname goodness was always odious: for we read, that for that very sin of *David,* God's name was evil spoken of amongst the wicked. So *Solomon* the Son of seduced *Bathsheba,* if we censure him by many of his actions, perhaps *Jeroboam,* and *Ahab* that made *Israel* to sin, were not personally addicted to so much excess of bodily lust, and pollution, nay perhaps many Heathens and *Turks* have detested his enormous lubricities.

I speak not this to countenance sin, but to discountenance rash censures of sinners, wishing all that think themselves frail and mortal, to turn their eyes inwards, and to lay their hands upon their own mouths, for bearing to censure all sins, but most especially the most latent and obscure of all sins, hypocrisy.

Solyman the magnificent is held the honestest of all the Princes which reigned in his time, not excepting Christian Princes, nay not excepting the great Father of them all, the Apostolic man of *Rome:* yet this is no shame to Christianity, but to Christians rather; nay I wish it might be accounted rather a rebuke, than a shame; rather a rebuke to humble them, than a shame to confute them. For *Christ* tells us that many times the first are last, and last first, God sees not as man sees , and yet he that will judge uprightly ought to see as God sees, and not as Man. So much of the extensive infamy of this word *Puritan,* now of its intensive malignancy: but little more needs to be spoken hereof, for he which tells you who is a Puritan, for the most part tells what is a Puritan.

The Papist we see hates one kind of Puritans, the Hierarchist another, the Court Sycophant another, the sensual Libertine another; yet all hate a Puritan, and under the same name many times hate the same thing. He which is an enemy to our Religion which is the truth, hates the Puritan as an enemy to Truth; He which is an enemy to Piety, Policy, Morality, charges the Puritan of being the same: Wherefore whatsoever is hated by the perverted and disaffected in Religion, Piety, Policy, Morality, is a Puritan, and whosoever is a Puritan, is censured, hated, and slandered as a man perverted and disaffected in Religion, Piety, Policy, and Morality.

This sufficiently appears by the common slanders of all goodness in these days, and particularly by the Bishop of *Downe,* for as he justifies Jesuits, Anabaptists, and the Powder-Traitors before Puritans; so he describes, and proscribes whole Religions, Sects, and Kingdoms for Puritans.

In the year of grace 1588, when the *Spanish Armada* had miscarried, notwithstanding that his holiness of *Rome* had so peremptorily christened it, and as it were conjured for it, One of that Religion was strangely distempered at it, and his speech was as 'tis reported, God himself was turned *Lutheran:* By which, for certain, he meant Heretical. 'Tis much therefore that my Lord of *Downe,* now that Episcopacy is so foiled in *Scotland,* has not raged in the like manner, and charged God of turning Puritan: but surely, if he has spared God, he has not spared anything else that is good; and if he has spared to call God Puritan, he has not spared to call Puritan Devil: but to conclude, if the confused misapplication of this foul word Puritan be not reformed in *England,* and that with speed, we can expect nothing but a sudden universal downfall of all goodness whatsoever. *Aelius Adrianus* the Emperor, about an hundred years after our Savior, having been certified by *Serenius Granianus, Proconsul* of *Asia,* that the Christians in those parts were illegally oppressed by the malice of unjust Sycophants, sends this his imperial edict to the next successor *Menutius Fundanus.*

If the Provincials can prove ought against the Christians, whereof they charge them, and can at the bar of justice make good the same, let them proceed in a judicial course: but let them not approach the Christians merely for the name, by clamoring, and railing scandals against them: for it is expedient, if any be disposed to accuse, that the accusation be throughly known, and judicially tried by you; therefore if any accuse the Christians that they transgress the Laws, see that you judge and punish according to the quality of the offense, but if any upon spite or malice by way of calumny complain against them, see you chastise such for their malice, and repay them with condign punishment. I began with a *Marquesse,* I end with an *Emperor:* both read the same lecture, both teach us a difference betwixt privy malicious calumny and open judicial accusing, or impleading; God send us to hearken to both, as much as the necessity of our case requires it.

FINIS

TO THE READER.

READER,

I Have said enough to make myself condemned for a *Puritan,* and by consequence all which I have said to be condemned for *Puritanical:* but verily, if thou art not an *Antipuritan* of the worst kind, I am not a Puritan. In my opinions I am not scrupulous or precise, in my life I am not strict, or austere, the more is my blame; if thou art a downright *Protestant,* and no more, I am the same, and no more. If thou thinkest some men religious which affect not the name of *Puritan,* I think so too: if thou thinkest most men irreligious which hate the name of *Puritan,* I think so too: if thou art not to me a violent *Antipuritan,* I have no quarrel with thee; nor am I a *Puritan* to thee: if thou art, hate me as a profest *Puritan,* and I will thank thee for the honor of it. Farewell.

Thine to fear thee, more than hate thee, and
> to fear thy malice rather than justice,
> > *Philus Adelphus.*

10

John Bastwick

The Confession, 1641

JOHN BASTWICK (1593–1654) studied at Emmanuel College in Cambridge and later received his M.D. degree in Padua. He supported himself by the practice of medicine and wrote numerous works, first in fluent classical Latin and later in English, on ecclesiastical controversies of the day. His vigorous attacks on episcopacy soon cost him a fine of one thousand pounds and a brief imprisonment in the Gatehouse; later, in 1637, when he was tried with William Prynne and Henry Burton, he was sentenced to pay a fine of five thousand pounds, to have his ears cropped, and to remain in prison for life. In 1640 he was released from prison by the Long Parliament and compensated for his fines. In 1642, serving as a captain in the parliamentary army, he was captured and again imprisoned, though briefly. He emerged to write against the bishops and later against the Levellers as well.

Bastwick's confession lives up to its title. It is a highly personal utterance, partly self-serving in its attempt to exculpate the author from charges of disloyalty. As a definition of puritanism, it gives no details of religious practice or belief, focusing instead on moral character and demeanor. About the puritans Bastwick makes several interesting observations. During his youth he heard the term *puritan* used frequently in extreme reproach, and even in condemnation, though in his locale very few people could be designated by it. Yet the few so-called puritans he met then and the many he met later turned out to be the most honest, trustworthy, and happy of all men. This concept of the happy puritan contrasts directly with the popular notion of the puritan forever troubled, groaning, rolling his eyes up to heaven, and wringing his hands, or with the equally familiar descriptions of the puritan as an intemperate, fiery zealot. Bastwick seems to have the stereotypes in mind as he draws his picture of a puritan serene in his faith, relied upon and trusted in extremities even by his abusers.

Against the honest, maligned puritan, Bastwick opposes the arrogant, prosperous bishop. He does not attack episcopacy itself; he expresses due regard for bishops who remain subservient to the authority of the king. Apparently he accepts the bishop in a pastoral, but not in a political, role. But the distinction between good and bad bishops is almost lost in the vehemence of his attacks upon those who set themselves above civil power and law to usurp the authority of civil officers—and who have fined and imprisoned Bastwick for a work in which his arguments were held invalid because they were based only on Scripture. The fundamental opposition here places loyal and happy puritans, humble bishops, Bastwick himself, and the king on one side and bishops who wield secular power on the other.

The Confession Of the faithfull Witnesse of *Christ,* Mr. *John Bastwick* Doctor of Physick. Wherein he doth declare his *Education,* and the grounds of his *Conversion,* and *Constancie, in the true profession of Faith.* With the Reasons wherefore hee became an Adversary to our *Bishops,* whom he proveth to be the *Toes of Antichrist,* and dangerous *Prelates* to abide in our *Church. With a Relation of their great pride, in setting the Kings Picture over their Dresser in the High Commission Court, with his hat off, and his Crown and Scepter laid downe before their Worships, like a Delinquent. By John Bastwick Doctor of Physicke.* London printed, and are to bee sold by H. W. 1641.

The confession of Master *John Bastwick* Doctor of *Physick.*

I have heard many Sermons at the Court, yet never did I hear any, wherein I saw not the PURITAN brought up, with one scorn or other, and some notorious lies told of them. So that I wonder not that those poor men are thought so evil of, though a most innocent and harmless people as any lives upon the Earth. For when the place of God itself, from whence truth should only sound, is made a Theater of lying and false accusations, no wonder that the King's Majesty, and Nobles of the Kingdom, have a prejudicate opinion of them they call *Puritans,* when they expect nothing but truth and veritable narrations from that place.

In my younger days (that I may in something relate my own condition) *I was bred in as great a hatred of Puritans,* as my tender years were capable of, as it is well known, and thought those men not worthy to live, yet knew not any of them, (our Country having then scarce two in it) neither was there a Sermon perhaps in half a year thereabouts, and that read out of a paper book, and half of it commonly was railing against the *Puritans.* But when it pleased God that some of those, that spake evilest of them (through surfeiting, and excess had brought themselves to languishing sickness and after to Death itself) I say, when those men, in their greatest extremities, chose rather to trust them, yea and to prefer them, before their own brethren and nearest kinsfolks, and bequeath their children and Estate into their hand, and then being also demanded the reason of such trust, and confidence in them, whom they had reputed the worst of men before, and most of all traduced, and hated, they then openly declared themselves, and their opinion of them, saying that they were now dying men, and that it was now time to speak the truth, and that they in their hearts believed they were the true servants of the Lord, howsoever despised and contemned in the world and withal they desired that their souls might go the way that theirs went.

I say, when I saw such a wonderful change in these men, who were many of them, of knowledge and understanding in all Religions, and some of them travelers and Courtiers, and that now on their deathbeds, they should give such an approbation, and so honorable testimony of those men, of whom they had in their prosperity spoken so maliciously, I being then of years of discretion, and better able to discern and judge of things that differ, began more seriously to consider of that matter, and so much the more studious I was, because I had in some sort, seen the vanity of all pleasures, having indeed been bred in nothing else. The right way then to find blessedness, was my only aim: which through God's special favor and benediction upon my earnest endeavors, daily reading of the Word and holy Scriptures, private duties, godly society, and frequent hearing of the word, which is only able to save our souls, I found out, to the praise and honor of his name be it spoken. And I then well perceived, looking into the lives and manners of men, that those that were commonly branded with the name of Puritans, were the happiest, and that if any were eternally blessed, they were such of them as squared their lives in sincerity according to their profession.

And lest that I might through an overweening conceit of some seeming blessedness in them, be mistaken; I contented not myself with home-comparing of men and domestical experience, but I resolved to seek out still a more excellent way, if there were any; whereupon I went into foreign Nations, and lived amongst all sorts of men, and in the greatest Princes' Courts convers-ing among all ranks and orders of them, and that many years, and amongst all professions, Courtiers, Soldiers, Scholars, Citizens, Merchants, and among all sects, of factions, and religions, and examining all those in the balance of judgment, I found none in life and death happy, and truly comfortable, but those that are branded with the name of *Puritans,* or at least those that live and die in their Faith. And for my own particular, to speak now my Conscience, I had rather go the way of the meanest *Puritans,* that live and die according to their profession, than of the greatest Prelates that ever lived upon the earth; and this I speak in the presence of God, for of the one's happiness I am as sure, as the Word of God is sure, and of the other's I can promise nothing he living in Rebellion to God all the days of his life, and his Repentance not known unto me.

And notwithstanding, I say, all this, that these are such an holy people: yet are they made but the off-scouring of the world, and of all things and brought upon every Stage, and into the Pulpit, as fittest for ludibry by the Players, Priests, and Prelates, yea and in their Courts it is enough to ruin a man's cause, if his adversary can but taint him with the name of a Puritan; but most especially are they vilely abused by the *Priests and Prelates* in their pulpits.

Now, I say, if it be lawful in them, to make plays of honest men, and to feign what they please against them: I pray let it be lawful in me, in merriment to speak the truth of them, which as near as I can I will not transgress. If some shall say, they have not so great trains nor so much ado in their marching; I affirm, that at all times, *they go more like Princes, than humble Ministers of Christ, and the Apostles' Successors,* of whom we never read they came ever in Coach or on horseback, but when *Paul was mounted by authority;* or that they had ever a servant to attend them, much less such pomp and State: and yet one of them converted more souls in one day, than all the Prelates ever did that ever I read of: neither to speak truly have I heard of any they ever converted, but of many thousands they have confounded. But now to the matter in hand, because one of their abetters said not long since, that they had not such attendance as I accuse them of. I say, if they have less company one day, they have more another, and whether they be their own or others' Servants, when they are in their company, be they the nobles themselves, they are all their attendants, and the best of them most heartily glad if by their service they can please them, and we know it usual that the demonstration of the retinue is always from the greatest, and they are found to be his followers. And I have heard the Pursuivants often brag of the greatness of their Master's attendance, and in such ample manner as I think the King's Majesty hath not commonly greater: and therefore that cannot be denied, which is daily practiced, And for their servants' insolency I have frequently both seen it and felt it. Now whereas you think, it will not be well taken *that I call Bishops, Priests, and Deacons, Antichrist's little toes;* and in my LITANY desire deliverance from them, and withal seem to accuse them of incontinency, all which you think will be censured of unadvisedness at least, if not thought scandalous and punishable.

To this I answer, first, that *By Bishops I understand the Prelates,* and by *Priests their own creatures, a generation unknown in the Church of Christ: and by Deacons the under Priests in this Kingdom,* Officers of which the Scripture knoweth nothing likewise. For *the Deacons* such as the Churches chose, and were allowed by the Apostles, they were men of gravity, full of faith and the Holy Ghost, men of wisdom and good government and honesty, and were the treasurers of the faithful and the Church of God, and distributed the liberality of the Saints amongst the poor indigent and necessitated brethren. *Now I know never a* Deacon in England *either guilty of any of those virtues before specified, or that was ever employed in that Office, or was thought fit to be trusted, with the treasury of the poor, or took the least care of them, whom ordinarily they trample upon and most reproachfully abuse with the name of rascality.* So that such Deacons as I pray against are limbs of the *Beast,* and the inferior order of shavelings and *such as ought to be spewed out of the Church as profitable for nothing but increase of wickedness.*

And for *Bishops* such as God appointed I honor them, and will maintain their dignity to the last drop of my blood, so far I am from praying against such. Neither did I ever speak unreverently against the *King's Bishops* and those that were appointed as an order in the State, till they had in their open Court renounced his authority, and run themselves by that, and many other notorious proceedings into a *Praemunire,* and so had made themselves enemies to his Prerogative royal, and delinquents against his Majesty, and under his Highness' displeasure, as by the statutes of the Kingdom they are proclaimed to be, and by the defenders of their proceedings in their Ecclesiastical Courts: who in a book set forth by their common consent, do conclude all these in a *Praemunire,* that challenge their authority *Jure divino* as the Pope and Clergy of *Rome,* which at this time they do.

And for your better satisfaction, look in the *Apology for proceedings in Courts Ecclesiastical* (a book made by the *Prelates'* own creatures) and in the first Chapter, you shall see all the Prelates by their own witness in a *Praemunire,* and delinquents against his Majesty in a high degree of contumacy.

And truly I think there was never such an affront put upon regal Dignity, as on that day I was censured, never such dishonor put upon the Scriptures, by such as would be thought Ministers of the word, and the Bishops and Pastors of Christ: Neither were the Scriptures ever more blasphemously abused, than they were at that time, in their open assembly, I shall briefly therefore tell you that day's work, of which there are a thousand witnesses, as also impious words against the most sacred word of God and divine Oracles of holy writ, by all which, you will see, I have good reason to call them ANTICHRIST'S LITTLE TOES, and to pray against them; for they are as desperately impious, and equally to be detested of all such as truly fear the Lord and the King. For if we compare them together, there will no disparity appear between them, they being every way as malicious against the word of God and his dear servants, *and as diametrally opposing regality as Antichrist himself.* But that all things may the more clearly be evidenced unto you, let me tell you that day's proceedings.

You must take notice, that howsoever, they had feigned some trivial Articles against me, they were all by the general consent of the Court thought so poor, as they openly averred they would not condemn me for them, and so much the rather, because those that had sworn to them, were proved to be my Capital enemies, and also, in their depositions to have sworn point-blank one against another, and like evil witnesses could not agree in swearing: therefore they condemn me only for my book which I writ in defense of Christ and his Kingdom, and of the King's most excellent Majesty's prerogative Royal, and supremacy against the Pope and Popish Bishops, provoked thereunto by a Papist; to which duty I was bound both by the law of God and the law of the land, and my special oath, all which I alleged at the bar, and furthermore added that in writing against the Bishop of *Rome, I* intend no such *Bishops as acknowledge their authority from Kings and Emperors, but only such Bishops that usurp authority over Kings and Emperors, and their fellow brethren and the Church of God jure divinos and so I had preferred in my* Book, *which I openly read here.*

And to speak the truth, I looked for favor and assistance in this combat, from the *Prelates;* never suspecting that they would have been my enemies for this endeavor, especially I having also in that place alleged the Acts and Statutes established by the public consent of the whole Kingdom in which it was ratified, that the Prelates have all their authority and jurisdiction which they now exercise, from the King, as immediately derived from him, and to affirm the contrary, is to be *ipso facto* an enemy of his Crown and Dignity. And as the Prelates were an order established by the King and State, I was so far from opposing them, that I never impeached their dignity in the least thing in all the book; neither would I ever have meddled with them, if they had kept their standing; but they like the evil Angels out of pride, not keeping their station, but openly renouncing the King's authority, and affirming, that Jesus Christ made them Bishops and that the holy Ghost consecrated them, and that they were Princes and had their thrones, and that before Kings, and all this *Jure divino:* by all which, they made me their enemy, they being delinquents against the King. And because I had ratified, whatsoever I had said in my book by the Word of God; they as they had before renounced the King's authority, and barbarously reviled me for my pains, most impiously, likewise vilified the holy Scripture, saying in their Sessions, that they looked for some great matter in my book, finding me so confident, but more diligently reading of it they found nothing but Scripture in it, which was the refuge of all Schismatics and Heretics: and that the Scripture could not be known to be Scripture, but by the Fathers, nor distinguished from the Apocrypha, but by the Fathers: nor the meaning of the Scripture could not be known but by the Fathers: and because the Fathers, as they find, were in their interpretation diverse from me (which notwithstanding is not so) therefore they condemned me.

But I pray, are not all these blasphemous, Popish, and Damnable assertions, could worse have been forged in the very conclave of hell? Is not this I pray you, to tell the spirit of God to his face he lies, and to teach another way to heaven than by the Scripture; which Christ the Son of God sendeth us to, and all the Prophets and Apostles, as to the Instructors of the simple, and able to make the man of God wise to salvation and perfectly furnished to every good work, and the which the holy Ghost compares to a Guide; and a Lantern for direction; and a light to conduct us in this our Pilgrimage and peregrination through the errors of the world, and to keep our feet in the paths of truth, and with the Prelates this great and glorious light; this Scripture must be so obscure, as it must be inferior to all things that have a power in themselves to declare and demonstrate their own nature, as fire to be fire, gold to be gold, light to be light. But the Scripture only that cannot be known, but by the help of others, to be the Word of God, it cannot be the word of God without the Fathers and their Interpretation of them; for the Scriptures themselves they are the only refuge of Schismatics, the cause of all errors, and that that cometh confirmed and proved only from Scripture, is ever to be suspected with the Prelates. *O*

Blasphemy, yea the book that hath nothing but Scripture, must be adjudged to the fire, and the Author of it given over to the Devil, fined 1000 £s, and censured to pay the costs of suit, and be debarred of his practice, only support left for the relief of his distressed family, to the utter undoing of him his poor wife and children, and all this forsooth, because there was nothing but Scripture in it. O horrible Impiety! The truth is, howsoever they seemed to condemn it; because it had nothing but Scripture that was not the occasion, but the very cause was, because I writ against the Pope Father *Antichrist,* such correspondency there is now between the Pope and the Prelates, that one cannot write against him, but the Prelates say by and by, that they are meant by it. *The Grolls.*

It is worth the looking on, to see the pride of the Prelates, in setting the King's picture over their dresser in the high Commission Court; for they have placed his Highness standing, with his hat off before their Worships like a delinquent, his Crown and Scepter laid low, as the poor Emperors and Kings were wont to stand before his impiety, the Pope, when they were cited to his Courts. Of which stories you may read many in King *James,* his Apology, to go no farther and in this very manner, have they set up the Portraits of our renowned King. And the very intrinsical Marrowbone of the matter is, they trample upon his Imperial dignity, while they seem to honor him, with whom they make themselves in the meantime Checkmates: for they say, they were before Christian Kings, and had their thrones, and that they were not beholding to them for their Honor and Dignity of Episcopality, for they were *Jure Divino,* that they were.

FINIS.

11

Some Considerations Tending to the Undeceiving Those,

Whose Judgements Are Misinformed by Politique

Protestations, Declarations, Etc., 1642

S*ome Considerations Tending to the Un-
deceiving Those, Whose Judgements Are Misinformed by Politique Protestations,
Declarations, etc.,* written at the beginning of the civil war, is a plea for the
unity of all protestant clergy in support of the Parliament. The work is
carelessly printed and haphazardly punctuated. Yet to impose a modern
system of punctuation upon it would be to destroy its rhetorical flavor and
to resolve—sometimes no doubt incorrectly—the numerous ambiguities
of syntax faced by its contemporary readers.

The author professes loyalty to the king but antagonism toward his evil
advisers, thus making a fairly standard, diplomatic distinction between
monarchy as an institution and the conduct of the reigning monarch. The
writer also denounces Cavaliers and the church ministers who flourished
under episcopacy. Although implicitly accepting a distinction between
puritans and protestants, the author attempts to minimize the difference
and, on the whole, to support the more thoroughgoing reformers. The
pamphlet appears to be addressed mainly to the more religious of the
conservative clergy who opposed the parliamentary reforms. The only fault
it attributes to the puritans is excessive zeal.

Among the puritan actions noticed by the author is the destruction of
organs, crosses, and surplices. Because the audience is protestant in general, the actions are not defended but instead minimized as dealing with

trivial matters. The scruples of the puritans should be respected on the logical ground that if any tenet or practice is very important to a conscientious person, it should be accepted by one who sees it as unimportant, and objections should be honored similarly. This plea for tolerance implies a distinction in zeal between the puritan and the protestant, the latter's seeming almost careless or lukewarm in religion. Opposed to both are the bishops, who stand for tithes, conformity, and arrogance in their use of oppressive power. But their worst fault, or at least the fault most forcefully addressed in this tract, is their attempt to subvert the revolution by setting many well-intentioned clergymen against the puritans and thereby fostering disunity in the parliamentary ranks.

Political considerations seem more important than religious issues in the author's mind. Because armed conflict has begun, he addresses the military situation. He belittles the strengths of the Cavaliers and heartens his audience by noting the strength of the Parliament's militia, army, and navy. In this context the past opposition of the puritans to George Villiers, first duke of Buckingham, and to Sir Thomas Wentworth, first earl of Strafford, deserves mention, since it makes the puritans defenders of the Parliament's cause even before the Parliament took up arms. The puritans emerge as extremely loyal, steadfast, and dependable allies.

Some Considerations Tending to the undeceiving those, whose judgements are misinformed by *Politique Protestations, Declarations,* etc. Being a necessary discourse for the present times, concerning the unseasonable difference between the *Protestant* and the PURITAN.

[1642.]

The end of the Parliament's consultations, and actions, is to free the Kingdom (the care whereof is to them by the Kingdom committed) from all those heavy tyrannies and oppressions which for many years, against express Laws, and cautions to the contrary, have surrounded and overwhelmed the Kingdom, all which, if we have not a desire to let them slip our memories, the Parliament's first Remonstrance will fully present unto us. Those men that do oppose the Parliament, are generally such as some way or other have thrived under those pressures, as being made instruments and actors in them, or else being addicted to vice and looseness, found that connivance and indulgence, than which, in times more reformed they cannot expect. Those men that do now side with, and assist the Parliament, are such as in those corrupt times were trodden under foot, such as were vexed and impoverished by insulting Courts, and Court-officers, forced against conscience to persuade to the breach of the Sabbath, compelled to fly their Country, or separate from the Church, by inducing vain and empty Ceremonies, which direct our minds from consideration of God's love to us in Christ, and are utterly inconsistent with the true, and spiritual worship of God; and indeed therefore pressed upon us, that thereby their friends might be known from their foes, the easy to be abused from the more difficult, that they might be embraced, and have all encouragements both from the Minister, and men of high places; and these disgraced, prosecuted, and though of never so honest lives, yet if in all things not conformable, scandaled, and made odious. Ceremonies were therefore too pressed upon us, that by them the Church becoming more pompous, and outwardly specious, the Clergy (by whom the Statesmen were especially to do their ill-intended work) might win greater esteem, and grown more and more reverenced by the people, who seldom they know dive into the reasons of things, but are usually carried away by outward shows and appearances. The Parliament's other friends are such as have been tormented with the permitted corruption of Lawyers, those devouring Locusts, no less ravening than the Egyptian ones that overspread that Land; such likewise as had lost the liberty of Trade, for the gaining of which, they served a long and tedious apprenticeship, by unlawful engrossments, and Patents; and all the multitude of good men; who are sensible either by their own, or their neighbors' sufferings, of the injuries of former times, or desirous to prevent and divert our oppression and slavery for the future: Now as it is a notable policy of evil men, though of quite different and opposite conditions to combine and associate together against all that oppose them, bearing with, and passing by anything for the present, though at other times much distasteful. So how much more does it behoove the honest men of this Kingdom, who are likely to taste equally the sweets of liberty, or the bitter pills of slavery, however they may be persuaded otherwise for the present, to unite themselves heart and hand, to join together as one man, against all those whom they shall discern either to oppose the Parliament, or endeavor to raise divisions and differences among themselves. The only way for our enemies to do their work, is not by strength, and force of Arms, for whatever their brags be, and how great soever their boasts by which they would seem to have what they have not, that thereby they may encourage their party, and dishearten their adversaries, yet indeed their forces are but small, their provisions scanty, their means and money only supplied by rapine, which cannot be lasting, having neither Forts, nor Shipping, so that it cannot be that by strong hand they should have any hope to do their work: No certainly, and yet notwithstanding they still dare to hold up the Cudgels, seem as confident as ever, bear up, as if the world were of their side; what should be the reasons thereof, reasons there are, we must persuade ourselves, it is not to be supposed that they are foolhardy, or that the sense of their many mischiefs have made them desperate, because past hope of reconcilement (though they well may) their Councils are notable, and surely come not short of the most able the world affords, their subtleties exceeds the Fox's, or the Serpent's, Rome's or Spain's; whose most damnable glory it is, that from mean beginnings they, by their wits especially, have raised themselves to the most extended tyrannies in the Christian world: and why should our politic enemies then despair? Since their wits are as quick, their consciences as deeply pained and senseless, many of our people as easy to be deluded as ever men were, having the assistance of former contrivances in making men slaves, furnished with Machiavil's, and *Stafford's* instructions from *Florence,* with all the assistance Rome's consistory, or Spain's can afford: and what force cannot do, deceit may: a subtle deceitful Declaration may do much more mischief than an Army, the one kills men outright, and so leaves them unserviceable for both sides, but deceitful words, when for want of consideration, unsettledness of judgment, and weak information, they captivate men, they make them not only dead to good men's assistance, and their Country's service, but promoters likewise of their deluder's interest, to the insensible ruin and slavery of their brethren, and in conclusion, of themselves. Deceits and delusions are the principal weapons with which the evil Counselors now fight; by which they subdue and captivate the understandings and affections of men; to scatter these, they hurry about from one County into another, and there at Assises, and other forced Assemblies practice, in one place they color and gloze over their own evil actions, with seeming pretenses of Law, Religion: in another, they scandalize and traduce the Parliament, for as they cannot want paint to make foul and unsightly actions seem fair and specious, so neither can they want dirt and mire to disfigure the best formed, and most honest enterprises in the world; words are never defective to make evil seem good, and good evil: what villainy was there ever committed, or what injustice, but words and pretenses might be found to justify it: Monopolies were once pleaded legal, and very wholesome for the people, we were once persuaded Ship-money was lawful, and now Commission of Array; if unjust things were offered to us, as they are, without disguise and artificial covering, they would appear so odious, as that each man would cry out upon them, and therefore it is a high point of policy to make the worst things show fairest, speak best, when they intend most mischief. In other Counties the people were thanked for their affections and assistance, when they found them wiser than to yield any; and when they were driven by necessity to a place, they would seem to be invited by love and certainty of compliance, when God knows in many places they found it much otherwise, and would likewise elsewhere too, but that the people were necessitated to their assistance by force, rather than forward, out of any liking. Well, their policies and delusions are most numerous, and every day increasing, and therefore it behooves every wise man to stand upon his guard, to be wary and watchful that he be not apprehended by their subtleties: in nothing there is required greater care, their invasions being insensible, and having once seized upon a man, he no longer dislikes, but approves of them, they force a man to love what erewhiles he hated, what he but now cried down, to plead for, and not to observe, because his intentions are honest, and he means no ill, that he is even against his knowledge his Country's enemy: He that can give any cautions how to resist their wiles, or show wherein we are already seduced by our cunning adversaries, doth do very good service to his Country, and deserves to be heard; this discourse was written principally for that end, namely, to discover to all good men how they have suffered themselves to be wrought upon by the adversary in a case very considerable, and thereby, though they observe it not, are become friends to their Country's chief foes, and foes to their principal friends. The work of evil Counselors, as it is to unite and join together their friends, so is it likewise to separate and divide their foes amongst themselves: all such are their foes as truly love their own liberty, and desire to free themselves from their insulting tyranny: it must needs be very advantageous to them, if by any means they can divide these, for being disjoined, they cannot possibly be so powerful against them as otherwise they would be, did they continue at union: now amongst many other ways that they have used to accomplish this end, there is not one hath been more effectual than in raising, and cherishing differences concerning forms and circumstances about Religion, that so setting them together by the ears about shadows, they may in the meantime steal away your substance: there is no difference they full well know is so permanent, as that which any way touches upon Religion, and therefore like cunning Pioneers, have lighted upon what is likely to make the greatest breach, which by continual plying the work, the difference daily increasing, it is much to be feared that all the pains the

Parliament takes, the assistance of good men, the hazards of our resolute soldiers, or whatever endeavors else are used for the accomplishing of good men's desires, will by this one difference, if continued, be utterly frustrate, and come to naught: for it is almost come to that pass, that the Puritan and Sectaries, as they are called, are more odious to the Protestant, than the Cavalier, Malignant, or Papist: all our discourses are diverted now by the cunning practice of the Politician from our forepast calamities, plots, and conspiracies of lewd men, from thinking what will be the best ways to speed and advantage our undertakings for our liberty, to railings against the Puritan, to cross and oppose the Puritan, to provoke him by many insolencies, and affronts to disorders, and then to inveigh with all bitterness against his disorders: if at such times as these, when so great a work is in hand, as the freeing of us from slavery, we can be so drowsily sottish as to neglect that, for the satisfying our giddy and domineering humor, what can be said of us, but that our fancy is dearer to us than our liberty, that we care not what goes to rack, though it be our substantial Religion, Laws, and Liberties, so we do but please ourselves in crying down our Brethren, because they are either more zealous, or else more scrupulous than ourselves: These things my friends, (for all good men are such) do show that you are not considerate, nor do not sufficiently bear in mind what was told you in the Parliament's first Remonstrance, that it was (and still is) one of the principal works of our common enemy, to sow division between the Protestant and Puritan, you have been too easy, and quickly wrought upon by him for the accomplishing that work: I would to God you would lay it to heart; the Puritan intends no mischief to any, you may assure yourselves he does not: if you inquire you shall find that they had no hand in our former oppressions, they were no maintainers of any unjust courses, or Courts, unless by those many fines which were extorted from them, for that they of all men had the courage to withstand their injuries: we hear of daily plunderings, rapes, and murders of the Cavaliers, women with child run through, and many other butcheries, and yet we pass by these, as if by no interest they concerned us, and let fly our speeches only against the Puritan for plucking a rail down, or a pair of Organs, a Surplice, Crucifix, or painted window, which are indeed no way conducible to the substantial worship of God, and yet retained by the ill-disposed Clergy, as fuel to yield matter to that discord they would continue amongst you: See how much to blame we are, see how exceedingly the politician has deluded us, that we should do thus, and yet see not that we do unwisely. If thy brother be weak and thou strong, bear with his weakness, or if the Puritan esteem thee weak and himself strong, it will be a good lesson to him; if we be strong we should bear with them that are weak; if we are weak we should not judge them that are strong, it will be no shame for anyone to take the Apostle's advice; let not slight and indifferent things divide our affections; let them not especially when substantial things be at the stake; it is all one as if our enemy being in the field with full purpose and speed to destroy us, we should turn aside to exclaim against a man that flung dirt upon us or laughed at us: and wholly neglect altogether to defend ourselves: what a shame will it be unto us, when hereafter it is said that the English might have freed themselves from oppression and slavery, but that in the doing of it they neglected their common enemy, and fell at variance among themselves for trifles. Ceremonies and other things that occasion difference, are stickled for by the Protestant, not for that they think them necessary, for surely unless it be for some indirect end they cannot be urged to be so, but for that they are not yet taken down by authority: The Puritan they would have them taken away for that they conceive them vain, unwarrantable by God's Word; relics of the Romish Religion not thoroughly purged away, and therefore they desire they should be left off by us, which are the principal cause of their separation from us: In all differences to be unwilling to reconcile, shows not a spirit of love, which Christians should ever be possessed withal, but of pride and contention, the Protestant hath not the engagements of conscience upon him, as the Puritan has, and therefore may the easier bear with the Puritan's infirmities, if meat offend my weak brother I will eat no meat as long as I live, what an excellent thing were it if we could have that holdfast over ourselves that the Apostle had to refrain from anything how pleasant and dear soever unto us, rather than give any offense, or occasion any difference between ourselves and weak brethren: let every man think of the answering this question to himself: whether if lewd men do get the better over the Parliament and honest men of the Kingdom, either Protestant or Puritan are likely to be any other but slaves: Certainly if any of them do persuade themselves otherwise, they are like the stiff-necked and unwieldy Hebrews, that wished they were slaves in *Egypt* again, where the much loved flesh pots were, for that it was troublesome and dangerous passing through the *Wilderness* into *Canaan,* a land of plenty and lasting liberty. Be not deceived with deluding thoughts of former times, when plenty covered our oppressions, and because of peace we could not see our slavery: it was a time when such as *Buckingham, Strafford,* domineering Bishops, corrupt and lawless Judges, grew rich and potent: when *Court's* Minions for no services but slavery and luxury were exalted, when offices were not conferred on foreseen virtue and honest desert, but were bought and sold;

when honors that ought to be the rewards of virtue, were by gold purchased, and they only deemed fit Subjects for both, that were easy to be corrupted, such as had stupid consciences, and would suffer their masters to undertake any dishonest employment. He that wishes for former times wishes for such times wherein it had been much better for a man to let go his right of inheritance, though never so apparently his, to any varlet that would have laid but any colorable claim to it, rather than have been worried by Court Mastiffs, and eaten to the bare bones by griping Judges and avaricious Lawyers; wherein a murder in one man was not so much punished as a word in another, wherein a poor man was hanged for stealing food for his necessity, and a luxurious Courtier of whom the world was never like to have any other fruits but oaths and stabs, could be pardoned after the killing the second or third man: wherein in a word, knaves were set upon honest men's shoulders, all looseness was countenanced, and virtue and piety quite out of fashion: In these times, who kept themselves so steady as the Puritan, who opposed against those exorbitant courses, and by that means who smarted more than they: sure, I think their sufferings are yet in each man's memory, who but they, or they especially withstood all Church innovations, and other taxes and impositions, for which both the Bishops and Clergy, as also the corrupt Statesman, and Projector were their profest and open enemies, and even then to make them odious, invented ridiculous names for them, and studied scurrilous tales and jests against them, and ever signed new devices concerning them, to direct our thoughts from our everyday's oppressions, to sport at the Puritan. The ways of wicked men are like the way of a Ship in the Sea, so quick and speedily covered, that without much observancy we cannot trace them: So that we see these endeavors to make the Puritan odious is no new policy, nor yet the reasons why it is endeavored, and how great a blemish it is unto our judgment, that though this deceit hath been so long in practice, and so apparently mischievous to good, and advantageous to bad men, we should not yet discover it, or being discovered and declared unto us, we should not lay it to heart, and endeavor to avoid it. Sure I think there is no more evident mark of our disaffections to the Parliament, than our invectives against the Puritan, whom the Parliament and all good men ought in all reason to esteem well of, for that they have been so abundant in their contributions, so forward in their services, so neglective of their private, to advance that necessary and most allowable work, both by God and all reasonable men in the world, of freeing us and our posterity from loathsome Tyranny and oppression: whatsoever faults the Puritan hath, this is not a time to cast them in his dish, neither are we certain that they are faults, we have but so digested them to ourselves, what he can say for himself, in his own justification, is not yet heard, nor is there yet a time of hearing: we may assure ourselves that the Parliament will endeavor all that possible they can to give all sorts of men that will not prove obstinate, and unsatisfiable, the best and largest satisfaction: If they should now go about it, or if they should at any time heretofore have enterprised it, they might in the meantime have had their throats cut, it is and hath been the endeavor of the King's evil advisers, to urge them always to the settlement of the Church, a work they know requires much time for the performance of it, and so must of necessity have diverted all considerations and provisions for their safety, when in the meantime those advisers would have been most active and vigilant, losing no jot of time, nor balking no opportunity or advantage to have fortified themselves, made a prey of the Parliament, and in their ruins have buried all that's near and dear unto us: We see, that though the Parliament have only intended one business, the defense and preservation of themselves, and the Kingdom, so great opposition hath yet been made, and so difficult a work have they found it, that there is no man can say they are too forward: and therefore if we will not willfully make ourselves a prey to our common enemy, let us resolve for the time to come firmly to unite our affections beyond the policy of evil-witted men to dissolve: let those whom the malignant and inconsiderate call Puritans, endeavor all that they can possibly, to give no offense to the Protestant, and let the Protestant be slow in taking any at the Puritan: the Puritan indeed is to blame in his not observing all he can to win by love, gentle behavior, such as differ from him in opinion, in not endeavoring all he can to bridle his passion, and not suffer his different opinion to cool his love and affection to other men: what? We have all need one of another, and till such time things are thoroughly canvassed, and examined (however each man concludes himself to be in the right (we know we are partial to ourselves) he may be mistaken, and upon better reasons which as yet he sees not may alter his judgment and be convinced; let us unite together as one man to the extirpation of certain and discovered enemies both of our substantial Religion, our laws, and liberties, that so all being quiet, and we assuredly free-men, all stratagems dissolved, and the sun of peace again appearing, the Church may be so purged and so religiously settled, that the Puritan may have no cause of separation (which cannot be according to his desire but that to which by the instigation of his conscience he is necessitated to) and so may be no longer an eyesore and distasteful to the Protestant, but both may with mutual joy and peace of conscience join together in praises and thanksgivings to that God, who by the free, and alone death of his Son atoned and reconciled us to himself, and in giving us his Son hath together with him given us all things also. But to what purpose will this, or other discourses of this nature be, when there is a sort of people in this kingdom, who make it their study and bend all their endeavors for to increase and enlarge this difference: and yet have full permission, and all opportunity that may be to do their work; neither could the politician have ever made this breach or extended it to that business it is at, but for the certain assistance of the Clergy, who for that end bound them his instruments, by the liberal distribution of honors and preferments, by enlargements of dignity and livings, by giving them power in Courts and letting them taste the sweets of domination, by authorizing them in their advance of tithes, multiplying their duties, favoring them in their abundant differences, and restless lawsuits; and in all likelihood they must be their servants who pay them such large wages; insomuch that in all the time of this Kingdom's slavery and wicked men's oppressions of us, who were greater promoters of both than the Clergy; what was the politic subject of their Sermons then, and discourses, but the advance of prerogative, and unlimited sway; the gaining of estimation to themselves not by their doctrines or lives, for what could be more corrupt and scandalous, but by subtle delusions, and delusive sophisms; the fitting of our minds for slavery, the abasing of our courages against injuries in Church or State; by preaching for obedience to all commands good or bad, under deceitful terms of active and passive, by which means injurious men were heartened in enduring mischiefs, and good men moped and stupefied to a patient sufferance of them, their very tongues tied up and no liberty given so much as to motion against apparent injuries, or to discover to the world the iniquity of them: This use is made of those most admirable gifts we admire the Clergy for, to this good end serves their great learning and excellent parts; and as in former times by these and many other ways they only employed their studies to make us apt and easy to admit our slavery without grudging or gainsaying, so do they still continue the Statesmen's hirelings, to further that difference between the Protestant and Puritan, which makes so much for their advantage: And that they may be truly serviceable, to this end they are brought up in the Universities fitted for the purpose; no man there countenanced unless he is like to prove a champion against the Puritan; the greater their abilities are that way, their preferments are answerable, insomuch, that generally those Ministers are only good, that trusting only to themselves, and not taking the pleasing course, could expect no encouragement from the Bishop or others in high places, but very content-edly did betake themselves to such places their honest friends and deserts obtained for them, whereas men of that other strain were almost courted into benefices, where the former benefits did not more sway with to justify injustice, and sow division, than the longing expectation after greater and greater preferments; and what though some have refused preferments, and yet are zealous in your work; it is well known yet that they live in abundance, drink the sweet, and eat the fat of the Land, are recompensed with large gifts, and abundant Legacies; who by a cunning refusal of what they need not, and perhaps they think would be too troublesome, have taken so deep root in unwatchful men's minds, that there are none so great promoters of this work as they; who likewise being the most subtle of all the tribe, order the business so, that what by their abilities of speech, reverent estimation men have of their persons, of their functions, of their sincerity, they even delude them as they list, and have so far fomented this fire of dissension that it is to be feared it will very shortly break out into a flame: they have even heightened this hatred to an insurrection, the people rise up one against another, grow into factions and acquaintances by wearing colors, and public meetings, outfacing authority, and slighting the most sovereign power even of the Parliament itself: nor is this likely in short time to be extinguished, though much care be used, and great pains taken for the doing it, so long as a cunning malicious sort of men are suffered without control or just punishment to yield new matter to this destructive flame of contention; to curb the license, and punish the insolencies of those licentious Clergymen may very well be one of the principal works of the Parliaments, whose earnest endeavors and noble undertakings do find no greater opposition from any sort of men, no not from the Cavalier himself, or the King's evil Councilors, than from these men of malice and dissension; many of them are Delinquents, and so voted, others likewise would appear to be so, did the people think it a fit time to make their complaints. Many of them are of scandalous and debauched lives, all of them indeed are bound by the respects they have to their own safety to destroy the Parliament, by whom they know, were they at leisure they should be sifted, and their crimes censured, and to bring in again the former government, wherein they found so great connivance in all sorts of vices whatsoever: And now what more seasonable counsel can there be to all sorts of men, than to try and examine all that they hear, to entertain nothing for the opinion we have of the man, for the judgment is never so likely to be deluded as when the person is too highly esteemed, to see likewise in how many respects the Clergyman is bound to make the Puritan odious to the Protestant, and how greatly disadvantageous that is to the work, all honest men are bound in conscience to further, and likewise to conclude those Clergymen disaffected that shall hereafter endeavor it, and to let both them and others in authority know it, to be firm in their affections to the Puritan, past all their subtleties to disunite them, that so all honest men being heartily united, the greater may be their force, and the kingdom's enemies the speedier subdued: the Puritan, Sectary, Brownist, and Anabaptists.

The Ministers under pretense of railing against, do scandalize and defame all the honest men of the Kingdom, yea even of the Parliament themselves: so that if we be not the more cautious we may be so far deluded, as to disesteem even their actions, not for that to any reasonable discreet man they can appear to be any other than as the actions of the most wise should be, but because they are approved of by the honest Puritan: It is not safe they think to rave against the Parliament point blank, they would then indeed appear so palpably malicious and villainously disaffected, that men would have much ado to tarry their trial by law without doing present execution on them: and therefore like men full of subtlety, they wound the Parliament through the Puritan's side, and therein take so vast a liberty, that almost provokes an honest hearted man beyond his patience; sometimes they speak in a doubtful sense, so as that all who are misled by them can understand them, and yet they think that if they should be questioned, as out of guilt of conscience they cannot but expect it they shall be able to give such an interpretation to their words, that thereby they can delude the holdfast of Law and the censure of justice: thus they provide an excuse before they act their villainy, and proceed as far as they imagine that will bear them out; what high time it is that these men should be crushed, lest in time they sow so many tares in the hearts of men, that no wisdom of man shall be able to pluck up, but that they choke even the seeds of good doctrine, and root out of our minds the very principles of reason: Another villainous work they have in hand, is to take away our courages and dull our resolutions by commending peace unto us, when we are necessitated to take up our Swords; what fools they imagine us to be, as if we did not know what were the sweets of peace, but then it must be accompanied with liberty, the bondman is at peace; there is peace, there is peace in a dungeon, yet I think no man can be heartily in love with such kind of peace, no certainly, if our liberty and our religion be much dearer to us then our lives, as I think they are to every wise man, then sure they must be dearer to us than our rest, our swords are drawn for them, and so long as they are violated, what peace? what peace? so long as the insolencies and conspiracies of unjust men, and their usurpations are so many? what peace? so long as those that would free us from former oppressions, and would provide for our future liberties, are in no safety but in continual hazard of their lives? were we not necessitated to it, it were madness to think we could take pleasure in shedding of our own bloods: what shallow men do they imagine us to be, that think, that through their sweet words, and smooth faces, we do not see their foul and mischievous intentions: yes to their grief of heart and the joy of all good men they behold that, notwithstanding they have in many other things deluded us, in this they have not; the *Militia* is settled in safe and trusty hands, the Forts and strongholds made good, the Navy secured and commanded by a faithful and courageous lover of his country, that a strong and a well-furnished Army is afoot to the terror of wicked men and we hope to the suppression; they are quite frustrate of their ends, all their cunning discourses and subtle motions for peace, though delivered with never so much pretended piety, and seeming love to our safeties, come short of their purpose, they have not thereby lulled us asleep, and so made us too secure, no, we have the courages of men, of valiant provoked men upon us, provoked by an insight into all our injuries, which are now fresh in our memories, provoked by discovery of their delusions, and animated by the amiable sight of liberty which we may now if we will ourselves, obtain, of which for many years we have been deprived: and therefore it is not good nor honest that they continue their invitations to peace, so long as the Parliament see it needful to provide for war. This it is when they will be overwise and pass the bounds of their office, nor are they more mistaken in this, than in other matters, especially when they plead the King's cause, their engagements and flatteries here make them stark blind, and let them not see how under stickling for the King's prerogative they comprehend under that such things, the obtaining whereof if duly considered would make his Majesty's office the most hazardous, and fraught with least content of anyone in the Kingdom. A negative voice they much stand for, a power of calling and likewise of dissolving Parliaments; these things because they carry power with them, and seem to add much greatness and high prerogative to the King, they stickling for them, and see not that if the King should have them, he would be thereby ever liable to the blame, and censures of the people; for if anything should be consulted of by the Parliament, and by them concluded to be safe and necessary for the Kingdom, and that the King by that power they claim for him, should cross it if the people should in the time to come by necessity for the want of what the Parliament would have provided for them, and the King would not, whom have they then to blame but the King: and he likewise must of necessity be under their hard opinions, should the neglect of calling Parliaments bring oppressions upon the people: or the too soon dissolving them without consent of the House before their business were fully dispatched. Both which in their

book of Canons and constitutions ecclesiastical, where without once mention-
ing the Parliament, they take liberty to make the King's Prerogatives what
they please, there I say have they peremptorily concluded the power of calling
and dissolving all assemblies to be the King's undoubted right, and would
likewise have possessed the people so by the quarterly reading of those decrees
of theirs in Churches by their own order: It is true indeed these commons
[canons (?)] are most justly damned by the Parliament, but by the remembrance hereof we may palpably observe, what a power they then usurped to
themselves, and how notoriously they abused that power to the prejudice of
the King, his perpetual hazard and disquiet: The King past all question saw all
this when he so willingly assented to those two acts for the constant calling of
Parliament and not dissolution of this, both which the Clergy had no other
means to disannul and make of no effect, than by infusing into his Majesty's
ears, and insinuating to the people, that the King hath a negative voice by
which all that the Parliament shall do comes to nothing unless it pleases the
King to assent, which is not like to be but when those that are so powerful (his
evil counselors) over him shall give way to; by which means alone those evil
men have a power of crossing and making void all the debates and conclusions
of the Parliament, and though this be in effect to make the safety and freedom
of the people to depend upon one man's will and understanding, an absurdity
in government; a man would think these men could not have the impudence to
plead for, much less that the people should be so unadvised as to admit it to
enter their thoughts as a thing just and reasonable, yet indeed so impudent are
those as to plead for it, and so ignorant are the people as to admit it, which is
the ground and occasion of all the evils and mischiefs which at this day threaten
both his Majesty and the whole people. So that we see the King hath little to
thank them for their too hasty forwardness in claiming what is so unsafe for
him, and so likely to divide the affections of the people from him: But what
care they, the King getting power, they get advancement, credit, honor, and
what not? so little respect they what is safe for him or prejudicial to the people,
so their own ends be served; there comes no harm from good consideration, the
advice then cannot be amiss, to wish everyone to consider what they hear, to
examine all not timorously, nor prejudicially, but impartially by that uncor-
rupt rules of reason, and to give no credit to what is spoken for the credit or
estimation of the speaker, but because it is the truth, and nothing but the
truth.

FINIS.

193

12

An Exact Description of a Roundhead,

and a Long-Head Shag-Poll

1642

*A*n *Exact Description of a Roundhead,*
and a Long-Head Shag-Poll presents a lively defense of puritans and a
spirited, satiric attack on the Cavaliers. The unknown author does not
argue any substantive points; his main aims seem to be to display his
considerable wit and to identify the roundheads with the puritans, thereby
removing all obloquy from the term *roundhead* before an audience that finds
the term *puritan* laudatory. His terminology provides an interesting contrast with that of *The Round-Head Uncovered,* also published in 1642.

The relatively uncommon term *semi-separate* appearing here points to a
current distinction between such groups as being, possibly, the followers of
John Robinson (the organizer of the American pilgrimage) on the one hand
and the more radical Brownists and Anabaptists on the other. According to
the author, the terms *roundhead* and *semi-separate* derive from *puritan* or
serve as alternate terms for the same people. Distinctions in beliefs that
remind the reader of Polonius's classifications of plays into ludicrously
numerous and complex categories in *Hamlet* more frequently appear in
writers who uphold orthodoxy. In defenses of puritanism, writers more
frequently minimize differences; thus here the three terms are said to be
equivalent.

Interesting also is the author's use of biblical quotations. The wholly favorable description of the puritan relies heavily on Scripture, especially on Genesis. For the Shag-Poll, Revelation provides a few quotations, but in general the Bible is less often cited; denunciations of contemporary immoral practices take its place. The reader is tempted to infer that the puritans' conduct and beliefs are based on Scripture, whereas their opponents largely ignore it.

Although the author draws in strong, bold colors—and only in two colors—throughout the bulk of his essay, he shades his criticism near the end, when he grants that some good men may have long hair and some bad men, short hair; the physical characteristic that has supported his humorous argument is not the real issue. This sober qualification, however, does not materially affect the lively, exuberant, and even outrageous tone of his pamphlet.

An Exact Description of a Roundhead, and a Long-Head Shag-Poll: *Taken out of the purest Antiquities and Records.* Wherein are confuted the odious aspersions of Malignant Spirits: Especially in answer to those most rediculous, absurd and beyond comparison, most foolish Baffle-headed Pamphlets sent into the World by a Stinking Locust, viz. *The Devill turn'd Round-Head. The Resolution of the Round-Head. The Vindication of the Round-Head.* and Jourdin *the Players exercising. London,* Printed for *George Tomlinson,* and are to be sold in the *Ould-Baily.* 1642.

A True description of the Round-heads.

And first there is laid down in these eight general heads:

First, the Original of them both, *Gen.* 2.7. *Revel.* 9.

Secondly, where they were made, as in the same record you shall find.

Thirdly, of what made, the same records also declares.

Fourthly, by whom made, there you shall find it also.

Fifthly, how they are qualified, there you shall find it also.

Sixthly, of the number of either of them, that you shall find *Mat.* 7. 13. *Revel.* 9.

[Seventhly,] of their use and particular end *Psal.* 73.

Eighthly, and lastly of their last, and final end that is *Mat.* 25.

All these are severally handled more plainly and largely in their order by W. P.

A faithful soldier of the sixth legion belonging unto the chief general of the most victorious regiment of the Round-heads. Written upon the plain of the earth, in the midst of an innumerable rabble gathered together by the Devil of shag-poll locusts, for the destruction of the Round-heads.

And first to begin with the Round-head's Original:

His beginning was the sixth and last day of the world's creation, in time preceding and going before that of the Locust shag-polls, being of more antiquity, and therefore more to be had in honor of those that reverence antiquity of time more than your shag-poll Locusts are.

Secondly, for the place where your Round-head was made: why, he was made in a place incomparable, more excellent than wherein your shag-poll Locust was made, as you shall hear hereafter, he was made in a delicate place, even in Paradise a place of spotless purity, and delightful content; a place fit for a Roundheaded puritan and *semi*-separate to be made in: your *semi*-separate, puritan, and Round-head, are computable 3. objects comprehended in one subject, being all made of one and the selfsame matter, as also of one and the selfsame nature, differing only in the precedency of the titles, the title *semi*-separates, and Round-head, issuing out of the [puritan (?)] as the stream issues out of the fountain being all one as the fountain and his stream is.

Thirdly, by whom was your Puritan or Round-head made? Your Puritan or Round-head was made by him who made the round world, and all that therein is, by *Jehovah Elohim* in most perfect beauty, shape, and form, most admirable, composed in most comely proportion and order, his Round-head not Ass-Head like, but round indeed, which being looked upon by God himself, he saw that it was good, yea, most exceeding good and liked it wondrous well, so that he blessed his round-head by him made, bids him increase and bring forth fruit, yea even that fruit that should destroy the shag-poll locusts, all the works of the Devil from off the earth.

Fourthly, of what made? He was made of that matter which that name which God gave him signifies, of red earth this *Adam* which the shag-polls in derision calls a Round-head, was made of red earth or of red dust, which to prevent some foolish objection, signifies one and the same thing.

Fifthly, how is this Round-head qualified? admirably, with grace and virtue of unvalued worth, as, first with innocency of life composed and mixt with rare ingredients, of mercy, truth and love, as also with rare wisdom and understanding, so that he did know the composition, and secret natures of all the creatures in the world, and so was able to give them names according to their nature, and so he did; thus internally and externally was this Round-head qualified with Admirable Wisdom, Beauty, Comeliness, and strength.

Sixthly, for his number and increase: why, for his increase of number it was small, excellent for quality, but few for quantity, in regard as the time now is and ever was, but here and there one; excellent and exquisite things being always scant, and rarest to be found, and that is the thing, together with their secret virtue, that makes them be of such account with those that knows their worth, which knowledge of them, as they are, it is only in God and amongst themselves, for foolish shag-poll locusts have no knowledge of their excellency, nor are no more able to discern their splendor, than a blind man that never saw the Sun, is able to judge or discern the glory or the illustrious beauty of the Sun.

Seventhly, of the Round-head's use, what is he useful for? the Round-head's use is manyfold, of many sorts and kinds, but all for good; and first to set forth the splendid glory of the justice of God, his grace manifested to them in the face and favor of Jesus Christ, but never unto the shag-poll locusts. Secondly, to set or show forth the virtues of Jesus Christ, the second person in Trinity, that hath therefore called these Round-heads out of darkness into light, that they should show forth his virtues, and so they do as on the contrary the Shag-poll shows forth the vices of the Devil. Their third use is to be store houses of wisdom. Their fourth use to be temples of the living God. Fifthly, to be teachers and instructors of men for the praise and glory of God, his secrets being made known unto them only. Sixthly, to denounce his Judgments against the world. *Revel.* 18. about the beginning, for these Round-heads are called his *Angels. Revel.* 2. *Angel* being a name of Office, not of nature always. Seventhly, they are useful to keep off his Judgments, sometimes from the Shag-poll, as that Round-head *Lot* while he was among the shag-poll Locusts Sodomites, the fire and brimstone could not come down to burn them; also here in *England,* how does these Round-heads keep off the pestilence, sword, and famine from the shag-polls here, and are the cause that many temporal blessings doth come upon them, which not withstanding these shag-poll locusts know, that it is for their sakes that they receive these benefits, yet they cannot endure them.

Eighthly, and lastly, what is the final end of the Round-heads? their final end next the glory of God is the salvation of his own soul, his final is the redemption from all miseries in this mortal life here and forever, hereafter, which no shag-poll locust must enjoy, his final end is to be a king, to reign with Christ forever, to be an heir with Christ, an inheritor and possessor of all things with him to all eternity; as also to praise and glorify God forever in an everlasting state of blessedness in the highest heaven, out of which all slanderous lying, scorning, barking, shag-poll locusts must be shut, *Revel.* 22.15 without shall be dogs, shag-poll locusts, he means enchanters, whoremongers and Idolaters, and whosoever loveth lies or makes lies, be they Priests, or Peasants, or whatsoever.

And thus have we finished your Round-head.

The second general head to be handled is your Shag-poll locust original when it was.

The Shag-poll Locust's original was the opening of the bottomless pit *Rev.* 9. the smoky pit, out of that smoke, came those shag-poll locusts, that wear hair like women, which was long after the making of the Round-heads: therefore are they of no such antiquity as your Round-heads are: and therefore according to your own rules are not so honorable as your Round-heads are.

Secondly, the place where they were made: why, they were made in the bottomless pit, as is above mentioned, they came out of the bottomless pit, at the place from whence they came, there were they made.

Thirdly, by whom were they made? why, by the devil the father of all slanderers and liars, such as these locusts are, whether locusts teachers, or locusts hearers, who made them all in uncomely, and unmanly order, for they had hair like women, faces like men, and teeth like a Lion, *Rev.* 9. *ver.* 7. 8. all like deformed monsters, as well inside as outside, exceeding bad and vile, full of confusion and deformed disorder, as well the Priests as people.

Fourthly, of what made? why, as first his case or outside he is made of dust as your Round-head is, although he knows it not as your Round-head doth, but for his pitch or inside it is *semen incubae,* or *sperma diaboli* he is made of the seed or spawn of the Devil: as concerning the constitution of his mind, murderers and liars are they, and so is he.

Fifthly, how are they qualified? Why, clean contrary to your Round-heads, not with innocency of life, but with nocency, with gross and palpable ignorance and blindness in spiritual and heavenly things, full of conceitedness of having that which they are utterly empty of, but being full indeed of the spirit: now I know to hear the name of Spirit will vex them, for they defy such as are full of the Spirit: but to quiet them a little, I give them to understand, that that Spirit which they mean, is not the Spirit I mean, the spirit that I mean here that they are filled with; is the spirit of lying and slandering, and false accusing of the Round-heads, the spirit of whoredom and unsatiable lust, the spirit of envy, malice, and murder, of drunkenness, epicurism, and all manner of loose profaneness, the spirit of hatred against the appearance of any goodness, though never so little, for they nothing almost but profit impiety like the devil himself, which reigns effectually in them, and he it is that hath thus qualified them, and which hath also blinded them in their judgments, that they cannot discern the nature and difference of things, but judge good to be evil, and evil to be good, *John* 16. 1. 2. They shall excommunicate you and he that kills you shall think he doth God good service: whether this be so or no, I refer you to yourselves, all you shag-poll Locusts.

Sixthly, for their number and increase, it is wonderful, in number they exceed the Round-heads, to speak comparatively, more than the mosquitoes and flies exceeds in number the Eagles, they darken the light of the Sun with their multitude, as did the flies of *Egypt.*

They are not rare to be found, as are the Eagles and the Round-heads, there are whole swarms of them in every place; and as hurtful and troublesome to your Round-heads in old *England;* as your Mosquitoes are to your Round-heads in *New England,* and every way as evil to be dealt withal, for the more you strive to beat them off, the more they muster and swarm about you, so that there is no way of quietness for a Round-head but to avoid them.

Seventhly, for their use, that also is divers, but tending all to hurt, yet contrary to their minds it effects good, not to themselves, but to the Round-heads, whom their whole intent and desire is to hurt. Now their first use is, to afflict the Round-heads, which if your shag-poll did know, what good they did unto your Round-heads, by afflicting of them, by their wrongs and injuries they do unto them, then would they never do it unto them: for first they teach them experience of the world's vanity, secondly, they make them weary of the world, and wean them from the love of the world, the love thereof would be their destruction: thirdly, they make them by their outrageous wrongs and injuries they do unto them, more splendid, bright, and lovely in the sight of God and good men; fourthly by the shag-poll's hatred of them, they come to have certain knowledge, that God loves them, which otherwise they could not have: for if the shag-poll Locusts loved them, it were a certain sign they were hated of God, for your shag-poll loves none but such as God hates: fifthly they increase the Round-heads' glory in heaven, for the more they scorn them here, the more shall they be honored there: sixthly, the shag-polls by reason of their outrageous wrongs and injuries that they do unto the Round-heads they make this world a hell unto the Round-heads, wherein these shag-polls like devils do torment them, so that they shall have no hell hereafter, as your shag-polls shall: other sorts of uses that they serve for is, first to make vessels of dishonor: secondly to declare the justice of his wrath upon, and to teach the Round-heads, that though he do for a time spare his and their enemies, that yet he will not always spare them: and lastly to be such firebrands of hell, as shall never be taken forth.

Eighthly and lastly, of their final end, their final end next to the glory of the justice of God's wrath, is to be damned, for their end is damnation, they mind nothing but earthly things, their God is their belly, they glory in shameful things, their conversation is not in heaven, therefore by God his definitive sentence, their final end is damnation.

And thus much for your Round-heads and your Shag-polls.

Only this by the way of Advertisement to the honest-hearted Christian Reader, that though some do either through ignorance, or some infirmity occasioning, wear their hair longer than may in some men's judgment seem fitting, for men professing themselves to be Christians to wear; know you that we intend not a definitive sentence against any particular person for wearing of their hair, but yet do wish them for the better informing of their judgments to consider the Apostle's rule concerning hair, in 1 *Cor.* 11. 14. where he may have full satisfaction; and further also we give you to understand, that we are so far off from a particular sentence that we believe that there are many among the Long-heads, that may belong unto the Round-heads, and that may in time declare themselves; and this also, that there are many Locusts among the Round-heads, that now seem to be Round-heads, yet are not so, and will declare themselves to be but Locusts; yet notwithstanding that, all that wear long hair are not Locusts; as also, all that wear not long hair are not Round-heads yet is long hair the visible sign or mark to distinguish a Locust *Rev.* 9. 8. *And they had hair like women.*

> Not long agone a Champion came from Hell.
> To bid defiance to the host of Heaven:
> But with the Puritans he hath no mind to deal,
> Because with them to no end he hath striven.
>> A periwig instead of Helmet on his head he wears,
>> To prove, if he by that can hide his *Midas* ears.
>
> His armor loose profaneness is, and Hatred strong,
> Disdain, contempt of God and goodness all:
> Murderous desire, by him retained long:

By which at last he hopes to make to fall
The Puritan, which now he Round-head call:
    A term by which he thinks to overthrow,
    And beat all goodness from the earth below.

By this design: he doubts not but to stop
The breath and life of goodness in this land:
And spoil that strength that Puritans have got,
And by this title Round-head to set all good at stand.
    But silly Long-head that hair is not thine own,
    'Tis but some harlot's, though by thee it's worn.

FINIS.

13

The Round-Head Uncovered

1642

*T*he *Round-Head Uncovered*, dated July 27, 1642, in the Thomason copy, was written shortly before the beginning of the civil war, apparently by an Anglican with a conciliatory attitude toward reformers. The author tries to foster peace by dissociating those called puritans from separatists and other radical dissenters; the latter groups he stigmatizes with the name *roundheads*. Throughout the work the name *puritan* is not used dyslogistically.

The anonymous author seems to feel that religious conformity has been the rule in England until nearly the time when he writes, and that controversy over religious practices has appeared only recently. He speaks of the "long liberty . . . enjoyed of the Gospel," wondering why dissension should have arisen. He accepts the Book of Common Prayer as being entirely drawn from the word of God and seems surprised that anyone could find fault with it; thus he adheres to a principle that the nonconformists rejected and against which they argued at length in the controversy over subscription. Variety of opinions and proliferation of sects he sees as phenomena of his own time, and he attributes the confusion to the arrogance of men who try to interpret Scripture for themselves, who dispute interpretations of texts without the guidance of learned authority. Eccentric ministers and their unlearned followers have caused turmoil and disunity within the church, have alienated the Parliament from the king, and now threaten armed conflict.

So strong and thorough going a supporter of the Anglican establishment could be expected to criticize puritans. Instead, however, he chooses the term *roundhead,* which was equated with *puritan* by the author of *An Exact Description of a Roundhead,* and surprisingly calls the roundhead an anti-puritan. Thus the puritans, by implication, become part of the establishment. Probably Josias Nichols, for example, would have been gratified by the laudatory use of *puritan* and happy to be considered completely loyal, but at the same time he certainly would have been puzzled by the notion that his time was free of turmoil. Nichols would have agreed with the idea that eccentric interpretations of the Bible cause trouble but not with the notion that men had enjoyed liberty in religious practice, and especially not with the statement that the Book of Common Prayer was "every word Scripture." What this tract indicates most significantly is that by mid-1642 radical and diverse opposition to the establishment had come into the open and gained popularity to such an extent that the so-called puritans of earlier years now seemed by comparison not far from the supporters of the establishment; also, the puritans' former opposition on some points had come to appear relatively benign. At least they had not approached civil insurrection.

The Round-Head *Uncovered.*
Being a moderate triall of his spirit. With a distinction betwixt the Round-heads, and such as Papists call Puritans.
London, Printed for *George Lindsey,* 1642.

The Round-head uncovered.

The soul of man being so excellent piece of workmanship of the Almighty Creator, and then so dearly ransomed by his only Son; she must needs be more tenderly loved, cherished and preserved by all the friends of God, than the rest of the Creatures, and consequently more hated, envied and chafed by his enemies. Hence it is that the Devil and his Angels, (her old professed enemies) *Ambit quasi Leo rugens.* Goes about her like a roaring Lion, traceth her steps, and by a long practice in temptation and a deadly rancor, by so much the more cruel, by how much it grows inveterate, doth continually lay traps and ambushes for her destruction; takes all occasions and inclinations to work upon; and together with her other confederate foes makes continual war against her.

Now this war being only visible to the intellectual sense, or inward eyes of the soul, and those eyes bleared and dimmed with mortality, bodily corruption and frailty; She is often beguiled, misled with illusions and false lights in her earthly pilgrimage: And the Devil being all Spirit, and (as our Savior saith) transforming himself (by permission as he had to tempt *Job*) into the shape of an Angel of light to deceive us; our poor Souls are thus apt to be induced into manifold errors and schisms.

By which means doubtless it cometh to pass that in this long liberty we have enjoyed of the Gospel (when most reformed Christians take leave to make their own way, in point of exposition of Scripture, as well as in other points of Christian duty) there are sprung up so many strange heresies and opinions. For as in the Primitive Church when the Laity and unlearned sort were contented with the plain rule of faith set down in the Apostles Creed without further peeping into mysteries, or comparing parts of Scripture, to try or question the truth of other parties; the lives and conversations of humble and devout Christians, and especially of their Pastors; were the bright lamps that lighted them in their way to God: So in these later times, through an unconfined liberty of expounding, and over public and unseasonable reasoning and disputing upon that subject; everyone presuming of his own Talent either of wit or grace; the sacred Text is so abused and mangled with variety of Opinions that it is become the common subject of discourse, as well in taverns and upon Alehouse benches, as, in private houses and out walkings. No marvel then that there are now well-nigh as many Sects and different opinions sprung as there be professors. But this redounds to the great disparagement of the reformed Church in general; especially to ours, which hath so long flourished and shined in the world's view in an Orthodox and settled discipline, without any material interruption, and still would flourish but for a crew of Hypocrites and Round-Heads, who taking the advantage of these late unlucky differences betwixt the King and his great Council, have partly by their loud whispers, and the libelous Pamphlets, and partly by their mutinous assemblies, not only sent his Highness a dangerous voyage into the North; and thereby deprived the whole Kingdom of that happy union betwixt him and his Parliament, which might otherwise have been expected: But by poisoning the hearts of many a thousand good Protestants, have new made a wide overture amongst many of the illiterate People (of *London* especially) to let in Innovations, both of doctrine and discipline into our Church: which cannot choose but produce some sad effect of a civil dissension amongst us: forasmuch as there is nothing that so much urgeth man's patience, as to be thrust out of a long continued possession upon new-found pretenses, and principally of a settled form of Divine worship;

which commonly foreruns a change of Religion itself. But because we are not yet (thanks be to God) come to that; I will break off from this tender point, to fall into the description both of that Zealous sort of Christians, which the Papists have long distinguished from the colder, and more remiss sort of Protestants, by the name of Puritans: And of that other sort who for their hypocrisy may be termed *Anti*-Puritans, or Round-Heads.

For the first, as it was given them by that common Adversary the Papists, but by way of mockery for their zeal in God's cause against them, so in regard the word Puritan carries no sense of disgrace. I could wish them to accept of it, and by making good the Title (as our late Protestant Princes have done that of Defender of the Faith contrary to the *Pope's* intention) to confront and beat down their specious Title of Universality and Superstition, with Christian purity and plainness, and the only way to be pure indeed.

But here let me pause a little, to give some of the unlearned sort of them, also this Christian Caveat; That whilst they condemn the Papists for relying too much on their own merits, they give them not as just occasion to condemn them for as great a presumption; which is to trust to their own sense in the exposition of mysterious points of Scripture: But rather to read and practice those other parts that conduce to a good and virtuous life, without expense of their feeble faculties, or perplexing their minds with things above their reach, as if they studied the Philosophers-stone.

For though it be granted that God's grace is never wanting to a devout soul, yet is it a question whether every man's self-seeming devotion be guided by a right spirit. Therefore it is that St. *Paul* bids us work our Salvation with fear and trembling. For Satan is a cunning Cheater, and like a *Hocus Pocus,* spies now and then occasions to throw in his false flashes into the soul, upon the sudden extinguishment of those true lights of grace, which sometimes are as soon put out as kindled, by the stinking lamp of some odious, unrepented sin, which passing for current, and embraced by presumption, for want of a right examen and trial of the heart, the mind is led awry with an *ignis fatuus,* or a Will with the wisp towards some dangerous precipice.

And it is upon the most spiritual and inaccessible soul that the black Engineer practiceth most of these wild-fires or illusions, such as make conscience of their ways, and are impregnable by the shot of Worldly and Fleshly provocations.

Is it not therefore pity that the weed of false zeal should be so fertile in these our times, and so prevalent, as to overrun the wholesome herb of Integrity? Is it not indeed a lamentable case that by means of this Gallimaufry of strange new Sects (united only in unity of mischief) our Book of Common Prayer (being every word Scripture) penned doubtless by the finger of God, and our decent and our orderly discipline in the House of God, should be thus shamelessly questioned and controverted, not only by a few of our over singular Divines, but by the Rabble of the illiterate Laity: who under the specious pretext of opposing Popery, and apprehensions of dangers to the Religion and State of England, do hazard by these uncontrolled disorders the ruin of them both?

Is it not pity (I say) that our eminent English Church after this long prosperity, should (like a fair ship at Sea) be overwhelmed by a shoal of Herrings: a swarm of buzzing *Round-heads;* a flock of straggled sheep, who misled by some scared Bellwethers, do thus leap and frisk all after each other, over their lawful bounds into unknown dangers.

For admitting the State or Religion were in peril, would it stand with honor of either of them to accept of their preservation from an unmarshalled and disorderly Rout of Round-heads such who for the most part for their unconformity in Religion, are as malign and dangerous as the common Enemy? God forbid. There be regular men enough, and true-hearted to the State and Religion here established, to be intrusted with the defense and conservation of the public liberty and Privilege of Parliament without them.

It is a wonder to me how these Round-heads (unless perhaps there be many of them Turners or Wheelers) have thus with their whimsies and devices turned the head of many a good Protestant as round as their own. And though I believe the name of Round-head was invented by some maligner of Parliamentary Privileges. Yet is it evident, by the time of its first raising, that it was upon occasion of their mutinous clamors and assemblies to the no small disturbance of the King and Parliament.

But this term is grown too general, for though all Citizens and many other civil persons that wear no locks are by most of the Cavaliers and Soldiers of this time (for antipathy sake) comprised in the number of Roundheads, yet am I of opinion, that in judgment of few wise and impartial men they will be so esteemed.

For conclusion, I will only admonish my Reader (whoever he be) to refrain siding, or to blow the already too much glowing coal of Sedition on either side, and with Christian humility to resign all to God's Providence, and to the managing of the superior Powers. For that can be no right spirit (without doubt) which delights in aggravation of offenses, especially in this weighty cause betwixt our Sovereign and his highest Council the Parliament.

FINIS.

14

John Geree

The Character of an Old English Puritane,

or Non-Conformist

1646

JOHN GEREE (*ca.* 1601 – 1649)
was educated at Magdalen Hall, Oxford, receiving his M.A. degree in
1621. He served briefly as a pastor in Gloucester, but from 1624 to 1641
he was without a position in the church because of his refusal to accept the
prescribed ceremonies. Throughout his life he opposed episcopacy but
acknowledged royal authority and felt a strong attachment to the king. His
published writings include arguments for infant baptism and arguments
against separatists. His preoccupation with infant baptism shows itself in
the last paragraph of his *Character of an Old English Puritane, or Non-
Conformist,* where he notes that a work written against his position caused
him to append the paragraph, almost as an afterthought, after his essay was
completed. This work has been reprinted, with a brief profile of the author,
by Maurice Hussey in the *Church Quarterly Review,* CXLVIII (1949,
pp. 65–71).

Geree draws an idealized picture. Although his work belongs to the
character genre developed by Sir Thomas Overbury and John Earle, it is to
some extent a self-portrait and a self-justification reflecting what we know
of its author's life and opinions. Ethically his subject is a very good man; he
is pious, hardworking, charitable, humble, and above all moderate, as
though Geree were seeking to defend puritans against the charge, mentioned only in his final paragraph, of excessive zeal and willfulness. In

religious practice the puritan holds to many of the nonconformist tenets. He believes that ceremonies should be grounded on Scripture, not on human traditions. He uses extemporaneous prayer suited to the time and occasion, but he would not reject set prayers. On Sunday he hears two sermons and avoids all recreations, though he admits that some are lawful. Although not denying entirely the efficacy of reading and lectures, he places great emphasis on preaching. In fact, Geree goes to considerable length in his discussion of preaching, even specifically citing as the best the sermon organized according to method, reason, and use. Unlike some dissenters, however, his puritan will not desert the local minister with inferior gifts and go elsewhere to hear a more effective preacher. It seems unlikely that he would seek out preaching tradesmen.

In his attitude toward church government, Geree's puritan, though called a nonconformist—perhaps as a reflection of the author's own refusal to conform—would be hard to distinguish, because of his moderation, from some reluctantly conforming Anglicans. Actually, like Geree, this puritan finds best the presbyterian form of church government, which he calls "aristocratical," or government by elders; he rejects the "monarchical" (government by bishops) or the "democratical" (a form of government found among some separatists). He will not join a sect outside the church, preferring to work for reform from within instead of setting up a competing organization. Above all, he dissociates himself from Anabaptists, again reflecting Geree's strong support of infant baptism. The puritan justifies his moderation on the matter of church government by the principle that the ideal, in the church as elsewhere, is rarely achieved in this world. Although rejecting some prescribed ceremonies, he will not cause turmoil within the church; he opposes authority modestly when his conscience does not permit him to obey, and he accepts punishment without complaining. In his conclusion, or appendix, Geree specifically argues that although some puritans were too zealous, the norm for the group was peaceful demeanor and willingness to suffer wrongs to maintain convictions. The view is essentially nostalgic, and Geree, writing in 1646 and using the past tense throughout his description, sees the connotations of the term *puritan* as wholly favorable.

The Character of an old *English Puritane,* or Non-Conformist. By *John Geree* M.A. and Preacher of the Word sometime at *Tewksbury,* but now at Saint

Albons. *Published according to Order*. London, *Printed by W. Wilson* for *Christopher Meredith* at the *Crane* in *Pauls* Church-yard 1646.

The Character of an old ENGLISH PURITAN,
OR NON-CONFORMIST

The Old English Puritan was such an one, that honored God above all, and under God gave every one his due. His first care was to serve God, and therein he did not what was good in his own, but in God's sight, making the word of God the rule of his worship. He highly esteemed order in the House of God: but would not under color of that submit to superstitious rites, which are superfluous, and perish in their use. He reverenced Authority keeping within its sphere: but durst not under pretense of subjection to the higher powers, worship God after the traditions of men. He made conscience of all God's ordinances, though some he esteemed of more consequence. He was much in prayer; with it he began, and closed the day. In it he was exercised in his closet, family, and public assembly. He esteemed that manner of prayer best, where by the gift of God, expressions were varied according to present wants and occasions; yet did he not account set forms unlawful. Therefore in that circumstance of the Church he did not wholly reject the Liturgy, but the corruption of it. He esteemed reading of the word an ordinance of God both in private and public; but did not account reading to be preaching. The word read he esteemed of more authority, but the word preached of more efficacy. He accounted preaching as necessary now as in the Primitive Church: God's pleasure being still by the foolishness of preaching to save those that believe. He esteemed that preaching best wherein was most of God, least of man, when vain flourishes of wit, and words were declined, and the demonstration of God's Spirit and power studied: yet could he distinguish between studied plainness and negligent rudeness. He accounted perspicuity the best grace of a Preacher: and that method best, which was most helpful to understanding, affection, and memory. To which ordinarily he esteemed none so conducible as that by doctrine, reason, and use. He esteemed those Sermons best that came closest to the conscience: yet would he have men's consciences awakened, not their persons disgraced. He was a man of good spiritual appetite, and could not be contented with one meal a day. An afternoon Sermon did relish as well to him as one in the morning. He was not satisfied with prayers without preaching: which if it were wanting at home, he would seek abroad: yet would he not by absence discourage his Minister, if faithful, though another might have quicker gifts. A Lecture he esteemed, though not necessary, yet a blessing, and would redeem such an opportunity with some pains and loss. The Lord's day he esteemed a divine ordinance, and rest on it necessary, so far as it conduced to holiness. He was very conscientious in observance of that day as the mart day of the Soul. He was very careful to remember it, to get house, and heart in order for it: and when it came, he was studious to improve it. He redeemed the morning from superfluous sleep, and watched the whole day over his thoughts and words, not only to restrain them from wickedness, but worldliness. All parts of the day were alike holy to him, and his care was continued in it in variety of holy duties: what he heard in public, he repeated in private, to whet it upon himself and family. Lawful recreations he thought this day unseasonable, and unlawful ones much more abominable: yet he knew the liberty God gave him for needful refreshing, which he did neither refuse nor abuse. The Sacrament of Baptism he received in Infancy, which he looked back to in age to answer his engagements, and claim his privileges. The Lord's Supper he accounted part of his soul's food: to which he labored to keep an appetite. He esteemed it an ordinance of nearest communion with Christ, and so requiring most exact preparation. His first care was in the examination of himself: yet as an act of office or charity he had an eye on others.

He endeavored to have the scandalous cast out of Communion: but he cast not out himself, because the scandalous were suffered by the negligence of others. He condemned that superstition and vanity of Popish mock-fast: yet neglected not on occasion to humble his soul by right fasting: He abhorred the popish doctrine of *opus operatum* in the notion. And in practice rested in no performance, but what was done in spirit and truth. He thought God had left a rule in his word for discipline, and that Aristocratical by Elders, not Monarchical by Bishops, nor Democratical by the people. Right Discipline he judged pertaining not to the being, but well-being of a Church. Therefore he esteemed those Churches most pure where the government is by Elders, yet unchurched not those where it was other ways. Perfection in Churches he thought a thing rather to be desired, than hoped for. And so he expected not a Church state without all defects. The corruptions that were in Churches he thought his duty to bewail, with endeavors of amendment: yet would he not separate, where he might partake in the worship, and not in the corruption. He put not holiness in Churches, as in the Temple of the Jews; but only counted them convenient like their Synagogues. He would have them kept decent, not magnificent: knowing that the Gospel requires not outward pomp. His chiefest music was singing of Psalms, wherein though he neglected not the melody of the voice, yet he chiefly looked after that of the heart. He disliked such Church-music as moved sensual delight, and was an hindrance to spiritual enlargements. He accounted subjection to the Higher powers to be part of pure religion, as well as to visit the fatherless and widows: yet did he distinguish between authority, and lusts of Magistrates, to that he submitted, but in these he durst not be a servant of men, being bought with a price. Just laws and commands he willingly obeyed not only for fear but for conscience also; But such as were unjust he refused to observe, choosing rather to obey God than man: yet his refusal was modest and with submission to penalties, unless he could procure indulgence from authority. He was careful in all relations to know, and do duty, and that with singleness of heart as unto Christ. He accounted religion an engagement to duty, that the best Christians should be best husbands, best wives, best parents, best children, best Masters, best servants, best Magistrates, best subjects, that the doctrine of God might be adorned, not blasphemed. His family he endeavored to make a Church, both in regard of persons and exercises, admitting none into it but such as feared God; and laboring that those that were born in it, might be born again to God. He blessed his family morning and evening by the word and prayer; and took care to perform those ordinances in the best season. He brought up his children in the nurture and admonition of the Lord, and commanded his servants to keep the way of the Lord. He set up discipline in his family, as he desired it in the Church, not only reproving but restraining vileness in his. He was conscientious of equity as well as piety: knowing that unrighteousness is abomination as well as ungodliness. He was cautelous in promising, but careful in performing, counting his word no less engagement than his bond. He was a man of a tender heart, not only in regard of his own sin, but others' misery, not counting mercy arbitrary, but a necessary duty: wherein as he prayed for wisdom to direct him, so he studied for cheerfulness and bounty to act. He was sober in the use of the things of this life, rather beating down the body, than pampering it: yet he denied not himself the use of God's blessing, lest he should be unthankful, but avoided excess lest he should be forgetful of the Donor. In his habit he avoided costliness and vanity, neither exceeding his degree in civility, nor declining what suited with Christianity, desiring in all things to express gravity. His whole life he accounted a warfare, wherein Christ was his Captain, his arms, prayers and tears. The Cross his Banner, and his word *vincit qui patitur*.

He was ἀνὴρ τετράγωνος, immovable in all times, so that they who in the midst of many opinions have lost the view of true religion, may return to him, and there find it.

Reader, seeing a passage in Mr. *Tombes* his book against paedobaptism, wherein he compares the Nonconformists in England to the Anabaptists in Germany, in regard of their miscarriages, and ill success in their endeavors, till of late years; I was moved for the vindication of those faithful and Reverend witnesses of Christ to publish this Character: whereof if any shall desire proof in matter of fact, as in matter of right the margent contains evidence: let him either consult their writings, or those who are fit witnesses by reason of age, fidelity and acquaintance, having fully known their doctrine, manner of life, purpose, faith, long-suffering, love, patience, persecution, and affliction, etc. 2 *Tim.* 3. 10. 11. And I doubt not but full testimony will be given, that their aim and general course was according to this rule: some extravagants there be in all professions, but we are to judge of a profession by the rule they hold forth, and that carriage of the professors, which is general and ordinary.

FINIS.

Part II
Negative Portrayals of Puritanism

15

James I

Basilikon Doron, 1603

(Excerpts)

JAMES I (1566–1625), king of England from 1603, reigned also in Scotland, from 1567, as James VI. Having had difficulties with the ministers who ruled the Scottish church under a presbyterian form of church government, he insisted upon an episcopal establishment in England. Proud of his erudition, he was ever willing to exhibit it in controversy, as well as to gain fame as a writer; at the same time, however, he wanted peace and stability in both domestic and foreign affairs. The *Basilikon Doron,* or "king's gift," is in effect a treatise on kingship written in the form of instructions to his eldest son and heir, Prince Henry, who did not live to succeed to the throne.

The *Basilikon Doron* was written in 1598 and printed in a few copies in 1599. A new edition with many changes designed for English readers came out in 1603 and achieved wide circulation both in Britain and on the continent. Ironically, both editions were printed by Robert Waldegrave, who had printed some of the Marprelate tracts and had since become the royal printer in Scotland. Subsequently the 1603 edition was reprinted in collections of James's English works in 1616 and 1620; thus the work remained easily accessible to English readers for a generation. Its early history was turbulent. Apparently the 1598 edition came to the attention of the Scottish churchman Andrew Melville, an advocate of theocracy on the Genevan model whose party had been outvoted by more moderate reformers siding with the king in the General Assembly of the Church of Scotland. Melville extracted from the book eighteen points on which he thought the king particularly vulnerable to attack; these were presented by other churchmen to the synod of Fife and aroused some controversy. In an attempt to conciliate some of the radical reformers in Scotland and to make himself more acceptable to the English, James refined and limited his definition of puritanism in an epistle to the reader, which first appeared in the 1603 edition. The relevant part is here reprinted. However, James did not significantly alter the strictures on puritans in the body of his work; these appear in the excerpt from the second book of the *Basilikon Doron*. The texts of James's manuscript and of both early editions can be found in James Craigie (ed.), *The Basilicon Doron of King James VI*, The Scottish Text Society, New Series, Nos. 16, 18 (2 vols.; Edinburgh, 1944, 1950). The first sixteen pages of volume 2 are especially relevant.

Of Melville's eighteen points, four directly concern puritanism. He points out that James has said, "No man is more to be hated of a King nor a proud Puritan" (point 6); "Puritans are pests in the Commonweal and Kirk of Scotland" (point 11); "The principals of them are nocht to be suffered to bruik the land" (point 12); and "For a preservative against their poison, there mon be Bishops" (point 13). The excerpt from the second book indicates that Melville summarized James's position accurately enough. In his prefatory "To the Reader," James attempts to quiet the succeeding controversy and to avoid offending many zealous reformers in England by defining the term *puritan*, limiting it to those who would cause a disturbance in the state. Specifically he cites the Anabaptists and names as examples the Family of Love and two individuals: the separatist Robert Brown and the Marprelate author John Penry. Strictly speaking, Brown, Penry, and the Familists were not Anabaptists, nor are they the best examples of seditious behavior, but James's intent was apparently to cite persons and groups who were both unpopular and in various ways extreme in their beliefs. To earn the goodwill of most nonconformists, James insists that he does not label as puritans either those who dislike some ceremonies of the church or those who do not support the episcopal system of church government, as long as they obey whatever laws are promulgated by the ecclesiastical and civil authorities. His entangled motives and principles thus produced a variety of statements about puritans that could be cited in their favor by both establishment Anglicans and nonconformists, depending on which statements each chose to emphasize.

In addition to the preface, "To the Reader," the *Basilikon Doron* consists of three "books." The first and shortest has the title "Of a King's Christian Duty Towards God." Here James takes up such matters as the fundamental importance of religion in the state and in the king's life, the proper use of Scripture, the correct form of prayer, and the nature and role of conscience. The unifying theme is the need to ground all religious practice on Scripture. For prayer, the Psalms and the Lord's Prayer in the New Testament are the models, and conscience must always be disciplined by the guides set forth in the Bible. It is interesting that James rejects the Apocrypha as being of little value; later, in the Bible that in popular terminology bears his name, he ordered the Apocrypha printed along with the canonical texts.

In the second book, "Of a King's Duty in His Office," James deals at some length with church government, arguing the need to control the overly zealous and willful by giving authority to sober-minded and moderate clergymen. He begins the book by making a distinction between a king and a tyrant, and then goes on to treat the proper relationship of a king not only to the church but also to the Parliament, the nobility, and the third estate of craftsmen and merchants. Among the subjects treated are the conduct of foreign affairs in both war and peace; the administration of justice; the king's choice of a wife (her religion being an important consideration); the king's behavior toward his children; the management of the royal court; the place of such studies as liberal arts and mathematics in the king's education (particularly his need to be governed in studies by practical, not antiquarian, interests); and the need for such virtues as humility, magnanimity, and liberality in the king's demeanor.

In the third book, "Of a King's Behavior in Indifferent Things," topics range from the advice to place no trust in dreams to the use of sports and games (especially hawking and hunting) and even to the style of writing (where James advocates a plain, sober style for a king). The comments on puritans, considering their relative brevity, should be inconspicuous in all this wealth of advice on such a large array of subjects, in which James quotes ancient and modern authorities and gives some details from his personal experience. However, such was the intensity of his religious feeling, particularly on questions focusing on the issue of puritanism, that his comments on the topic became the most widely publicized and, for James, the most troublesome.

ΒΑΣΙΛΙΚΟΝ ΔΩΡΟΝ.

Or His Maiesties Instrvctions to His Dearest Sonne, Henry the Prince. Edinbvrgh Printed by Robert Walde-graue Printer to the Kings Majestie. 1603. [Excerpts: sigs. B3–b3; pp. 38–44.]

To the Reader [Excerpt]

To come then particularly to the matter of my book, there are two special great points, which (as I am informed) the malicious sort of men have detracted therein; and some of the honest sort have seemed a little to mistake: whereof the first and greatest is, that some sentences therein should seem to furnish grounds to men, to doubt of my sincerity in that Religion, which I have ever constantly professed: the other is, that in some parts thereof, I should seem to nourish in my mind, a vindictive resolution against England, or at the least, some principals there, for the queen my mother's quarrel.

The first calumny (most grievous indeed) is grounded upon the sharp and bitter words, that therein are used in the description of the humors of Puritans, and rash-heady preachers, that think it their honor to contend with Kings, and perturb whole kingdoms. The other point is only grounded upon the strait charge I give my Son, not to hear, nor suffer any unreverent speeches or books against any of his parents or progenitors: wherein I do allege my own experience anent the Queen my mother: affirming that I never found any, that were of perfect age the time of her reign here, so steadfastly true to me in all my troubles, as these that constantly kept their allegiance to her in her time. But if the charitable reader will advisedly consider, both the method and matter of my treatise, he will easily judge, what wrong I have sustained by the carping at both. For my book, suppose very small, being divided in three several parts; the first part thereof only treats of a King's duty towards God in Religion: wherein I have so clearly made profession of my Religion, calling it the Religion wherein I was brought up, and ever made profession of, and wishing him ever to continue in the same, as the only true form of God's worship; that I would have thought my sincere plainness in that first part upon that subject, should have ditted the mouth of the most envious *Momus,* that ever hell did hatch, from barking at any other part of my book upon that ground; except they would allege me to be contrary to myself, which in so small a volume, would smell of too great weakness, and slipperiness of memory. And the second part of my book, teaches my son how to use his office, in the administration of justice, and politic government: the third only containing a King's outward behavior in indifferent things; what agreeance and conformity he ought to keep betwixt his outward behavior in these things, and the virtuous qualities of his mind: and how they should serve for trunchmen, to interpret the inward disposition of the mind, to the eyes of them that cannot see farther within him, and therefore must only judge of him by the outward appearance. So as if there were no more to be looked into, but the very method and order of the book, it will sufficiently clear me of that first and grievousest imputation, in the point of Religion: since in the first part, where Religion is only treated of, I speak so plainly. And what in other parts I speak of Puritans, it is only of their moral faults, in that part where I speak of policy: declaring when they contemn the law and sovereign authority, what exemplary punishment they deserve for the same. And now as to the matter itself whereupon this scandal is taken, that I may sufficiently satisfy all honest men, and by a just apology raise up a brazen wall or bulwark against all the darts of the envious, I will the more narrowly rip up the words, whereat they seem to be somewhat stomached.

First then, as to the name of Puritans, I am not ignorant that the style thereof doth properly belong only to that vile sect amongst the Anabaptists, called the Family of love; because they think themselves only pure, and in a manner, without sin, the only true Church, and only worthy to be participant of the Sacraments; and all the rest of the world to be but abomination in the sight of God. Of this special sect I principally mean, when I speak of Puritans; divers of them, as *Browne, Penrie,* and others, having at sundry times come in Scotland, to sow their popple amongst us (and from my heart I wish, that they had left no scholars behind them, who by their fruits will in their own time be manifested) and partly, indeed, I give this style to such brainsick and heady preachers their disciples and followers, as refusing to be called of that sect, yet participates too much with their humors, in maintaining the above mentioned errors; not only agreeing with the general rule of all Anabaptists, in the contempt of the civil Magistrate, and in leaning to their own dreams and revelations; but particularly with this sect, in accounting all men profane that swears not to all their fantasies; in making for every particular question of the policy of the Church, as great commotion, as if the article of the Trinity were called in controversy; in making the Scriptures to be ruled by their conscience, and not their conscience by the Scripture; and he that denies the least jot of their grounds, *sit tibi tanquam ethnicus & publicanus;* not worthy to enjoy the benefit of breathing, much less to participate with them of the Sacraments: and before that any of their grounds be impugned, let King, people, law and all be trod under foot. Such holy wars are to be preferred to an ungodly peace: no, in such cases, Christian princes are not only to be resisted unto, but not to be prayed for. For prayer must come of Faith, and it is revealed to their consciences, that God will hear no prayer for such a Prince. Judge then, Christian reader, if I wrong this sort of people, in giving them the style of that sect, whose errors they imitate: and since they are contented to wear their livery, let them not be ashamed to borrow also their name. It is only of this kind of men, that in this book I write so sharply; and whom I wish my Son to punish, in case they refuse to obey the law, and will not cease to stir up a rebellion. Whom against I have written the more bitterly, in respect of divers famous libels, and injurious speeches spread by some of them, not only dishonorably invective against all Christian princes, but even reproachful to our profession and religion, in respect they are come out under color thereof: and yet were never answered but by Papists, who generally meddle as well against them, as the religion itself; whereby the scandal was rather doubled, than taken away. But on the other part, I protest upon mine honor, I mean it not generally of all Preachers, or others, that likes better of the single form of policy in our Church, than of the many ceremonies in the Church of England; that are persuaded, that their Bishops smells of a Papal supremacy, that the Surplice, the cornered cap, and such like, are the outward badges of Popish errors. No, I am so far from being contentious in these things, (which for my own part I ever esteemed as indifferent) as I do equally love and honor the learned and grave men of either of these opinions. It can no ways become me to pronounce so lightly a sentence, in so old a controversy. We all (God be praised) do agree in the grounds, and the bitterness of men upon such questions, doth but trouble the peace of the Church; and gives advantage and entry to the Papists by our division. But towards them, I only use this provision, that where the Law is otherways, they may content themselves soberly and quietly with their own opinions, not resisting to the authority, nor breaking the law of the country; neither above all, stirring any rebellion or schism: but possessing their souls in peace, let them press by patience, and well grounded reasons, either to persuade all the rest to like of their judgments; or where they see better grounds on the other part, not to be ashamed peaceably to incline thereunto, laying aside all preoccupied opinions.

And that this is the only meaning of my book, and not any coldness or crack in Religion, that place doth plainly witness, where, after I have spoken of the faults in our Ecclesiastical estate, I exhort my son to be beneficial unto the good men of the Ministry; praising God there, that there is presently a sufficient number of good men of them in this kingdom: and yet are they all known to be against the form of the English Church. Yea, so far I am in that place from admitting corruption in Religion, as I wish him in promoving them, to use such caution, as may preserve their estate from creeping to corruption; ever using that form through the whole book, wherever I speak of bad preachers, terming them some of the ministers, and not Ministers or Ministry in general. And to conclude this point of Religion, what indifferency of Religion can *Momus* call that in me, where, speaking of my son's marriage (in case it pleased God before that time to cut the thread of my life) I plainly forewarn him of the inconveniences that were like to ensue, in case he should marry any that be of a different profession in Religion from him: notwithstanding that the number of Princes professing our Religion be so small, as it is hard to foresee, how he can be that way, meetly matched according to his rank.

Basilikon Doron. The Second Book [Excerpt]

The natural sickness that have ever troubled, and been the decay of all the Churches, since the beginning of the world, changing the candlestick from one to another, as *John* saith, have been Pride, Ambition, and Avarice: and now last, these same infirmities wrought the overthrow of the Popish Church, in this country and diverse others. But the reformation of Religion in *Scotland,* being extraordinarily wrought by God, wherein many things were inordinately done by a popular tumult and rebellion, of such as blindly were doing the work of God, but clogged with their own passions and particular respects, as well appeared by the destruction of our policy; and not proceeding from the Prince's order, as it did in our neighbor country of England, as likewise in Denmark, and sundry parts of Germany; some fiery spirited men in the ministry, got such a guiding of the people at that time of confusion, as finding the gust of government sweet, they begouth to fantasy to themselves, a Democratic form of government: and having (by the iniquity of time) been overwell baited upon the wrack, first of my Grandmother, and next of my own Mother, and after usurping the liberty of the time in my long minority, settled themselves so fast upon that imagined Democracy, as they fed themselves with the hope to become *Tribuni plebis:* and so in a popular government by leading the people by the nose, to bear the sway of all the rule. And for this cause, there never rose faction in the time of my minority, nor trouble sen-syne, but they that were upon that factious part, were ever careful to persuade and allure these unruly spirits among the ministry, to spouse that quarrel as their own: where-through I was ofttimes calumniated in their popular sermons, nor for any evil or vice in me, but because I was a King, which they thought the highest evil. And because they were ashamed to profess this quarrel, they were busy to look narrowly in all my actions, and I warrant you a mote in my eye, yea a false report was matter enough for them to work upon: and yet for all their cunning, whereby they pretended to distinguish the lawfulness of the office, from the vice of the person, some of them would sometimes snapper out well grossly with the truth of their intentions: informing the people, that all Kings and Princes were naturally enemies to the liberty of the Church, and could never patiently bear the yoke of Christ, with such sound doctrine fed they their flocks. And because the learned, grave, and honest men of the ministry, were ever ashamed and offended with their temerity and presumption, pressing by all good means by their authority and example, to reduce them to a greater moderation, there could be no way found out so meet in their conceit, that were turbulent spirits among them, for maintaining their plots, as parity in the Church: whereby the ignorants were emboldened (as bayards) to cry the learned, godly and modest out of it: parity the mother of confusion, and enemy to Unity which is the mother of order. For if by the example thereof, once established in the Ecclesiastical government, the Politic and civil estate should be drawn to the like, the great confusion that there upon would arise, may easily be discerned. Take heed therefore (my Son) to such PURITANS, very pests in the Church and commonweal: whom no deserts can oblige; neither oaths or promises bind; breathing nothing but sedition and calumnies, aspiring without measure, railing without reason, and making their own imaginations (without any warrant of the word) the square of their conscience. I protest before the greater God, and since I am here as upon my Testament, it is no place for me to lie in, that ye shall never find with any Highland or Border thieves greater ingratitude, and more lies and vile perjuries, than with these fanatic spirits. And suffer not the principals of them to brook your land, if ye like to sit at rest: except ye would keep them for trying your patience, as *Socrates* did an evil wife.

And for preservative against their poison entertain and advance the godly, learned, and modest men of the ministry, whom of (God be praised) there lacketh not a sufficient number: and by their provision to Bishoprics and

Benefices (annulling that vile act of Annexation, if ye find it not done to your hand) ye shall not only banish their conceited Party, whereof I have spoken, and their other imaginary grounds; which can neither stand with the order of the Church, nor the peace of a commonweal, and well ruled Monarchy: but also shall ye reestablish the old institution of three Estates in Parliament, which can no otherwise be done. But in this I hope (if God spare me days) to make you a fair entry; always where I leave, follow ye my steps.

And to end my advice anent the Church estate, cherish no man more than a good Pastor, hate no man more than a proud Puritan: thinking it one of your fairest styles, to be called a loving nourish-Father to the Church; seeing all the Churches within your dominions planted with good Pastors, the Schools (the seminary of the church) maintained, the doctrine and discipline preserved in purity, according to God's word, a sufficient provision for their sustentation, a comely order in their policy, pride punished, humility advanced, and they so to reverence their superiors, and their flocks them, as the flourishing of your Church in piety, peace, and learning, may be one of the chief points of your earthly glory: being ever alike ware with both the extremities, as well as ye repress the vain Puritan, so not to suffer proud Papal Bishops: but as some for their qualities will deserve to be preferred before others, so chain them with such bonds as may preserve that estate from creeping to corruption.

16

William Covell

A Modest and Reasonable Examination,
of Some Things in Use in the
Church of England, 1604

(Excerpts)

WILLIAM COVELL (*ca.* 1560–*ca.*
1614) was educated at Christ's College, Cambridge, where he took the
B.A. degree in 1584 and the M.A. degree in 1588. In 1589 he became a
fellow of Queen's College, Cambridge, and in 1601 he was granted the
D.D. degree. For the rest of his life he held various ecclesiastical positions
earned by his writings in defense of the establishment as well as by his
training and abilities. Apparently his *Modest and Reasonable Examination, of
Some Things in Use in the Church of England* was called forth by Josias
Nichols's *Plea of the Innocent* (1602) and may have been commissioned by the
government or by the church authorities. He wrote also in support of
Richard Hooker's *Laws of Ecclesiastical Polity* (1594, 1597).

A *Modest and Reasonable Examination* consists of a long, detailed defense
of the established church, including its government, discipline, and ceremonies. Covell tries to refute criticism of the establishment by the authors
of admonitions to the Parliament, by Marprelate, and by other earlier
writers, but in his full title he mentions by name only Josias Nichols's *Plea
of the Innocent,* which he sees in part as a summary of earlier statements, not

as an original work. The excerpts here reprinted treat Nichols's arguments directly. In his third chapter, Covell argues the inopportuneness of Nichols's plea at the beginning of James's reign and portrays the church as stable, peaceful, and tolerant. His preface, "To the Reader," charges that "in the midst of an universal joy" Nichols's book "sounded a seditious alarm." Then, in his third chapter, Covell turns Nichols's request for unity back upon itself, arguing that it will cause only disunity. In dealing with the name *puritan,* Covell contradicts Nichols directly, pointing out first that it is applied only to those who "would seem upright" (a small minority) and insisting upon their kinship with the ancient heretics and the Anabaptists and Martinists—in short, with all those from whom Nichols tried to dissociate himself.

Covell begins his work with an assertion of the right and duty of kings and princes to establish an ecclesiastical discipline with a set form of church government, a prescribed liturgy, and definite articles of belief. He draws upon historical precedents and cites as negative examples the ancient Donatists, who held that the monarch should not prescribe any religion, and the contemporary Anabaptists, who were generally thought rebellious. Positive examples, also generally accepted by the public, are Solomon, Constantine the Great, and Justinian I. The appeal to tradition provides an argument for innovations, since the Bible, the apostolic church, and the church fathers constantly developed new practices and modified old ones. For Covell the Elizabethan settlement of 1559 forms the standard pattern for the English church; however, he feels that a reigning monarch can alter the settlement if changes in English society so require. Finding warrant for all practices in Scripture seems needless and even pointless, since even within scriptural times, changes were made. Moreover, the church fathers, through their recommendations and practices, also provide a sanction for contemporary church practices.

The necessity of a set discipline justifies the use of subscription, the agreement by all ministers to adhere to the same articles of faith and to use the same ceremonies. In answer to Nichols's pleas for freedom of conscience, Covell urges the need for humility and obedience. Like Nichols he sees nothing as truly indifferent, but unlike Nichols he believes that everything commonly so designated should be accepted out of a sense of duty; if it is a small matter, the minister need not object to it, and if it is an important matter, the monarch has the duty to enforce conformity. The established church government by bishops finds its justification in the edicts of the monarch and its precedent in "all ancient churches." Covell points out that metropolitans, or archbishops, appeared as early as 255 A.D., called forth by the growth of the early church in population and area. Covell grants the importance of a preaching ministry, but whereas Nichols finds no shortage of excellent preachers, Covell argues that the universities have not produced a sufficient number of preachers both gifted and learned and that the reading of Scripture and prayers can be of more service than a bad sermon. A nonpreaching minister can provide more edification than a bad preacher. On similar grounds of necessity, Covell justifies nonresidency and the plurality of ecclesiastical holdings by one person; both practices will, under adverse conditions, give the people the best ministry possible.

In his twelfth chapter, Covell takes up objections to the Book of Common Prayer and answers them one by one. The objections he lists might serve as touchstones to define puritanism were he not so thorough, wide-ranging, and lacking in emphasis; he seems to have included every reservation he has heard, even from loyal, perfectly conforming members of the established church. In fact, occasionally he shares the dissenters' misgivings and falls back simply upon the necessity of obedience to, and respect for, authority to justify the practice. A sampling of his assertions may be worthwhile, the objections being always easily deducible from his defense. Thus he argues that the prayer book follows the Roman missal only where the missal follows the church fathers. Unlike reformed prayer books, such as the Genevan, the English prayer book best suits its time and place. Using excerpts from the Epistles and Gospels is justified by tradition and by the fact that chapter divisions do not date back to antiquity. Long prayers do not interfere with preaching; few prayers are truly long, whereas many sermons are prolix. It is right to pray to be "defended from all adversity," because the Lord's Prayer includes the petition "deliver us from evil." Praying for deliverance from tempests and lightning in winter is appropriate, because these phenomena are manifestations of God's wrath and may strike whenever he wills. The "Nunc Dimittis" and similar prayers are no more objectionable than the Psalms. Baptism administered by women is not recommended but may be necessary under special circumstances. Communion given to the sick is justified, because the sick are a part of the religious community. The ring in marriage is an appropriate symbol. Confirmation strengthens faith. The burial service edifies the living, as do prayers for the dead. The sign of the cross in baptism could be omitted but does no harm, for it is not given sacramental significance. To pray that all may be saved is consistent with Hope. Prayers for the help of the angels are nowhere forbidden. In his responses, Covell implicitly or explicitly uses reason and tradition to show that the practice in question does not violate any doctrinal principle and that being at worst harmless, it may be prescribed.

To Nichols's plea for toleration, Covell answers in effect that toleration applies to those outside the church. In other words, members of the Church of England must be bound by its rules, but nonmembers in various categories may be tolerated in various ways. Surprisingly, Jews receive the most lenient treatment: They may be permitted to reside in a kingdom and even to establish synagogues, under supervision. In historical fact, Jews had been expelled from England in 1290 and were not officially readmitted until 1655; therefore Covell advocates a policy not permitted by the laws of his time, though apparently these particular laws were not strictly enforced. Idolaters, a category that includes Roman Catholics, may live in the state but may not set up their own churches. Finally, heretics should be treated charitably, with a view to their conversion. Members of a fourth category, the Anabaptists, appear only in Covell's final chapter, where they are considered a danger to the religious and civil peace of a kingdom. Where the persistent nonconformists fit is not clear; by inference from Covell's other statements, some may be tolerated as quiet heretics, but the more active nonconformists could be linked with Anabaptists as a seditious group.

A Modest and reasonable examination, of some things in vse in the Church of England, sundrie times heretofore misliked, and now lately, in a Booke called the (Plea of the Innocent:) and an Assertion for true and Christian Church policy, made for a full satisfaction to all those, that are of judgement, and not possessed with a preiudice against this present Church Gouernment, wherein the principall poynts are fully, and peaceably aunswered, which seeme to bee offensiue in the Ecclesiasticall State of this Kingdome. By *William Covell,* Doctor of Divinitie. At London, Printed by Humfrey Lownes for Clement

Knight, and are to be solde at his shop at the Signe of the holy Lambe in Saint
Paules Churchyard. 1604.

[Excerpts: pp. 25–31, 39–45.]

Chap. III.

The Censure of a Book called the *Plea of the Innocent*.

Where the persons of men, have so near affinity with the actions performed by
them, it will require great moderation and care, so to censure the one, as that
we may not justly be suspected to disgrace the other: the neglect of this, (a
fault which is too common both in the times before us and in our age) hath
turned the confutation of errors to personal reproofs, and hath made the
defenders', weakness, or Indiscretion, the greatest adversary to a good cause;
and howsoever some partial men are carried with as much love to all they do, as
they are to themselves that do it; and with like disposition, are impatient to be
touched in either; yet no man of wisdom or understanding, can think it to be
all one, to have his action or his person, censured; some Actions I confess there
are of that nature, which are the defects of our ordinary weakness; and therein
though not Excusable, yet carry some reason to challenge a favorable compassion, extending either to forgiveness or to concealments; (which both doubtless are the effects of men that are truly virtuous) whereas some others, as it
were by covenant are performed to that end, that they rest amongst all men,
and in all ages, liable to that censure which time shall give them, And they
merit. *Of the first sort are our sins, in which kind our profession hath had some evil
Confessors;* of the Latter are Books, which as they are acts performed, with the
best of our judgment, voluntary, with deliberation, and with a resolution by
covenant either to answer or endure what Censures shall light upon them, it
cannot be any breach of Charity, or modesty, where the opinions misliked are
defended, to censure the Books, which are made in defense of them. And
although every man in reason is tied, to be careful of his good name, yet seeing
that both every hard Censure, is not a proof to continue error, nor every error
an imputation to a man that deserves well; It is not all one to say such a Book is
evil written, and to say such a one is not an honest man: The first is allowed in
the warrantable liberty of all learning, but the latter, Charity, and Humility,
do both forbid, as being but the dangerous effect of too much pride. Things
that are evil in manners, are evil in that they are done, and are a just imputation to the party in that they are known; but writings that are Censured, carry

not ever that sentence among them, which some ignorant, or partial opposite, shall impose upon them; nor even do men censure, as some enemies peradventure would make them speak. There are Commentaries we know upon Saint *Luke,* which pass under Saint *Ambrose* name, of which *Ruffinus* in his second Book of *Invectives,* maketh Saint *Jerome* to give this Censure, that he dallied in the words, and *slept in the sense.* Which surely as the best writers are of opinion, was rather forged by *Ruffinus,* to make Saint *Jerome* odious, than spoken by Saint *Jerome,* to disgrace Saint *Ambrose.* Doubtless it were great pity, that seeing the world so much erreth in the choice of friends, that this so necessary an office rather than omitted, should not be performed by our worst acquaintance, and the resolution of all men ought to be this (which I thank God I find in myself) if thy friend chide justly in his Censure, he hath profited thee, if undeservedly yet he meant to do thee good, so that to the first being bound for that which he hath done, and to the other for that which he would have done, in reason for this good office, were tied to both; and for myself I never wrote any thing, with that mind to have it published in print (although some things I have done for which with Master *Beza* I crave pardon) but I am very willingly content to be Censured for them; when the chief troubles of the Church for discipline were either appeased with discretion, or else buried with the Authors of them, suddenly in the year 1602 came forth a Book written by Master *Nicholles,* as an Apology for the dealing in that cause *Intituled* the *Plea of the Innocent.* Wherein as there were many things, that served to little use, saving only to express that honest desire to be well thought of, which peradventure the Author had, so the first thing, though not the greatest in my opinion to be misliked, was the want of due consideration of the time, for surely if *Solomon* said true (which no man hath reason to make doubt of) that there was a time for all things; a time to keep silence and a time to speak, in my weak judgment, it had been much fitter (considering the eager contention amongst those of the Church of *Rome*) to have been lookers on, rather at the event of that quarrel, than to have been Authors of any new disagreement amongst ourselves; but so different are the dispositions of men, that what one man taketh to be a reason why a thing should be done, and other peradventure taketh it to be a reason why it should not be done; to have forborne a little had been much safer for the Church, and in all reason more honorable for yourselves. I wish the Author of that book had those three ornaments, which S. *Jerome* calleth the foundation of all virtue; a patience to be silent, an opportunity to speak, and a contempt of riches. Doubtless to renew an unnatural contention that was almost buried, and especially at that time, when all proceedings in the Church were without rigor, as it could not choose but be labor evil spent, so it was likely to bring little advantage unto God's Church. Peradventure I mistake the cause, which moved him then to undertake that Treatise, we will hear himself in his Preface what he saith, we have suffered (meaning himself and others that have labored for reformations), "and endured much reproach, and contempt, which we have patiently borne, and with great silence, for divers years sustained, that on our part the sacred word of righteousness, might not be evil spoken of, and as much as in us lieth, we might cut off all occasions to the common adversary to prevail against the holy Church of Christ which is among us." This surely was just reason, and if it were performed as he saith, it was not performed without Just cause; for doubtless there is nothing of so small moment that hath brought greater disadvantage to our Church, than that with so much violence we have differed amongst ourselves and blessedness surely shall be their portion, who in this kind have been forward to make peace; but it is not these embracings of *Joab*, nor the kisses of *Judas*, that can bury from the world's eye, those bitter *Invectives*, of *Whittingam, Goodman, Knox, Buckanan, Gilby, Martin, Throgmorton, Penury, Fenner* and sundry other, most odious and unsavory books (besides a great number of others without name) all which must needs testify, that for this whole time of our happy peace, whatsoever the occasions were, the matter hath been carried with little silence, and less patience. These men in this case (how well soever they have deserved otherwise,) have not been for bitterness of speech much inferior to the Heretics of former times, and of whose followers I may say, with Saint Chrisostom; "In age they are younger but in malice Equal; the Brood of serpents are of less stature, but have not less poison. The Whelps of Wolves, though they cannot hurt so cunningly, yet will hurt with biting, and desire to suck Blood." The sum of all is as *Sidonius* speaketh; "openly they envied, basely they forged, and servilely they were proud"; and that which made all this to be much worse, was that the Authors of this evil-speaking, made Religion to be a warrant to speak evil; and whilst they offended upon this ground, others were desirous to offend, that they might not differ, from their example so that a double fault lieth upon the first Author; one that they offended in their own person, the second that they were examples to others to the like offense. But why continued you not in this silence still? notwithstanding all this (say you) "The state of things is worse than ever before and I cannot tell whether our *connivance* in suffering of evil speeches against us, hath done the Church harm. For now Papists begin to comfort themselves, yea they challenge unto them the name of honest and true men, and good subjects, and by the reproachful name of *Puritan,* All godly

Protestants are most cunningly depraved." *Give me leave quietly to tell you this much;* That (unless I mistake it) you have little reason or any that hath labored in that cause to think that the state of *things is worse than before,* At that time when you wrote thus what men were committed for their disobedience? arraigned for their treasons? or where was that *assault* as you *call it of Subscription?* besides, all Godly Protestants are not termed *Puritans;* no it is but the singular affection of a some few, that would seem upright, which have gained that name, wherein they do much glory, last of all if by your sufferance, some Priests grew insolent, and were not afraid in comparison to make themselves to be more righteous than you, this was no reason so unreasonably to provoke the *Reverend Fathers* of the Church against you; but rather all to have joined and yourselves foremost against them, and yet he not guilty that is accused, but he that is convinced in this cause. But to let pass the occasion of that treatise; give me leave without offense to give you my opinion of the whole Book: it is a verbal reiterating of the same things; handled and discoursed by some of those with whom by some occasion you have much nearness, I speak it not that I think you had their help, for to this there needs none, but to show that the labor might well have been spared seeing others with far better success, had travailed in that same cause; Contradictions there are divers and all is unsaid in the last Chapter, which before you have handled in the whole Book; speeches that savor of flattery too plain. First of the Queen whose worthiness far exceeded whatsoever you could speak of her, but surely you cannot possibly commend her government, who as it seems by your complaints was no more careful to have the Church reformed, as you deal with the Queen so you deal with the Council, nay rather than fail you will flatter the Bishops also. You reckon up a true Catalogue of their excellent uses in this Church; and yet notwithstanding, if any harm should have come to our late Queen, you threaten a little after to lay it to their charge. Much like unto the Author of the demonstration of discipline who saith that the Bishops by their government give leave to a man to be anything, but a sound Christian; nay yourself fear not to say, (which certainly is not true,) "they that were incensed against the Puritans, by the Papist's means"; nay you spare not our first *Bishops,* in our late Sovereign's time, which having fled in Queen *Mary's* days, were not likely in reason to be favorers of the Church of *Rome;* hereunto I may add your often repetitions of the same things; besides is not this a strange phrase? "We cannot tell whether we might by the laws and order of this Realm subscribe, although it were otherwise lawfully by God's word." As if the Laws of this Land could be a restraint for subscribing being warranted in God's word, which they so earnestly impose only in this respect because it is so warranted. I omit false English, which could not be the Printer's fault. The principle points which you seem to handle we will answer, God willing, in the Chapters following; and with this desire rather to find out the truth than to confute you, the one is a duty, but the other can be small honor. Neither are you to think me over arrogant in this censure, seeing I may much better do it to you than you to his Grace whom you ought to all duty not to have named, but with greater honor, having showed unto you more favor, as yourself cannot but confess, than many others of your quality and desserts. I will therefore conclude this point, saying with that learned man (whom I must ever reverence) as he spake of Master *Cartwright's* second Reply. "Let me not live if ever I saw anything writ more loosely or almost most Childishly," and after much to the same effect, the conclusion is this, he is altogether unworthy to be confuted by any man of learning. Surely there is nothing we do taste worse than to have a true censure of those things, which oftentimes either out of ignorance or affection are much esteemed, which serveth in the end only to delude ourselves and deceive others; but though the flattery of *Parasites do seem pleasant, yet the wounds of a Lover are much better.*

Chap. IV.

The proceeding of the Reformers wholly unlawful.
[Excerpt]

The Book which we Censured in the former Chapter, called the *Plea of the Innocent,* undertaketh (very strangely in my opinion) the defense of the proceeding in this whole cause. For although the Author himself might have assurance of his own sincerity, whereof I cannot accuse him (though some do) yet surely he could not be so ignorant of what had passed, since the beginning of her late Majesty's Reign, nor so charitable to excuse the manner of it, that a defense of the whole Story might have been better spared than written at that time, and doubtless if all other means of opposition had failed, their own dealing was an overthrow sufficient to that cause. The first thing that he misliketh is that they are called *Puritans;* and in the clearing them from all affectation of this name, he spendeth the whole Chapter; making other of his brethren that seemed to be less Religious, and the Universities (places which in duty he ought to have more honored) to be the principal Authors of this name, for to term them *Puritans.* But seeing the end of names is but to distinguish, and those who first used it amongst us, did rather show what their own followers did esteem of them, and what themselves affected, than what they were; It cannot in reason be an imputation to any, that they were termed by that name. Neither do I think (although divers of them did glory to be so termed) that this name first proceeded from us, but rather that the Church of *Rome,* seeing us to reform ourselves to a purer Religion than they professed, and that divers amongst us not content with that, desired yet to be more pure, accounting all of us to be Heretics, these by a special name, as affecting to seem more holy than others, (a common practice of the Heretics in old time) they termed by the name of Puritans; so that the fault which he layeth upon us, doubtless had his original from those of the Church of *Rome;* and therefore one *Rushton* in a Table dedicated to Cardinal *Allen* then Governor of Douai maketh *Puritanism* an Heresy which began in the year 1563. neither do I think it can easily be found that any Protestant in England before that time, in any public writing, used the name of Puritan; for no man can be ignorant but that he who was the strongest and first opposite to this new discipline, and handled this argument with greatest learning, was himself in all preciseness far purer, than those that most gloried in that name; and was never an adversary to any of this cause, that was not either malicious, arrogant, or an hypocrite; neither is it fit to lay that distinction upon the University, of youths and *Precisians,* (as this pleader doth) as though all that were not for this new *Reformation* were like one *Athacius* who bending himself by all means against the heresy of *Priscillian* (the hatred of which one evil was all the virtue he had) became so wise in the end, that every man careful of virtuous conversation, studious of Scripture, and given unto any abstinence in diet, was set down in his Calendar of suspected *Priscillianists.* For whom it should be expedient to approve their soundness of faith, by a more licentious and loose behavior; neither do I think unto a great number that desired this name, could anything more fitly be applied than that unto the *Cathari,* a sect of Heretics, not clean but worldlings; or as Epifanius calleth them, pure impure ones. But surely if either the *Cathari,* the *Novatians,* the *Pelagians,* the *Donatists,* or any sect of the papists at this day worthily deserve to be termed by the name of *Puritan,* then surely it is no great error to apply that name to a number amongst us, who are ever ready to boast of their innocency, and in respect of themselves, to account all of a contrary faction unholy, and profane. Others this Author accounteth old barrels. And yet if he had well remembered what he saith in any other place; "That whoso feareth an oath or is an ordinary resorter to Sermons earnest against excess, riot, Popery, or any disorder, they are called in the University, Precisians, and in other places Puritans." Surely if this description of a *Puritan* were true, neither were there much reproach in the name, nor would a great number be left out of that sect, who in all humility, religion and conscience, have learned to submit themselves to the present States; and I doubt not but very truly a great number of the *Reverend Fathers* of the *Church,* might more fitly be called precise, than those that for the earnest affectation of a new discipline, desire by their followers to be called pure. For surely in all those things mentioned as notes to discern a *Puritan,* many that are very far from that peevish singularity of some amongst us, have done the Church more service in one year, and lived with greater sincerity their whole life, than the principal of those who are distinguished by that name; Is it not a strange presumption to *Impropriate Conscience, Holiness, Innocency,* and *Integrity* only to some few, as if all the rest who have severed themselves from the Church of *Rome,* were no better than Atheists, time-servers, profane, and irreligious, only in this respect because by their authority and learning, they have resisted this unreasonable desire of a new discipline? So hardly do we temper ourselves, when we are strongly persuaded of our own fancies, but that all that are contrary or repugnant to us, we traduce them to the world, as men without conscience, only for this that they are opposite. A practice which alone is able is discover to the world, our exceeding pride, and intolerable self-love; for no man can doubt but the adversaries to this cause have exceeded the other, in all that wherein they are or would seem to be most excellent; only they have learned to obey, which is much better than all the sacrifice of fools. But seeing words have so many Artificers, by whom they are made, and the things whereunto we apply them, are fraught with so many varieties, it is not always apparent what the first inventors respected, much less what every man's inward conceit is, which useth their words; doubtless to distinguish things that are of a different condition, is the most ordinary, and the safest use of names, seeing necessarily to collect what things are, from names by which they are called, can have small warrant, these being but effects oftentimes of malice, sometimes of ignorance, mistaking sometimes of some particular accident; all which serve but in the construction of wisemen, to make their estimation by a better rule; and where things are not in nature such, not to condemn them, though they be called by evil names. *The name of Puritan or Precisian* no man hath reason to use it as a disgrace, seeing with us it serveth, but to signify such, as being more strict for observation of Ceremonies, than others (both parties being opposite in that) they both notwithstanding may be equally distant from the Church of *Rome,* and therefore as I cannot excuse such, as profanely make it any imputation to be precise, (a duty which surely ought to be performed by us all in a stricter manner) so neither do I think the proceeding of those to be altogether lawful, who under this name having shrouded themselves, account all men besides, to be profane Atheists, and the resistance which they find in their violent course, to be a cruel persecutor of innocent men in a good cause. They that teach the world to think and to speak thus, must needs be judged both to slander the profession of the Gospel amongst us, and to make themselves the best part of that Church which is severed from the customs of the Church of *Rome.* But lest peradventure none of them either mislike the name, or make the original of their sufferings to be their innocency, let us hear one of them plead for the rest, "Men which make conscience of many things, which the Reverend Fathers and many learned men affirmed to be lawful, and for this they were called Puritans"; There is no man can think, but in matters of this nature, the judgment of the Reverend Fathers, and many other learned men that were not Bishops, might have overswayed the stiffness of some few (for so they were at the first) without enforcing any faction or breach of the Church's union; this phrase is usual in that Book (the goodness of our cause) and the innocency of our persons, *God delivered his innocent servants;* and being reproved for their proceeding, their answer is, the "innocency of our cause doth constrain us," and that the world may know the reason of their sufferings, they say "the chiefest cause of their trouble and reproach, is their careful and zealous following of God's holy Word, and their tender conscience in offending God." Would not a man think that the Church of England which hath severed itself not without many dangers from the Church of *Rome,* had looked back and become a Harlot and a bloody Kingdom? surely there cannot be a greater blemish laid upon this Church (which both is, and is desirous to be thought reformed) than that it hath persecuted for their conscience, *men holy, religious, Innocent,* and it a good cause. The whole tenor of that plea of the Innocent runneth on in this course as if it were the sighs and mournings of a Church upright and pure, laboring under the burden of persecution, because they cannot in conscience yield unto *Superstition* as others do; from hence are these speeches. They seeing our Innocency that of mere conscience "our uprightness makes us poor innocent men." And in another place to the same purpose. "We can boldly and in the sight of God protest our Innocency, we and our honest and just cause. It is now at the least three and thirty years since our troubles began to be heavy upon us, let them show how we have moved our finger against our dread Sovereign," and in defense of all those who have labored in this cause he is not afraid to say: "Was not all our doings by humble Supplications, honest and Christian

Apologetical writings, and by lowly and earnest suing by our friends?" And further: In this "we have done no other way than all Christian Ministers may and ought to do." And if any man marvel how the Bishops became their enemies he answereth; "Bishops were our enemies by the Papist's means." Could any man Imagine that either so much without cause against the *Bishops*, or so many things without truth for themselves, could have been uttered, if an opinion peradventure of that wherein themselves were Innocent, did not carry them with overmuch charity, both to think all which was against them to be too vehement and too much, and all for them over modest and too little. Can it be thought that the Author of the plea of the Innocent, should be persuaded that the Papists had made any of the Bishops to be their enemies? or that those libels which passed under the name of *Admonitions, Supplications, Demonstrations, Martin, Dialogues* and such like should by any indifferent reader be thought to be either humble, honest, or Christian? or that they had done nothing in this cause more than all Christian Ministers may, and ought to have done? no surely; the Christian part of the world to whom our unnatural, violent, and unholy contentions have come, are able to witness too well that he who hath brought a willingness to speak evil, and hath performed it (in how unseemly a manner soever) hath been thought by the patrons of that cause, to have merited sufficiently the name of a brother, and to have been a deserved partner of their liberal contribution; This to many young men hath been a dangerous temptation (I mean those of the meanest sort,) who in themselves naturally have a double advantage to give strength to this dangerous weakness, The one a disposition to reprove wherein their own innocency is thought greatest when they dare in unseemly terms take upon them to control others; The other a hasty desire to seem of some account, which, in an ordinary course without great labor is not easily attained, whereas evil speaking and unseasonable railings (Commonly called *Zealous* preaching) bringeth them (at least among their partial followers) into an opinion of learning, innocency, and purified *Zeal;* But let these men understand, that where readers are of Indifferency (as sometimes their Books fall into the hands of such) (though for the most part they are dispersed amongst the Brethren of the cause) they gain this Just *Censure, That that cause cannot be good which hath not other patrons to support it, than those who have learned nothing, but only to speak evil.* I am sorry the inferior sort of our Clergy, are both so ignorant themselves, and have possessed their auditors with the same error, that we may not allow anything used in the Church of *Rome,* no more than anything used in any assembly of the Heathen whatsoever; So that whilst over bitterly we distaste everything, which is in use in that Church (whose greatest part is infected with much error) we breed an opinion in those who are not fully resolved, that we rather mislike many things because they use them, than for that we are able to give a reason why we do mislike them. The best course in this had been first to have made Demonstration that the same things being used by divers are all one; or that those things contended for by authority in our Church, were not in the better and former times of the Church or are not of an indifferent nature, neither can be made lawful by any circumstance. These things being neglected and other means used, less reasonable, and less honest, we conclude that the proceeding of the *Reformers* hitherto, hath been altogether unlawful and without warrant.

17

Oliver Ormerod

The Picture of a Puritane

1605

(Excerpt)

OLIVER ORMEROD (*ca.* 1580–1626) was educated at Emmanuel College, Cambridge; he received his B.A. degree in 1599. His staunch defenses of the Church of England against both radical reformers and Roman Catholics were published in a short space of time, 1605 to 1606. From 1610 he served as rector of two parishes successively and apparently devoted himself to his pastoral work. *The Picture of a Puritane* is a lengthy attack on English puritans and German Anabaptists that argues a similarity between the two in belief and conduct. The characterization of a puritan found there is practically mirrored in *Puritano-papismus,* a treatise appended (or "annexed") with separate pagination, to *The Picture of a Puritane.* The dialogue here reprinted is the first of three dialogues in the appended work and provides a representative, as well as fairly concise, view of Ormerod's concept of a puritan, whom he seeks to associate with both the separatists of his time and the heretics of past ages.

Ormerod dedicates *The Picture of a Puritane* to all those, and only to those, whom the puritans have slandered. Specifically he mentions Queen Elizabeth, King James, the Privy Council, the bishops, the cathedral churches and their officers, and the universities; a noteworthy omission is the Parliament. At the outset of what he notes is his first work, he reveals his thoroughgoing loyalty to the establishment and his respect for authority in intellectual, civil, and religious matters. He writes in dialogue form; his initial and longest section consists of alternate statements by a German and an Englishman, the former describing faults of the Anabaptists and the latter matching, and often exceeding, them with accounts of parallel actions and works drawn from the English puritans. The indictments fall under the general heading of rejection of duly prescribed ceremonies in the church, errors in theology, and resistance to authority in both church and state. The two speakers make extensive use of quotations from Anabaptists and puritans, both prominent and obscure, as examples of reprehensible attitudes; each speaker counters his opponents with quotations from the church fathers and reformed theologians, and frequently also with biblical texts.

The English religious figures cited as puritans are a disparate group. The signers of the Millenary Petition are treated as a unit, and their specific requests are denounced. A large number of quotations derive from the works of Thomas Cartwright, who repudiated the designation of puritan but received praise from the Marprelate authors. Cartwright, a professor of divinity at Cambridge, disputed learnedly and was treated with respect by his Anglican opponent John Whitgift. Cartwright had little in common with the other specific exemplars of puritan behavior cited by Ormerod: the fanatics William Hacket, who proposed to dethrone Queen Elizabeth, and his equally fanatic admirer Edmund Coppinger. Although Ormerod sees puritanism as varied and changeable in form, the juxtaposition of these three figures gives the term a wide range of meanings indeed. At the same time, William Perkins, another Cambridge scholar often listed among the puritans by modern scholars, is quoted several times in opposition to puritan tenets. Apparently statements attributed to Cartwright in *A Second Admonition to the Parliament* (1572) and Cartwright's controversy with Whitgift made him seem an activist, unlike Perkins, and therefore unacceptable.

The appearance of John Calvin and Theodore Beza, as well as Perkins, in support of antipuritan arguments may be explained by a scrutiny of Ormerod's extensive use of quotations and themes from the works of William Whitaker; this master of Saint John's College in Cambridge from 1586 until his death in 1595 showed considerable favor to nonconformist ideas in church discipline. A staunch Calvinist in theology, Whitaker was highly regarded by Whitgift (and even by Robert Bellarmine, although Whitaker wrote extensively against Roman Catholicism) for his wide, profound learning, particularly concerning Scripture and the church fathers. At a time when Calvinistic theology dominated both Church of England and nonconformist thinking, Ormerod can disregard suspicious tendencies in religious practices and discipline because of his respect for doctrinal orthodoxy, learning, and high position in the universities. The church fathers and the reformed theologians stand together in his mind against the controversialists who lack respect for authority; and the university scholars, unless they speak out directly against the establishment, seem part of it.

Another interesting dichotomy in *The Picture of a Puritane* sets Peter Ramus against Aristotle. The puritans are accused of making errors in their use of scriptural warrant for their positions because they use the faulty Ramistic logic, a form of dialectical reasoning, instead of traditional Aristotelian logic. Specific examples of Ramistic methods in argumentation are not given, but specific principles of Aristotelian logic appear in refutations of some puritan arguments. For example, the puritans confuse cause with effect by calling the surplice a source of dissension. Again, in arguing against benefices, they confuse the institution with the man: The existence of a benefice itself should not be attacked simply because some men pursue and gain it by reprehensible means. Reliance on a pagan philosopher is justified by the fact that Paul, in his Epistles, quoted Aratus, Menander, and Epimenides and thus gave biblical sanction to the use of pagan learning in religious matters. Here, as elsewhere, Ormerod seeks the help of, and remains deferential to, authority; Aristotle is useful in his argument, and the example of Paul justifies the use of Aristotle.

Puritano-papismus, appearing under the same cover though with separate pagination, supplements *The Picture of a Puritane* with three dialogues. In each, a puritan and a protestant are the speakers. The puritan is allowed his point of view only to a limited extent; much of the time he merely asks questions that lead the protestant to explain puritan errors. At other times the puritan raises objections to the church of Rome only to have the protestant show that the same criticism applies to the puritans. At the beginning, Ormerod rejects the notion that puritans oppose Roman Catholics more strongly than do the Anglicans, arguing instead that both types of establishment opponents have much in common. The original list of similarities given in the first dialogue does not advance the argument very far; for instance, to argue that two groups are akin because both profess loyalty to the king seems meaningless at a time when almost no one would profess disloyalty. But later in the first dialogue, more significant questions are raised as the protestant shows the similarity in belief between puritans and each of a large number of heretics, ranging in time from the contemporary Brownists back to the early Cathari and Donatists.

The second dialogue, "Treating of Their Perseverance in Schisme, and of Their Ghostly *Idolatrie*," asserts more briefly Ormerod's favorite point: the need for conformity. Church fathers, chiefly, are quoted to show the importance of a uniform discipline and of uniform ceremonies within a church. Where the puritan argues that his party differs from the church authorities only in external and accidental matters, the protestant notes in rebuttal only one substantial difference: The puritans are said to show lack of orthodoxy in the explanation of the Article of Religion concerning Christ's descent into hell. Here Ormerod seems to have difficulty in finding specific puritan departures from orthodoxy in theology or doctrine. Another charge, that of idolatry, turns back against the puritans a criticism they frequently made against the Church of England but proves hard to document; Ormerod notes merely that the puritans worship their own opinions—thus again rejecting authority.

The third, very brief dialogue brings in a new argument for conformity: It would be inequitable to ask some ministers to conform and to allow dispensations to others. Hence tolerance, even in indifferent things, should not be permitted. The final impression the reader gains from Ormerod's work is that obedience to authority in matters of religion is essential and that the need for uniformity within the church justifies both the enforcement of subscription and the removal of nonconformists from the ministry.

The Picture of a Puritane: Or, A Relation of the opinions, qualities, and practices of the *Anabaptists* in Germanie, and of the Puritanes in England. Wherein is firmely prooved, that the Puritanes doe resemble the Anabaptists, in above fourescore seuerall thinges. By *Oliuer Ormerod, of Emmanuel* Colledge in *Cambridge.* Whereunto is annexed a short treatise, entituled, Puritano-papismus: or a discoverie of Puritan-Papisme. Newly corrected and enlarged. *London* Printed by *E. A.* for *Nathaniel Fosbroke,* and are to be solde at his Shop, at the West end of Paules. 1605.

Puritano-papismus: Or *A Discoverie of Puritan-papisme:* made by way of Dialogue or conference, betweene a Protestant and a Puritane.
[Excerpt: pp. 1–18.]

The 1. Dialogue.

Wherein is plainly shewed, that the Puritans have in sundry things joined with the *Pharisees, Apostolics, Aerians, Pepuzians, Petrobrusians, Florinians, Cerinthians, Nazarens, Beguardines, Ebionites, Catobabdites, Catharists, Enthusiasts, Donatists, Jovianists, Brownists* and *Papists.*

The Protestant.   Come neighbor, let us shake hands and be friends.

The Puritan.   Shake hands with a Formalist?

The Protestant.   Why not with a Formalist? you will not stick to shake hands with a papist.

The Puritan.   Do we shake hands with the Papists? "Whilest you compare us to the Anabaptists, some friend of yours might think that you said truly, because such, always seeking dark and solitary places, might happily have some favorers which are not known. But when you join us with the Papists, which are commonly known to all men, whose Doctrine we impugn as well as you, whose marks and badges we can less away with than you, whose company we fly more than you, whose punishment we have called for more than you for your part have done: and therefore are condemned of them as cruel, when you oftentimes carry away in the name of mildness and moderation, which forsooth know no commandment in the Scriptures to put Heretics to death: when I say, you join us thus with the Papist, you do not only lose your credit, in these untrue surmises (wherein I trust with the indifferent reader, you never had any) but you make all other things suspected, which you affirm, so that you give men occasion to take up the common proverb against you, I WILL TRUST YOU NO FURTHER THAN I SEE YOU."

The Protestant.   *Pilate* and *Herod* were at great odds about private matters between themselves, but when they had to deal with Christ, they could then become friends, and conjoin together for his destruction: The *Pharisees* and *Sadducees* were of contrary sects, yet were they both enemies to Christ and his Doctrine.

The Anabaptists agreed not with the Papists, yet they both sought to deface the church of Christ, and did cleave together in their devices against Christ, as the Scales of *Leviathan:* even so you, though ye be at enmity with the papists; though you impugn their Doctrine; though ye cannot away with their marks and badges; though ye fly their company; though ye call for their punishment; yet, in defacing and depraving of this Church of England, you fully join with them against us. So that as there was a day, when *Herod* and *Pilate* were made friends, so there is (I see) a day when Papists and Puritans are made friends. And for this cause did our reverend Brethren, of the University of Oxford observe this seven-fold semblance betwixt you and the Papists.

"1. You both entitle yourselves, the Kings afflicted subjects, and above all other, his devoted Servants.

2. You both pretend an enforcement of a speedy recourse to his Majesty, for a present redress and reformation.

3. You both complain, of being overwhelmed with enduring persecution through loss of living and liberty.

4. You both ground your Doctrine and Discipline upon the sacred Text of God's word and Gospel.

5. You both condemn the obedience of us Protestants to the laws established, to be, not for conscience and zeal: but for moral honesty, and fear of temporal punishment, say the Papists; for their own quiet, credit and profit in the world, say you.

6. You both renounce a public alteration and dissolution of the state ecclesiastical.

7. You both deny, that you exhibit your petitions, with a tumultuous spirit, or with a disloyal and schismatical mind."

The Puritan.   What tell you me of these things? these are but matters of circumstances; but have you observed any semblance in any matter of substance?

I tell you plainly, that we defy the Pope and his Religion: we say that he is Antichrist, because he advanceth himself above all that is called God. For when Kings and Emperors (to whom the name of God is communicated) do come into the presence of his holiness, they must (forsooth) after obeisance done in three several distances, fall down before him and kiss his feet.

And if they be in presence when he taketh horse, the chiefest of them must hold his right stirrup, and likewise when he lighteth off do the same.

Take an example of his insolent and Antichristian behavior. Pope *Alexander* the third excommunicated the Emperor *Frederick Barbarossa*, and took his Son prisoner in *Venice*. And when he came into the Church of

243

Saint *Mark* there, to the end that he might be absolved, and his Son restored, the Pope having commanded him to prostrate himself upon the ground, and so to ask pardon, set his foot in the neck of the said Emperor, saying: it is written, "Super aspiden & basiliscum ambulabis, & conculcabis Leonem & Draecaonem."

The Protestant. If the Doctrine of your consistorians and disciplinarians might take place, our Kings of England (I fear) would in short time be brought to the like slavery: for do not they teach that Princes ought to submit themselves to the Seniors of the Church, and that they ought to be content to be ruled and governed, to be punished and corrected, to be excommunicated and absolved by their discretion, and at their pleasure? "Christian Princes must remember" (saith T.C.) "to subject themselves unto the Church, to submit their Scepters, to throw down their Crown before the Church: yea to lick the dust of the feet of the Church." Doth not this Puritan-popish Doctrine smell of Antichristianism?

But to proceed, wherein do your chief writers, dissent from the Popish writers?

The Puritan. Wherein do we not?

The Protestant. Insist in some particulars.

The Puritan. Cardinal *Bellarmine, Cardill, Harding* and the rest of the Popish Doctors teach, "that Councils and Synods may be assembled without the Knowledge of the Emperor."

The Protestant. Do not your Doctors teach the same Doctrine? have they not had many assemblies and classical Synods, whereunto the authorizement of the Prince was not had? is not their opinion answerable to their practice?

The Puritan. The Papists also teach, that the Emperor ought not to be over-ruler, or determiner in Councils and Synods.

The Protestant. Doth not T. C. teach the selfsame Doctrine? "No civil Magistrate" (saith he) "in Councils or Assemblies for Church matters can either be chief moderator, over-ruler, Judge or determiner."

The Puritan. Yea, but do any of our teachers deny the King's supremacy, as the Papists do?

The Protestant. What say you to T. C. who speaketh most clearly, and seemeth to be on the Pope's side in this matter. His words are these: "The Christian Sovereign ought not to be called the head under Christ, of the particular and visible Churches within his Dominions."

The Puritan. But do any of our writers, spoil the Civil Magistrate of all government in Ecclesiastical matters, as the Papists do?

The Protestant. Yes, the Admonitors say in plain terms, that "to these three jointly, that is, the Ministers, Seniors, and Deacons, is the whole regiment of the Church to be committed."

Now if the whole government of the Church, be to be committed to Ministers, Seniors, and Deacons, what authority remaineth to the civil Magistrate in the government of it?

The Puritan. I answer in the name of the Authors of the Admonition, "that the Prince and civil Magistrate hath to see, that the laws of God touching his worship, and touching all matters and orders of the Church, be executed and duly observed: and to see that every Ecclesiastical person, do that office whereunto he is appointed: and to punish those which fail in their office accordingly. As for the making of the orders and ceremonies of the Church, they do (where there is a constituted and ordered Church) pertain to the Ministers of the Church etc."

The Protestant. I reply with the words of the late Reverend Archbishop. "What? no more but to see them executed? how differeth this from Papist? The Papists give to the Christian Magistrate in Ecclesiastical matters potestatem acti & non juris, that is, to see those laws executed and put in practice that the Pope and his Clergy shall make, and to be as it were their executioner, but not to make any laws in Ecclesiastical matters: for doth not *Saunders* a popish writer say the same? Although I do not deny" (saith he) "that the knowledge of a fact that belongeth to the Ecclesiastical law, may be committed to Kings and Magistrates: and before the Ecclesiastical cause be determined, the King may use his authority to this end, that there may be some quiet place prepared where the Bishop shall consult, and that the Bishops be called to the same place at a certain day, and that in the meantime while the matter is in determining, common peace may be preserved even among the Priests themselves. To conclude, after the cause be determined and judged by the Priests, the King may punish him with the sword (which he carrieth not in vain) or by some other corporal punishment, which shall refuse to obey the sentence of the Priests."

Musculus also setteth out this Popish opinion, touching the authority of the civil Magistrate in Ecclesiastical affairs, very plainly in these words: "Those whom they call Ecclesiastical Persons, and we call them Papists,

245

will not commit to the Magistrate, any further authority in Religion, than to be the keeper and revenger of it, and of their Ecclesiastical Laws, that the Ecclesiastical policy may remain immovable: wherefore they deny him to have authority, in that he is a Magistrate, to make or to publish any Ecclesiastical laws, because such things pertain to those that do represent the Church; whose decrees and constitutions must be maintained and defended by the authority of the Magistrate."

But to leave this resemblance, what arguments do the Popish Doctors use against the Prince's authority in causes Ecclesiastical?

The Puritan.   *Saunders, Harding* and other of them do quote 2 *Chron.* 19:8. 11. which place maketh indeed fully against them: for *Jehosaphat* had chief authority and government both in things pertaining to the Church, and in things pertaining to the Commonwealth; but for better execution of them, the one he did commit to be executed by *Amaziah* the Priest, the other by *Zebadiah* a Ruler of the house of *Juda:* even as the King's Majesty, being in all causes, both Ecclesiastical and Temporal, within these his Realms and Dominions, supreme governor, committeth the hearing and judging of Ecclesiastical matters to the Reverend Fathers of the Church, and of Temporal matters, to the Right honorable, the Lord Chancellor and other Judges.

Now had *Jehosaphat* nothing to do with Church matters, because he made Amaziah Priest judge in the same? they may as well say, that he had nothing to do in Temporal affairs, because he also appointed *Zebadiah* to hear and determine them.

The Protestant.   True, and yet T. C. quoteth the selfsame place, to prove the selfsame thing, "look" (saith he) "in the second Book of the Chronicles in the 19. Chap. and in the 8. and 11. verses, and you shall see that there were a number appointed for the matters of the LORD, which were Priests, and Levites, and there were other also appointed for the King's affairs, and for matters of the Commonwealth etc."

The Puritan.   But in what other things agree we with the Papist?

The Protestant.   1. The Papists would not have the scriptures read in the Church to the people: No more would your Puritan-popish writers: for they blush not to say that "reading is no feeding, but as evil as playing upon a Stage, and worse too."

2. The Papists condemn our Book of common prayer, set out by public authority, and the whole order of service: so do you.

246

3. The papists say that our Sacraments are not rightly ministered: so say you likewise, as hath been already shewed.

4. The Papists say that we have no right ministery in England, no Pastors, no Bishops, because they be not rightly and canonically called to these functions: and the selfsame do you affirm, as hath also been shewed.

5. The Papists avouch that we are not the true church, no that we have not so much as the outward face and shew of the true Church: and the selfsame thing do your Puritan-popish teachers avouch, in their first Admonition, page 33. and in their second admonition, page. 6.

The Puritan. All this notwithstanding, we come far short of the Papists: for Popery is (as a one truly saith) "an hotch-potch and miserable mingle-mangle of all Satan's forgeries and devilish heresies. With *Carpocratian* Heretics they set up the image of Christ, and other Saints; with the *Anthropomorphits,* they paint God the Father like an old man with a grey beard: with the Pelagian Heretics, they maintain free will, power to justify ourselves, and to fulfill the commandments: with the *Messalians,* they mumble their Matins, Paternosters, and seven Psalms by number, upon a pair of Beads; with the *Tatians, Cataphryges, Montanists,* and *Ebionites,* they seek sanctification in eating and not eating, in marrying and not marrying, etc."

But not to insist in the enumeration of their Heresies can you shew that we have revived any old Heresies?

The Protestant. I can shew, that there was scarce any Heresy invented by old Heretics, which either the *Papists* or the *Puritans* have not revived and renewed with fresh and new colors. And besides their opinions, you have also their tricks, qualities, and conditions.

The Puritan. Insist I pray you in us, whom you call *Puritans:* can you prove that we have joined with any old Heretics?

The Protestant. Yes, you have joined with the *Pharisees, Apostolics, Aerians, Pepuzians, Petrobrusians, Florinians, Cerinthians, Nazarens, Beguardines, Ebionites, Catobabdites, Enthusiasts, Donatists.*

The Puritan. To begin with the *Pharisees,* wherein have we joined with them?

The Protestant. The *Pharisees* sewed Pillows of self-liking under their own arm-holes, and took no knowledge of beams in their own eyes; but evermore excepted against their brethren, as men not worthy the ground they trod upon. "Why eateth your Master" (said they to Christ's Disciples) "with Publicans and Sinners?" The like exception (to my knowledge) did some of your faction lately take against a Minister, that chanced to eat with one that was suspected to be a Papist. "Why eateth our Minister" (said they) "with one that is a Papist?"

2. The *Pharisees* separated themselves from other people as more holy than they, and therefore some think that they be called "Pharisees, quasi segregati, quod vita sanctimonia, a vulgi moribus & vita seperati essent, non aliter atque Monachi, quot Carthusianos vocant, as separated from the common sort in holiness of life and conversation, much like unto the Monks which be called Carthusians."

And do not you come near the *Pharisees* herein, when you despise all those that be not of your sect, as polluted, and not worthy to be saluted, as hath already been shewed?

3. *Josephus* observeth this to be another property of the *Pharisees, viz:* "that whatsoever their own reason persuaded them; id sequuntur pertinaciter, that they stubbornly followed." And the selfsame thing have I observed to be the property of stiff and stubborn Puritans in these days.

4. The *Pharisees* were (as the same *Josephus* witnesseth) "astutum hominum genus, arrogans, & interdum quoque regibus infestum, etc." that is, "a subtle kind of men, arrogant, and sometime deadly enemies to Kings": and so are you.

For it is not unknown to any that hath had any dealing with you in worldly affairs, how crafty and subtle you are in all your dealing.

As for your arrogancy and contempt of superiority, this is not unknown to the King's Majesty himself.

Puritans (saith his Highness) "are ever discontented with the present government and impatient to suffer any superiority, which maketh their sect unable to be suffered in any well-governed commonwealth."

Thus you see, that we have just cause to term you English *Pharisees* and to say with *Nazianzen:* "Pharisaion ou genos alla tropos ergasetai, not the nation but the conversation maketh a *Pharisee.*"

The Puritan. But wherein I pray you do we join with the *Apostolics, Aerians, Petrobrusians,* and the rest of those old Heretics before named?

The Protestant. The *Apostolics,* neither considering the diversity of times for Ecclesiastical policy; nor the true liberty of Christian Religion in things indifferent nor the authority of christian Magistrates, concerning the same, would have nothing to be used in the Church in these days, which was not used in the days of the Apostles; Now let it be imagined, whether your Preachers do not resemble them herein, when they complain, as hath been shewed, that we "have Surplices devised by Pope *Adrian.* etc. which the Church of God in the Apostles' time never knew and therefore they are not to be used."

Aerius (of whom the *Aerians* took their name) was condemned of Heresy both by *Epiphanius* and Saint *Austen,* for that he held, that Fasts appointed by the Church were not to be kept, and next, for saying that a "Presbyter should not be distinguished from a Bishop by any kind of difference." How then can you wipe away the blot of Heresy, that reckon (as hath been shewed) Saints' Eves, and Lent for "*Romish fasts*"; Archbishops and Bishops, for "new Ministers never ordained by God."

The *Petrobrusians* held, that holy-days are *Ethelothresceiai,* and no man hath, nor ever had, since *Moses,* authority to institute them in the old testament, nor in the new, except the Apostles, who instituted (as they say) the Sunday only. To this heresy of these *Petrobrusians,* did our Admonitors fully subscribe: for they condemned the observing of holy days, as a thing "contrary to the word of God, and as a piece of the Pope's portuise." But to proceed:

There were certain Heretics called *Beguardins,* who held, that "a spiritual man is not subject to human obedience": Now let it therefore be judged with indifferency, whether you Puritans have not some touch of this Heresy, who will not submit your necks and souls to the yoke of human obedience in things indifferent.

There were also other Heretics called *Acephali,* or *Catobabditae,* who would not suffer any Bishop to have any jurisdiction over them. Now if these *Catobabdites* were for this very cause reputed Heretics, what shall we say of you Puritans, that do tread in their steps? What reason can you bring that this should be an Heresy in them and none in you? where got you that exemption? or if it be an Heresy in both alike, why should you not be condemned for Heretics both alike.

The *Enthusiasts, Pepuzians,* and other old Heretics depended on dreams, visions, and revelations: and so have some of your Puritan preachers done, as hath been already proved.

The *Ebionites, Cerinthians, Nazarens,* and *Florinians,* were reputed heretics, because they tied men to a strict observation of Mosaical ceremonies. Now this old Heresy was renewed by one of your faction in Oxfordshire, (who as an Oxford Doctor testifieth) "when his father's ribs were broken, would not ride for a bonesetter on the Sabbath day."

The *Jovinianists* were condemned for Heretics, because they hold all sins to be equal. Now this Heresy have some of your faction begun to revive. For example sake and verifying what *I* have spoken, I will acquaint you with the very words of some of them.

To insist again in an Oxfordshire man, "there was one that went out of Oxford, and preached in a Market-town in Oxfordshire, that it is as great a sin to do any servile work upon the Sabbath, as to do murder and commit adultery."

And there was another *Individuum vagum*, that preached in a market-town in Somersetshire, that "it is as great a sin to throw a bowl on the Sabbath day as to kill a man." Yea some have not blushed to say, that "it is as great a sin to kill a man's Cock, as to kill his Servant."

But let us leave the *Jovinianists,* and come to the *Donatists.*

The Puritan.   Do we agree with the *Donatists?*

The Protestant.   Yes, the *Donatists* divided themselves from the congregations of other men, and had their private coventicles: so have you.

Again, the *Donatists* held the minister to be "de ipsa baptismi essentia, of the being of Baptism": and so do you, as hath already been shewed.

Yea, T. C. came not far short of the *Donatists,* when he taught, "that children of Heretics and of such as by excommunication, are cut off from the Church, may not be baptized." But let us come to our *Brownists,* which are indeed the very brood of the *Donatists.*

The Puritan.   Do we agree with the Brownists too.

The Protestant.   Yes, and that in so many things, as that I can hardly find any difference betwixt them and you.

To insist in some particulars, the *Brownists* strive about external matters, and separate themselves from us: for things ceremonial, as appeareth by the very confession of the "Overseers, Deacons, and Brethren of the English Church at Amsterdam in Holland, exiled," (as they falsely report) "for the Gospel of Christ." Their confession is this: "We testify by these presents unto all men, and desire them to take knowledge hereof, that we have not forsaken any one point of the true, ancient, Catholic, and Apostolic faith, professed in our land: but hold the same grounds of Christian religion with them still, agreeing likewise herein with the *Dutch, Scottish, German, French, Helvetian,* and all other Christian reformed Churches round about us, whose confessions published, we call to witness our agreement with them, in matters of greatest moment, being conferred with these Articles of our faith, etc." Now, as the *Brownists* do (by their own confession) "strive about external and ceremonial things": so do you likewise. And therefore we may fitly say unto you both, as Saint *Paul* said unto the like in his time: "If any man lust to be contentious, we have no such custom, neither the Churches of God."

2 The *Brownists* deny our Church to be the true Church of Christ. These are their impious words: "These Ecclesiastical Assemblies, remaining thus in confusion and bondage, under this Antichristian ministry, courts, canons, worship, ordinances, etc. without freedom and power to redress any enormity among them, cannot be said in this confusion and subjection, truly to have Christ their Prophet, Priests, and King, neither can be in this estate, (whilst we judge them by the rule of God's word) esteemed the true, visible, orderly gathered or constituted Churches of Christ, whereof the faithful may become or stand members." And the like words have some of your faction likewise uttered against our church. "We in England" (say the Admonitors) "are so far off from having a Church rightly reformed, that as yet we are scarce come to the outward face of the same.

3 The black-mouthed *Brownists* do rail thus on our *Hierarchy:* "The present Hierarchy retained and used in England of Archbishops, Primates, Lordships, Metropolitans, Suffragans, Deans, Prebendaries, Canons, Peticanons, Archdeacons, Chancellors, Commissaries, Priests, Deacons, our half Priests, Parsons, Vicars, Curates, Hireling roving preachers, Churchwardens, Parish clerks: also their Doctors, Proctors, and other officers of their spiritual courts; together with the whole rabble of the Prelates and their servitors, from, and under them, set over these Cathedral and Parishional assemblies in this confusion, are a strange and Antichristian Ministry and offices." And the like libeling and railing, these and your Teachers used. "Our Bishops" (say they) "are Antichristian Prelates, ordinances of the devil, Petty Popes, Petty Antichrists, cogging and cozening knaves, robbers, wolves, simoniacs, persecutors, sowers of sedition, and discontentedness, and that the worst Puritan, is an honester man than the best Lord Bishop in Christendom."

4 The forenamed *Brownists,* have "sued to the Prince and Parliament, to have Bishops removed out of the Church, as being the limbs of Antichrist": so have your Puritan Preachers likewise done, in their admonitions and supplications to the Parliament.

5   The *Brownists* would have Pastors, Teachers, Elders, Deacons, and
Helpers, instead of Archbishops, Lord-bishops, Suffragans, Deans,
Archdeacons, Chancellors, etc. and so would you too. "Of necessity" saith
Martin, "all Christian Magistrates, are bound to receive this government
by Pastors, Doctors, Elders, and Deacons, and to abolish all other Church
government."

6   It is an article of the *Brownist's Creed,* that every "Congregation
hath power and commandment, to elect and ordain their own Ministry,"
so it is an article of your Creed also, that the common people of every
Congregation should elect their own Ministers.

7   The *Brownists* cry out against our Cathedral Churches, and
complain that we have "Organs, Queresters, singing men and boys, as in
times past in popery": so do your leaders cry out against our "chief
chanters, singing men, Organ players, and squeaking Queresters": as they
call them.

8   The absurd *Brownists* say, that "degrees in Theology, enforcement
to single life in Colleges, and the study of heathen Writers, with other
like corruptions," (as they term them) in Schools and Academies, should
be removed and redressed: and the like say you, as hath already been
shewed.

9   The *Brownists* have exhibited a supplication to the King's Majesty,
and therein craved, that "no Apocrypha writings, but only the Canonical
Scriptures be used in the Church": and so have you.

10   The *Brownists* would not have Homilies to be read in the Church,
no more would you.

11   The *Brownists* dislike our prescript form of prayer, and so do you.

12   The *Brownists* bear the world in hand, that "our Service Book is
verbatim gathered out of the Mass-book": so do you, that it is "culled and
picked out of that popish dunghill, the Portuise and Mass-book."

13   The newfangle *Brownists'* blame is, for "keeping the old fashion of
psalms, Chapters, Epistles, Gospels, Versicles, Responds, Te Deum,
Benedictus, Magnificat, Nunc dimittis, Our Father, Lord have mercy
upon us, The Lord be with you, O Lord open thou my lips, Glory be to
God on high, Lift up your hearts, O come let us rejoice, Glory be to the
father, Quicunque vult, etc." and the selfsame do you.

14   The *Brownists* dislike our *Letany* and *Collects:* so do you.

15   The *Brownists* dislike our "Prayers over the dead at burial": so
do you.

16   The *Brownists* would not have Preachers to preach at burials: No

more would you, as appeareth by your Book of *Discipline,* wherein are these express words: "In funeribus desuescendum est commode, ab habendis concionibus, quod periculum sit, ne superstitionem quorundam foveant, aut vanitati inserviant": The Preachers must leave off by little and little, as they may conveniently, to preach at burials, least thereby they nourish the superstition of some men, or give over themselves to the preservation of vanity: Yea the Admonitors were not ashamed to compare funeral Sermons to Trentals.

17   The *Brownists* crave, that "the Church be not urged to keep any holy-days, save only to sanctify the Sabbath": so do you, as hath already been shewed.

18   The *Brownists* do reckon Saints' Eves, and Lent, for Romish fasts: so do you.

19   The *Brownists* dislike the Ring in marriage: so do you.

20   The *Brownists* would not have "women to be churched": no more would you.

21   The *Brownists* have slandered our Ministers, and blazed abroad, that they take upon them to forgive men their sins: and so have you, as hath been shewed.

22   The *Brownists* also falsely report, that we "permit Midwives to administer Baptism": so do you.

23   The brainsick *Brownists* would not have children to be "Baptized in Fonts": no more would you; because "Fonts" (as you say) "were invented by Pope Pius."

24   The *Brownists* dislike of "Crossing in Baptism": so do you; because (forsooth) it is a piece of Popery.

25   The *Brownists* dislike that children should have godfathers and godmothers at their Baptism: so do you.

26   The *Brownists* would not have *Interrogatories* to be ministered to Infants; no more would you.

27   The *Brownists* blame us for "Ministering the communion to the people kneeling": so do you.

28   The *Brownists* hold Surplices to be Popish corruption: so hold ye them to be "known liveries of Antichrist."

29   The *Brownists* would have nothing to be used in these days, which was not used in the days of the Apostles: no more would you.

30   The *Brownists* think it unlawful for us, to use any rite or ceremony in our Church, which is used in the Church of *Rome:* and so do you.

To conclude, the Brownists and the Puritans do agree together in all things (their separation only excepted) as even as two pieces of cloth, that are of the same wool, of the same thread, of the same color, and of the same breadth and length.

The Puritan.　　But to put you in mind of one particular, before we make an end of this our conference; why do you usually call us by the name of *Puritans?*

The Protestant.　　Why? because you agree with certain old Heretics, which were so called in former ages.

The Puritan.　　Wherein do we agree with them?

The Protestant.　　The old *Puritans* "sought for a church," saith master *Calvin,* "wherein there should want nothing that might be desired": even so do you as appeareth by these words of your chiefest Writer: "The Church in the whole and general government and outward policy of it, may be pure and unspotted."

Secondly, we call you *Puritans,* not because you are purer than other men are, no more than were the *Puritans* in ancient time; but because you think yourselves to be purer than others, as the old *Puritans* did.

God almighty give you grace to become "pure in heart," and "in simplicity and godly pureness," to have your "conversation in the world."

18

David Owen

Herod and Pilate Reconciled

1610

(Excerpts)

D AVID OWEN (*ca.* 1580–*ca.* 1642)
was educated at Cambridge, where he received his B.A., M.A., and B.D.
degrees. In 1618 he became a doctor of divinity. His writings in both Latin
and English concern chiefly a defense of royal authority, especially in ecclesiastical matters.

Herod and Pilate Reconciled, a very learned, fifty-seven-page booklet, deals
solely with the question of whether anyone—the pope, statesmen, or the
people in general—has the right to fight against, depose, or kill a king.
Owen's thesis, appearing in the title of his first chapter, is that kings "are
not punishable by man, but reserved to the judgment of God." Possibly the
work was called forth by the assassination in 1610 of Henry IV, king of
France, by the fanatic monk François Ravaillac. Apparently this act,
together with memories of the Gunpowder Plot of 1605, caused King
James to issue his proclamations against Roman Catholics, especially
Jesuits, in 1610 and 1611, and in turn prompted replies by Jesuits beginning in 1610. If Owen wrote his work either in reaction to the assassination or in support of James's first proclamation, as Peter Milward
suggests in *Religious Controversies of the Jacobean Era* (Lincoln, Neb., 1978,
pp. 119–21), then we must admire Owen's learning, which is shown
specifically by his ability to muster so quickly a host of arguments ranging

in time from the Bible to his contemporaries. Also noteworthy, and more significant here, is the amount of space Owen gives to puritan statements on the question of the king's authority. The work shows that a staunch defender of the king's absolute supremacy saw a grave threat to the monarchy in much protestant political theory and as early as 1610 suspected the people called puritans of tending toward regicide. Not unexpectedly we find that the work was reprinted in 1643 with a new title, *Puritano-Jesuitismus, the Puritan Turned Jesuit,* but with no change in content.

The nine chapters of the work fall into two distinct parts, the second of which is here reprinted. The first six chapters muster quotations from the Bible, church fathers, and medieval churchmen in support of Owen's thesis. Having established his argument by authorities going back to antiquity, Owen then cites the reprehensible, erroneous opinions of both Roman Catholic and reformed thinkers to the contrary in order to point out their falseness and their danger to the state.

The first chapter cites biblical examples and statements in support of royal authority. The second, dealing with the fathers of the first three hundred years A.D.—among them Justin Martyr, Tertullian, and Cyprian—points out that even when Christians formed a large, powerful group within the Roman Empire, they made no effort to overthrow the emperor. The third chapter, covering the next three hundred years of the Christian era, uses such illustrious figures as Athanasius, Gregory Nazianzen, Cyril of Alexandria, Ambrose, Augustine, Chrysostom, and Gregory the Great in support of the principle that when men cannot obey the king, they must accept the consequences patiently. The fourth chapter carries the argument through the years 600 to 900 A.D., citing such figures as Isidore of Seville and Fulgentius of Ruspe (who is here apparently confused with Fulgentius of Ecija). The fifth chapter covers the period from 900 to 1200 A.D. (here Saint Bernard appears); the sixth, starting with the year 1200, comes up to the Reformation, citing among respected authorities Thomas Aquinas, the Parliament of England during the reign of Edward I, and Aeneas Sylvius (who became Pope Pius II). In addition to these luminaries, Owen also cites very obscure people in each period.

Because Owen's arguments do not vary significantly, the first six chapters have been omitted, and only chapters 7 through 9, which treat puritans directly, have been reprinted here. Chapter 7 begins with the pope's assumption of authority over kings and goes on to quote erroneous ideas of Roman Catholic controversialists. Owen does not make fine distinctions;

he quotes Robert Bellarmine and Alexander Carerius without noting the considerable differences, leading to quarrels, that existed between the two in their views of the authority of the papacy. And the chapter goes beyond defenders of the pope to cite as opponents of kingship and its prerogatives two protestant—in fact, Calvinist—theologians, François du Jon (Junius) and Lambert Daneau. Roman Catholics and some protestants appear in general agreement on ends, though not on means; whereas the former hold that the pope can depose a king, the latter give this right to the king's subjects.

In his eighth chapter, Owen focuses exclusively on puritans, citing numerous writers. Such prominent names as John Calvin, Theodore Beza, and John Knox appear, though Calvin seems to be treated with some deference. Ironically Thomas Aquinas is quoted approvingly in Owen's refutation of reformed theologians. Finally chapter 9 continues to cite reformers and brings in a few Jesuits near the end to prove the similarity between them and the puritans. The term *puritan* in Owen's use seems to apply to any member of the reformed churches who will argue for the deposition of the king upon any grounds or by anyone, especially by the nobility, by statesmen, or by the general population. And any puritan appears to be a potential regicide.

Herod and Pilate reconciled:

Or, The Concord of Papist and Pvritan (Against Scripture, Fathers, Councels, and other Orthodoxall Writers) for the Coercion, Deposition, and Killing of Kings. Discovered by *David Owen* Batchelour of Divinitie, and Chaplaine to the right Honourable Lord Viscount Hadington. Printed by Cantrell Legge, Printer to the Universitie of *Cambridge* 1610 and are to be sold in Pauls Churchyard at the signe of the Bishop
[Excerpts: preface; pp. 36–57.]

To the Dutiful Subject.

The Puritan Church Policy, and the *Jesuitical society* began together: the one in *Geneva,* 1536. and the other in *Rome,* 1537. Since their beginning, they have bestirred themselves busily (*as he that compasseth the earth, or they that coasted sea and land,*) each one in his order. The *Puritan* to break down the wall of *Sion,* by disturbing the peace of the *reformed Church:* the *Jesuit* to build up the ruins of *Babylon,* by maintaining the abomination of the *deformed Synagogue.* These (though brethren in sedition and heady) are *head-severed,* the one staring to the *Presbytery,* and the other to the *Papacy,* but they are so fast linked behind, and *tail-tied* together with *firebrands* between them, that if they be not quenched by the power of Majesty, they cannot choose (when the means are fitted to their plot) but set the *Church* on fire, and the *state* in an uproar. Their *many and long prayers,* their *much vehement preaching,* and stout opposition against *orders established,* their show of austerity in their conversation, and of singular learning in their profession, (*as the evil fiend transformed into an angel of light*) brought them first to admiration. Whereby they have not only *robbed widows' houses* under pretense of prayer, and ransacked their *seduced disciples* by show of devotion, but also battered the *courts of Princes,* by animating the *Peers* against *Kings,* and the *people* against the *Peers* for pretended *reformation.* And whereas God hath inseparably annexed to the *crown of earthly majesty, a supreme ecclesiastical sovereignty* for the protection of *piety;* and an absolute *immunity* from the judicial *sentence,* and Martial *violence,* for the preservation of *policy:* These sectaries bereave Kings of both these their *Princely prerogatives, exalting themselves* (as the son of perdition) *above all that is called God:* Lest they might seem *sine ratione insanire,* to sow the seeds of sedition without show of reason, *Caedem faciunt scripturarum* (as the heretics in *Tertullian's* time were wont to do) *in materiam suam,* they kill the Scripture to serve their turns: and pervert the holy word of the *eternal God,* by strange interpretation, and wicked application against the meaning of the *Spirit,* by whom it was penned; the doctrine of the *Church,* to whom it was delivered; and the practice of all the *Godly,* (as well under the *Law* as the *Gospel*) that did believe, understand, and obey it; to maintain their late, and lewd opinions. I have in my hand *above forty several places of the old and new Testament,* which both the brethren of the enraged opposite faction do indifferently quote, and seditiously apply, in defense of their dangerous opposition, and damnable error, against the *Ecclesiastical supremacy,* and the *indelible character of royal inunction.* Unto the which places, falsely expounded, perverted, and applied, I have added the interpretation, of the learned *Protestants* since the time of *Martin Luther,* who began to discover the nakedness of the *Romish Church,* 1517. More especially insisting in the most mighty Kings, the most reverend Prelates, honorable Lords, loyal Clergy, and other worthy men, that have in the Church of *England,* learnedly defended the Princely right, against disloyal, and undutiful opponents: which by *God's* help I mean to publish, when I have added the exposition of the *Fathers,* to confute the falsehood of the

Puritan-popish-faction, and to confirm the truth of the *Protestants' Doctrine* in each particular quotation. I protest in all sincerity, that I neither have in this treatise, nor mean in the other, *hereafter to be published,* to detort anything, to make either the *cause* itself, or the *favorers* of it more *odious,* than their own words, (published with the general approbation of their several favorites) do truly infer, and necessarily enforce. I hope the loyal subject, and *Godly* affected, will accept in good part my endeavor, and industry, intended for the glory of *God,* the honor of the *King,* and the discovery of *the seditious.* The displeasure of the *malcontented factions* (which can no more abide the truth, than the Owls can light, or the frantic the Physician) I neither regard nor care for. Farewell.

The seventh Chapter showeth the concord of Papist and Puritan for the deposition of Kings, and their discord about the means and persons to be employed in the execution of their designments.

Childerick was deposed, and *Pipine* crowned King of France about the year 750. The truth of which history is this. *Childerick* void of all princely gravity, gave himself over to pleasure and wantonness, leaving the burden of the state to *Pipinus,* that was his Lord *Marshall:* Who conspired with the Nobles, to advance himself, by the deposition of the king his master. To set a better color on the matter, *Pipine* sent his Chaplain to Pope *Zachary,* to have his answer to this Question: *Whether should be King, he that bare the name and did nothing, or he that governed the kingdom?* The Pope gave sentence with the Marshall against the King, whereupon, *Childerick* was made a shorn Monk, and *Pipine* a crowned King.

It is a wonder to see how these opposite sectaries, do insist upon this fact of the Frenchmen, to justify their dangerous doctrine, and seditious conspiracies against Princes. As Cardinal *Bellarmine de pontif. lib. 2. cap. 17. Thomas Harding* against the *Apology* of the Church of *England fol.* 181. *Franc. Fevardentius* in his commentaries on *Hester pag.* 85. *Boucher alias Raynolds de justa abdicatione Henrici.* 3. *lib.* 3. *cap.* 14. *Ficklerus de jure magistratuum fol.* 30. *Alexander Carerius patavinus de potestate papae lib.* 2. *cap.* 3. *D. Marta de temporali & spirituali pontificis potestate, lib.* 1. *cap.* 23: and *Doleman in his conference touching succession part.* 1 *cap.* 3. *pag.* 48. And also these *Puritans, Christopher Goodman in his treatise of obedience pag.* 53. *George Buchanan de jure Regni apud Scotos pag.* 47. *Danaeus de politia Christiana lib.* 3. *cap.* 6. *pag.* 221. *Brutus Celta de jure magistratuum, pag.* 286. *Phyladelphus dialogo* 2. *pag.* 65. *Franc. Hottomanus* in his *Francogallia cap.* 12. and *Speculum tyrannidis Philipi Regis pag.* 27. The *Papists* which ascribe this deposing power to the pope, endeavor by tooth and nail, to disprove that interest which the *Puritans* grant the peers or the people. First, this example served *Gregory* 7 to excuse his presumptuous practices against *Henry* the fourth. *Quidam Romanus pontifex.* A certain Bishop of Rome deposed a king of France, not so much for his ill life, as for that he was not fit for government, and placed *Pipine,* which was father to *Charles* the great, in his place: absolving all the Frenchmen from the oath of allegiance, which they had sworn to their king. Thus far *Gregory* in an epistle to one *Herimanus,* that was Bishop of Metz in France.

Thomas Harding concludeth from this fact, a divine power in the pope. Can you not see (saith *Harding*) what strength and power is in the pope, which is able with a word, to place and displace the mightiest King in Europe? with a word, I say, for I am sure you can show us of no army, that he sent to execute his will. Is it in the power of a man (think you) to appoint kingdoms? can the Devil himself, at his pleasure set up and depose Kings? no surely. Much less can any member of his do the same. Remember you what Christ said, when the Jews objected, that he did cast out devils in the name of the prince of devils? beware you sin not against the holy Ghost, who confess that the Pope hath pulled down and set up Kings. Which thing undoubtedly he could never do profitably and peaceably, but by the great power of God, etc. So far *Harding.*

Cardinal *Bellarmine* the grand-master of Controversies, cannot endure to hear that this deposition was done by any other than the papal authority. The Pope (saith he) *Judicavit licere Frauncis, regnum Childerici in Pipinum transferre.* The Pope gave judgment that the Frenchmen might lawfully transfer *Childerick*'s kingdom to *Pipin:* and did absolve them from the oath which they had sworn unto him. No man that hath his right wit can deny this to be lawful. For the very event hath proved, that change to be most fortunate: seeing the kingdom of France, was never more potent, nor religion more flourishing, than under *Pipin* and *Charles* his son. Thus far *Bellarmine.*

This Cardinal's reason from the success to the approbation of the fact, will conclude well for the Turk, who hath longer continued, more flourished and enlarged his state, than the house of *Pipin.* Hear in a word the true success of *Pipin*'s posterity out of *Benventus Imolensis* and *Paulus Aemilius.* The first of that line was *Charles* the great, in whose time the Empire was divided. The second was *Ludovicus Pius,* against whom *Lotharius,* an unnatural son, did conspire: who thrust his father to a cloister, and placed himself in the throne, where he sat like a tyrant, till he was also deposed. The fourth was *Ludovicus* secundus, a man unfortunate in all his doings. The fifth was *Ludovicus* tertius, whom they call *Ludovicus nihili,* or *Lewes* nobody. The sixth was *Charles* the *bald,* a very coward. The seventh was *Carolus Crassus,* as very a Fool. *Arnulphus* the eight of that progeny, was eaten with lice. The ninth was *Ludovicus* 4. in whom that race ended.

Alexander Carerius inferreth the absolute sovereignty of the *Pope* over all Kings, even to depose them, and to transpose the Realms, from the insufficiency of the Nobles and people. *Esto quod verum sit Papam, non deposuisse Regem Franciae:* Be it true that the Pope did not depose the king of France, but gave consent to the Peers and people to depose him, this is a most manifest proof of our intent: that kings have one, if not many superiors, *viz.* the Barons and people of their kingdom: and overthroweth their position and conclusion, *That Kings have in temporal things no superior,* no, not the Bishop of Rome. But seeing the Barons and people, could neither judge nor deprive him, because they wanted coactive power, which Vassals or subjects have not over their sovereign, it followeth necessarily, that the Pope by his princely power, as superior to the King in temporalities, might lawfully depose him. Thus far *Carerius.*

D. Marta, is as peremptory for the Pope, against the pretended claim of the Peers or the people. *Childericus privatus est Regno Franciae ob stupiditatem & Ineptitudinem in administrando:* Childerick was deprived of the kingdom of France, for his stupidity and unfitness to govern. They that say he was not deprived by the Pope alone, but by them that desired another king, do not answer the reasons alleged for the Pope's sovereign power in temporalities: nay they confirm the Pope's power. *Baldus* asketh this question, when the Emperor is unprofitable, or mad, or a drunkard, may the people depose him, or assign him a coadjutor? No, saith he, the Pope must do it, *for the Pope is the crown and brain of the people.* And we have proved before, that God did give no jurisdiction to the people, but to *Moses* and his successors. Wherefore the vassals or Peers which represent the people, have no power common with the Pope, in the deposing of Princes: And in that they say, that the Frenchmen desired another king, it is a great confirmation, that the Pope hath right to dispose of kingdoms. He useth to desire, who hath not of his own: or cannot of himself effect that, which he would have done: Thus far *Marta.*

They that plead for the state of the *Laity,* are as confident against the Pope and clergy. *Ut paucis dicam* (saith *Junius*) *hoc fecit Zacharias ut dominus aut ut mandatarius, authoritate instructus a domino,* that I may use few words, the Pope deposed *Childerick* either as his Lord, or as a mandatary having authority from the Lord; but he did it neither way. Not as Lord, how could he be Lord in France, that in those days had no Lordship in Rome? he did it not as mandatary, for then he ought to have showed his authority, which he neither did, nor could show. Christ would not divide a private inheritance, shall *Zachary* then presume to depose kings or transpose kindoms? Thus far *Junius.*

Caeterum quod monachus iste (saith *Lambertus Danaeus*) whereas this monk *Bellarmine* contendeth, that *Childerick* was lawfully deposed by Pope *Zacharias,* a stranger, a Priest, no Magistrate, but (in this respect) a private person, though he were Bishop of Rome. Will he ever be able to prove or defend his assertion? Can *Zachary* have authority in *France,* being a stranger? can he depose the public Magistrate, being but a private person? or transfer that principality to *Pipin* that he hath no right unto? and commit so many sacrileges and impieties, stealing from *Childerick,* and giving to *Pipin* another man's right? authorizing subjects to violate their oaths, which they had sworn to their king? transposing kingdoms from one man to another, whereas it doth only belong to God to depose kings, and dispose of kingdoms? thou mayest see (*Bellarmine*) how many outrages this thy *Zachary* hath committed, beside that he did thrust his sickle into another man's harvest, and meddled with the cobbler beyond his last, in that, being but a Priest he took upon him the decision of the right of kingdoms. Thus far *Danaeus,* who is not so violent against the Pope, as he is virulent for the deposing power of Peers, or states of the kingdom. The kings (saith he) of Lacedemonia had the *Ephori* to control them. The statesmen of the Roman commonwealth, deposed the Emperors, which were tyrants, and abused their authority. The French-state hath often dethroned their kings: The Nobles of Spain may do it by their law: And the history of the Scottish affairs (excellently well written by *Buchanan*) doth report that the statesmen of that country, have many times deprived the kings of Scotland. Finally, natural reason, and the practice of all nations doth confirm, that the statesmen in every kingdom, may depose kings, that are peccant. So far he. *Hottoman* in his *Franco Gallia,* hath a long chapter to prove that this might be done lawfully, by the Peers, or the people, but in no case by the Pope or the clergy.

Men cannot say (as it is in the proverb) *nimium altercando veritas amittitur,* seeing that in this opposition, the truth is not lost, but divided among them. For their premises, brought together, will unavoidably conclude, that this deposing power, is neither in the Pope, the Peers, nor the people. Though it were, the reason of the seditious *Papist* and *Puritans, a facto ad jus,* is sophistical in the schools, where nothing can be concluded *ex meris particularibus,* of mere particular instances. Absurd in law, *quia legibus non exemplis vivitur,* for men must do as the law requireth, not as other men practice. Erroneous in divinity, *non ideo quia factum credimus, faciendum credamus, ne violemus praeceptum dum sectamur exemplum:* We may not do that, which hath been done by other men, lest we break the law of God, in following the example of man. And dangerous in policy, as my *Lord of Northampton,* the ornament of learning, observeth. The fly (saith that noble Earl) sitting on the cart wheel, might as well wonder at the dust raised in the way, as *Gregory* or *Zachary,* draw counsel to power, and make that fact their own, which was hammered in the forge of ambition, countenanced with the color of necessity, and executed by *Pipin,* a minister, that being weary of subordination, resolved by this trick, when the means were fitted and prepared to the plot, to make himself absolute. The case of Kings were pitiful, if *ex factis singularibus,* it were lawful to draw leaden rules in their disgrace. Thus far the Earl.

> *The eight Chapter sheweth the danger of this Doctrine, and the original of the Puritan position, concerning the power of statesmen to punish and depose Princes in Monarchies.*

These desperate attempts, suggested by the Devil, executed by the people, encouraged by the state, and approved by the Pope, must serve as admonitions to Princes, to humble themselves before God: *Qui non dabit sanctos suos in captionem dentibus eorum,* who will not give his Saints for a prey to their teeth. For it is not heard (as our great King remembreth) *That any Prince forgetteth himself in his duty to God, or in his vocation? But God with the greatness of the plague revengeth the greatness of his ingratitude.*

These practices therefore must be no precedent for Peers, or people to follow, because God hath forbidden Christian subjects to resist, though kings reign as Tyrants; and commanded them to endure with patience, though they suffer as Innocents. And also, because that instead of relieving the Commonwealth out of distress, which is ever the pretense of seditious practitioners, they shall heap mischief on it, and desolation on themselves: as (*Aquinus*) if he be the author of the book *de regim. principum,* sheweth manifestly. *Esset multitudini periculosum & ejus rectoribus:* It were dangerous to subjects and governors, that any should attempt to take away the life of princes, though they were tyrants: for commonly, not the well-disposed, but the ill-affected men, do thrust themselves into that danger. And the government of good Kings, is as odious to bad men, as the rule of tyrants to good people. Wherefore the kingdom, by this presumption would be rather in danger to forgo a good prince, than a wicked tyrant. So far *Thomas*.

They that are the authors or abettors of sedition, can neither avoid shame in earth, nor escape eternal damnation. Though God the great Judge do sometime permit rebels, in his Justice to prevail against Kings, for their contempt of the law of the highest, and the neglect of their own duty. The reward of rebellion shall be no better than the recompense of Satan, who is the instrument of the Lord's wrath for the punishment of all disobedience. It is most true that as sick men, near their death, have many idle fancies, so the world before the end thereof shall be troubled with many errors. In these declining days of the world, many countries, Cities, and Cantons, renounced their old government, and submitted themselves to such a new regiment as they best liked: for confirmation of which practices, there wanted not politic Divines, (what wine is so sour that some hedge grapes will not yield) to invest the people and Nobles with the power over Kings, to dispose of their kingdoms. The heathen *Politicians* from whom this politic Divinity is derived, knowing not the true God, and having no rule to direct them, but natural reason, thought him no murderer, but *a defender of his country that killed tyrants*. But this pagan principle, being a plant, that *Christ* hath not planted, must be plucked up by the roots. I can find no ground of this lewd learning, beyond 220. years in the Christian world: the first authors of it being *Johannes de Parisiis, Jacobus Almain,* and *Marsilius Patavinus: Ubi peccat rex in temporalibus,* saith *Johannes de parisiis, papa non habet ipsum corrigere:* when the king offended in the temporal government, the Pope hath no authority to correct him, but the Barons or Peers of the Realm, and if they either cannot, or dare not meddle with him, they may crave the Church's aid to suppress him: so far *John of Paris*.

Tota communitas (saith *Jacob Almain*) *potestatem habet principem deponere*. All the communalty, hath power to depose their Prince, which power the communalty of France used, when they deprived their king, not so much for his impiety, as for his disability to manage so great a charge: so far *Almain. Regis depositio & alterius institutio* (saith *Marsilius patavinus*) the deposition of a king, and the institution of another in his place, belongeth not to the Bishop of Rome, to any priest, or the college of priests, but to the universal multitude of the subjects. So far he.

From these, the *Puritans* have learned their error, of the *power of Statesmen over Kings,* than which, no opinion can be more dangerous: where the Nobility are as ready to practice, as the *Puritan* preachers are to prescribe. What presumption is it in men, to pass the bounds which God hath set them, to control the wisdom of the Lord, and his unspeakable goodness, when he maketh trial of the patience of his Saints, by the outrage and tyranny of cruel kings, that they which are found patient in trouble, constant in truth, and loyal in subjection, may be crowned with glory. Were we persuaded, that the *hearts of Kings are in God's hand,* that the hairs of our head are numbered, and that no affliction can befall us, which God doth not dispose to the exercise of our faith, the trial of our constancy, or the punishment of our sin, we would as well admire the justice of God, in permitting tyrants, that our sins may be judged, and punished in this world, as praise his mercy and favor, in giving rest to his servants, under the protection of godly and gracious princes.

The ninth Chapter sheweth the general consent of the Modern Puritans touching the coercion, deposition, and killing of Kings whom they call tyrants.

The Citizens of *Geneva,* changed the government from a *Monarchy* to *Democrity* in the year of Christ, 1536. In the which year, *John Calvin* came into that City, to visit his friend *Farellus;* And was chosen the public reader of divinity. At his first coming thither, he published his *Theological institutions.* Wherein he doth very learnedly, and Christianly intreat of the authority of princes, and the duty of subjects. One only place is harsh, and dangerous: delivered in obscure, and doubtful terms, to excuse (as I conceive) the outrage of the Citizens, against their prince, whom they had not many weeks before expelled: not to authorize other men to attempt the like against their sovereign Magistrates. His words are these, *Si qui sunt populares Magistratus, ad moderandam regum libidinem constituti.* If there be any popular Magistrates, to restrain the licentiousness of Kings, of which kind were the *Ephori* opposed against the Lacedemonian Kings, the Tribunes of the people, which curbed the Roman Consuls, and the Demarchy which bridled the Senate of Athens; And such peradventure as things now stand are the three states in every kingdom, assembled in Parliament. I do not deny, but these in regard of their duty, stand bound to repress the unruliness of licentious kings: Nay, I affirm, that if they do but wink at those kings, which peevishly make havoc of their people, and insult against their communalty, that they want not the guilt of heinous treachery, because they betray the liberty of the people, whose guardians they know themselves to

be appointed. Thus far *Calvin*. Since which time all *Puritans* have turned his
conjunction *conditional*, into an *illative*, his adverb of *doubting* to an *affirmative*,
and his permissive, *non veto*, into a verb of the *imperative mode*, in their books of
regiment secular, and discipline Ecclesiastical.

Christopher Goodman, published a treatise of obedience at *Geneva*, not without the very good liking and approbation of the best learned in that city, 1557.
wherein he affirmeth, That if Magistrates transgress God's law themselves, and
command others to do the like, they lose that honor, and obedience which
otherwise is due unto them: and ought no more to be taken for Magistrates:
but to be examined and punished as private transgressors: so far *Goodman*.

Much about the same time was *Knox* his *appellation* printed in the same
place, wherein he feareth not to affirm, That it had been the duty of the
Nobility, Judges, Rulers, and people of England not only to have resisted
Mary, that *Jezabel* whom they call their *Queen*, but also to have punished her to
the death, with all such as should have assisted her, what time that she openly
began to suppress Christ's Gospel, to shed the blood of the Saints, and to erect
that most devilish Idolatry, the papistical abominations, and his usurped
tyranny. Thus far *Knox*.

Ann. 1560. *Theodore Beza* printed his *Confessions*, wherein he avoucheth,
That there are vices inherent in the persons of Princes, though they be lawfully
established, by succession, or election, *viz.* Ungodliness, covetousness, ambition, cruelty, luxury, lechery, and such like sins which tyrants delight in.
What shall be done in this case to these Princes? I answer (saith he) that it
belongeth to the superior powers, such as are the 7. electors in the Empire, and
the statesmen of the kingdom almost in every Monarchy, to restrain the fury of
tyrants, which if they do not, they are traitors to their countries, and shall
before the Lord give an account of their treachery. Thus far *Beza*.

1561. The very year after there was a contention between the Nobility and
Clergy of Scotland about his matter, (as *Buchanan* reporteth:) let him tell his
own tale. *Calendis Novembribus Regina ad Missam:* The Queen upon the feast of
All Saints, added to her private Mass all the solemnities and superstitious
ceremonies of the Papists; The Ministers of the Gospel took it very ill, com-
plained thereof to the people, in their public congregations, and admonished
the nobility of their duty in that behalf: whereupon rose a controversy in a
house of private meeting, between the Nobles and Preachers, whether the
Nobles may restrain Idolatry, that is like to break out to a general destruction:
and by rigor of law, compel the chief Magistrate to his duty, when he exceedeth
his bounds? The Ministers of the Church stood steadfast in opinion, as they

had formerly done, that the chief Magistrate may be compelled even by forcible means to live according to law: but the Noblemen because of the *Queen's* favor, hope of honor, or love of lucre, did a little waver, and thought otherwise than the Ministers: and so in the end judgment passed with the Nobles, because they were more in number and of better esteem and reputation. Thus far *Buchanan*.

1568. The outlandish Churches in London concluded this Canon in a classical Synod, *Si quisquam repugnantibus legibus patriae:* If any man usurp Lordship, or Magistracy, against the laws and privileges of the country, or if he that is a lawful Magistrate, do unjustly bereave his subjects of the privileges, and liberties which he hath sworn to perform unto them, or oppress them by manifest tyranny, the inferior officers must oppose themselves against him, for they are in duty bound before God, to defend their people, as well from a domestical, as a foreign tyrant. Thus far they.

1574. We had swarms of caterpillars: namely, *Disciplina Ecclesiastica* from Rochel, to teach us, that the senate Ecclesiastical hath the chief moderation of the Christian society, and ought to provide that no Magistrate be defective in his charge, and by common care, counsel, and authority to oversee, that every governor carry himself faithfully in his Magistracy. Thus far that author.

Franco Gallia from *Colen,* wherein we find that the people hath power to dethrone their Princes.

Junius de jure Magistratuum (as some think from *Geneva,*) wherein it is said, that the people have the same right to depose kings that are tyrants, which a general council hath to displace a Pope that is an heretic.

Eusebius Phyladelphus from *Edenbruge,* wherein we read, that it was as lawful for his brethren of France, to defend themselves against the tyranny of *Charles* the ninth, King of that name in France, as for wayfaring men to resist and repel thieves, cutthroats, and wolves: nay further, I am (saith he) of opinion with the old people of Rome, that of all good actions the murder of a tyrant is most commendable. Thus far he.

1577. Came forth the *Vindiciae contra Tyrannos,* with this resolution, That Princes are chosen by God, established by the people: every private man is subject to the Prince: the Multitude and the officers of state which represent the Multitude, are superiors to the Prince: yea they may judge his actions, and if he make resistance, punish him by forcible means. So far he.

1584. *Danaeus* finished his book of Christian policy, wherein among many other he propoundeth, and answereth a *Noble question,* as he termeth it. *Nobilis quaestio sequitur.* A noble question followeth, whether it be lawful for subjects to change and alter their government? Yea whether it may be done by godly men with a good conscience? his answer is. The chief Magistrate, that notoriously and wilfully violateth the fundamental laws of the kingdom, may be displaced by godly subjects, with a good conscience. And this is his reason, *Reges summique Magistratus,* Kings and chief Magistrates are the vassals of the kingdom, and of the Commonwealth where they rule: Wherefore, they may be dispossessed and dejected when they shall obstinately attempt anything, against the feudal laws of the kingdom where they govern, as Kings and chief Magistrates. And it is truly said, that as a general council, is above the Pope, so the kingdom or the Peers of the Land, are above the King. Thus far *Danaeus.*

1585. *George Buchanan* proclaimed rewards as well for murdering kings as killing tigers. If I (saith he) had power to make a law, I would command tyrants to be transported from the society of men into some solitary place, or else to be drowned in the bottom of the sea, that the evil savor of dead tyrants should not annoy living men. Furthermore I would award recompense to be given for the slaughter of tryants, not only of all in general, but of everyone in particular, as men use to reward them for their pains which kill wolves or bears, and destroy their young ones. *haec ille.*

The same year *Thomas Cartwright* commended *Dudley Fenners* his *Sacra Theologia* (as they call his book) to the world, wherein men are warranted by sundry texts of Scripture, most miserably abused, to destroy tyrants. Therein he (following the common opinion of the *Puritans*) maketh two sorts of tyrants, *Tyrannus sine titulo,* and *Tyrannus exercitio.* For the tyrant without title: He is confident, that any man may cut his throat. *Huic quisque privatus resistet, etiam si potest e medio tollat,* Let every private man resist him, and if he can, take away his life. For the Tyrant exercent: having described him to be a Prince, that doth wilfully dissolve all, or the chiefest compacts of the commonwealth, he concludeth against him, *Hunc tollant, vel Pacifice vel cum Bello, qui ea potestate donati sunt ut regni Ephori vel omnium ordinum conventus publicus:* The Peers of the kingdom or the public assembly of states, ought to destroy him, either by peaceable practices, or open war. *haec ille.*

Anno 1588. *Hermanus Renecherus* published observations upon the first *Psalm,* wherein he investeth the *Presbytery* with all the *Pope's* prerogatives. Concerning the *Presbyterian power* over kings. This is his notable annotation: God (saith he) hath ordained the Civil Magistrate for the good of the ecclesiastical order, therefore the ecclesiastical state is the highest throne of god's earthly kingdom, the supreme seat of all excellency, and the chiefest court wherein God himself is president, to distribute eternal gifts to his servants.

Whereas the political empire is but as it were an inferior bench, wherein justice is administered according to the prescription of the ecclesiastical sovereignty: Thus far *Renecherus.*

Robert Rollocke, a man otherwise very learned, is carried with the current of this error, and borrowed his assertion of M. *Fenner,* whose words he expoundeth by way of *paraphrasis,* in his commentaries on *Daniel* printed at *Edinburge,* 1591. Though the chief lawful Magistrate (saith M. *Rollocke*) do many things unjustly and tyrannously, he may not rashly be violated, by them especially which have not authority: but the Nobles or the public assembly of states, must reduce him to his duty, by reproof and all other lawful means, I.Sam. 14. 46. If he do still persist in open and desperate tyranny, wilfully dissolving all or the chiefest compacts of the commonwealth, private men must not yet meddle with him, only the Peers, or the public assembly of all states to whom that charge belongeth, must provide that the Church and Commonwealth come not to desolation: though it cannot otherwise be done, than by the death and destruction of the tyrant. Better it is that an evil king be destroyed, than the Church and state together ruined. Thus far *Rollocke.* For proof he referreth his reader first to the 1.*Sam.* 14. 46. *viz. Then Saul came up from the Philistims, and the Philistims went to their own place: ergo* Kings that are wicked may be reduced to their duty by the Peers, or assembly of states according to the rules of the new *Puritan logic.* Secondly, for the killing and destroying of kings, he referreth his readers to the 2. *regum* C. 11. v. 4. 5. 6. 7. which place I think he never vouchsafed to look upon, but set it down as he found it quoted in *Fenner's* divinity, from whom he hath taken all the rest.

I will make an end with *William Bucanus,* whose book was published at the request, and with the approbation of *Beza* and *Goulartius,* main pillars of the Church of *Geneva.* 1602. They (saith *Bucanus*) which have any part of office in the public administration of the Commonwealth, as the Overseers, Senators, Consuls, Peers, or Tribunes, may restrain the insolency of evil kings. Thus far he.

This *Puritan dangerous* error is directly repugnant to the Law, the Gospel, the precepts of the Apostles, the practice of Martyrs, and the doctrine of the Fathers, Councils, and other classical Writers, as I have proved in the six former Chapters: and will more directly shew (by the grace of God) in my other book: wherein the holy texts of Scripture, which the *Papists* and *Puritans* do damnably abuse against the ecclesiastical and Civil authority of Kings, shall be answered by the godly Protestants: whose labor God used to reform his Church since the year of our Lord, 1517. and by the ancient Fathers and orthodoxal

Writers in every age of the Church. This *Puritan position,* which authorizeth Nobles and assemblies of States against wicked kings, is the very assertion of the most seditious *Jesuits,* that have lived in our age, as I will demonstrate by two or three: *Johannes Mariana,* whose book seemeth to be written in defense of *Clement* the friar, who stabbed *Henry* the 3. king of France. The faults and licentiousness of kings (saith *Mariana*) whether they reign by consent of the people, or right of inheritance, are to be borne and endured, so long as the laws of shamefastness and honesty, whereto all men be bound, are not violated: for Princes should not rashly be disturbed, lest the commonwealth fall into greater misery and calamity. But if the Prince make havoc of the commonwealth, and expose the private fortunes of his subjects for a prey to other men, if he despise law, and contemn religion, this course must be taken against him. Let him be admonished and recalled to his duty: if he repent, satisfy the Wealpublic, and amend his faults, there ought (as I think) to be no further proceeding against him. But if there be no hope of his amendment, the commonwealth may take away his kingdom. And because that cannot be done (in all likelihood) without war, they may levy power, brandish their blades against their king, and exact money of the people, for the maintenance of their war: for when there is no other help, the Peers of the commonwealth, having proclaimed their king a public enemy, may take away his life. Thus far *Mariana.*

The Statesmen of the Kingdom (saith *Franciscus Fevardentius*) have a sovereign power over their Kings: for Kings are not absolutely established, but stand bound to observe laws, conditions, and compacts, to their subjects: the which, if they violate, they are no lawful Kings, but thieves and tyrants, punishable by the states. Thus far *Feverdentius.*

Inferior Magistrates (saith *Johannes Baptista Ficklerus*) are the defenders and protectors of the laws and rights of the state, and have authority (if need require) to correct and punish the supreme King. So far *Ficklerus.*

An English fugitive, which was the author of the book *de justa abdicatione Henrici tertii,* affirmeth, That all the Majesty of the kingdom, is in the assembly of Statesmen, to whom it belongeth to make covenants with God, to dispose of the affairs of the kingdom, to appoint matters pertaining to war and peace, to bridle the kingly power, and to settle all things that belong to public government. So far he.

And the most seditious *Doleman* saith, that all human law and order natural, National, and positive, doth teach, that the commonwealth, which gave Kings their authority for the common good, may restrain or take the same from them if they abuse it to the common ill: so far *Doleman,* and of this opinion are many other as may appear by D. *Morton* by whom they are discovered and refuted.

How far this gangrene will extend, I know not. The kings of Christendom are daily crucified, (as Christ their Lord was) between two thieves; I mean the *Papist* and *Puritan,* which have prepared this deadly poison for Princes, whom they in their own irreligious and traitorous hearts, shall condemn for tyranny. I hope neither Peers nor people will be so fond to believe them, or wicked to follow them, which pretend the reformation of religion, and defend the subversion of Christian states. If inferior officers, or the public assembly of all States, will claim this power, it standeth them upon, (as they will avoid everlasting damnation) not to derive a title from Rome, Lacedemon, or Athens, (as *Calvin* doth, whom the rest follow) but from the hill of *Sion,* and to plead their interest from the law or the gospel. *Si mandatum non est praesumptio est, & ad paenam proficiet, non ad praemium: quia ad contumeliam pertinet conditoris, ut contempto Domino colantur servi, & spreto Imperatore, adorentur Comites.* If their opposition against Kings be not commanded of God, it is presumption against God: for it is a contumely against God the creator of all states, to despise Lords and honor servants, to contemn the sovereign Emperor, and to reverence the Peers of the Empire. So far *Augustine. My son* (saith *Solomon*) *fear God and the King, and meddle not with the seditious: for their destruction shall come suddenly, and who knoweth the end of them?* The conclusion of all is, That Kings have supreme and absolute authority under God on earth, not because all things are subject to their pleasure, which were plain tyranny, not Christian sovereignty: but because all persons, within their dominions, stand bound in law, allegiance, and conscience, to obey their pleasure, or to abide their punishment. And Kings themselves, are no way subject to the control, censure, or punishment, of any earthly man, but reserved by special prerogative to the most fearful and righteous judgment of God, with whom there is no respect of persons. He whose servants they are, *will beat them with a rod of iron, and break them in pieces like a potter's vessel,* if they abuse that great, and sovereign power, (which God hath endued them withal,) to support error, to suppress truth, and to oppress the innocent. God, of his great mercy, grant us the spirit of truth, to direct us in all loyalty, that we being not seduced by these seditious Sectaries, may grow in grace, stand fast in obedience, embrace love, follow peace, and increase more and more in the knowledge of our Lord Jesus Christ. To whom be all praise, power, and dominion now and forever. Amen.

FINIS

19

George Wither

Abuses Stript, and Whipt

1613

(Excerpt)

GEORGE WITHER (1588–1667)
studied briefly at Oxford. He wrote voluminously all his life, during the
five times when he was imprisoned no less than when he was at liberty, in
many genres and rhetorical forms. In religion he was a conforming, but
tolerant, Anglican. During the civil war he served rather ineffectively as an
officer in the parliamentary army.

Abuses Stript, and Whipt satirizes aberrant behavior under a number of
abstract headings. It consists of twenty satiric verse essays divided into two
books, with some introductory poems, a conclusion to book 1, and a final
"Scourge." For its time the work, in which Wither announces his intention
to tell the truth fearlessly, was sufficiently outspoken to earn its author a
prison sentence. The essays in book 1 deal with "fond" love, lust, hate,
envy, revenge, choler, jealousy, covetousness, ambition, fear, despair,
hope, compassion, cruelty, joy, and sorrow. All are short, and only a few
deal with positive qualities. The second book examines at greater length
only four topics: vanity, inconstancy, weakness, and presumption. The
lines here reprinted appear early in the last essay and criticize presumption
in religion. The term *puritan* allows Wither to castigate the irreligious who
use it to mock piety, as well as those who create disturbances by insisting
dogmatically and intemperately upon their own eccentric beliefs. Thus

Wither clearly recognizes at least two disparate ways in which the term is used. The vehemence of his attack on the "counterfeit elect" logically places the selection in the antipuritan category. Throughout the brief discussion, the term *puritan* itself is dyslogistic, though many so-called puritans are considered truly religious.

Abvses Stript, and Whipt.

Or Satirical Essayes. By George Wyther. Divided into two Bookes. At London, Printed by G. Eld, for Francis Burton, and are to be solde at his shop in Paul's Church-yard, at the signe of the Green-Dragon. 1613.

[Excerpt: The II. Booke.
Of the Vanitie, Inconstancie, Weaknes, and Presumption of Men, and First of Vanitie. Of Presumption. Satyra. 4, pp. 232–34.]

> Also, in this abominable time,
> It is amongst us now, a common crime,
> To flout, and scoff at those which we espy
> Willing to shake off human *Vanity,*
> And those that gladly do themselves enforce,
> Unto a strict and more *religious* course
> Than most men do; (although, they truly know,
> No men are able to pay half they owe
> Unto their *God*) as though their wisdoms thought
> He might be served better than he ought,
> They count precise and curious more than needs,
> They try their sayings and weigh all their deeds;
> A thousand things that they well do, shall be
> Slightly passed over, as if none did see:
> But one thing ill done, though the best does ill,
> They shall be certain for to hear of still;
> Yea notwithstanding they can daily smother,
> Millions of ten-times greater faults in other:
> Who are so hated, or so often blamed,
> Or so reviled, or scorned, or so misnamed?
> To whom do we now our contentions lay?

Who are so much termed *Puritans* as they
That fear *God* most? But 'tis no marvel men
Presume so much to wrong his children; when
As if they feared not his revengeful rod,
They can blaspheme, and dare to anger *God*.
Now by these words to some men it may seem,
That I have *Puritans* in high esteem;
Indeed, if by that name you understand,
Those that the vulgar *Atheists* of this Land
Do daily term so, that is such as are
Fore-named here, and have the greatest care
To know, and please their maker: then 'tis true,
I love them well, for love to such is due:
But if you mean our *busy-headed sect,*
The hollow crew, the counterfeit elect:
Our Dogmatists, and ever-wrangling spirits,
That do as well contemn good works, as merits:
If you mean those that make their care seem great
To get souls food, when 'tis for bodies meat.
Or those all whose Religion doth depend,
On this, that they know how to discommend
A Maygame, or a Summerpole defy,
Or shake the head or else turn up the eye,
If you mean those, however they appear,
This I say of them would they all might hear,
Though in a zealous habit they do wander,
Yet they are God's foes and the Church's slander;
And though they humble be in show to many,
They are as haughty every way as any.

20

Sir Thomas Overbury

A Wife

1614

(Excerpt)

SIR THOMAS OVERBURY (1581–
1613) took his B.A. degree at Oxford in 1598 and studied law at the
Middle Temple. For a time he served as a diplomat and nourished ambi-
tions for a high appointment at the royal court. But he antagonized the
king and others by his opposition to the marriage of Robert Carr (a royal
favorite and later earl of Somerset) to Lady Frances Howard, whose character Overbury impugned. Court intrigues led to Overbury's imprisonment
and murder in the Tower of London.

Overbury's literary talents were recognized by Ben Jonson. Today his
reputation depends upon his "characters," or character descriptions, which
were attributed, when first published, to Overbury and "other learned
Gentlemen." The essays in the collection treat various social, moral, and
psychological types, with each sketch providing a vehicle for the display of
wit. "A Puritane" appears to be a good representative expression of a courtier's view. Although its authorship cannot be determined with absolute
certainty, Overbury himself seems to be a very strong candidate.

The sketch of "A Puritane" focuses on external appearance and behavior.
What apparently impressed the courtier was the puritan's objection to
ceremonies and vestments, especially the use of the ring in marriage, the
playing of the organ, and the wearing of the square cap. There is no

discussion of opposition to the bishops, but the mention of nonresidency is an indication of its prominence in the writings of the day. The nonconformists' refusal to accept tradition as a warrant for religious practice appears among the few more fundamental issues. Indirectly hypocrisy is charged against the puritan when he is portrayed, with concrete references to food, as a glutton. Finally, the work is an interesting testimony to the importance and high visibility of women among the opponents of the establishment.

A Wife:

Now The Widow of Sir Tho: Ouerbvrie Being a most exquisite and singular poem of the choyse of a Wife. Wherevnto are added many witty Characters, and conceited Newes, written by himselfe and other learned Gentlemen his Friendes. The fifth Impression, enlarged with more characters than any of the former AEditions. London Printed by T. C. for Lawrence Lisle, and are to be sold in Paules Chur-chyard, at the Tygres-head 1614.
[Excerpt: sigs. F—Fv.]

A Puritan

Is a diseased piece of *Apocrypha,* bind him to the Bible, and he corrupts the whole text; Ignorance, and fat feed, are his Founders, his Nurses, Railings, Rabbis, and round breeches: his life is but a borrowed blast of wind; For between two religions, as between two doors, he is ever whistling. Truly whose child he is, is yet unknown; For willingly his faith allows no Father, only thus far his pedigree is found, Bragger and he flourished about a time first; his fiery zeal keeps him continual costive, which withers him into his own translation, and till he eat a Schoolman, he is hidebound; he ever prays against *Non Residents,* but is himself the greatest discontinuer, for he never keeps near his Text: anything that the Law allows, but Marriage and March beer, he murmurs at: what it disallows, and holds dangerous, makes him a discipline. Where the gate stands open, he is ever seeking a stile: and where his Learning ought to climb, he creeps through; give him advice, you run into *Traditions,* and urge a modest course, he cries out *Councils.* His greatest care, is to contemn obedience, his last care to serve God, handsomely and cleanly; He is now become so cross a kind of teaching, that should the Church enjoin clean shirts, he were lousy; more sense than single prayers is not his, nor more in those, than still the same petitions; from which he either fears a learned Faith, or doubts God understands not at first hearing. Show him a Ring, he runs back like a Bear; and hates square dealing as allied to Caps, a pair of Organs blow him out o' the Parish, and are the only glister pipes to cool him. Where the meat is best, there he confutes most; for his arguing is but the efficacy of his eating, good bits he holds breeds good positions, and the Pope he best concludes against in Plumbroth. He is often drunk, but not as we are, temporally, nor can his sleep then cure him, for the fumes of his ambition makes his very soul reel, and that small Beer that should allay him (silence) keeps him more surfeited, and makes his heat break out in private houses: women and Lawyers are his best Disciples, the one next fruit, longs for forbidden Doctrine, the other to maintain forbidden titles, both which he sows amongst them, honest he dare not be, for that loves order; yet if he can be brought to Ceremony, and made but master of it, he is converted.

21

[John Earle]

Micro-cosmographie

1628

(Excerpt)

JOHN EARLE (*ca.* 1600–1665) took
his M.A. degree at Cambridge in 1632 and his D.D. degree at Oxford
in 1640. His early poems in Latin and English gained some recognition,
but his *Micro-cosmographie,* a series of character descriptions first published
in 1628, established his lasting position in the history of the English
literary essay. Earle pursued a successful career in the church and became
the tutor of the future Charles II. When he lost his ecclesiastical preferments during the interregnum, he served Charles in exile as an adviser.
After the restoration of the monarchy Earle held high positions in the
church, including, successively, the bishoprics of Worcester and of Salisbury. Throughout his life he was known for his good humor, tolerance, and
integrity, and while he served as a bishop he had the respect of nonconformists, including Richard Baxter.

In his printed essays, Earle did not criticize puritans by name. But his
character sketch of "A she precise Hypocrite" is titled "A Shee-Puritan" in
his holograph manuscript; see the facsimile, *The Autograph Manuscript of
Microcosmographie* (Leeds, 1966, pp. 115–21). The change in title perhaps
reflects Earle's reluctance to offend many of those called puritans by his
contemporaries: apparently, like George Wither and others, Earle saw the
term used indiscriminately, and being concerned specifically with hypo-

critical nonconformity, he avoids calling it puritanism. His specific criticism focuses on religious practices at issue in many attacks on the puritans. His hypocrite leaves her own parish to hear an inferior sermon elsewhere; she likes a two-hour sermon; she does not use a ring in her own wedding. In most instances, by favoring one practice she rejects a more important one. For example, her stress on faith causes her to neglect charity; her love of preaching causes her to neglect prayer. Throughout Earle paints a picture of misguided zeal and false values, as well as the intolerance that he himself tried to avoid in his dealings with nonconformists.

Micro-cosmographie.

Or, A Peece of The World Discovered; in Essayes and Characters. London, Printed by William Stansby for Edward Blount. 1628.

[John Earle. Excerpt: character 45.]

45. A she precise Hypocrite. ["A shee-Puritan" in the manuscript]

Is one in whom good Women suffer, and have their truth misinterpreted by her folly.

She is one, she knows not what herself if you ask her, but she is indeed one that has taken a toy at the fashion of Religion, and is enamored of the Newfangle. She is a Nonconformist in a close Stomacher and Ruf of Geneva print, and her purity consists much in her Linen. She has heard of the Rag of Rome, and thinks it a very sluttish Religion, and rails at the Whore of Babylon for a very naughty Woman. She had left her Virginity as a Relic of Popery, and marries in her Tribe without a Ring. Her devotion at the Church is much in the turning up of her eye, and turning down the leaf in her Book, when she hears named Chapter and Verse. When she comes home, she commends the Sermon for the Scripture, and two hours. She loves Preaching better than Praying, and of Preachers Lecturers, and thinks the Weekday's Exercise far more edifying than the Sunday's. Her oftest Gossipings are Sabbath-day's journeys, where (though an enemy to superstition) she will go in Pilgrimage five mile to a silenced Minister, when there is a better Sermon in her own parish. She doubts of the Virgin Mary's Salvation, and dares not Saint her, but knows her own place in heaven as perfectly, as the Pew she has a key to. She is so taken up with Faith, she has no room for Charity, and understands no good Works, but what are wrought on the Sampler. She accounts nothing Vices but

Superstition, and an Oath, and thinks Adultery a less sin, than to swear by my Truly. She rails at other Women by the names of *Jezabel* and *Dalilah:* and calls her own daughters *Rebecca* and *Abigail,* and not *Anne* but *Hannah.* She suffers them not to learn on the Virginals, because of their affinity with the Organs, but is reconciled to the Bells for the Chimes' sake, since they were reformed to the tune of a Psalm. She overflows so with the Bible, that she spills it upon every occasion, and will not Cudgel her Maids without Scripture. It is a question whether she is more troubled with the Devil or the Devil with her: she is always challenging and daring him, and her weapons are Spells no less potent than different; as being the sage Sentences of some of her own Sectaries. Nothing angers her so much, as that Women cannot Preach, and in this point only thinks the Brownist erroneous: but what she cannot at the Church, she does at the Table, where she prattles more than any against sense, and Antichrist, till a Capon's wing silence her. She expounds the Priests of *Baal* Reading Ministers, and thinks the Salvation of that Parish as desperate as the Turk's. She is a main derider to her capacity of those that are not her Preachers, and censures all Sermons but bad ones. If her Husband be a Tradesman, she helps him to customers, howsoever to good cheer, and they are a most faithful couple at these meetings: for they never fail. Her Conscience is like others' Lust, never satisfied, and you might better answer *Scotus* than her Scruples. She is one that thinks she performs all her duty to God in hearing, and shows the fruits of it in talking. She is more fiery against the May-pole than her Husband, and thinks he might do a Phineas his act to break the pate of the Fiddler. She is an everlasting Argument; but I am weary of her.

22

Owen Felltham

Resolves

1628

(Excerpt)

OWEN FELLTHAM (*ca.* 1604–
1668), poet and essayist, seems to have been educated by private tutors. He
was royalist in political sympathy and conversant with the literary world of
his time, especially the Jonson circle. His *Resolves* grew from fairly short
resolutions in his first edition (*ca.* 1623) to longer, more reflective essays in
the second edition (1628), in which "Of Puritans" was first published.
A variorum edition of *Resolves,* by Ted-Larry Pebworth, appears in three
manuscript volumes (Ph.D. dissertation, Louisiana State University, 1966).

Felltham's thoughtful essay reveals much about contemporary usage of
the term *puritan.* He sees it as a new word, hard to define and used in
various ways, but generally a "name of infamy." The few who embrace it do
not understand its true meaning; possibly Felltham is thinking of the
Greek word *catharoi,* which it translates. Granting that some so-called
puritans are really pious men, he finally settles on a tentative definition,
calling the puritan a "Church-Rebel" and hence unsympathetic. Felltham
dislikes refusals to accept ceremonies prescribed by authority and sees in the
rejection a tendency to cause strife. Moreover, he believes fully that recreations allowed by law should not be condemned because of the scruples of a
few, mainly because he sees religion as joyful and any melancholy demeanor
as a perversion of its true spirit. He cannot identify any specifically puritan

tenets; he sees puritanism more as an attitude than as a complex of beliefs, and in this perception he is no doubt typical of many of the conformists of his time.

Resolve's A Duple Century one new and another of a second Edition by Ow.: Felltham. London: Imprinted for Henry Seile and are to be sould at the Tygers Head in S. Paules Churchyard. 1628

Resolves or, Excogitations. A Second Centurie. London: Printed for Henry Seile, at the Tygers head. in St. Pauls Church-yard. 1628
[Excerpt: pp. 9–12.]

V

Of Puritans

I Find many that are called *Puritans;* yet few, or none that will own the *name.* Whereof the reason sure is this; that 'tis for the most part held a *name of Infamy;* and is so new, that it hath scarcely yet obtained a *definition:* nor is it an *appellation* derived from one *man's* name, whose *Tenents* we may find, digested into a *Volume:* whereby we do much err in the application. It imports a kind of *excellency* about another; which *man* (being conscious of his own frail bendings) is ashamed to assume to himself. So that I believe there are men which *would be Puritans:* but indeed not any that *are.* One will have him one that lives religiously, and will not revel it in a shoreless excess. Another, him that separates from our *Divine Assemblies.* Another, him that in some *tenents* only is *peculiar.* Another, him that will now *swear.* Absolutely to define him, is a work, I think, of *Difficulty;* some I know that rejoice in the *name;* but sure they be such, as least *understand* it. As he is more generally in these times taken, I suppose we may call him a *Church-Rebel,* or one that would exclude *order,* that his *brain* might rule. To *decline offenses;* to be careful and conscionable in our several *actions,* is a *Purity,* that every man ought to labor for, which we may well do, without a sullen *segregation* from all *society.* If there be any *Privileges,* they are surely granted to the Children of the *King;* which are those that are the Children of *Heaven.* If *mirth* and *recreations* be lawful, sure such a one may lawfully use it. If *Wine* were given to cheer the *heart,* why should I fear to use it for that end? Surely, the *merry soul* is freer from intended *mischief,* than the *thoughtful man.* A bounded *mirth,* is a *Patent* adding time and happiness to the crazed life of *Man.* Yet if *Laertius* reports him rightly, *Plato* deserves a *Censure,* for allowing *drunkenness* at *Festivals;* because, says he, as then, the *Gods* themselves reach *Wines* to present *Men. God* delights in nothing more, than in a *cheerful heart,* careful to perform him service. What *Parent* is it, that rejoiceth not to see his *child* pleasant, in the limit of a *filial duty?* I know, we read of *Christ's weeping,* not of his *laughter:* yet we see, he graceth a *Feast* with his *first Miracle;* and that a *Feast of joy:* And can we think that such a *meeting* could pass without the noise of *laughter?* What a lump of *quickened care* is the *melancholic man?* Change *anger* into *mirth,* and the Precept will hold good still: *Be merry, but sin not.* As there be many, that in their life assume too great a *Liberty:* so I believe there are some, that abridge themselves of what they might lawfully use. *Ignorance* is an ill *Steward,* to provide for either *soul,* or *Body.* A man that submits to reverent *order,* that sometimes unbends himself in a moderate *relaxation;* and in all, labors to approve himself, in the sereneness of a healthful *Conscience:* such a *Puritan* I will love immutably. But when a man, in things but *ceremonial,* shall spurn at the grave Authority of the *Church,* and out of a needless *nicety,* be a Thief to himself, of those benefits which GOD hath allowed him: or out of a blind and uncharitable *Pride,* censure, and scorn others, as *reprobates:* or out of obstinacy, fill the World with *brawls,* about *undeterminable Tenents.* I shall think him one of those, whose *opinion* hath fevered his *zeal* to *madness* and *distraction.* I have more faith in one *Solomon,* than in a thousand *Dutch Parlors* of such *Opinionists.* Behold then; what I have seen good! That it is comely to eat, and to drink, and to take pleasure in all his labor wherein he travaileth under the *Sun,* the whole number of the days of his life, which GOD giveth him. For, this is his *Portion.* Nay, *there is no profit to Man, but that he eat, and drink, and delight his soul with the profit of his labor.* For, he that saw other things but *vanity,* saw this also, that it was the *hand of God.* Methinks the reading of *Ecclesiastes,* should make a *Puritan* undress his brain, and lay off all those *Fanatic toys* that jingle about his *understanding.* For my own part, I think the World hath not better men, than some, that suffer under that name: nor withal, more *Scelestic Villainies.* For, when they are once *elated* with that *pride,* they so *contemn* others, that they infringe the Laws of all *human society.*

23

Giles Widdowes

The Schysmatical Puritan

1630

(Excerpt)

G ILES WIDDOWES (*ca.* 1588–
1645) was educated at Oxford, receiving his B.A. degree in 1608 and his
M.A. degree in 1614. From 1610 to 1621 he served as a fellow of Oriel
College. In 1619 he was granted a parish in Oxford, where he continued to
serve for the rest of his life. He was also chaplain to Katherine, duchess of
Buckingham, and in high favor with Archbishop Laud. His defense of
Anglican ceremonies in *The Schysmatical Puritan* evoked a lively response
from William Prynne, whom Widdowes had tutored at Oriel.

The Schysmatical Puritan consists of a sermon with a long preface titled
"To the Puritan." Logically the preface should explain the sermon, but
actually a brief look at the sermon defines Widdowes's religious orientation
and clarifies his intentions in the preface. Widdowes preaches on the text
"Let all things be done decently and in order" (1 Corinthians, Chapter 14,
verse 40) and relates it to the Twentieth Article of Religion of the Church of
England, especially the first part of the article: "The Church hath power to
decree rites and ceremonies, and authority in controversies of faith." The
rest of the article, which prohibits as unlawful anything contrary to Scripture or any interpretation of one scriptural passage in such a way that it
contradicts another, gave rise to much controversy; however, Widdowes
largely ignores this section to concentrate on the question of authority. He

liked to outline topics; his approach in the sermon is to subdivide his text and develop the meaning of each word or phrase at some length, a common enough procedure here carried out with remarkable orderliness. The word *let* receives two pages of exposition, the point being that it constitutes an authorization or command. The words *all things* receive eight pages and are most relevant to the preface, because Widdowes interprets them to mean all details of ecclesiastical discipline, as well as all rites and ceremonies. The words *be done* are explained in eight pages, with stress on the right of authority to demand performance and the necessity of obedience. Finally, the words *decently and in order* call, in eight pages, for decorum. In support of his interpretation, Widdowes draws extensively upon the rest of the Bible, as well as the writings of the church fathers.

The very orderliness and proportion so clearly visible in Widdowes's handling of his text signal his dislike for nonconformity and for any tolerance of varied practices within the church. His stress on authority indicates his impatience not only with disobedience but also with protests. Finally, his interpretation of *all things* leaves nothing to be called indifferent, and his comments on decency and order suggest that he will find intemperate zeal objectionable. The attack on nonconformists in his preface grows naturally out of his biblical text as he expounds it in his sermon.

The preface, which is here reprinted, takes notice of the word *puritan* and its uses. Widdowes sees two possible meanings, one favorable and another both popular and dyslogistic. Consequently he divides all puritans into two general categories: the truly pure (who are to be commended) and the hypocritical (who try to seem more pure than the conforming members of the church). The latter he calls "fallacious puritans," and with these he concerns himself in the rest of the essay. First he defines them as "protestant nonconformists" and then subdivides them into ten groups. The perfectist believes that no one can sin after baptism and simply revives the ancient heresies of the Cathari and the Novatians. The factious sermonist, like most of the others, is wholly contemporary. He deprecates set prayers, preferring his own ill-conceived formulations, and especially preferring sermons to prayers, whereas Widdowes holds that both prayer and preaching are equally necessary. The adjective *factious* points to the sermonist's rejection of authority. The separatist is a modern pharisee, who thinks his own way of life more pure than that prescribed by the church. The Anabaptist denies the existence of original sin and so rejects directly the Ninth Article of Religion. The Love's Familist believes in a community of goods, contrary to biblical teachings. The Brownist rejects church buildings, holding his own services outside them, even in woods and fields. The precisian is here narrowly defined as a person who refuses to swear (to take an oath). The Sabbatarian rejects the observance of holy days, observing only the Lord's day, and even then he errs by favoring unauthorized prayers and sermons. Widdowes insists upon the holy days recognized by the Church of England and argues that a day is kept holy by use of the Book of Common Prayer. The antidisciplinarian does not acknowledge the king's authority in matters of religion. Finally, the presuming predestinarian arrogantly feels assured of his own election.

Presumably any one person can belong to more than one subgroup, and explicitly all nonconformists have in common some divergence from the Articles of Religion, from the Book of Common Prayer, and from the canons of the Church of England. Yet the ten groups represent disparate types of nonconformity. The definitions are narrow and brief because they serve merely to distinguish the groups from one another; all groups share a broad spectrum of differences from the established church. Notably only the Anabaptist and the predestinarian err in fundamental points of theology, and in rejecting the doctrine of predestination Widdowes goes beyond most antipuritan writers to attack a controversial tenet of Calvinist theology. Also, since the separatist, Brownist, Anabaptist, and Love's Familist are outside the Church of England, Widdowes does not limit his definition of puritans to reformers within the church. In effect any protestant except a conforming member of the church is a puritan—specifically, a fallacious puritan.

The Schysmatical *Puritan*.

A Sermon Preached at Witney concerning the lawfulnesse of Church-*Authority, for ordaining, and commanding of Rites, and Ceremonies, to beautifie the Church*. By Giles Widdowes Rector of St. Martins Church in Oxford. *Printed at Oxford for the Author*. 1630.

[Excerpts: dedicatory epistle; preface, pp. 1 – 18.]

To his Gracious Lady, Katharine, Duchess of Buckingham Her Grace, all health, prosperity, and salvation through Jesus Christ.

MADAM

Importunity of friends hath with unanswerable persuasions constrained me, to imprint this Sermon: because an ignorant zeal of some hasty spirits, would cry down the lawful Authority of the true Doctrine, and discipline of our Reformed Church. I therefore desire your Grace's favor most earnestly, to accept these my first fruits, sacrificed on the Press; and to wish them safe protection. My obliged duty directs, and necessitates me, to be thankful unto you, for your special favors beyond my desert, to dedicate myself, and these my orthodox labors to so good, and Gracious a Lady. The Lord Crown your merits with spiritual, and temporal blessings for Christ Jesus' sake, and that for the hearty prayers of

Your Grace's most humble servant and Chaplain

GILES WIDDOWES.

TO THE PURITAN

It is your practice, to run from the Church. I am sorry, that so learned, and so holy men, as you would seem to be, do want true Christian patience, to hear orthodox holy doctrine. But let me entreat you, to understand me this one time. I hope it will be for your edifying. This is my prayer unto Almighty God through Jesus Christ. My business with you is the *Puritan:* whose name distinguished, whose essence rendered in the very property, and whose several kinds essentially differing, I give into your own hands, that you may see, and learn true Reformation.

Concerning the name (*Puritan*) it is ambiguous, and so it is fallacious. For some good men are called *Puritans:* and they are *Puritans* indeed. They are pure in heart, and so blessed, that they shall see God. *Mat.* 5. 8. And some evil men are called *Puritans,* who desire to seem to be just, and holy; but in their doctrine, and discipline, they are the underminers of our True, Protestant, Reformed Church. Are you angry, because I tell you the truth. *Be angry but sin not,* and I will tell you, the essential definition of this fallacious *Puritan.*

A *Puritan* is a Protestant Non-Conformist. A Protestant, this is his Genus, his kind of being. A Non-Conformist: this is his *differentia*, his essential difference, his essential Quality. A *Puritan* is a kind of Protestant. For he will be tried by the Scriptures concerning his faith, and his Christian moral life, so far as his Spirit will endure the text. But the scriptures' deducible sense in

Essentials, Essentiates, Efficients, Finals, Subjects, Effects, and their Modalities, being opposite to their tenets, confounds this Professor, and overthrows his Chair: but he ashamed to forsake his seducing profession a long time vehemently clamorous, taketh fast hold only on the letter, and chapter of the text. So then this *Puritan* is a sullen fallacy of the Reformed Church: being confuted, he will not learn to turn: still he is pure, not really, but in his own suppose. The Lord grant him grace to reform.

This *Puritan* is a Non-Conformist. For he is oppositely set, a Contradictist to the Scriptures' deducible sense in three things. The first is the 39 Articles of our Church's Reformed faith. The second is our Common Prayer-book. The third is the Canons of our Church. And yet the doctrine of the Articles, the faith of the common prayers, and the lawfulness of the Canons, are contained in the deducible sense of holy Scriptures. The Articles of our Reformed Church's faith, which he opposeth are these: the 3. 6. 9. 16. 17. 20. 21. 23. 26. 27. 33. 35. 36. 37. 38. 39. This is proved in the several kinds of this irregular scripturist. The prayers in the common prayer-book, which he contradicts (being collected, and translated out of the Mass-book, yet corrected, and purged from gross errors) those selected prayers he refuseth every one, because they were thence collected. The Absolution he disliketh, because he makes a query, whether the congregation did faithfully, and penitently confess their sins. The Lord's prayer he will not say, because he will make a prayer like to the Lord's prayer. *Nunc dimittis, etc.* he rejects, because he will not any prayer, or hymn, but such as he thinks fit according to his own will. The Litany he saith is composed of conjuring, and swearing, and of unnecessary and unlawful Invocations. The collect on Trinity Sunday, he saith is composed of an Impossibility. And that the last collect but one read at holy Communion is composed of untruths. He is ill-disposed, oppositely affected against prayers at Christenings, Confirmations, and Burials.

I make answer thus. To pronounce, He pardoneth, and absolveth all them, which truly repent, and unfainedly believe; is the actual duty of Evangelical Priests, and so good a duty is no sin. Ministers (must) say the Lord's prayer. The Lord hath said it. *Luk.* 11. 2. And they must make their prayers according to the form of the Lord's. It is the text, they must use no vain babbling: their form of prayer must be effectual, not vain; brief, not stuffed with tautologies, and iterations. Read *Matth.* 6. *ver.* 7. 8. 9. God did regard us with a Savior, in that he did regard the Blessed Virgin with a Son, and a Savior, therefore we say the Magnificat. We shall be saved by the same faith, as old Simeon was, therefore we say *Nunc dimittis.* In the Litany we pray to be delivered from sin, and punishment. And how must Christians pray for to be delivered, but by

Christ's agony, and bloody sweat, etc.? And is this swearing, or conjuring? Is praying in the Winter, to be delivered from thunder, and lightning, unnecessary? Lightning, and thunder are God's secret judgments: he may afflict sinners with them in the Winter: though naturally summer be the time for those terrifying Meteors: but because they are God's secret judgments, therefore we pray always for deliverance. Is praying for thieves, and whores unlawful, the one being included in all men, travailing by land, or by water; the other being included in all women laboring with child? Our Savior saith, that his Heavenly Father *is merciful to the just, and unjust,* and that all God's people must be so merciful *Math.* 5. 48. etc.: And S. *Paul* saith, *do good unto all. Gal.* 6. 10: and therefore we must pray for all. On Trinity Sunday we pray to be delivered from all adversity; and it is thus in the Lord's prayer. *Deliver us from all evil:* And shall we not pray, as the Lord hath taught us? In the last Collect but one at the holy Communion, we confess our unworthiness, and blindness: And wheresoever sin is inherent, and a fighter, there must be *necessitate causae,* (sin being an actual cause,) and unworthiness of God's favor, and blind ignorance; not in the necessary precepts of faith, but in Contingents, with what particular blessing, when, where, and how God will bless sinners. Prayers at Baptism do regenerate: though you deny this. 'Tis the text: *Ask, and you shall have.* To pray is to *Ask.* To be Regenerate is to *have.* The blessed Apostles did confirm the Churches, which they before had converted. *Act.* 14. 22. *Act.* 15. 32. *For confirmation is a Principle of the doctrine of Christ* next to baptism. *Heb.* 6. 1. 2. Therefore S. *Peter* and S. *John* did pray and impose hands to confirm the Church with the holy Ghost. *Act.* 8. 17. And little Children being more weak in the state of Grace, than such Converts, must necessarily be confirmed by the Bishop, the Apostle of the Diocese; though not by miraculous, *yet by seven, of the holy Ghost's gifts.* We must pray for the dead. *Thy kingdom come.* Oh Lord raise the dead prisoners in the grave. And herein we pray for their souls, and bodies. God be with them, to comfort their souls deprived of their bodies; I say to confort them with hastening the Reunion, and the consummate joy of soul and body. Thus the Primitive Fathers: *Junius, B. Bilson, Mornay, Chameirus.* This is not to defend Purgatory, but the received answer against Purgatory.

These things being thus answered: observe that this *Puritan* would obstinately cast out of the Church, *God's saving mercy, saving hope, saving charity, and the seven gifts of the holy Ghost.* And what then is his religion, but faction? *But mark those, that cause division in the Church, contrary to the doctrine, which you have received. For they, that are such, serve not the Lord Jesus, but their own bellies; and with fair speech, and flattering, deceive the hearts of the simple. Rom.* 16. 17. 18.

289

The third thing in which this *Puritan* is Non-conformist, is the Canons of our reformed Church. These, 1. 2. 3. 4. 5. 6. 7. 8. 9. 10. 11. 12. 13. 14. 15. 24. 29. 30. 31. 48. 49. 54. 55. 56. 57. 58. 60. 61. 73. 127 etc. But who is this *Puritan?* What is his name? Mr. *Rogers* in his Preface to the 39 Articles, saith, that since the suppression of *Puritans* by Archbishops, *Parker, Grindall,* and *Whitegift,* none will seem to be such irregular Professors. But the eye that beholds their daring oppositions in the Church, may very well believe, that such Rebellions are taught in their *Conventicles.* What Rebellions? Their teaching against the King's Supremacy, a rejecting of our Reformed faith, a refusing of God's holy worship written, which is the Common Prayer-book; a despising of Canonical obedience; a repugning against our Reformed Church. Yet this seditious Schismatic would be the most true Reformist of Church, and Religion: but read the Survey of the Pretended holy discipline and hence it is evidently proved, that he knows not what he is, nor what he would be. Therefore for his better edifying, let him learn to believe, to pray, and obey according to the understanding Rules of this Reformed Church. For the 39 Articles are true precepts of faith; all Collected out of holy writ. The Common prayers are godly prayers. The Canons are true, and wholesome laws. Therefore he, that will not believe, pray and obey according to this established estate of Church government, *is no pure man in heart.* He studies Confusion of Church, and Commonwealth. The specifical kinds of *this Puritan* promise neither truth, nor goodness: and therefore let no man favor their unrighteous dealing; and let our Church stand fast in her faith, instruct, correct, rebuke: that this Non-conformist may be a true Reformist.

The species; specifical kinds of this *Puritan* are these. 1. *the Perfectist.* 2. *the factious Sermonist.* 3. *the Separatist.* 4. *the Anabaptist.* 5. *the Brownist.* 6. *Lovesfamilist.* 7. *the Precisian.* 8. *the Sabbatarian.* 9. *The Anti-disciplinarian.* 10. *the Presuming Predestinatist.* These ten kinds *in their opinions* are the best Christians: and every one differs *in the Reciprocal Quatenus* (i.e.) in his proper essential Quality from other, as much as white, and black: yet the same subject of inhesion (man) may be all these ten, as the same eye is white, and black: though whiteness, and blackness differ essentially.

The *Perfectist* is he whose pureness is *continuata perseverandi actio sanctificans;* never to sin after baptism. This is the Novatian Catharist. But St. *Paul did sin after baptism. Rom.* 7. This is a perfect keeper of God's law. Thus he is a Papist. but S. *Paul could not do the good, which he would, but the evil which he would not.* His opinion is, that a Christian sinning after baptism is damned. Our Reformed faith is: That by the grace of God, he may Repent, and amend: and thus S. *John, if we confess our sins, he will forgive.* 1. *John.* 1. This *Puritan* sins against the 16. Article.

The *factious Sermonist*, is he, whose pureness is, to serve God with sermons, and extemporary prayers made according to his supposititious inspiration. His opinion is vain glory: Preachers Composed not according to this hasty rule, he saith are unworthy, and therefore they must not be heard to preach, nor resorted to, at holy Communion. Then *S. Peter,* (if unworthiness might depose Preachers) should never have preached *after his forswearing his master.* Our reformed faith is, that we may use the ministry of *Unworthy Ministers.* And 'tis strange that he commends himself to be worthy: whereas *S. Paul* is not a teacher of his opinion. 2. *Cor.* 2. 16. in these words, *who is sufficient for these things?* This sinneth against the 26. Article. Another opinion of his, is that *preaching is better than Prayer.* But both being most necessary: Preaching for to instruct the people; and prayer to worship God, instrumentally to cause regeneration by baptism etc. It follows, that this Sermonist is a peevish disturber of Religion. A third opinion of his, is, that *private Prayer* made by a tardy comer to Church is *the sacrifice of fools.* As if too late coming to Church were not a sin to be repented of: and that one so ill prepared to join with the congregation, should not pray for remission, and God's blessing, and then praise the Lord with the whole Assembly.

The *Separatist* is he, whose Pureness is Pharisaical. He commends himself in the Temple to be far above all others for holiness: Our Savior saith that the *Publican repenting was more just than he. Luke* 18. 14. His opinion is, *that only he is the Elect, the Regenerate, and faithful child of God.* And that all others are reprobates, the wicked, the unregenerate, and the damned: *But God's judgments are unsearchable. Rom.* 11. 33. *And who art thou that judgest? why dost thou Judge etc. Rom.* 14. 4. 10. 11. 12. 13. The judgment of our Church is, that all that are baptized are regenerate: Thus, *Seeing that this child is regenerate and grafted into the body of Christ's congregation etc.* And the Church regulated by scriptures *is the pillar and ground of truth.* 1. *Tim.* 3. 15. therefore believe our Church. Regeneration is by infusion of grace, by sowing the good seed: it differs from increase of grace, and perseverance. Regeneration is *ortus boni seminis,* the springing of good seed: *This good seed did grow in stony and thorny ground.* Regeneration is the individual act, making Christians. Increase of grace and perseverance preserve Christians. And moral persuasion cannot regenerate stony and thorny hearts dead in sin. Therefore regeneration being the individual act of God bound to his Church by his own convenant, judge as our Church doth, concerning the baptized; that all baptized are regenerate.

The grace of God's covenant doth admit of no *Separatists:* for it did not separate, but bind *Issac* and *Ismael* unto God in obedience: neither doth it separate, but unite the baptized unto Christ. As for the separating judgment according to the merciful decree of election who are the saved; this belongs only to God to pronounce. But let all Christians religiously pray and live according to the grace of restitution, and humbly submit their judgments, concerning the secrecy of personal election. The *Separatist* sins against the 17. Article, which saith that *God's election is secret to us, for we know not the elect by their particular names.* He sins against the 35 article at the 2. 4. 5. 6. 7. 10. 11. 15. 19. 20. 21. homily. For these do charitably exhort the whole congregation to obey and honor God; whereas the separatist is no friend of Publicans and sinners: but the uncharitable accuser of our Savior's pitied company.

The *Anabaptist* is he, whose pureness is a supposed birth without original sin. And yet our bodies are parts of *Adam's* nature, that did sin. And no man was born without sin, *Christ only excepted.* His tenet is, that infants must not be baptized. *Yet Isaac was circumcised the eighth day.* And to be *circumcised,* and *baptized* are one, and the same in effect. And *Abraham's* Religion, and ours are the same. *Gal.* 3. 9. 14. 15. 16. 17. And therefore by a necessary seal of the Covenant, we must do, as *Abraham* did; *bind little children in Covenant to God.* This *Puritan* sins against the 9 and 27 Articles. The one affirmeth *that infants are born in original sin,* the other *that infants must be baptized.* If infants be born without original sin: then 'tis no controversy; That original sin foreseen is not the meritorious cause of reprobation. The sinner deserves, and the judge intends punishment. So 'tis certain, that sin is not the foreseen intending efficient of that preordained punishing decree. And it is without question, that God's Supremacy may pardon or punish *pro absoluto beneplacito,* only as he will, seeing 'tis the prerogative of supremacy, he being supreme Judge. But he *cannot be just in decree,* if he so reprobates, but for sin foreseen. For the law was not, that any should die in *Adam,* if *he* had not eaten of the forbidden fruit: *and therefore this law in prevision transgressed is the meritorious efficient of reprobation.*

The *Brownist* is he, whose pureness is to serve God in woods and fields. He is a wilderness of pureness. His opinion is, that Idolatry cannot be reformed without pulling down of Churches. But King *Hezekiah* commanded *the Levites to sanctify the house of the Lord, and to carry forth the filthiness out of the sanctuary etc.* 2. *Chron.* 29. 5. And our Savior *whipt the buyers and sellers out of the Temple:* though it was profaned, yet without any pulling down, he calls it *the house of prayer. Mat.* 21. 12. 13. This *Puritan* sins against the 35. Article, at the 1. homily, which teacheth a decent keeping of the Church.

Loves-familist is he, whose pureness is to serve God as well at his Neighbor's charge, as at his own. *Omnia sunt Communia:* no one saith, that the things, which these Love-Masters possess are their own, but all are Common. Yet S. *Paul* saith, *that he is worse than an Infidel that provideth not for his own family.* If he be poor, his poor pureness must not labor with his hands to get his living, though he be a Mechanick, he must only meditate on the word. Yet the text saith *he that will not Labor, let him not eat.* He in his conceit is a greater Saint than S. *John the Baptist,* and that he is in persecution for the Gospel; and therefore *Ananias* doth sell his possessions, that the poor brother may participate of his brotherly kindness. Concerning S. *John* our Savior saith *that he was as great a Prophet,* as any born of a woman. Concerning *Ananias* S. *Peter* saith *that he dissembled with the holy Ghost: Concerning this poor Saint's persecution for the Gospel:* his punishment is justly to be inflicted on him for abusing the gospel with his deceit to maintain idleness: His neighbor seduced to sell, *is undone:* this is injury which must not escape unpunished. This *Puritan* sins against the 38 Article. For this truth is to be believed, that as in persecution, the rich did relieve the poor Saints: So in the time of peace, all able men must labor, to preserve the Commonwealth. Here, note, that *Loves-familist* in the 38 Article is called the *Anabaptist:* and 'tis true *subiectiue; sed non formaliter.* The same man may be *Loves-familist,* and *Anabaptist:* but to be formally the *Anabaptist,* is not to be *Loves-familist;* their definitions differ.

The *Precisian* is he, whose pureness is, not to swear before a Magistrate. Yet *this kind of swearing* is commanded *Deut.* 6. 13. He teacheth that unlawful *swearing* is a greater sin, than murder. God indeed is greater than man, Hence is the compare, But the effect destructive is greater by murder, for thereby man's life is destroyed, but unlawful *swearing* cannot wound so deep. And God commands that the Murderer die the death, *blood must be shed for blood;* he deals not so severely with the swearer. This *Puritan* sins against the 39. Article: which teacheth that 'tis lawful to swear before a magistrate.

The *Sabbatarian* is he, whose pureness is to preach down all holy days. Preaching; the instrumental directing cause to keep holy the sabbath day, he makes to be the keeping holy the Sabbath; but God's holy worship, common prayer is this keeping holy the sabbath day. For preaching the holy direction teacheth holy worship common prayers to be the holy practice of that day to praise the Lord for our Redemption etc. This is the sole principal end of preaching on the Lord's day. The Sabbatarian's preaching is a *Sylua synonymorum,* Tautologies, Iterations. His praying is too much brainsick babbling. His opinion is; *Labor thou six days: therefore there must be no holy days,* but the Lord's day. 'Tis true in an understanding judicious sense: Thus. Thou must praise God for the Creation, Redemption, Restitution, and preservation of the world: To praise God for these Causes, *only the 7. day is set* apart. Which is not the *Jews'* Sabbath, the sabbath only for the creation. But this is the day following: when Christ rested from subduing sin, hell, and death: when the *Lord Jesus ceased from his work. Heb.* 4. He then *appointed a certain day by saying today ver.* 7. And because Christ rested from his work of restoring his kingdom to Israel in the same manner, as God did from his, *ver.* 10. appointing the first day after the creation to be the sabbath. Therefore the first day of the Jews' week, the scripture calls, and 'tis instituted for to be the Lord's day; *for this is the day of Christ's rest religiously to be celebrated with holy worship in remembrance of our justifying, sanctifying, saving, victorious, and triumphing Redemption.* But concerning other holy days *there were seven together, in the time of the law. Deut.* 16. Therefore when God was to be praised for preserving Israel in tents, when he brought them out of Egypt etc: then the text saith not, *labor 6. days, but keep holy 7. days* etc. So when God is to be *praised for the Angel's good news to the Blessed Virgin, for the Nativity of our Savior, for his circumcision etc.:* then the Church teacheth not 6. days labor, but to praise the Lord on the holy time appointed. This *Puritan* sins against the 35. Article at the 7. 12. 13. 14. 16. and 17 homilies. For these do teach the holy observing of feasts unto the Lord.

The *Anti-disciplinarian* is he, whose pureness is above the King's Supremacy. Imperious Imagination! His holiness is the Church's greatest Authority, and as good a Rule for to know the Reformed true faith, as holy writ. He is a strict observer of the law, therefore his Religion is the best religion. But our Savior teacheth, that *mercy is the best part of Religion. Matth.* 9. 13. And he never learned, *that Christ's king's office is above Christ's Priest's office, in spiritual things:* forasmuch as Christ a Priest, died for to make satisfaction for our sins, to God the Supreme Judge, who is Christ a king: and that from this office of Christ a king, the king is derived: and that the Priest is derived from Christ's Priest's office. This *Puritan's* tenet is, *that kings must be subject to the Puritan-Presbyter's Censure, submit their Scepters, throw down their Crowns, and lick up the dust of their feet.* Thus *Mr. Rogers* in the 11. page of his Preface to the 39. Articles: and thus *T. C. teacheth in his Reply,* page 180. Thus the oath of Supremacy, and allegiance are broken. This *Puritan* is an Arch-traitor. His proud holiness sins against the 21. Article, which affirmeth, that *Princes in their Dominions have supreme Authority to gather together General Councils,* and against the 35. Article at the last homily, which *preacheth down Rebellion:* and against the 37. Article, which saith, that *the King is supreme Governor of Church and Commonwealth next, and immediately under Christ in his Dominions; in all causes, and over all Persons Ecclesiastical, and Civil.* His tenet is, that all Priests should be Equal. But who ever gave all Priests authority to ordain, and did exalt inferior Priests, and pull down Superiors for that equality; but *Farellus,* and *Viretus* (by Sermons) two *Geneva-Presbyters.* But by what Law? Whence was that authority? This *Puritan* sins against the 23. 33. and 36. Articles, which teach the lawfulness of *Archbishops',* and *Bishop's Superiority,* and *Jurisdiction.* This *Puritan* is an enemy to Church-Ceremonies, as if God's Ministers, and his house should be *naked,* without all external beauty. He saith, that he is only for *essentials* at baptizing, etc. And yet Metaphysical divinity is far beyond the sphere of his *plainly, and briefly,* etc. For the Scriptures' deducible sense transcends his capacity. This *Puritan* sins against the 20. Article.

The *Presuming Predestinatist* is he, whose pureness is an inspired knowledge, that he shall be saved by God's absolute election. He is so sure of his salvation, as if he were now in heaven: as if there were no life in him, *but God's essential glory.* This is to sin without fear or wit. He considereth not, that the World, the flesh, and Devil are such cruel, and subtle enemies, that they did so terrify *S. Peter* as that he denied, with an oath, that he knew *the Rock of Salvation,* and the other *Apostles* fled. And pray thou Continually, that thou enter not into temptation. Thus the 17. Article teacheth thee. And presume not that thou art absolutely certain of salvation, for *in denying Christ's soul's local descent* into Hell, which is against the 3 Article, thou deniest a part of *Christ's subduing evil spirits,* and *his triumph over the power of hell:* for this end *Christ descended to the spirits, that were disobedient in the days of Noah.* 1. Pet. 3. 18. 19. 20. and thou seemest to deny *that good works are the striving instrumental causes for salvation,* in that thou regardest not Examples of good life, by abhorring *Apocrypha scripture,* which is against the 6. Article. Suffer the words of exhortation: be not factious in the Church, *to maintain an Imperious ruinating holiness, to amaze silly people, to gain a competency, by way of collection.* God hath given *the tenth part in all Israel for an Inheritance,* to maintain the Priesthood. *Num.* 18. 21. And if the human positive law hath not made provision according to this divine law, stay the Lord's leisure, till he shall assist the king, and the general Council of this land, to reform this thing, as yet full of difficulty. If thou hast no Benefice; faction can never bring thee any *de jure;* but reformation may. Down on thy knees; repent, and amend: and praise God Almighty, forasmuch as thy Dread Sovereign Lord, and king, hath spared thy life so long; thou being nothing better *in tenet, than an Arch-Traitor.* Down on thy knees and give hearty thanks to God; in that the Most Reverend Archbishops, and the Right Reverend Bishops, thy holy and Ghostly Fathers, have not delivered thee over to Satan, *Maiori Excommunicatione,* cursing thee forth, from the Church, and all human society, thou being a most *contumacious Schismatic.* It is not sufficient, that thou deny, that thou art any such *Puritan;* for thy faction is visible (almost) everywhere in this land. Down on thy knees, and pray for God's holy spirit's illumination; that thy zeal may be according to the infallible knowing faith, and that God may thus incline thy heart to our *true, faithful, reforming Christian Religion.* The Lord Almighty, and most merciful, make the light of his countenance to shine upon thee, and to reform thee. Then the Church shall enjoy her much desired unity: In which how happy a thing it is for Brethren to dwell together, for Christians to live, and die; I desire you, to consider; I pray you; I beseech you: Even I, though I am very disdainfully hated of you, am so charitably affected; and I labor always to the utmost of my prayers, and studies, to instruct you with true sanctifying reformation, and so shall till death remain,

Your hearty well-wisher to solid Reformation,
GILES WIDDOWES.

[Excerpt from the second edition, (Oxford, 1631), Sig. C3.]

There you have the 10 kinds of *Puritans,* although they have been censured by pragmatical fantastics, yet they cannot be Confused by a Solid School divine. For they differ really, they have their several real differences.

The real and formal essence of

1   The perfectist is, an impossibility to sin.
2   The factious Sermonist is, a professed contradiction of common prayers.
3   The Separatist is, his judging separation of the sheep from the goats, a judging election, contrary to Church Regeneration.
4   The Anabaptist is, Original righteousness.
5   The Brownist is, a Wilderness of pureness.
6   Loves Familist is, *Omne Commune.*
7   The Precisian is, the prohibition of lawful swearing.
8   The Sabbatarian is the prohibition of holy days thanksgiving.
9   The Anti-disciplinarian is, a masterless subjection.
10   The presuming Predestinatist is presumptuous glory.

And are not these 10 several realities? or is any one of them really the same with the other? what now will the babblers say?

Carpere vel noli nostra, vel ede tua

24

John Taylor

A Swarme of Sectaries, and Schismatiques

1641

(Excerpt)

JOHN TAYLOR (1580–1653), the
self-styled "Water Poet," had little formal education but much wit and
initiative. By occupation he was first a Thames boatman, later a tavern
keeper, and always a prolific writer. A staunch royalist in high favor with
Elizabeth, queen of Bohemia, he encountered some difficulties with the
authorities after 1649 but escaped serious punishment. The two brief
stanzas from his *Swarm of Sectaries, and Schismatiques* point out that in his
view the term *puritan* can be applied to either of two radically different
groups: the truly pious (who are stigmatized with the name *puritan* by the
less religious) and the hypocrites (who would seem pure but use their
appearance of piety to hide some basic wickedness). In both cases Taylor
sees *puritan* as a term of reproach, and his testimony is especially interesting
because of his thorough knowledge of popular attitudes.

The contents of the rest of Taylor's pamphlet are clearly indicated by the
title page. He supports the establishment and rejects all self-authorized
preachers; his criticism of them takes the form of ridicule, pointing out the
disparity between their training and the learning needed by sound preachers. Most receive very brief comment, but Samuel How, the preaching
cobbler, is described at some length. In his desultory way Taylor also adds
an account of some of the miracles of the Apostles and then moves to

a general denunciation of preachers who lack credentials from church authorities. Thereupon the name *puritan* shows up in an interesting passage. Beginning with an invective against the heretics of the early church, Taylor proceeds:

> For in Saint Austin's time, he made complaint,
> That eighty-two Sects did the Church attain:
> Since when, could I all Heresies recount,
> The number (trouble) treble will amount;
> Yet in that Father's days, that reverend man
> Did ne're hear of the Sect called Puritan,
> And sure the name of Puritan doth yield,
> A good man's nickname, and a bad man's shield,
> It is a cover for a cheating Knave,
> And 'tis a jeer, a good man to deprave;
> But both the good and bad, whate're they be,
> They get no name of Puritan from me.
> I write of Separatists, and Schismatics,
> Of shallow-pated, harebrained Heretics,
> Such as do make the Text a Lesbian rule,
> Whose faith or reason (like the Horse or Mule)
> Whom neither Law, or sense can curb, or bridle,
> Who ne're are well employed, nor never idle. (p. 17)

Of course Augustine did not hear the word *puritan,* because no one in his time spoke modern English; however, he was familiar enough with its Greek equivalent, *catharoi.* In this passage Taylor seems to indicate that the name is too good for the troublers of the church and too bad for the truly religious; also, it leads to confusion. Like Thomas Fuller, Henry Parker, and others, he feels it should be avoided.

A Swarme of Sectaries, and Schismatiques:

Wherein is discovered the strange preaching (or prating) of such as are by their trades Coblers, Tinkers, Pedlers, Weavers, Sow-gelders, and Chymney-Sweepers. By John Taylor. Printed luckily, and may be read unhappily, betwixt hawke and buzzard. 1641.

[Excerpt: introductory verses.]

The odds or difference betwixt the Knave's Puritan, and the Knave Puritan.

And first of the Knave's Puritan.
He that resists the world, the flesh, and Fiend,
And makes a conscience how his days he spend
Who hates excessive drinking, Drabs, and Dice,
And (in his heart) hath God in highest price;
That lives conformable to Law, and State,
Nor from the Truth will fly or separate:
That will not swear, or cozen, cog, or lie,
But strives (in God's fear) how to live and die:
He that seeks thus to do the best he can,
He is the Knave's abused Puritan.

The Knave Puritan.
He whose best good, is only good to seem,
And seeming holy, gets some false esteem:
Who makes Religion hide Hypocrisy,
And zeal to cover cheating villainy;
Whose purity (much like some devil's Ape)
Can shift himself into an Angel's shape,
And play the Rascal most devoutly trim,
Not caring who sinks, so himself may swim:
He's the Knave Puritan, and only He,
Makes the Knaves's Puritan abused to be.

For (in this life) each man his lot must take,
Good men must suffer wrong for bad men's sake.

25

Antibrownistus Puritanomastix [Pseud.]

Three Speeches

1642

Three Speeches, "published by Anti-brownistus Puritanomastix," consists of the speeches of a warden, his wife, and the wife's chambermaid. All three satirize puritan and roundhead religion, intelligence, and morals. Somewhat expanded versions of the speeches of the warden and his wife were published independently, and these longer versions are here reproduced, followed by the chambermaid's speech from *Three Speeches*. The greater coherence of the expanded versions suggests that the speeches of the warden and Mistress Warden were first printed separately and then later condensed, with the maid's speech added to round out the collection.

In a satiric introduction the warden—apparently the warden, or head, of a company of merchants—shows his ignorance by misuse of language (by here, as elsewhere, ironically applying derogatory terms to himself). Five separate topics then come up for discussion in his speech: the liturgy; the militia; the papists; Ireland; and by way of conclusion, "fears and jealousies." In treating the liturgy of the church, the author satirizes the unlearned nonconformists' ignorance of Latin and Greek and has the warden praise Hebrew, of which he is totally ignorant. With amusing double entendres, the members of the company are accused of licentiousness consequent upon their religious ceremonies and doctrines. Untrained preachers also come under ridicule. The discussion of the militia shows the warden to be an opponent of the king—essentially a rebel—as he praises the fourteenth-century insurrectionists Wat Tyler and Jack Straw. The topic "extirpation of the Papists" leads to more criticism of extemporaneous preaching and ridicule of the argument that all vestiges of popery should be eliminated from religious practice. The characterization of dissenters goes beyond comment on their lack of knowledge to accuse them of substituting a highly dubious "feeling" for "reason and sense." The question of Ireland shows the warden and his fellows to be interested solely in the money to be gained from Irish estates and callous to the suffering of English soldiers in the Irish wars. Finally the fears and jealousies are essentially sexual, revealing a concern about the illicit behavior of wives and daughters—behavior that here also is promoted by eccentric religious beliefs and unorthodox religious services.

Mistress Warden tracks her husband's argument with some repetition of ideas but with slightly different emphasis and new examples. Throughout her disquisition she repeatedly exhibits the vices of gluttony, greed, lechery, vanity, and ignorance. She opposes the Book of Common Prayer, the monarchy, and the use of "reason and sense." She speaks favorably of the churches of Scotland, Amsterdam, and New England, as well as of the Anabaptists. Also she favors "aristocratical government," the doctrine of predestination, and the use of conventicles instead of churches. Whereas protestants are her adversaries, she finds many affinities with subversive Jesuit beliefs. On most topics she speaks more vehemently than does the warden. Her chambermaid, in a briefer discourse, is more outspoken still in her dislike of papists and of "reason and sense," favorite terms of the author. Her observation that the youthful elect reveal themselves by being "furiously obstinate in zealous anger" describes the tone of both her speech and that of her mistress.

The word *puritan* appears only once, in the maid's speech, whereas *roundhead* occurs several times. However, the pseudonym identifies the author as antipuritan and makes a connection between puritans and Brownists that is exploited particularly in reference to their highly unconventional places of worship; Giles Widdowes had indicated that the rejection of specifically "church" buildings was a highly visible characteristic of the Brownists. Obviously reformers within the church, heretics, and separatists are grouped here as opponents of the Church of England, of learning, of morality, of the king, and even of monarchy as an institution.

Three Speeches.

Being such Speeches as the like were never spoken in the City. The first by Master *Warden* to the fellowes of his Company, touching the Affaires of the Kingdome. The second by Mistris *Warden,* being her observation on her Husbands Reverent Speech, to certain Gentlewomen of Ratliffe and Wapping. The third by Mistris *Wardens* Chamber-maid as she was dressing her Mistris, The Wisedome and Learning whereof will amaze your judgements. Published by Antibrownistus Puritanomastix. Printed at London for *S. R.* 1642.

The Speech of a Warden to the Fellowes of his Company: Touching the great affaires of the *Kingdome.* Wherein your Judgement will stand amazed to decide whether his Wisdome or Learning did exceed. And doubtlesse is such a Speech as was never spoken by any Warden since the Citie was made a Corporation. Published by *Antibrownistus Puritanomastix.* Printed for *N. V.* 1642.

Brethren and fellow Councilors of this never too-wise assembly: Before I begin my discourse, my duty binds me to render you all humble thanks for your general Election of me, to wag my beard amongst you this day, for the good of the Commonwealth: I confess myself as very a Woodcock as the best of you, and as far unfit for this great employment, yet (with your patience) I will endeavor to express the simplicity of my zealous affection to the Weal public, with as much vigor and outrageous spleen, as my shallow capacity can perform.

The first thing I am bound in conscience to present to your consideration, is the *Liturgy* of the Church, which is a thing in these days generally spoken against, and that by our most eminent, grave and orthodox Coachmen, Weavers, and Brewers' Clerks; nay it is grown odious to our She-divines, whose eyes do perpetually look asquint with the very thought of it. For my part, what this *Liturgy* is, I know not, nor care not, yet as simple as I am, I am confident it is a hard word. And in my judgment is either Greek or Latin or both: from whence I must necessarily conclude, that there ought no hard words, no Greek nor Latin, nor any that know them come within the Discipline of the Church, nor any Language or Linguist, but plain Hebrew and English. Let us therefore avoid this *Liturgy* as a thing whereof we are utterly ignorant, uncapable, and undeserving. And if it concern the Common Prayer (as my singular wife saith it doth) then questionless (if the new Convocation be but endued with wisdom correspondent to mine) they will doom it to be burnt with such a fire as will consume it, yea till it be consumed even as the Logs in Lincolns-Inn-fields were. And great reason, for it hath been the only cause why the Gospel hath prospered so slenderly under the ministry of preaching trades-men and Lay Clergywomen, who have coupled themselves together, in a joint labor for the procreating of young Saints to fill up the number of this new faith: To which purpose, how often, and how long have Barns, Stables, Woods, Sawpits, Old Ditches, Cellars, yea houses of Office been their Synagogues, places of excellent privacy, and free from the eyes of the sinful, and such of the wicked as will speak worse than they mean, for certainly their speaking is worse than our doing. But (to come to my subject again, for I had like to have rambled from it,) if this *Liturgy* (that heathen word *Liturgy*) were blotted out of the Church, what an infinite increase, and multiplication of spiritual chil-dren would they suddenly beget, insomuch that the parishes would even swarm with them. And that in regard of the Liberty they might then use, for they are altogether so strong of Spirit (by reason of high fare) and as I may say so zealously impudent, that I persuade myself, they would go toot even in the open streets, and never fear or shame to be discovered. But I will conclude this argument as Goodman *Green* did in the Hebrew tongue in *Hatcham Barn* last fasting day after dinner quoth he very excellently, *Quicquid libet cuquodlibet,* which according to the best translation is, away with the *Liturgy,* away with it, and so say I.

The second thing I must vex your patience withal, is the *Militia,* which (although I know not the meaning of it) yet it is argument sufficient to me to conceive it absolutely requisite, because the King doth absolutely oppose it. This same *Militia* is likewise a hard word: And if it be Hebrew (as for ought I know it may be) I should love it the better; but from hence I must needs observe, that hard words are fitter for the Camp than the Church: And there-fore I hold it very necessary that those who are Scholars and understand hard words, should be compelled (as I think they will be) to apply themselves to Military Offices; and in their stead those that understand nothing be in-structed with Ecclesiastical Discipline. And further: Touching this *Militia,* what a glorious sight it is to see the Leaders, and their horses armed in gold and silver lace, Gorgets, and Leading-Staves, of beaten plate, Ornaments of excellent use in War, for the enemies to make prize on, and is perhaps a witty policy (in case of surprisal) to carry their Ransoms in the habit of Armor: And then again, to see the unstained Buff and Scarlet, never blemished with so much as one Crimson Drop, the new-painted Drums, and unweatherbeaten

Ensigns, and chiefly the courageous Batteries made upon the fresh air, with full as much alacrity and undaunted spirit as if the enemy himself had been there ready pitched for an encounter or more, I verily believe. What say you to me myself that never discharged a piece in all my life before it did my heart good to hear my gun crack though I could not see it, for indeed I winked, and yet *I* think in my conscience *I* could have hit the great Tent (durst *I* have charged a Bullet) at more than twenty foot off. Well this *Militia* is a brave thing, and as necessary an invention to consume powder, and to keep us in a weekly employment in these times of small trading, as heart can wish: In my opinion it is fit to be encouraged: And that it be ordained (enacted I believe it will not be) Colonel of all the hard words that ever came into the City since the valiant Conquest of *Wat Tyler* and *Jack Straw,* performed by a Citizen and predecessor of ours.

This Militia (being established) leads me on to my third argument which I doubt not but (by your grave favors) to go through, with as much desecration as I have done the two former.

And that is the extirpation of the Papists. O let us elevate our perspicuous Noses to smell out their treacheries that we may be able to root them out, (but not with our Noses, for that would be swinish:) And rather than be such beasts let us be horned beasts, (as our Ancestors and predecessors in all ages have been) that we may yoke ourselves together in full strength, and plow them up, as it were the bowels of the earth: Let us heap so many crosses upon them till they be afraid to cross the way on us, or to cross the proverb or to cut any cross Capers, lest we interpret every such act to be direct Popish superstition. And to perfect this extirpation let all men whosoever that are not directly and absolutely of our opinion mind habit, (if it had been possible I would have said wisdom) be reputed *Papists.* (And so they are already) but I mean let them fall within the limitation and censures of all laws established against Popery and popish innovation. And therefore let him that honors the name of *Jesus* be reputed a *Jesuit,* him that takes degrees at the *universities* be held a *Seminary,* and so consequently let them both be hanged, drawn, and quartered for high Treason, for that's the doom my charity can afford them: Nay let not a woman wear Beads, lest we judge she numbers her prayers by them (unless it be Pearl beads in a Hatband because my wife herself (That impregnable piece of devout obstinacy) hath adjudged and followed that fashion as a decent wearing, and special vestment, to give evidence of the haughty and vainglorious pride of a Citizen's wife. And further, for this purpose: Let us draw the King (if it be possible) to become no natural man; that is, never to reflect on any man for his excellency of learning, pregnancy of wit, affability and sweetness of behavior, fluency of language, or any other perfection of Art or Nature whatsoever, unless he can likewise give sufficient Testimony of his affection to Round-headism, that he never heard any Common prayers but can pray himself four hours with more vehemency, than the best Divine in Christendom that prays but a quarter. That he believes it not possible that a sermon in any language under Heaven can save a soul, except *English* and *Hebrew*. Now truly, for my part I cannot very perfectly speak this same *Hebrew tongue* I mentioned so often; but I honor it because I take it to be the language they speak at *Amsterdam*, where the most famous Lay-Doctors in all the World do exercise. But I say what a glorious Court would men of these qualities and faith make: the King's graces before meat and after meat would be longer than his morning and evening prayers are; the reversion of his Diet not given away, but all eaten, as swiftly as a *Cormorant* swallows an Eel: Ambassadors would be answered before they had an Audience, even by instinct of the spirit; long locks would be converted to large ears; Masques and Plays to Conventicles, and Psalm-singing; the very sight or ugly aspect of them would fright these same pretty Taffeta-beauties out of the Virge, so that no sinners but themselves, should come near the Throne of Majesty, whereby they would be (as their ambition ever was) the prime sinners of the Kingdom. How fit would these men be for State employment too? Would not *How* the Cobbler make a special Keeper of the great Seal, in regard of his experience in Wax? Or *Walker* the spiritual Ballad-writer, become the Office of Secretary of State? Or the *Locksmith* that preached in *Crooked Lane*, make an excellent Master of the Wards? And the *Taylor* at *Bridewell-Dock*, might be Master of the Liveries. Who fitter to be Master of the Horse than my Lord *Whatchicallum's* Groom? I tell you plainly, he is able to do more service in the Stable (besides what he can do in the Pulpit) than he that enjoys the place. And would not *Browne* the Upholsterer, make a proper Groom of the Bedchamber? Why, I myself am Warden of my Company, and could not I think you as well be Warden of the Cinque Ports? Well, well, I am verily persuaded we shall never attain to these preferments; but it doth me good to build a Castle in the Air with the thought of it, to think how we should firk the Popish and Malignant party, what now in them is but Petty larceny, should then be accounted high Treason; what now is but Superstition, should then be blasphemy. Innovation should be Heresy, and Latin in a Sermon should be reputed flat Damnation. O there was never any Tiger,

Dragon, or Elephant did reign, domineer, rule, and tyrannize as we would do; we would be very Lions in the *Naemean* woods, Hydraes in the *Lermean* Fens, Eagles in the Skies, Whales in the Seas, Pikes in the River, and *Neroes* in the Empire; nay, all the Devils in hell, Hags, Furies, Witches, and Instruments of damnation whatsoever, should never parallel us for inventions to plague these lukewarm Locusts, these Mercurials of Religion that stand upon Philosophy, Reason, Sense and *I* know not what; as if reason and sense, and such fooleries, were pertinent to religion and the graces of the Spirit. This Rapture had almost begot an ecstasy in me but that a proverb amongst the wicked came in the nick to cool the fumosity of my Choleric rheum, that the curst Cow hath short horns: And truly now *I* think better on it, whatsoever our mad frenzies do persuade us to imagine ourselves, yet we are not the people that must have all the sway, the King's part will bear half; for let us think what we will of ourselves, the truth is the wiser sort do hold us but Roundheads, silly rascals, ignorant coxcombs, indiscreetly zealous fools, yea even Cuckolds, and know us to be so too, yet *I* have only intimated my proper zeal and customary desires unto you, that you might all with my affection expect this happy change, which we would call by the name of Reformation, for this (might it come to pass as it never will do) were a sure way to banish Popery, and bring the Kingdom into a way of extempory preaching and spiritual blasphemy. And here *I* end with the Papists. *I* should have prolonged my invection against them, but that *I* say the Proclamation for executing Laws upon them, wherefore (Though *I* do not love them) yet *I* think the better of them because the King pursues them so eagerly.

The next thing which I will plunder my brains and beat out the very quintessence of my noddle about, is the design for *Ireland,* upon which subject I doubt not but to belabor my invention so strongly, that you would think *Tully* were making an oration against *Cataline,* or that an Apple-wench were scolding with a Peddler in *Bartholomew fair* about a standing; or that a railing Lecturer were preaching a Sermon of damnation in a reprobate Auditory: nay, I fear not but you will crown me Cob-warden of all the Wardens in Europe or *New-England;* which is more.

The great necessity of this Design appears to my conscience, but in two particulars only. First, the reparation of our losses past: and secondly, the expectation of a mighty profit to come; for which two causes only (without any collateral or other consideration of bloodshed, or anything else) I do urge this unto you. As for our losses, they are more than Arithmetic can number; and that is a great deal you will say, yet it is true, though he that counts it easy to multiply the Sands and the Stars were to be the accountant. And thus it appears, many of us here present and many hundreds more have wittily taken the opportunity of the Rebellion in *Ireland,* to compound their debts here, under pretense of losses there; which in my judgment is a most inscrutinous and unsearchable pretense; and he that gave the first example thereof deserves to be made Master of the Company of Bankrupts; I would have you all learn it. And I confess, I myself would follow it, but that it doth not agree with the rules of City pride; for then I should be compelled to forsake my *Wardenship,* and my wife to give the wall, which would break her heart, or else breed such a dissension betwixt us, that she would break mine. But I say, by virtue of this ingeniously mischievous pretense, you might enrich your debt Books to a treble estate, and never come within the compass of controllment, and so cozen your Creditors and the Commissioners of Bankrupts with a clearly neat excuse, and invisible piece of knavery. I even tickle with the conceit of it: you may thereby preserve your money to buy land in *Ireland,* and so after the Conquest, have that estate there in reality, which now you do but pretend to have. Now truly I thank you all for that loving Hum, it is a most evident token of your proneness to take my advice; and I doubt not but to my glory and your comfort, it will be followed with speedy effect, especially if the King be not pacified and return home again. The second cause why I press this Design (as I said before) is the mighty benefit which thereby will accrue; he that adventures two hundred pounds for a thousand Acres, purchaseth for the said two hundred pounds, five and twenty pounds a year at six pence an Acre *per annum,* (I made my man *Jehosaphat Singularity* cast it up this morning.) And this kind of profit is peculiar only to us money-mongers. The benefit which will redound to the Soldiers is of another nature, *viz.* that transparent and invisible treasure called Honor, the proper advancement of all resolved spirits: For alas, what should they do with Lands or estates, to hinder their brave achievements and re-doubted undertaking. It is enough they come home with half their limbs, thereby enabled to be Pensioners of the County Treasury, under the limitation of maimed Soldiers, in genteel rags, and not a louse that creeps upon those rags, but a gentleman by the Law of Arms; the total of their whole Revenue consisting of honorable scars, and rusty Whinyards that will not be pawned; arguments of more validity for them to swagger, and damn and sink withal, than infinite wealth could be; and may but their idol Fortune be so favorable as to afford them means to procure Ale and Tobacco, why they will live as happily as the great *Turk;* though meat and clothes be things utterly worn out of their memories. And so much for this Design.

Now for my period, my *ultimum,* my *nil ultra,* the very Garland of my good Will to the Public; and that is the fears and jealousies which do now possess the Kingdom; I will but only grunt you out a modicum, a touch, a relish, a short twang of them, and then end with the same modesty, gravity, and wisdom that I began.

Concerning these Fears and Jealousies; they are of a most dangerous nature and high consequence, the greatest that ever was in any Time or Nation; but truly neither I nor any man living can tell what they are, or from whence they should arise: but without all doubt there is great cause, or else there would not be such talking of them: And it appears by an example here present, for all you that now snore so loud, could not have been so sleepy had not *Fears* and *Jealousies* kept you waking: Besides, now I think on't, there are some apparent causes, as myself do fear lest *Jehosophat* should get my Daughter *Dorcas* with child, for *Jehosophat* is a notable boy, and hath said prayers at a Conventicle, and the girl hath a strain both of Father and mother in her. You neighbor Gripe do fear lest your wife should know you keep a whore at Putney, and you brother *Brush* fear lest you should be hanged for speaking high treason against the King; and truly we all fear one thing or other. And for our Jealousies, all of us here present, that have handsome wives are jealous of them, and not without good cause: and those that have not, are jealous of other women, and some are jealous of their servants; so that you see there are both Fears and Jealousies grounded upon considerable causes. Now truly how to prevent the effects of these Fears and Jealousies is not within the compass of my Ingenuity: For it is not the *Militia,* the stopping of Ports, and holding Garrison Towns, that can keep our Wives, Daughters, and Servants honest, if they have a mind to cuckolds, or try whether they be able to fructify: No, no *Italian Locks* will not do it: nay, for ought I know, your wife neighbor *Spider* may be just now at it, for I saw *Green* the felt-maker go that way as I came to the Hall: O tremble not neighbor, she hath (no doubt) discretion to do nothing but what is spiritual and secret, merely to take down the price of the flesh, for I'll assure you that Act is as great a help to the mortification of fleshly desires, as the longest fast that ever was kept. Now there are other Fears and Jealousies; but as I said, so I say again, I cannot imagine from whence they should proceed, unless we should fear lest the Devil should too soon take a swift Vengeance on us for our damnable Extortions, and Cozenage in the sale of our Commodities: And yet why should we fear that we are already sure on. Well, since there is no remedy;

we will fear still, and be jealous still: And (without all question) when the danger comes upon us, we shall know the cause thereof: In the meantime, I will sit down and fall asleep, and hold my peace.

FINIS.

Mrs. Wardens Observations Upon Her Husbands Reverend Speech In the Presence of certaine Gentlewomen of Ratcliffe and Wapping. [1642]

The right Worshipful Mr. Warden, calling for his flowered Satin-sleeves with the Canvas-back, his Wife perceived by that, and the brushing of his Demi-caster, it was *Hall*-day. His *Breeches* were Velvet, entailed to the Heirs male of his Family, ever since the *Scottishman* begged the Wardrobe. Thus put into Print (his Garters composed into a true-love's knot, and his Shoes shining to the terror of poor people) away He trots, with as much grace as an *Hartfordshire* horse, leaving his thrice reverend Wife with a penny-pot of *Alligant* and a toast in her hand: I say, his *Thrice* reverend Wife, as she had been sometimes a *School-Mistress,* now a *Midwife,* and Mrs. *Warden.* She had scarce licked her lips after the first glass, but five or six of her Daughters from *Ratcliffe* and *Wapping,* came to offer their Eggs and Muskodell unto her. They had lately delivered a *Petition* concerning their opinions in redress of matters in State, and had elected Mr. Warden (since the fame of his *Speech* had spread him) to be their Spokesman when occasion should offer.

Now after some three or four Quarts, and a little bawdy talk the Eggs provoked, one of them very demurely rising drops a *Wapping* curtsy, simpers twice or thrice, casts up her squints, and begins (with a look like skimmed Milk) as morally as the Song of *Toll, Toll, Toll, gentle Bell for a soul, etc.* to be very Religiously angry with the King and a Malignant party of Nobility, Clergy, Judges, Gentry, and Reprobate Cavaliers; nay, and in truth it is feared (saith she) that three parts of the Kingdom have their eyes blinded with a kind of Duty and Conscience, and what is the root of all this unrighteousness, but that abominable Profane, Superstitious, Idolatrous, Babylonish, and conjuring book of Common————. Here her face grew black, and she sat down to take breath: whilst another of the Nymphs, called Gammer *Toad-fish,* starts up in her place and cries: Nay, Mother, there be some that blush not to talk of a Prerogative, and I know not what, as if we of the Elect could speak Treason; Nay, (profane wretches) there want not some that dare laugh and gibe at Mr.

Warden himself, and his thrice endowed *Speech,* at our *Petition* too, though it were penned by as Zealous a Brewer's Clerk, as ever prayed in *Hebrew.* With that the very ancient Gentlewoman (in a kind of anger, like an Ape when it is mocked) throws a clean Partlet upon her shoulders, and nestling in her Chair like a Bear, that is to show tricks, after three or four mops and mows, thus bespoke attention.

Most pure and chosen of the Times, my Daughters and Companions in *Predestination,* I know you will not doubt that truth, which a most Learned man and friend of ours, hath very ignorantly and impudently set forth, that *Democracy, Aristocracy, etc.* (he might have added *Hypocrisy*) are as much from God, as *Monarchy.* By which position (to speak truth) he shows his wisdom in his Ignorance by proving nothing. It may hold that a *Stable,* or an house of *Office* are places, and as ancient as *Churches;* therefore as Sacred and proper to teach in. And by the same belief (when He shall but please to say it) are we to obey and confide in our own opinions before all *things.* Which inference and your assertion throws me very pregnantly upon my Husband's argument of the *Malitia.*

The *Malitia* (dear Daughters and Sisters of the *pint*) hath already been most faithfully handled by one great *Observator,* and not unlearnedly by my *Husband,* on which I raise my first observation. That, as the Philosophers have a *Maxim, we are born for our Country,* so the *Lawyers* have a Rule, *That every man is next to himself:* By which it will follow (and must) If men be bound either to hazard their *Lives,* or *words* for their Country, that *Lege talionis,* their *Country* is bound to hazard their *Estates, Wives,* and *Children* to requite and uphold them; for what are their estates, wives, and children, if not protected and secured theirs? So that to an easy judgment it will appear, the *Militia* is but a mutual bond and interchange of men's estates and affections, and (as that worthy lover of his King saith) a very legal invention to keep the City loyal to the King, and to make the King confide in the City. Beside the great and unknown benefit it bringeth to *Feather-makers, Brokers,* and other dutiful Subjects, whereas the *Commission of Array* is another thing, and if any be so presumptuous to think it *legal,* yet by the same Author we are informed, there is an *equity* in the *Law* beyond the *Letter,* by which we may dispense with our *estates* and our *consciences* as we please, believe what we list, and take up new *Opinions* and *Arms,* as we shall think fitting for Church or Commonwealth. Nor stand we bound (an happiness of these present times before any other) to confide in any such exposition of Judges or Lawyers before our own: But as I have often heard my learned and double-combed Husband say, Oh what a flourishing Commonwealth should we see, if it were contrived into *Halls* and *Companies,* and governed by *Wardens* and *Masters!* Indeed this would come very near that Model of *Church government* laid down by that most hypocritical and seditious *Fox* of the *Church*, who begot the *Protestation protested* (pardon me Elect Members of the *Conventicle*) they be *Hieroglyphic* terms to express his zeal, learning, and boldness by. And now I am come so near the *Church* I will place my observation upon my *Husband's* point as it stands, and only peep in at the window, because I know you are all *Gentlewomen* of the function, and showed your abilities in all those places by him mentioned. It is nothing what language their *Liturgy* is in, for they confess the most unlearned may know enough to be saved by: *Ergo,* Learning is needless, and if needless, why not *profane?* Nay I gather further thus: If learning were either necessary or convenient, the *Scriptures* would enjoin it as it doth other things that are so, but the most unlearned may be saved, nay are saved; *Ergo,* Learning is neither necessary nor convenient: and so from the *major* consequently to the *minor;* if not *Learning,* neither *Reason* nor *Sense.* For as that man of Revelations Mr. *Greene* proves it fully, *Ignorance* and *Noise,* are marks sufficient enough whereby to know our *Election:* and the other with the sanctified Lungs, Mr. *Hunt,* in his *tale of a Tub,* both maintaineth and maketh good, Learning to be a mere trouble and vexation to Religion. By which reasons we can (if it please us) as easily prove it as lawful for *women* as *men* to be *Bishops* (if *Bishops* were lawful at all) which we must deny. And therefore I hope it shall not need much breath to prove them *Antichristian,* where it is so orthodoxly believed already; not because of their *estates* and *honors* (for *riches* and *honor* are not to be despised, if placed upon the right *Saints*) but because they will not resign them to us and our righteous *seed,* who ought to inherit the Earth. And here again, we have just cause to vent our *holy* malice against the *Laws* for putting a *profane* bridle on us; but thanks be given, the bowels of our *hope* is somewhat enlarged.

The *Anabaptists* most excellently deny a great part, if not almost all the *Scriptures* that make against them any way, and do not we as religiously leave our divers *Epistles* making against us, or call them *Apocryphal?* By which *Spirit,* I hope it is no hard thing to prove a *Barn,* or *Stable,* or any hole, places most proper to our *doctrine* and *conversation;* for it is *Religion* makes a *church,* not the *Church* Religion; therefore any place may be made a Church. Besides you know we congregate together in the Spirit, to feel as well as hear; and I pray, in what Church of our opposites have you that free conveniency? Then for the universality of it, what Church can be more universal for *Simplicism, dotagism,* and *Hypocrisism?*

As for the Babylonish Rags and Antichristian Wardrobe, let us leave them to the Kirk of *Scotland* and *Amsterdam;* their Surplices to make sarks, and their

Copes to make cushions: Only our observation voluntarily here thrusts itself in, in which I must heartily admire our brothers of Scotland, that at their first coming hither, they could forget (for what it had been for them to remember a greater matter?) and overlook all this needless trumpery in the Church, when they begged the leads of it: Which if I could but believe they assayed, I should think their modesty not the less meritorious, though they hardly missed.

Now concerning the pearl Hatband my most ever Round-headed Husband yawns at in his Speech, you shall see it, but truly I confess I never wore it with that pride and delight since he compared it to Popish beads, a word so unnatural to me, that verily I must drink the other cup to reconcile my stomach; but let me tell you ingeniously, it is more for the Pope's sake and the King of *Spain's,* than the Religion merely itself; for in sooth there be many principles in that Religion which we do not deny for wholesome and Orthodox, only we scorn to own them from the Jesuits, our own inventions being the only and infallible rule of all our *Faith, Hope,* and *Charity:* As first, that Church holdeth *Ignorance* the Mother of *Devotion,* and Article of our Faith. Then they have their *Revelations, Visions, Dissensions,* so have we. They have private *Shrifts,* so we. They call it a *Venial sin* with a sister, and in case of necessity can forgive a Neighbor's wife, so we. They allow *Deposing* and *regulating of Princes* by tumults and other ways, so do we. They endeavor to domineer over *Church* and *State,* so would we. They hatch *Factions,* and say it is good fishing in troubled streams, so do we. And lastly, they *deny* all this in plain words, but *grant* it in effects, and so do we.

And although we cannot endure a Surplice, or Cross, the Pope's Bulls, nor his fiercer beasts the Jesuits, yet we hold it lawful by the same virtue of equivocations, and mental reservations, to cheat, swear, and lie with any that is not one of us, nay even among ourselves, if there be an holy cause. And to say which is the best subject, or most honest, the Jesuits or we, would be a very hard question, if we were suffered to make our own laws: Yet by my Husband's leave, though he speak in the abundance of his good will to the advancement of the holy Brethren, methinks it would be a more heavenly sight to see Mr. *How,* or the grave *Observator* himself in his *Bar-gown,* mounted upon the steps at the Banqueting house in *Whitehall,* expounding Chapters to the *Courtiers* and *Cavaliers,* and to have all the Privy Council chosen out of the Elect, the Pensioners Lay doctors, and the Guard devout Elders; then for Lord *Chamberlain,* Groom of the stool, and Bedchamber (places indeed most consonant to women) some of the Holy Sisters, who received their education against the world, the flesh, and the Devil in the *Zion* of *New-England,* that both the King and State might the more securely confide in their Continence and purity. Let us all fling up the whites of our eyes in an holy hope, that the strong breathing of the spirit may stir up some worthy instruments to say *Amen* to the work.

But to draw to a conclusion, because I perceive by the fervent twinkling of your eyes, and ardent licking of your lips, you would be at your devotions, I shall but wag my petticoat at the first of his two last reasons concerning *Ireland*. And I observe that the spirit doth never leave us destitute of sanctified shifts to overreach our adversaries the Protestants; for if we be constrained to break in knavery or beggary, yet we still have some refuge or land of *Promise* to fly to. Yet sincerely for living in *Ireland* (though I confess the advantage great we have wrought of it and the present times) I know not what to say, because no venomous beast will live there; nor need we care, since *New-England* (as I verily believe) was found out to that purpose: For the design there I will speak little now, because (as the case standeth) for my part, I had rather all the Soldiers were in *Hull* than in *Ireland;* for if the King once take that, by the help of his loving and dutiful Subjects (as he calleth them) it will put the Brethren to a great many of hard texts and tedious prayers, if it do not break the heart of our conventicle: And what jealousy and fear can be like that? I appeal to any Reverend Round-head that is not a Cuckold (if there be such an one,) therefore it is high time to bestir us, (and so please you Mistress *Spritsayle* but lend me the Chamber pot) we will have the other quart, and I will conclude, as the same Gentlemen began, applying all in these words, that as our case is not like *Scotland*'s, so *Scotland*'s never was, nor (I think) can be ever like ours.

Dixi. J. B.

A Speech made by Mistris Wardens *Chamber-maid.*

Mistress Warden's Chambermaid called *Abigaile,* was a pretty white-faced thing, of a right Puritan complexion, and thought (as other maids do) to get a Husband by a simpering show of Religion. She had offended her Mistress in bringing up her clean warm smock too late one morning when she was to go very early to a Conventicle, and being chidden for this delinquency, to vindicate her diligence, and continue her words, through passion she said 'twas true by the Mass. Her Mistress presently taking notice of the abominable word Mass, grew exceeding angry with *Abigaile,* and called her Reprobate, and baggage Papist. The color in *Abigaile*'s cheeks rose at her words, scorning the word, much more the name of a Papist; biting the lip a while and pouting, at last her zealous anger for being called Papist flew out in this Speech, consisting of many parts starched together.

I must tell you forsooth good Mistress, that though I was brought up in the Country, yet my Father being Sexton of the Church in the Market Town, would after Evening Prayer was done make his house ring with singing of Psalms, and though I say't, I was bred as well as any of the elect Maids here in London, so that I had rather you had called me a zealous dissembler (as some of our Sisters be) than a Papist. For I am so absolutely against them, that if all Papist's heads were on one neck I would cut them off with one blow, that so in Country Towns I might be drawn in the painted cloth like *Judith* cutting off Holofernes' head. A Papist is in my conceit an abominable creature, and holds damnable opinions, some bad and some good, whereof I was never guilty; I count fasting to be but a foolish thing, for our Cupboard at home stood always open, and on Fridays or fasting-days I could go to it, and take what I list without any resistance of the Spirit, for Religion must lie in a maid's heart, though her fortune doth sometimes lie in her belly, and for good works, I never loved them since I left my Sampler, and then I was out of Charity with them because they were wrought in Cross-stitch: and another Reason was because (as you know forsooth) embroidery was much used in times of Popery for Copes and other Idolatrous apparel; so that not only their opinions, which I naturally detested, being as I said, a Sexton's Daughter of the reformed Religion, but also their Persons have been odious in my sight, and if I were as my Master, and you good Mistress, (for you are wise learned, and can be as Religiously angry as he) I would i'faith tickle these Papists, and firk them out of the Parishes in London, my Mr. talks of yoking themselves like horn-beasts to plow them up, but now let us rather with Hay-forks taken out of Barns, where we exercise zealously, prick them forward, till for very fear they leap over Sea and utterly forsake the Land. If Master Warden would but play the Devil's part in punishing and plundering, and plaguing these Papists, I myself when I come amongst any of them am fully resolved to scratch out their eyes, for it is a proper sign of an elect young man or maid to condemn that we understand not, and to be furiously obstinate in our zealous anger. Therefore good Mistress I wish in your presence, that are a great spiritual observer (as appears by your learned observation on my Master's wise Speech) that I may never see Conventicle more, but that if I had the power I would be worse than all the Devils in Hell, Hags, Furies, Witches, and instruments of Damnation whatsoever to punish these Papists.

O Mistress! you know not how stiff maids are in their opinion, and if they once get a thing by the end they will hold it fast; and I will ever hold that Papists are in a certain state of Damnation, as certain as the Elect and the Brethren and Sisters of Predestination are sure of salvation. Thus have I proved myself no Papist, now I will tell you (good Mistress) my opinions, which jump just with yours as a Chambermaid should do, I like Hypocrisy as well as Monarchy; and that a Barn, or Stable may be a Church: our old Church in the Country being decayed, was like a Barn or Stable, I never loved Learning nor learned men, sir *Roger* our Curate deceived me in a deep point, therefore learning is no Religion nor learned men are not always zealously religious, and learning Mistress (as you say) is profane, and sense and reason in Religion are unnecessary, for though we can have feeling other ways, yet we can have no sense of Religion, and feeling I hope is a sense respected much of us the Elect, and therefore though you banish sense and reason, yet let there be always a religious feeling in and amongst us. This said, she finished the dressing of Mistress Warden, and so ended her speech.

FINIS.

26

The Speech of a Cavaleere to

His Comrades

1642

The Speech of a Cavaleere to His Comrades appears to date from the beginning of the civil war, before any major battles had been fought. Puritans are not mentioned by name, but the work deserves inclusion here because it is professedly inspired by the satiric *Speech of a Warden* (1642). The author is far from being an uncritical adherent of the royalist cause.

Like the warden, and especially like Mistress Warden, the Cavalier drinks intemperately. Ironically, unlike the warden and his wife, the Cavalier is shabbily dressed; the Cavaliers who claim high social status wear cast-off clothing, whereas the warden and his group, affecting simplicity and humility, wear and admire elaborate clothing. On the warden's five topics the Cavalier has ironic comments that sometimes contradict and sometimes extend the criticism to the warden's opponents. The liturgy suits the Cavalier well enough, but he understands nothing of it and it appeals to him solely because of its resemblance to secular music. Its equivalent among the roundheads has a good aspect, the four-hour banquet; it also has a bad side, the "howling" of Psalm 119, which—it may be noted—is distinguished among the Psalms by its extraordinary length. The militia appears to be hopelessly incompetent, but its Cavalier counterpart no less so. Here the affectation of gentility by people of very humble rank among the Cavaliers is described in some detail. The threat of the papists is minimized, and the old equation between puritan and Jesuit appears in a reference to the menace of the "Protestant Jesuit." Concerning Ireland the Cavalier talks only of the miseries of military service there. Finally, the Cavalier scorns all fear and jealousy, simply because he is full of drunken bravado.

The author ridicules both sides in the civil war. However, his lack of concern about the papists and his use of the term *Protestant Jesuit* place him on the side of the establishment, though not without qualifications.

The Speech of a Cavaleere to His Comrades, In answer to the Wardens Speech. Written by *Agamemnon Shaglock Van Dammee, Clerke of the Regiment.* *London,* Printed Anno. Domini 1642.

The Speech of a Cavalier to his Comrades: In Answer to the Warden's Speech.

Brothers and Commanders of this never too civil society, Before I give fire to those Squibs and Crackers I am to discharge, my courtesy thinks it fit to present the compliment of your poor servant, for your general choice of me to shake my locks before you this day for the honor I confess, of the Cavalry; which I doubt not (by that unaccustomed quality amongst you called patience, and upon condition you will not outswagger me) but to finish as well as the maddest roarer here present. And for testimony of my acknowledgment of your favors, and as a preparation to the work in hand here is a health of three glasses, when that is gone round I will proceed you out the business itself in as new coined asseverations as my vaporing Genius can perform.

You are now to conceive in what time and upon what occasion this discourse is grounded. The time is now, just now that I have received my pay, newly repaired my threadbare outside, and once more do enjoy that miraculous blessing of clean Linen, before my Feather and Scarf be ruffled, or the dew of Heaven hath fallen upon them, my pockets furnished, my brain inspired with raptures and enthusiasms insinuated by the corroborative virtue of this excellent and never too much admired Cavalry. The occasion, since high treason and hanging matters are become but market talk only but a game at Shittlecock wherein the bold world dare toss betwixt King and State every idle fear, and frivolous suggestion which fancy or imagination doth prompt and frame, in their half lost wit, and this kind of desperate communication grown more customary than the French tongue or fashion. Why should not we as well as all the world besides take some liberty to prate of great matters to little purpose. And therefore as these two glasses more shall enable me, I will go forward with such matters as the heat of my blood and the vertigo in my brain shall drop into my language.

My Antagonist the Warden begins his Cinquepace with the Liturgy of the Church, wherein his Scotch Bagpipe whines you out his Antipathies thereunto in such abominable out of tune chords that the unparalleled harmony rather begets ridiculous mirth than any solitude or soul-sympathizing pleasure. Now touching this subject, I must ingeniously confess (Gentlemen) but pardon me for it, that the time hath been I have seen the inside of a Church, although not often nor lately, and there although the Organ did exceed the noise of the voices, whereby not a plain syllable more than *O* and *yaw,* he and *aise,* could be distinguished, yet I verily believe the Vicars and song-men do mean well by their ejaculations and gaping upwards and shaking their gray beards. And although the Organist do as a Praeludium to the Anthem play Sellengers-round, yet I must tell you that it is done with so much division both on the treble and base keys, that nobody but himself can tell what to make of it, unless he tell it to a friend as once he did, which friend began immediately to dance, and being asked by a Vicar what he meant (quoth he) to serve God as he was never served in his life, but let that pass I have seen books with good plate covers, gilt Candlesticks, Plush Carpets, etc. and so far am I from thinking any hurt of all this, that I must acknowledge I have many times wished this kind of Liturgy in mine own chamber, that I might have made much of it, and used it more frequently than I did. Now for form or essence of worship, I know (Gentlemen) you will easily give me credit, and not stand upon that needless trouble of proof, that I have been no extraordinary student therein, nor much addicted to the discourses thereunto pertaining, whereby I cannot but hope you will pardon me if I do not give you satisfaction in it. But concerning the Warden's church which is a conventicle, you may please to understand, that before I was in service, in regard I owed some money in town, I took occasion to walk without my Periwig or my Sword, which I left with my then Landlord for his service, thereby to obscure myself from my Tobacco-Grocer, my Ale-draper, and my Thimble-merchant, and others into whose book I had (by many faithful persuasions and honest protestations) damned myself in a matter of four Nobles. And having likewise at that time by a woeful mischance gotten an imperfection in my nose, whereby I could not choose but speak the right

318

tone, I was by this means generally taken for a Roundhead, and being on a time invited to the duties I went along with the party, who conducted me into a chamber one pair of stairs and half below stairs, which presented itself a Cellar, and a Kitchen, where there were a matter of twenty persons of both sexes. The men saluted me with welcome dear brother, I wish you had brought along with you a yoke-fellow that might be edified: The women told me they should be glad to discover unto me the path wherein I was to tread, and so presented me with a cup of Muscadine and Eggs, and thus ended the salutation, for being all very hungry the Bibles were presently laid under the Dresser, and the meat brought to the table, and thus far, ne'er a man breathing could complain of their Liturgy; marry after dinner which was finished in less than four hours, they fell to (I cannot call it singing but) howling the 119. Psalm, the sudden squeaking whereof frighted me out of the house, and hath made me look thus madly ever since. Now for these reasons, I see no hurt in the Liturgy, and therefore as I love it, so deep will I drink to the full confirmation and continuation thereof.

The next thing which his Wardenship's wisdom flies upon as eagerly as a Hawk, or a Buzzard fells a Partridge or carrion, is the Militia, of which kind of Militia I will not speak one word, it was so well done, (if not overdone by the Warden himself) but I will dilate upon our own Militia, that of us the Cavaliers, and Gentlemen of this present society. In which you must understand, I mean not the Cavaliers that belabored themselves so bravely at *Westminster,* nor they that now attend at *York,* for such as they are a thought too great to be jested withal, and are or may be our paymasters: no, I mean us the newmade Gentlemen of the times, us that have won our Arms by feats of Chivalry done in the *North* of *England,* where we did nothing at all, and I say what though we cannot prove the descent from our ancestors. 'Tis no matter, the greater glory hangs upon our Swords, and the world shall study new heraldry purposely to enable us with the Arms of the Gentry. Thou *Tom Trimwell* wast Sir *John Sucklin's* Tailor, in making the doublets didst reduce as much shavings as made thyself a suit, so became a Trooper and art now a Cavalier. Thou Master *Fawne* wast thy Captain's man got his cast clothes, and are now a formal Cavalier, hast the garb, the oaths, the vapors, and all things in a Tavern pertaining to the function, I myself was a Gentleman before indeed, for I was a gentleman usher to the Lady at *Charing Cross* that hath vowed never to sin with any but Soldiers and hath been famous with so many of them, by her commendations I was made a Corporal, and am therefore an absolute Cavalier: And now Gentlemen that we may perfectly attribute the title to ourselves, if there be any amongst us that bears the name of any great Family in the Kingdom, let him pretend himself of the same house and blood, 'twill carry it amongst those that cannot contradict it. Or besides by the adding, diminishing, or exchanging a letter or syllable of your own names into other men's it is easily done: And therefore he whose name is, *Person* may call himself *Percy, Barton* may change to *Bartue, Cliff.* to *Cliford,* or *Cliftin,* and then again let the want of means be supplied with excess of swaggering, and domineering, a kind of testy pragmatical bearing, and scorning to answer any man that questions your birth, all easy ways to preserve yourselves under the title of Cavaliers, which very bare title is enough to make you of that Militia, which service we hope will not be much more difficult than that Militia the Warden mentions, so long as one Array continues at *York,* and the other at *London,* and howsoever well their protectors do agree, yet I hope their Armies may never come nearer than they are, and that partly for the Commonwealth's sake, and partly for our own sakes, for truly these meeting services are not half so comfortable as those six, or seven score miles distance, And to be a warrior, a Cavalier, a Soldier, and lie in a featherbed, eat and drink like Epicures, not to be lowly, why it [is] almost as easy a perfection as to be a Roundhead, although the Roundhead be far unfit to be a Cavalier, for surely the steel Helmet would chafe his ears to pieces, there being no hair to defend them. Besides the noise of the Guns would run like an Axle through his ears, and turn his head round about it, for you know he's giddy already; No, no we are the men that must charge at distance, and stand for the good of that party that will pay best, and doubt not to defend them boldly against no resistance, But I will end this argument lest my cock-brains should hurry me into such circumstances, as would bring me into question without redemption.

The third discourse his grave frenzy throws him on is the extirpation of the Papists that giving Religion, that leaves their great Legacies in the hands of the Priests to be distributed to charitable uses, and make their children beggars for their better mortification, if they but dare to stir, let us alone with them now their arms are taken away, Marry if the Protestant Jesuit were but as well tamed as they are there would be no use for us in *England,* we might even trudge as Volunteers to the other Kingdom, where we should hardly find so good entertainment; and yet we should make pretty work with them, if they were but disarmed as the papists here are. And Gentlemen, when the seditions are appeased let us expect no other employment. But this Discourse tends to my next argument, therefore I will touch it but sparingly, only six glasses to their destruction before we come, that we may have the easier service; if we be called, I pray you pledge it, that it may be known we can wish them mischief thus far off, and that at a nearer we might be called on to do something too upon any reasonable odds in Arms and Ammunition.

Then my adversary proceeds to beat out the quintessence of his noddle, Would that employment of beating out had been mine. I would have done it to some purpose. But that is of the Irish expedition, in which I will say nothing of the benefit thereof, more than appertains to ourselves, which consists of these conveniences, naked Arms appearing out of Shammy doublets like Peddlers or Glass-carriers with half breeches, footless stockings, and over them drawn a pair of Leather buskins, which in former days had been boots of a decent wearing, and near to the primitive nakedness. For diet, think not scorn of moldy Biscuit, and a fat Colt boiled in his own skin, if you can catch it: for want of diet that precious vapor of *Virginia* in a leaguer pipe is a singular prevention to stop the yawning of the hungry stomach; and grudge not now and then to be magnificently starved to death for want of these commodities too; and the sports and recreations that belong to this employment of standing sentinel four long hours in a frosty night, or lying *per diem* in a trench of cold water, which is a sovereign provocative to that comfortable malady called the Bellyache, and yet there may be better accommodations if the Adventurers will but bring in their money fast enough; but in case they do not the aforesaid solaces and preferments are like enough to ensue. Now Gentlemen, you know we are the men must actually and personally hazard ourselves in these affairs, whereas that cowardly slave the Roundhead, if he were called to the employment, would be hanged here for disobedience to his Colors, rather than stir a foot towards it; and yet at home dares preach against us, yea and pray too till his eyes be almost started out of his head with praying for our confusion, that must defend him to live at ease snarling like a dog in a manger, and will neither do good himself, nor permit others to do it, he vexes me to the heart, but I will drown sorrow in this Bear-bowl of Sack, and so end this business.

Lastly, he proceeds to his period, his pudding prick, his *nil ultra* coxcombry, his fears and jealousies; for our part Gentlemen, we are now armed *cap a pie* with a good grape Armor, and is this a time for us to fear? No, I fear not the devil himself in any shape whatsoever. I could now outstare a Basilisk, poison a Crocodile with one puff of my smoke reeked nostrils, I durst do anything that ever any man or men combined to any other creature ever attempted, O for any Army of such as we now are ready pitched, to assault all the Rebels in *Ireland* joined before us, S. *Patrick* himself, were his legend true, should find, that mortal creatures inspired with immortal sack were able to vanquish an Army of such as himself. nay, since I am now like to be in the Array of one side or other, let me tell you, I fear not a Roundhead, which of all shapes else I am the most afraid on, if afraid I could be. But Gentlemen, I have dilated so long, that I can hold open my eyes no longer. I will therefore comply with the Warden in one particular, and fall asleep, And that without a quarrel first had too, which is no ordinary miracle.

FINIS.

27

A Puritane Set Forth in His
Lively Colours

1642

A Puritane Set Forth in His Lively
Colours, apparently written by an anonymous royalist, is dated in the
Thomason copy August 23, 1642, the day after King Charles raised his
standard at Nottingham. It draws heavily upon King James's denunciation
of puritans and equates them with roundheads. Some basic puritan tenets
are mentioned, but mainly the work consists of moral accusations of law-
lessness and hypocrisy; the final verses accuse the female puritan of such
moral failings.

The puritan is first defined, generally and briefly, as a libertine in morals
and religion who wants to establish a presbyterian form of church government and an "aristocratical" state in place of the monarchy. Essentially, he
promotes disorder and turbulence. Most of the prose essay, which takes up
half the pamphlet, quotes James's strictures on the puritans from the
second book of the *Basilikon Doron;* it takes no notice of James's hedging
and attempts to limit the definition of the term *puritan* in his preface. The
reign of James is nostalgically portrayed as a time of peace and tranquillity
in the church and kingdom.

The verses describing the roundhead's character bring up the familiar
charges of hypocrisy, obstinacy, hatred of learning, and opposition to
authority. A few specific points of religious practice are noted; for example,

the roundhead will not bow at the name of Jesus or use the sign of the cross in baptism. Also he sits during the communion service, and he refuses to use set prayers, favoring his own inventions. In the accompanying verses describing a "Holy Sister," *roundhead* and *puritan* are called equivalent terms, and other specifically puritan behavior is described. The holy sister likes to hear three sermons on Sunday, supports unlicensed preachers, sings Psalms even in the street, and prefers John Dod's exposition of the Ten Commandments to the Bible's. In addition, her lechery is duly noted.

The work is useful because of a few interesting touches. These include the reference to the very popular work of Dod; the equation of *puritan* and *roundhead,* which provides a contrast with many works that make a distinction between the terms; and the reliance upon the words of King James to condemn puritans, in contrast with Henry Parker's use of James to defend them.

A PURITANE Set forth In his Lively Colours: Or, *K. James* his description of a Puritan. Whereunto is added, The Round-heads Character, with The Character of an *Holy Sister*. All fitted for the times. *London,* Printed for *N. B.* 1642.

A PURITAN *Set forth* in his Lively Colors.

Whosoever will look with an impartial eye upon the face of things, and consider aright the headstrong and unruly zeal of those preposterous maligners of Monarchical Government, (who shaking off all Civil and Ecclesiastical Order, would (if it were in their power, and they do endeavor as much as in them possibly lies for to effect it) introduce a Presbyterian in the Church, and Aristocratical in the State, if any at all, for they are truly, as they would seem to be, Libertines, and seek to live without Laws as they list) He cannot but confess, what K. *James* of happy memory (whose motto was *Beati Pacifici, blessed are the peacemakers,* though their actions be the contrary, counting them only happy, which are the Peace-breakers) was the King of Prophets in these later times, and a Prophetical King. For he wisely foreseeing with the Promethean eye of judgment, what miserable consequents, and dangerous effects, would ensue and happen unto this Kingdom, if these turbulent spirits should get a head, or come into any place of authority, did in the second Book of his

Basilicon Doron, that Kingly gift, which he bequeathed unto our Royal King *Charles,* (whom God long prosper with his just and religious designs) as his last Will and Testament, among other of his Princely Admonitions, gave him this *caveat,* to beware of this monstrous brood. Take heed (saith he) of these Puritans, the very pests (or plagues) in the Church and Commonwealth; whom no deserts can oblige; neither oaths, nor promises bind; breathing nothing but sedition and calumnies; aspiring without measure, railing without reason, and making their own imaginations (without any warrant of the Word) the square of their conscience. I protest before the great God, and since I am here, as upon my Testament, it is no place for me to lie in, that you shall never find, with any Highland, or Border-thieves, greater ingratitude, and more lies, and vile perjuries, than with these fanatic spirits. And suffer not the principals of them to brook your land, if you like to sit at rest; except you would keep them for trying your patience, as *Socrates* did an evil wife. And (in the page before) he speaks thus of them: I was oft-times calumniated by these fiery-spirited men in their popular Sermons; not for any evil or vice in me; but because I was a King: which they thought the highest evil. So that then, if any man shall propound that old Quaere, *What is a Puritan?* We may resolve the Question, and describe him in his true colors, out of K. *James,* after this manner: A Puritan, is one of the pestilent party, the very plague of the Church and Commonwealth, whom no deserts can oblige, nor oaths, nor promises bind; one that breathes nothing but sedition and calumnies; aspiring without measure, and railing without reason; making his own imaginations (without warrant of the Word) the square of his conscience. He is a fanatic spirit; with whom you may find greater ingratitude, more lies, and viler perjuries, than amongst the most infamous thieves. And if the principals of them be suffered in a Kingdom, it can be to no other good purpose, but for the trial of the King's patience: for when they speak evil of Kings, it is not because Kings deserve it; but because it is natural in these men to deprave them.

This was the judgment and opinion of K. *James* of happy memory and learned experience: in whose days, we enjoyed the flourishing estate of the Gospel, with a great deal of peace, plenty, and prosperity. But now to our grief we see the truth of his Divine Prediction, and by woeful experience are too too sensible of their conditions.

And thus having shown you K. *James* his opinion of these kind of creatures, which he directed in *Prose;* please you to see the character of them, though under another notion, in *Verse;* it is, as followeth.

The Round-Head's Character,

If you will see the Character
Of a *Round-head,* lo it is here.
He that would holy seem in all men's sight,
Whenas he truly is an Hypocrite;
Would be thought humble, and not have descried
His obstinacy and spiritual pride;
Who hath enough of saving knowledge, though
He never yet could read his Christ-cross row;
That cries down learning, 'cause the simple spirit
Doth him inspire with all things against merit.
Who hates a Papist, yet approves this notion,
That ignorance is mother of devotion:
That's a good Christian, yet doth disallow,
At Jesus' name, his stubborn knee to bow
Though God commands it; will cut close his head,
Because he saith Saint *Paul* doth him so bid;
Loves decent things at home, at Church nought fitting,
And will not take the Sacrament but sitting;
That will not cross his child in Baptism,
Because 'tis contrary to Roundheadism,
That in a morning seven long miles on foot
Will stretch, to hear a Lay-Priest pray by rote,
Ricking in zealous sweat; that boldly dares
Reject our Savior's, and our Church's Prayers;
That hates a Scholar 'cause he's Orthodox,
Yet posts to hear such as in nasty frocks
Do prate at Conventicles; will be sick,
If he but hears of a Church Catholic,
Yet's well at the next Article; nor faints
When he's amidst the communion of Saints.
That will not swear, when's found fast with a sister,
But yet, by Yea and Nay, deny he kist her:
That will not do his neighbor the least evil,
Yet thinks to cozen him, God, and the Devil:
That utterly detests strange innovation,
Yet daily schisms doth procreate in our Nation:

Who hates, yet makes division, 'cause the sway
Of this our Kingdom should be ruled his way:
Who's never well employed, yet still in action,
Loves outward peace, but inward's lined with faction:
That is religious, will oppose nothing
But what's authorized by the Church and King:
That would be counted blameless from his youth,
    This is a very Roundhead in good truth.

    Now because you seldom or never can meet a *Puritan* or a
Roundhead (they are *termini aequivalentes*) without a holy sister,
which they dearly love, I think it not amiss to adjoin her character
under him, that so you may the better take notice of both.

The Holy-Sister's Character

She that can sit three Sermons in a day,
And of those three, scarce bear three words away;
She that can rob her husband, to repair
A Budget-Priest that noses a long prayer;
She that with Lamb-black purifies her shoes,
And with half eyes, and Bible, softly goes;
She that her pocket with Lay Gospel stuffs,
And edifies her looks with little ruffs;
She that loves Sermons, as she does the rest,
Still standing stiff, that longest are the best;
She that will lie, yet swears she hates a lier,
Except it be that man that will lie by her;
She that at christenings thirsteth for most sack,
And draws the broadest handerchief for Cake;
She that sings Psalms devoutly next the street,
And beats her maid i'the Kitchen, where none see't;
She that will sit in shops for five hours' space,
And register the sins of all that pass;
Damn at first sight, and proudly dares to say,
That none can possibly be saved but they;
That hangs Religion in a naked ear,

And judge men's hearts, according to their hair;
That could afford to doubt, who wrote best sense,
Moses, or *Dod* on the Commandments.
She that can sigh and cry, Queen *Elizabeth,*
Rail at the *Pope,* and scratch out sudden death;
And for all this can give no reason why,
    This is an Holy Sister verily.

                FINIS.

28

Religions Lotterie, 1642

Religions Lotterie, dated July 20, 1642, in the Thomason copy, is interesting because it provides, from a moderate establishment point of view, a list of sects or religious groupings recognizable as discrete entities on the eve of the civil war. Characterizations are very brief but touch fundamental issues. The puritans receive benign criticism and appear closely akin to true protestants.

The work has been attributed variously to John Taylor, "the Water Poet," and to Alexander Ross (1591–1654), of Scotland. However, it is not in the characteristic style of either: It is too scholarly and concise for Taylor, and it appears to be written from a point of view more appropriate to an Englishman than to Ross.

Some of the author's religious groups, such as the Adamites and Novolists, are obscure and seldom appear in writings against nonconformists. Also some of his definitions are unusual and even inappropriate. The Lutherans are here simply antiepiscopalians. The separatists appear to be presbyterians—wanting a government of the church by elders and laymen—and hence actually reformers within the church. The Brownists are distinguished by their extemporaneous prayers, not, as in Giles Widdowes's *Schysmatical Puritan,* by their meeting in ordinary houses instead of churches. Under the name *Arminians* the author seems to comprehend the Laudian church with its elaborate ceremonies, but he does not mention Arminian theology. Arians are not, as might be expected, antitrinitarians but rather are people who favor keeping the Mosaic law, even in rites and ceremonies. Timeservers are not simply conforming members of the established church but are followers of the Parliament's decrees in religious matters. In general the work indicates that by 1642 the proliferation of religious groupings differing from one another on such a wide variety of issues as church doctrine, religious practice, and church government had made definitions very uncertain. In the midst of such confusion, the people once designated as puritans seemed very moderate, and to at least the author of this work, their fault was no greater than a preference for the rites, discipline, and organization of the Church of Scotland.

RELIGIONS LOTTERIE, or the Churches Amazement. Wherein is declared how many sorts of Religions there is crept into the very bowels of this Kingdome, striving to shake the whole foundation and to destroy both Church and Kingdom. Namely these 16. hereafter mentioned. 1 *Papists* 2 *Arians* 3 *Arminians* 4 *Canonists* 5 *Athiests* 6 *Adamites* 7 *Familists* 8 *Anabaptists* 9 *Lutherans* 10 *Separatists* 11 *Brownists* 12 *Puritanes* 13 *Novolists* 14 *Time-servers* 15 *Rattle-heads* 16 *Round-heads*. Whereunto is annexed each of their severall opinions, with sufficient Arguments to confute each opinion, and to prove them Enemies to the peace of the Church and Kingdome.

London, Printed by *T. F.* for *F. S.* July 20, 1642.

Religion's Lottery, or, The Church's Amazement.

The first that I shall begin with in this discourse is the *Atheist,* he being indeed the worst of all creatures, as in this his definition may plainly appear.

Atheist.

An *Atheist* is one that believes that there is no God, only ascribes all things to the power of chance and fortune, he looks only upon the natural things of the world, not dreaming of any other Deity.

Answ. To confute this Argument, I will use but only this one Testimony, "The Heavens declare the Glory of God, and the Firmament sheweth the works of his hands," *Psalm* 19. *Verse* 1.

Papist.

The *Papists* among us are a people who would have a Church consisting of Cardinals, Archbishops, Bishops, Deacons, Jesuits, Friars, etc. independent to the Crown or civil Magistrate, he will acknowledge no High Priest but the Pope, from whom he expects remission of sins and absolution.

Answ. To confute this opinion of the Papists, I shall only use this Argument to prove that there is no High Priest but *Christ Jesus,* you may read in the 7. chap. of the *Hebrews,* at the 17. 23. 24. 25. verses, etc. The Lord testifies of Christ's saying, "Thou art a Priest forever after the order of Melchesideck." Likewise they have many Popes and many High Priests, because they are not suffered to continue by reason of death, but our High Priest, because he continueth forever hath an unchangeable Priesthood.

Arians.

The *Arians* among us are people that would maintain the *Mosaical* Law, with the same Levitical Ceremonies.

Protestant's Answer. The Old Law was abolished by the new Testament, "Even as by the first man Adam, all men was made sinners, so by the second man Christ Jesus, all men became Heirs unto salvation."

Arminians.

The *Arminians* among us are a people which would have the Church governed by Archbishops, Bishops, they are half Papists and half Protestants, they would have Altars, Cushions, Wax Candles, with the first and latter Service, one at the Desk, the other at the Altar, with many other superfluous Ceremonies.

Protestant's Answer. Either that these Ceremonies may be lawful or no I will not question, but I am sure they are not effectual to Salvation, but rather a Rock of offense at which many stumble; Therefore they ought to be abandoned, for "whosoever so sinneth against his Brother and woundeth his weak conscience, sinneth against Christ," Cor. 1. 12.

Adamites.

The *Adamites* are a people which would live under no command of Magistrate or Church, they would be mere Libertines and live as they list, following that place of Scripture, "Increase and multiply," and in their society they are so overcome with the flesh that they cannot pray.

Protestant's Answer. That this opinion is grounded on a vain and fruitless foundation may be easily discerned, for St. *Paul* tells us in his Epistle to the *Galatians, chap.* 5. *ver.* 13. this Lesson; "For Brethren though you have been called unto liberty, yet use not your liberty for an occasion to the Flesh, but by love serve one another."

Familists.

The *Familist* would have no Bishops nor governors in the Church, but all things common, as wife, children, goods, etc. and that no punishment should be inflicted on offenders, but only to pray for them and leave them to God's mercy.

Protestant's Answer. To confute these, I will use no other Argument but the word in the Commination, "Cursed is he that lies with his Neighbor's Wife."

Anabaptists.

The *Anabaptist* would have no Government at all in the Church, neither would they have any Baptized, but such as are of age, and they pray more for such a Church than for grace or faith.

Protestant's Answer. You may read that Christ rebuked his Disciples, saying; "Suffer little Children to come unto me, and forbid them not, for of such is the Kingdom of God," and if Children be Saints in the Church Triumphant, it cannot be denied, but that it is lawful by Baptism to be made Members of the Church Militant.

Novolists.

Novolists are those that change in their opinions oftener than the fashion, sometime they are *Papists,* sometime *Puritans,* they are never constant in one thing, but always wavering like a Reed shaken with the wind.

Protestant's Answer. To these I will only give a Christian-like admonition, "Examine yourselves whether ye be in the faith, prove your own selves, know you not that Jesus Christ is in you, except ye be Reprobates," Cor. 13. 5.

Time-servers.

Timeservers are always of the strongest side, they commend no description but what they are like to have, they are like Virgin's wax capable of any impression, Bishops or no Bishops, what the Parliament shall please to ordain that they will follow, and till then they are of all Religions, or as I may justly say of no Religion.

The Protestant's Answ. To these I will likewise bestow a friendly admonition, "make your Election sure, beware lest any man spoil you through Philosophy and vain deceit after the tradition of men and not after Christ, for in him dwelleth all fullness of grace," Colossians, 2. 8.

Canonists.

The *Canonists* desire the government of Bishops still to abide, because they stand upon Canon Law, likewise they stand for all Canonical *Ceremonies.*

Answ. I need quote no Scripture to prove this opinion unlawful, the Report strikes terror through the whole Kingdom, only I desire that all the Canons betwixt this and *Canterbury,* may be sent to the Tower, where they shall meet with a little Canoneer that will make them fly with a powder.

Lutherans.

The *Lutheran* would have no Bishops, but a Church government under the King, they would have all Ordinances agreeable to the Ordinances of the Primitive Church.

Protestant's Answer. That there was in the time of the Apostles Bishops, and that some of them were Bishops is apparently manifest, and that the Office of a Bishop is allowed of by St. *Paul,* you may find in the third of *Tim.* ver. the 1. "This is a true saying, if a man desire the Office of a Bishop he desireth a good work."

Separatists.

The *Separatists* are men that would have no Bishops but Elders, Ecclesiastical and Laic.

Prot. Answ. That the government of the Church especially in teaching do no way belong to Laymen, is made apparent in these words; "Having then gifts, differing, according to the grace that is given us, whether prophecy let us prophesy according to our proportion of faith," that is, "everyone must labor diligently in the calling in which he is placed," Rom. 12. 6.

Brownists.

The *Brownist* would have no *Common Prayer,* only extemporary Prayer, by the motion of the Spirit.

Answ. Their opinion is not much different from the *Separatist,* and may easily be confuted by the same Argument.

333

Puritans.

The *Puritan* is the most commendable of all the rest, for he would have a Religion for which he hath a precedent, *to wit,* the Kirk of *Scotland.*

Prot. Answer. To which opinion I can say little, only I conceive, that the difference in the Ordinance alters not the effect, since in the fundamentals we do perfectly agree.

Rattle-heads.

The *Rattleheads* are a company of shallow-pated hare-brained shittle-witted Coxcombs, that neither regard Law nor Religion, they regard nothing but to make mischief, build Castles in the Air, hatch Stratagems, invent Projects, and do mischief with dexterity, and after fly for it.

Answ. To these I have little to say, only I wish that they had more grace, so leaving them to the prick of conscience, and the lash of a Beadle's whip, I rest.

Round-heads.

The *Round-heads* are people that would have the Church and Service orderly performed, but yet they are the chief Ringleaders to all tumultuous disorders, they call the *Common Prayer* Porridge, and they will allow no Doctrine for good, nor no Minister a quiet audience, without he preach absolute damnation.

Protestant's Answer. To these men that are disturbers of the church I say with St. *Paul, Corinthians,* 13. 17. "If any man destroy the Temple of God, him shall God destroy. For the Temple of God is Holy."

Thus having finished my intended course I rest,

Praying to God the Author of true peace,
That truth may flourish and dissension cease.
FINIS.

Part III
A Focal Document

29

The Millenary Petition

1603

The Millenary Petition was so named
because it professed to come from a thousand ministers. Thomas Fuller,
who published this petition in his *Church-History of Britain* (London, 1655,
X, pp. 7, 21–23), uses the term *Millemanus Petition* as well, though he
notes, perhaps inaccurately, that it was actually signed by 750. Stuart
Barton Babbage, in *Puritanism and Richard Bancroft* (London, 1962, p. 46),
suggests that Fuller got his number from the Lincolnshire petition of 1604.
Whatever the precise number directly involved, the petition apparently
represents the views of a substantial number of the clergy. The author is
unknown, though Fuller says that Arthur Hildersam, a popular and frequently suspended preacher, was among those "intrusted to manage this
important business." The document was widely publicized and called forth
refutations from both universities. The text here reprinted from Fuller is
identical, except for two inconsequential differences in the use of singular
and plural nouns, with the text that appeared in *The Answere of the Vicechan-
celour, the Doctors, Both the Proctors, and Other the Heads of Houses in the
Universitie of Oxford* (Oxford, 1603, pp. 1–5).

The millenarists identify themselves as loyal subjects of the king and
members of the Church of England, not as schismatics. They have accepted
subscription reluctantly, some with conditions and others under protest.
They seek "Uniformity in Doctrine" but desire changes in some prescribed
practices and tolerance in others. Under the heading "Church-Service,"
they call for changes in the administration of baptism, in the use of

vestments, in the observance of Sundays and holy days, in church music, and in various other rites and ceremonies. Under "Church-Ministers," they object to nonpreaching ministers and nonresidency. Here and in the section treating "Church-Livings, and Maintenance," their plea goes far beyond the expected objection to plurality of holdings to consider taxes and fees. Finally, under the heading "Church-Discipline," excommunication, ecclesiastical penalties, the ex officio oath, and ecclesiastical courts are said to be in need of reform. Throughout the tone is moderate, with pleas for the reform, not demands for the abolition, of current practices. For instance, of the much-disliked ex officio oath, the ministers ask only that it "be more sparingly used."

No particular item receives special emphasis, but both the introduction and the conclusion seem to indicate general dissatisfaction with the Book of Common Prayer. The ministers are said to be "groaning, as under a common burden of Human Rites and Ceremonies." They call for subscription only to the Articles of Religion and to the king's supremacy, thus omitting the prayer book, which, incidentally, is never mentioned by name in the petition. And finally, they object to having ministers punished for failing to observe "men's traditions." They make no protests against a church establishment, a church governed by bishops, or the theology of the church. The document can be seen as a minimal list of the reforms deemed essential. If it is so viewed, its large number of separate items indicates that placating even moderate reformers would have been difficult.

The humble Petition of the Ministers of the Church of *England,* desiring Reformation of certaine Ceremonies, and abuses of the Church.
[The Millenary Petition, 1603; reprinted from Thomas Fuller, *The Church-History of Britain* (London; 1655), X, pp. 21–23.]

To the most Christian, and excellent Prince, our Gracious and dread Sovereign, *James by the grace of God, etc.* We the Ministers of the Church of *England,* that desire Reformation, wish a long, prosperous, and happy Reign over us in this Life, and in the next everlasting Salvation.

Most gracious and dread Sovereign, Seeing it hath pleased the Divine Majesty, to the great comfort of all good Christians, to advance Your Highness, according to Your just Title, to the peaceable Government of this Church and Commonwealth of ENGLAND: We the Ministers of the Gospel in this Land, neither as factious men, affecting a popular Parity in the Church, nor as Schismatics aiming at the dissolution of the State Ecclesiastical; but as the faithful servants of Christ, and Loyal Subjects to Your Majesty, desiring, and longing for the redress of divers abuses of the Church; could do no less, in our obedience to God, service to Your Majesty, love to his Church, than acquaint Your Princely Majesty, with our particular griefs: For, as Your Princely Pen writeth, "The King, as a good Physician, must first know what peccant humors his Patient naturally is most subject unto, before he can begin his cure." And, although divers of us that sue for Reformation, have formerly, in respect of the times, subscribed to the Book, some upon Protestation, some upon Exposition given them, some with Condition, rather than the Church should have been deprived of their labor, and ministry; Yet now, we, to the number of more than a thousand, of Your Majesty's Subjects and Ministers, all groaning, as under a common burden of Human Rites and Ceremonies, do, with one joint consent, humble ourselves at Your Majesty's Feet, to be eased and relieved in this behalf. Our humble suit then unto Your Majesty is, that these offenses following, some may be removed, some amended, some qualified.

I. *In the Church-Service.* That the Cross in Baptism, Interrogatories ministered to Infants, Confirmation, as superfluous, may be taken away. Baptism not to be ministered by Women, and so explained. The Cap, and Surplice not urged. That Examination may go before the Communion. That it be ministered with a Sermon. That divers terms of *Priests,* and *Absolution,* and some other used, with the *Ring in Marriage,* and other such like in the Book, may be corrected. The longsomeness of Service abridged. Church-songs, and Music moderated to better edification. That the Lord's day be not profaned. The Rest upon Holy-days not so strictly urged. That there may be a Uniformity of Doctrine prescribed. No Popish Opinion to be any more taught, or defended. No Ministers charged to teach their people to bow at the name of JESUS. That the Canonical Scriptures only be read in the Church.

II. *Concerning Church-Ministers.* That none hereafter be admitted into the Ministry, but able and sufficient men, and those to Preach diligently, and especially upon the Lord's day. That such as be already entered, and cannot Preach, may either be removed, and some charitable course taken with them for their relief; or else to be forced, according to the value of their Livings, to maintain Preachers. That Non-Residency be not permitted. That King

Edward's Statute, for the lawfulness of Ministers' Marriage be revived. That Ministers be not urged to subscribe, but, according to the Law, to the Articles of Religion, and the King's Supremacy only.

III. *For Church-Livings, and Maintenance.* That Bishops leave their Commendams; some holding Prebends, some Parsonages, some Vicarages with their Bishoprics. That double beneficed men be not suffered to hold, some two, some three Beneficies with Cure: and some, two, three, or four Dignities besides. That Impropriations annexed to bishoprics and Colleges, be demised only to the Preachers Incumbents, for the old rent. That the Impropriations of Laymen's Fees may be charged with a sixth, or seventh part of the worth, to the maintenance of the Preaching Minister.

IV. *For Church-Discipline.* That the Discipline, and Excommunication may be administered according to Christ's own Institution: Or at the least, that enormities may be redressed. As namely, That Excommunication come not forth under the name of Lay persons, Chancellors, Officials, etc. That men be not excommunicated for trifles, and twelve-penny matters. That none be excommunicated without consent of his Pastor. That the Officers be not suffered to extort unreasonable Fees. That none, having Jurisdiction, or Registers' places, put out the same to Farm. That divers Popish Canons (as for restraint of Marriage at certain times) be reversed. That the Longsomeness of Suits in Ecclesiastical Courts (which hang sometime two, three, four, five, six, or seven years) may be restrained. That the Oath *Ex Officio,* whereby men are forced to accuse themselves, be more sparingly used. That Licenses for Marriage, without Banns asked, be more cautiously granted.

These, with such other abuses, yet remaining, and practiced in the Church of *England,* we are able to shew, not to be agreeable to the Scriptures, if it shall please your Highness farther to hear us, or more at large by writing to be informed, or by Conference among the Learned to be resolved. And yet we doubt not, but that, without any farther process, your Majesty (of whose Christian judgment, we have received so good a taste already) is able of Yourself, to judge of the equity of this cause. God, we trust, hath appointed your Highness our Physician to heal these diseases. And we say with *Mordecai* to *Hester,* "who knoweth, whether you are come to the Kingdom for such a time?" Thus Your Majesty shall do that, which we are persuaded, shall be acceptable to God, honorable to your Majesty in all succeeding ages, profitable to his Church, which shall be thereby increased, comfortable to your Ministers, which shall be no more suspended, silenced, disgraced, imprisoned for men's traditions: and prejudicial to none, but those that seek their own quiet,

340

credit, and profit in the world. Thus, with all dutiful submission, referring ourselves to your Majesty's pleasure, for your gracious answer, as God shall direct you: we most humbly recommend Your Highness to the Divine Majesty; whom we beseech for Christ his sake to dispose Your Royal heart to do herein, what shall be to his glory, the good of his Church, and your endless comfort.

> *Your Majesty's most humble Subjects,*
> *the Ministers of the Gospel, that desire*
> *not a disorderly innovation, but a due*
> *and godly Reformation.*

Glossary

Brief identifications and definitions are given for names and terms not identified or explained by their contexts in this collection. In general, classical and biblical allusions have been omitted, because they seldom require explanation and their inclusion here would make the Glossary unwieldy. Some well-known religious and political figures have been included to make their dates immediately available.

ABBOTT, GEORGE (1562–1633). Archbishop of Canterbury from 1611; was considered too radical by the church hierarchy and lost authority after 1627.

ABBOTT, ROBERT (1560–1617). Elder brother of Archbishop George Abbott; bishop of Salisbury; anti-Arminian; engaged in controversy with Nicholas Sanders and Robert Bellarmine.

ACEPHALI. Egyptian sect (*ca.* 500); believed in the single nature of Christ, in opposition to the belief in two natures (human and divine).

ADAMITES. Early Christian group advocating a life of innocence similar to that of Adam before the Fall and including the practice of nudity; name and ideas were assumed by some separatist groups in the sixteenth and seventeenth centuries.

ADRIAN (or HADRIAN) I (d. 795). Pope from 772; friend of Charlemagne; interested in liturgy; supported and defined the use of images.

ADRIAN (or HADRIAN) IV (*ca.* 1100–1159). Pope from 1154; English ecclesiastic, born Nicholas Breakspear; in conflict with Frederick I (Barbarossa).

ADRIANUS, AELIUS (76–138). Roman emperor, better known as Hadrian; persecuted Christians.

343

AEMILIUS, PAULUS. PAOLO EMILI (d. 1529). Wrote a history of France: *De Rebus Gestis Francorum* (Paris, 1530).

AENEAS SILVIUS DE PICCOLOMINI (1405–1464). Poet, humanist, diplomat; became Pope Pius II in 1458.

AERIANS. Fourth-century sect, named for Aerius, a presbyter in Pontus known for his objections to praying for the dead.

ALEXANDER III (*ca.* 1100–1181). Pope from 1159; legal scholar; in conflict with Frederick I (Barbarossa); tried to suppress the Albigenses (or Cathari).

ALLEN, WILLIAM (1532–1594). Cardinal; one of the founders of the English Jesuit seminary at Douai, where he lectured on theology.

ALLIGANT. Variant of *Alicante,* a Spanish wine.

ALMAIN, JACQUES (*ca.* 1480–1515). French theologian; argued that the authority of church councils was superior to that of the pope.

AMBROSE (*ca.* 339–97). Bishop of Milan; influenced Augustine; asserted ecclesiastical authority over secular; refused communion to Emperor Theodosius.

AMES, WILLIAM (1576–1633). Calvinist theologian and militant reformer; was educated in England but lived on the continent during most of his active career.

ANABAPTISTS. Opponents of infant baptism; became politically active in Germany and the Netherlands in the sixteenth century.

ANDREWS, LANCELOT (1555–1626). Preeminent biblical scholar and Anglican preacher; noted prose stylist; leader of one group of King James Bible translators; holder of several ecclesiastical offices, notably dean of Westminster and bishop of Winchester; Anglican preacher.

ANTHROPOMORPHISM. A name that could designate anyone who tends to conceive of the deity in human terms, including attributing to God human senses and action.

APOSTOLICS. A name that could be applied to any Christian group or sect that claimed for its practices direct descent from the Apostles and that rejected the teaching of postapostolic theologians.

ARATUS (*ca.* 315–*ca.* 245 B.C.). Greek poet and physician, one of whose poems was quoted by Paul in Acts and was held to justify the use of pagan learning in sermons; *see also* EPIMENIDES and MENANDER.

ARIANISM. Antitrinitarian belief, early condemned as heresy; held that the Son is subordinate to the Father; name derived from its exponent, Arius (*ca.* 250–*ca.* 336).

ARMINIANS. Followers of Arminius, or Jacob Hermans (1560–1609), a

Dutch theologian; opposed Calvinistic determinism and asserted human free will.

ARNULPHUS. ARNULF (*ca.* 850–899). King of Germany and Holy Roman Emperor from 887.

ARUNDEL. PHILIP HOWARD (1557–1595). First earl of Arundel; son of Thomas Howard, third duke of Norfolk; Roman Catholic imprisoned for religious activities; died in the Tower of London.

ATHACIUS (or ITHACIUS) (fl. 381–388). Spanish bishop who opposed reforms of Priscillian; was deposed after 388.

ATHANASIUS (*ca.* 297–373). Theologian, staunch opponent of Arians; helped establish New Testament canon; was credited with the Athanasian Creed, which he publicized.

AUGUSTINE. AURELIUS AUGUSTINUS (354–430). Most famous of the church fathers; bishop of Hippo; was an opponent of the Pelagians and the Manicheans in controversy.

AVAL. An endorsement by an official on a bill, note, or writ.

AVISOES. Formal notifications or formal advisory statements.

AYLMER, JOHN (1521–1594). Marian exile; became bishop of London in 1576; conservative Anglican.

BAGSHAW, EDWARD (*ca.* 1586–1662). Writer on religious questions; was antiepiscopal during much of his life, but became a staunch royalist in the civil war and was imprisoned briefly.

BALDUS. BALDO DEGLI UBALDI (*ca.* 1320–1400). Italian legal scholar; taught at Perugia, Pisa, Florence, and Padua; was consulted by Pope Urban VI on legal matters; also known as Angelo Baldeschi.

BANCROFT, RICHARD (1544–1610). Bishop of London in 1597; archbishop of Canterbury from 1604; conservative Anglican.

BARNAUD, NICOLAS (*ca.* 1538–*ca.* 1607). French Calvinist; wrote on religious topics and on occult knowledge.

BAXTER, RICHARD (1615–1691). Clergyman; served as military chaplain for the parliamentary forces in the civil war; leader of dissenters after the Restoration and noted religious writer.

BEAME. Bohemia.

BEGHARDES. Heretical Christian sect, originating in the eleventh century; believed in communal living; visionaries who rejected the orthodox doctrine of grace and established moral law.

BEGOUTH. Began.

BEGUINES. Women's religious group, active in the Netherlands in the twelfth and thirteenth centuries; charitable; had mystical tendencies.

BELLARMINE, ROBERT (1542–1621). Cardinal; theologian and leading controversialist of the Counter-Reformation.

BÉNÉVENT, JÉRÔME DE (fl. 1611). French writer; wrote a laudatory chronicle of the actions of Henry IV of France.

BENVENUTO IMOLENSIS. BENVENUTO DA IMOLA (*ca.* 1336–1390). Italian scholar and political figure; ambassador to the papal court; chiefly known as a commentator on the works of Dante; also wrote a history of Rome.

BERNARD OF CLAIRVAUX (1091–1153). Theologian; established strict monastic discipline; supported the Crusades; wrote also on the relationship between the power of the pope and the emperor.

BERNARDUS DE LOGUES (BERTRAND DE LOQUE). FRANÇOIS DE SAILLANS (fl. 1577). Author of *Traité de l'Eglise* (Geneva, 1577).

BEZA, THEODORE (1519–1605). Swiss protestant theologian; Calvin's successor in Geneva.

BILSON, THOMAS (1547–1616). Bishop of Winchester; biblical translator.

BOND, NICHOLAS (1540–1608). Chaplain to the queen; later, president of Magdalen College and vice-chancellor of Oxford University.

BONNER, EDMUND (*ca.* 1500–1569). Bishop of London and enforcer of conformity under Queen Mary.

BOUCHER, JEAN (*ca.* 1548–1605). French theologian; opponent of Henry IV, the king of France.

BRIDGES, JOHN (*ca.* 1540–1618). Dean of Sarum; wrote a learned defense of the Anglican establishment.

BRISTOW, RICHARD (1538–1581). Roman Catholic apologist; taught at Douai.

BROOK. See GREVILLE, ROBERT.

BROWNE, ROBERT (*ca.* 1550–1633). Separatist; early congregationalist.

BROWNISTS. Followers of Robert Browne.

BRUTUS CELTA, STEPHANUS JUNIUS. Pseudonym used by HUBERT LANGUET.

BUCANUS, GULIELMUS. GUILLAUME DU BUC (*ca.* 1550–*ca.* 1603). Calvinistic theologian.

BUCER, MARTIN (1491–1551). Reformer; controversialist; was held in high esteem in England in the 1540s; professor of divinity at Cambridge (1549–1551).

BUCHANAN, GEORGE (1506–1582). Scottish humanist, historian, and neo-Latin writer; tutor to James I.

BUCKINGHAM. GEORGE VILLIERS, FIRST DUKE OF BUCKINGHAM (1592–1628). Favorite of James I; adviser to Charles I.

BULLINGHAM, JOHN (*ca.* 1530–1598). Bishop of Gloucester (1581–1598); conservative Anglican.

BURTON, HENRY (1578–1648). Militant reformer; wrote against Laud; was several times imprisoned for writing antiepiscopal tracts; was freed in 1640.

CALVIN, JOHN (1509–1564). Reformer at Geneva; perhaps the most influential protestant theologian.

CAMERARIUS, JOACHIM (1500–1574). German philologist, humanist, and scholar; discussed the reunion of the Lutheran and Roman Catholic churches.

CAMPION, EDMUND (1540–1581). Jesuit priest and martyr; preached privately in London (1580–1581).

CARDILL. Possibly GASPAR CARDELLO DE VILLALPENDO (1527–1581). Wrote commentaries on Aristotle and an apology for the Council of Trent.

CARERIUS, ALEXANDER (fl. 1599). Theologian; argued for temporal power of the papacy; opponent of Robert Bellarmine in the Counter-Reformation controversies.

CARIER, BENJAMIN (1566–1614). English clergyman, for a time chaplain to James I; converted to Roman Catholicism in 1613; wrote against the Anglican church.

CAROLUS CRASSUS. CHARLES LE GROS, or CHARLES THE FAT (839–888). King of France (884–887) and Holy Roman Emperor (881–887).

CARPOCRATIONS. Followers of Carpocrates, a Christian gnostic of Alexandria in the second century; believed that Christians could achieve a higher spiritual condition than did Christ himself.

CARTWRIGHT, THOMAS (1535–1603). Professor of divinity at Cambridge; advocated reform of the Anglican church.

CASSANDRIAN. *See* SPRINT, JOHN (d. 1623).

CASSENDER, GEORG (*ca.* 1513–1566). Flemish theologian who tried to reconcile opposing sides in disputes of the Reformation.

CATAPHRYGES. Another name for Montanists; also called Phrygians and Pepuzians.

CATHARI (or CATHAROI). Name applied to Novations (third century) but most often to Albigenses (eleventh century), a rigidly ascetic group.

CATOBABDITES. Another name for the Acephali.

CERINTHIANS. Followers of Cerinthus, of apostolic times; chiliasts; required circumcision.

CHADERTON, LAURENCE (*ca.* 1538–1640). Clergyman; friendly with nonconformists as master of Emmanuel College, Cambridge; biblical translator.

CHAMEIRUS. *See* CAMERARIUS, JOACHIM.

CHARLES THE BALD (823–877). King of France (840–877); Holy Roman Emperor (875–877).

CHARLES I (1600–1649). King of England from 1625; waged war against Parliament in defense of royal supremacy; was imprisoned, tried, and beheaded.

CHARLES THE GREAT. CHARLEMAGNE (742–814). King of the Franks from 768; emperor of the West from 800.

CHILDERICK. CHILDERIC III (d. 751). King of France (741–751); deposed by Pépin the Short.

CHRYSOSTOM, JOHN (*ca.* 345–407). Patriarch of Constantinople (398–404); fluent writer and eloquent speaker.

CIRCUITORES. Apparently another name for Circumcelliones.

CIRCUMCELLIONES. Militant Donatist sect, fourth and fifth centuries; name means "surrounders of dwellings" and refers to their attacks on opponents.

CLEAVER, ROBERT (b. *ca.* 1562). Religious writer; collaborated with John Dod on an extremely popular commentary on the Ten Commandments.

CLÉMENT VIII (1536–1605). Pope from 1592; wanted to restore the Roman Empire.

CLÉMENT THE FRIAR. JACQUES CLÉMENT (1565–1589). Dominican friar; stabbed and killed Henry III of France during an audience because of dissatisfaction with the king's lenient policy toward protestants; was killed by royal attendants.

CONSTANTINE THE GREAT (280–337). Roman emperor; converted to Christianity; aided its spread throughout the empire.

COOPER, THOMAS (*ca.* 1517–1594). Bishop of Lincoln in 1570; bishop of Winchester from 1584.

COPCOT, JOHN(*ca.* 1548–1590). Doctor of divinity; Cambridge scholar; chaplain to Archbishop John Whitgift.

COPPINGER, EDMUND (d. 1592). Supporter of William Hacket, a religious fanatic.

COSIN, RICHARD (*ca.* 1549–1597). Holder of many ecclesiastical offices, including those of dean of Arches and vicar general of the province of Canterbury.

COTTON, JOHN (1584–1652). Congregationalist who refused to conform; emigrated to New England.

CROOK (or CROKE), GEORGE (1560–1642). Judge and author of legal works; was antiepiscopal in his personal and legal opinions; was knighted.

CULPEPPER, MARTIN (*ca.* 1544–*ca.* 1599). Warden of New College, Oxford (1573–1599); vice-chancellor of Oxford, 1578.

CYPRIAN (*ca.* 200–258). Bishop of Carthage from 248; Christian martyr and influential religious thinker.

CYRIL OF ALEXANDRIA (376–444). Archbishop of Alexandria from 412; theologian and biblical scholar; defender of orthodoxy against the Novations; opponent of Jerome in religious controversy.

DANAEUS, LAMBERTUS. LAMBERT DANEAU (1530–1596). French Calvinist preacher.

DAVENPORT, CHRISTOPHER (1598–1680). English Catholic chaplain to Queen Henrietta Maria; friend of Laud; tried to reconcile the Church of England with the Roman Catholic church.

DAY, JOHN (b. *ca.* 1539). Doctor of canon law; vicar general of Bath and Wells.

DE JUSTA HENRY TERTII ABDICATIONE (1589). Antimonarchical protestant work; probably written by Jean Boucher.

DENT, ARTHUR (d. 1607). Religious writer whose devotional work *The Plaine Man's Pathway to Heaven* (1601) was frequently reprinted.

DOCETISM. An early Christian heresy that held that Christ's body was human in appearance only.

DOD, JOHN (*ca.* 1549–1645). Nonconformist whose commentary on the Ten Commandments, written in collaboration with Robert Cleaver, was published in 1604 and was frequently reprinted.

DOLEMAN, NICHOLAS. ROBERT PARSONS (1546–1610). Jesuit missionary to England and writer of controversial works.

DONATISTS. African separatists; named for Donatus, a religious leader in Carthage in the early fourth century; held ascetic beliefs.

DOWNE, BISHOP OF. HENRY LESLIE (1580–1661). Bishop of Downe in Ireland; strong supporter of Laud's ecclesiastical program.

DOWNHAM, GEORGE (d. 1634). Bishop of Derry; strict Calvinist; wrote against Robert Bellarmine.

DOWNHAM, JOHN (d. 1652). Devotional writer; nonconformist.

DRYDEN, ERASMUS (1553–1632). Baronet; sheriff in Northamptonshire; protector of nonconformist ministers.

EBIONITES. Early Jewish Christians; combined Judaic and Christian beliefs; also called Nazarenes.

EDWARD I (1239–1307). King of England from 1272; defied the authority of the pope in secular matters.

ELIZABETH, QUEEN OF BOHEMIA (1596–1662). Daughter of King James I of England; married Frederick V, elector of the Palatinate; very popular with English poets.

ELYOT, THOMAS (*ca.* 1490–1546). Diplomat; translator of Greek works on statecraft; author of the influential *Boke Called the Governour* (1531); was knighted.

ENTHUSIASTS. A name applied to many Christian movements and sects, including some Anabaptists, who claimed direct influence of the Holy Spirit on their thoughts and actions.

EPHORI. Literally, "overseers"; magistrates in Sparta and elsewhere who supervised the actions of kings.

EPIMENIDES (seventh century B.C.). Greek philosopher cited by Paul; *see* ARATUS.

EPIPHANIUS (*ca.* 315–403). Bishop of Salamis; defender of orthodox belief.

ESTIENNE, ROBERT (1503–1559). Noted French printer of classics and the Bible who established verse divisions in the Bible; became protestant and moved to Geneva in 1552.

ESTIENNE, ROBERT (1530–1570). French printer, son of Robert Estienne (1503–1559), remained Roman Catholic and a royal printer after his father moved to Geneva.

EUSEBIUS OF CAESAREA (*ca.* 265–*ca.* 339). Also known as EUSEBIUS PAMPHILI; bishop; defender of orthodoxy; best known for his *Ecclesiastical History* (*ca.* 325).

EUSEBIUS PHYLADELPHUS. Pseudonymous author of anticlerical works; identified variously as NICHOLAS BARNAUD, as THEODORE BEZA, and as FRANÇOIS HOTMAN (FRANCISCUS HOTTOMANUS).

FAMILY OF LOVE. Sect following the teaching of Henry Nicholas (*ca.* 1502–*ca.* 1580), a religious figure in the Netherlands; mystical; rejected many traditional rules of conduct, notably in approving communal marital relations; was active in England, in the late sixteenth and early seventeenth centuries.

FAREL, GUILLAUME (1489–1565). French reformer; associate of Calvin.

Glossary

FAWKES, GUY (1570–1606). Leading conspirator in the Gunpowder Plot (1605).

FENNER, DUDLEY (*ca.* 1558–1587). Cambridge reformer and follower of Thomas Cartwright; was suspended by John Whitgift.

FEVARDENTIUS. FRANÇOIS FEUARDENT (1539–1610). French Franciscan controversial writer and preacher.

FICKLERUS. JOHANN BAPTIST FICKLER (1533–1610). Roman Catholic controversialist; wrote against Queen Elizabeth.

FLORINIANS. Sect of Carpocratians; were sometimes thought (probably erroneously) to be followers of Florinius (late second century A.D.), a Roman presbyter with heretical notions of the origins of evil.

FRANCO GALLIA (1573). Antimonarchical protestant work; probably by François Hotman (Franciscus Hottomanus); perhaps influenced by Theodore Beza.

FREDERICK BARBAROSSA. FREDERICK I (*ca.* 1123–1190). Holy Roman Emperor and king of Germany from 1152; king of Italy from 1155; died during the Third Crusade.

FULGENTIUS (*ca.* 550–*ca.* 620). Bishop of Ecija in Spain; brother of Isadore of Seville; writings of Fulgentius of Ruspe are sometimes mistakenly attributed to him.

FULGENTIUS OF RUSPE (468–533). Bishop of Ruspe in Africa (510–512, 523–532); opposed Pelagianism and Arianism.

FULGENTIUS PERRANDUS (sixth century). Served as deacon at Carthage; opposed Arianism; opposed Justinian.

FULKE, WILLIAM (1538–1589). Friend of Thomas Cartwright; wrote controversial works against Roman Catholics.

FULLER, THOMAS (1608–1661). Clergyman; popular preacher; historian; moderate royalist.

GARDINER, STEPHEN (*ca.* 1483–1555). Bishop of Winchester under Henry VIII; lord chancellor under Queen Mary.

GARNETT, HENRY (1555–1606). English Jesuit; was convicted of participating in the Gunpowder Plot.

GATAKER, THOMAS (1574–1654). Clergyman; moderate reformer; noted for scholarship.

GILBY, ANTHONY (*ca.* 1515–1585). Scholarly disciple of John Calvin; Marian exile; biblical translator.

GLOUCESTER. GODFREY GOODMAN (1583–1656). Bishop of Gloucester from 1625; was in favor with Laud.

GOODMAN, CHRISTOPHER (1520–1603). Marian exile; friend of John Knox; opponent of the Anglican establishment.

GOODMAN, GABRIEL (*ca.* 1529–1601). Dean of Westminster from 1561; strict conformist.

GOULART, SIMON (1543–1628). French protestant clergyman; author of many religious works.

GRACCHUS. Family name of a number of Roman statesmen who held high offices, including those of consul and tribune, between 238 and 122 B.C.

GREENE, JOHN (fl. 1639–1646). A felt maker (hat maker); preached to a congregation in London.

GREGORY THE GREAT (*ca.* 540–604). Became Pope Gregory I in 590; theologian, biblical scholar, influential writer; promoted Christian missionary activity, notably in England.

GREGORY VII (*ca.* 1020–1085). Pope who excommunicated the Holy Roman Emperor Henry IV.

GREVILLE, ROBERT, SECOND BARON BROOK (1608–1643). Political leader and parliamentary general.

GRINDAL, EDMUND (1519–1583). Marian exile; archbishop of Canterbury from 1576, but in disgrace with the government after 1577 for reformist views.

GROLL. According to the *Oxford English Dictionary,* "a foolish or superficial person"; a term frequently used by John Bastwick.

HACKET, WILLIAM (d. 1591). Religious fanatic; looked for a new messiah; proposed to overthrow the monarchy.

HADINGTON. JOHN RAMSAY, VISCOUNT HADINGTON AND EARL OF HOLDERNESS (*ca.* 1580–1626). Officially declared to have saved the life of James VI of Scotland; remained in high favor with the king; patron of David Owen.

HAKEWILL, GEORGE (1578–1649). Preacher; controversialist; for a time was chaplain to Charles I, but later was banished from the court for radical views.

HALL, JOSEPH (1574–1656). Religious controversialist and writer of essays and poems; bishop of Exeter (1627–1641) and Norwich (1641–1647); friend of both Laud and some nonconformists.

HARDING, THOMAS (1516–1572). Chaplain to Edward VI; later became Roman Catholic; left England; wrote against the Anglican establishment.

HARKWIT. *See* HAKEWILL, GEORGE.

HASTINGS, FRANCIS (d. 1610). Member of Parliament; supported nonconformists; was knighted.

HENRY IV (1050–1106). Holy Roman Emperor from 1056; was excommunicated by Pope Gregory VII.

HENRY IV (1553–1610). King of Navarre (1572–1589) and king of France from 1589; converted from protestantism to Roman Catholicism when crowned king of France; was assassinated by François Ravaillac.

HENRY FREDERICK, PRINCE OF WALES (1594–1612). Eldest son of James I of England; was admired universally for his piety and his respect for learning and the arts.

HENRY III (1551–1589). King of France during the religious wars; agreed to a truce favorable to the Huguenots, but later disavowed it under political pressure.

HERMANUS. HERMAN OF METZ (*ca.* 1030–1090). Supported Pope Gregory VII in his disputes with Emperor Henry IV.

HERMANUS RENECHERUS. HERMAN OF REICHENAU (1013–1054). Also known as HERMANUS CONTRACTUS or HERMAN THE LAME; monk, scholar, historian.

HEYLYN, PETER (1600–1662). Theologian, historian, controversialist; supported the Anglican establishment.

HIERON, SAMUEL (*ca.* 1576–1617). Popular preacher; conformed to the Church of England but opposed some ceremonies.

HILDERSHAM (or HILDERSAM), ARTHUR (1563–1632). Clergyman and religious writer; was frequently suspended for failure to conform.

HOCUS POCUS. A trickster or magician.

HOOKER, RICHARD (*ca.* 1553–1600). Clergyman and theologian; noted prose stylist; wrote *The Laws of Ecclesiastical Polity,* a classic defense of the Church of England.

HOTTOMANUS, FRANCISCUS. FRANÇOIS HOTMAN (1524–1590). Wrote a history of France; criticized usurpations of thrones.

HOW, SAMUEL (d. *ca.* 1640). Cobbler by trade; established a separatist congregation; wrote the popular work *The Sufficiency of the Spirit's Teaching Without Humane Learning;* died in prison.

HOWARD, FRANCES (*ca.* 1573–1632). Countess of Essex as wife of Robert Devereux from 1590; became countess of Somerset in 1613 by marrying Robert Carr; was found guilty of murder in a plot against Thomas Overbury; was condemned to death but was promptly pardoned.

HOWARD, HENRY (1540–1614). Earl of Northampton; Roman Catholic; was noted for learning.

HUGUENOTS. French protestants; after 1562, opposed the French monarchy and sought both political and religious autonomy; were centered at La Rochelle.

HUTTON, RICHARD (*ca.* 1561–1639). Judge and legal scholar; was disliked by strict conformists; was knighted.

ISIDORE OF SEVILLE (*ca.* 560–636). Bishop of Seville *ca.* 600; theologian; learned scholar in many disciplines; compiled an influential encyclopedia of learning.

JEROME (*ca.* 345–*ca.* 419). Biblical scholar and religious controversialist; was best known for his translation of the Bible into Latin, the Vulgate.

JOHANNES DE PARISIIS. JOHN QUIDORT OF PARIS (*ca.* 1240–1306). Dominican theologian; wrote on the relationship of papal to civil power.

JOHN OF FULHAM. *See* Aylmer, John.

JOHN OF GLOUCESTER. *See* BULLINGHAM, JOHN.

JOSEPHUS FLAVIUS (37–*ca.* 100). Jewish scholar; wrote a history of the Jews; served as a Roman official.

JOVINIAN (d. *ca.* 405). Opponent of Jerome; wrote in favor of marriage; believed that the truly baptized cannot sin.

JULIANUS AFRICANUS (d. 552). Bishop; had unique views of the canonicity of various books of the Bible.

JUNIANUS (fl. 411). Donatist bishop in Numidia.

JUNIUS, FRANCISCUS. FRANÇOIS DU JON (1545–1602). Protestant theologian; studied in Geneva; wrote against Robert Bellarmine; tried to reconcile contending protestant groups.

JUSTIN MARTYR (*ca.* 110–*ca.* 165). Early Christian philosopher; wrote in defense of the Christian faith; early Christian martyr.

JUSTINIAN. JUSTINIAN I (483–565). Byzantine emperor (527–565); was noted as a statesman; expanded the empire; codified laws.

KATHERINE, DUCHESS OF BUCKINGHAM. KATHERINE MANNERS (d. 1649). Converted from Roman Catholicism to the Church of England to marry George Villiers, first duke of Buckingham and royal favorite under James I and Charles I, in 1620; was widowed in 1628 and remarried in 1635.

KENNOLD. JOHN KENNALL (*ca.* 1522–1592). Held ecclesiastical offices at Oxford, Rochester, and Exeter at various times.

KNOX, JOHN (1505–1572). Scottish religious reformer and political leader; Calvinist; established presbyterian church discipline in Scotland.

LAERTIUS. DIOGENES LAERTIUS (third century). Author of lives of Greek philosophers; interpreted and classified various schools of philosophy.

LAKE, ARTHUR (1569–1626). Theologian; bishop of Bath and Wells from 1616; noted for piety and for preaching; strict disciplinarian and staunch royalist.

LANGUET, HUBERT (1518–1581). French protestant humanistic scholar; corresponded with Sir Philip Sidney.

LAUD, WILLIAM (1573–1645). Theologian; held several bishoprics; enforced strict conformity as archbishop of Canterbury from 1633; was imprisoned in 1641 and was beheaded in 1645.

LESBIAN RULE. A regulation easily interpreted to permit whatever the interpreter desires to do.

LEVELLERS. A republican group appearing in the parliamentary army in 1647; opposed monarchy and later Cromwell's authoritarian rule; sought equality of all before the law; had John Lilburne (*ca.* 1614–1657) as the leading spokesman.

LEY, JOHN (1583–1662). Clergyman and religious writer; was considered by some to be the author of *A Discourse Concerning Puritans,* now generally attributed to Henry Parker.

LICHFIELD. *See* OVERTON, WILLIAM.

LONDON, BISHOP OF. *See* AYLMER, JOHN.

LOTHARIUS. LOTHAIRE (795–855). Holy Roman Emperor from 840.

LUDOVICUS PIUS. LOUIS THE PIOUS (778–840). King of France and Germany and emperor of the West from 814.

LUDOVICUS QUARTUS. LOUIS IV (*ca.* 921–954). King of France from 936.

LUDOVICUS SECUNDUS. LOUIS II (846–879). Called "le Bègue" or "the Stammerer"; king of France from 877.

LUDOVICUS TERTIUS. LOUIS III (863–882). King of France from 879.

LUTHER, MARTIN (1483–1546). Friar, scholar, religious reformer; professor of biblical studies at Wittenberg; launched the protestant reformation in 1517.

MACHIAVELLI, NICOLO (1469–1527). Florentine diplomat and political writer; author of *Il Principe,* a work frequently criticized during the Renaissance for advocating sacrifice of morality in government to political expedience.

MALVEZZI, VIRGILIO, MARQUIS DE (1595–1653). Italian scholar; wrote historical and political works, among others.

MANWARING, ROGER (1590–1653). Chaplain to Charles I; bishop of Saint David's; strong supporter of royal authority.

MARIANA, JOHANNES. JUAN DE MARIANA (1536–*ca.* 1623). Spanish Jesuit; wrote a history of Spain; apologist for regicide.

MARSILIUS PATAVINUS. MARSILIUS OF PADUA (*ca.* 1275–1342). Advocated the subjection of church to civil control; influenced Thomas Cranmer, a leading English Reformation theologian and writer in the 1540s.

MARTA, GIACOMO (or JACOPO) ANTONIO (*ca.* 1559–1628). Italian jurist and philosopher; taught at Naples, Rome, and Pavia; wrote on ecclesiastical and secular jurisdiction.

MARTIN, ANTHONY (d. 1597). Advocated the reconciliation of factions in the Church of England; wrote pleas for resistance against foreign invasion.

MARTIN, GREGORY (d. 1582). Roman Catholic scholar at Douai and Reims: biblical translator.

MARY I (1516–1558). Daughter of Henry VIII; queen of England from 1553; Roman Catholic; attempted a counterreformation of the English church.

MELVILLE, ANDREW (1545–1622). Scottish theologian, linguist, university scholar; knew Theodore Beza and Peter Ramus; helped organize a Scottish church on the presbyterian model.

MENANDER (*ca.* 343–*ca.* 291 B.C.) Greek author of comedies; cited by Paul; *see also* ARATUS.

MENTZ. Probably MAXIMILLIAN I (1573–1651). Duke of Bavaria from 1597; defeated Elector Frederick V in 1620.

MESSALIANS. Fourth-century Syrian mystical sect; believed they could achieve moral perfection.

MIDDLETON, MARMADUKE (d. 1593). Became bishop of Saint David's in 1582; very unpopular with reformers; was rumored to have two wives; was deprived of his see for misuse of church property.

MINUCIUS FUNDANUS (*ca.* 100). Proconsul of Asia under Hadrian; showed tolerance toward Christians.

MOMUS. God of ridicule and jests in Greek mythology.

MONTANISTS. Followers of Montanus, second century A.D.; had a special strict discipline and believed in direct revelations from the Holy Spirit; early on were declared heretical, but survived until the ninth century; also called Phrygians and Pepuzians.

MONTENSES. Donatist community in Rome, fourth century A.D.; derived their name from their meeting place, a mountain outside the city.

MORE, THOMAS (1478–1535). Roman Catholic scholar, statesman, writer; lord chancellor of England (1529–1532); was beheaded for refusing to deny papal authority in religion; was respected for learning by most factions; was knighted.

MORNAY, PHILIPPE DE (1549–1623). Titled Seigneur du Plessis; French protestant scholar, soldier, diplomat in the service of Henry IV; spiritual leader of the Huguenots.

MORTON, JOHN (ca. 1420–1500). Archbishop of Canterbury from 1486 and cardinal from 1493; provided the information for Thomas More's biography of Richard III.

MORTON, NICHOLAS (ca. 1525–ca. 1590). Theologian; Roman Catholic agent in England; was involved in a rebellion against Elizabeth.

MOULIN, PIERRE DU (1568–1658). Also wrote as PETER DU MOULIN and PETRUS MOLINAEUS; French Calvinist theologian; resided for a time in England to escape persecution; wrote in defense of James I and against Robert Bellarmine.

MUSCULUS, ANDREAS (1514–1581). Lutheran theologian; one of the authors of *Formula Concordiae* (1557), a formulation of Lutheran beliefs; anti-Calvinist.

MUSCULUS, WOLFGANG (1497–1563). German Lutheran theologian and biblical scholar; wrote against the supremacy of the civil magistrate; wrote *The Temporisour,* against timeservers, in Latin in 1550 (a work translated into French, translated from French into English, and published in English in 1555 and 1584).

NAZARENES. Jewish Christians of the first five centuries A.D.; kept Jewish law but accepted Christ as the Messiah; also known as Ebionites.

NAZIANZEN. GREGORY OF NAZIANZUS (ca. 330–ca. 390). Prominent theological writer of the Eastern Christian church.

NEAL, DANIEL (1678–1743). English clergyman known for his *History of the Puritans; or, Protestant Nonconformists* (1732–1738).

NICHOLLS, AUGUSTINE (1559–1616). Judge renowned for moral and fiscal probity; prosecuted Roman Catholics; patron of Robert Bolton; was knighted.

NORTHAMPTON. *See* HOWARD, HENRY.

NOVATION OF ROME (fl. 250). Leader of a party within the church; held to a very strict discipline.

NOVATUS (third century). Presbyter of Carthage; supported Novation of Rome.

NOVOLISTS. Possibly Novellers, a term applied (according to the *Oxford English Dictionary*) during the early seventeenth century to innovators in religion.

ORLÉANS. Staunchly royalist city during the strife between the French monarchy and its protestant opponents.

OVERTON, WILLIAM (*ca.* 1525–1609). Bishop of Coventry and Lichfield; well educated, but called unlearned by Marprelate.

PALSGRAVE (or PALTZ). FREDERICK V (1596–1632). Elector of the Palatinate (1610–1623); married Elizabeth, the daughter of James I of England, in 1613.

PARKER, MATTHEW (1504–1575). Archbishop of Canterbury from 1559; moderate in doctrine; supervised the establishment of the Thirty-nine Articles in 1571 and the publication of the Bishops' Bible (1563–1568).

PARMENIAN (d. *ca.* 390). Donatist bishop, orator, and theologian.

PARSONS (or PERSONS), ROBERT (1546–1610). Jesuit missionary and forceful controversialist; was educated at Oxford.

PAULUS AEMILIUS (late fourth century). Bishop of Beneventum; supported John Chrysostom against the empress of Byzantium in the struggle to reform the discipline of the Eastern Catholic church.

PELAGIUS (*ca.* 360–*ca.* 420). Ascetic Christian moralist; was known for his belief that man could free himself from sinfulness.

PENRY, JOHN (1559–1593). Welsh Calvinist, one of the Marprelate group; was hanged for sedition.

PÉPIN THE SHORT (714–768). Father of Charlemagne; became king of France in 751, with Pope Zachary's blessing, by deposing Childeric III.

PEPUZIANS. Another name for the Montanists, derived from the town of Pepuza in Greece, which served as their headquarters.

PERKINS, WILLIAM (1558–1602). Noted theologian and Cambridge scholar; was held in high esteem by nonconformists.

PERNE, ANDREW (*ca.* 1519–1589). Doctor of divinity; dean of Ely in 1559; held preferments under Henry VIII, Edward VI, Mary, and Elizabeth; contributed to the Bishops' Bible.

PETROBRUSIANS. Followers of Peter de Bruys (early twelfth century), a religious leader in southern France; objected to prayers for the dead, infant baptism, sanctity of churches, and the use of images in worship.

PHILIP IV (1605–1665). King of Spain from 1621.

PIUS V (1504–1572). Pope from 1566; supported recommendations of the Council of Trent; advocated conformity; called for deposing Queen Elizabeth I; revised the Breviary and the Missal.

PORTUISE. Handbook of devotional readings; medieval breviary.

PRAEMUNIRE. An illegal action consisting of the obtaining of a decree from the pope against the king.

PRISCILLIAN (d. 385). Bishop of Avila in Spain; attempted reform of the church in Spain; was executed for heresy but later was vindicated.

PRYNNE, WILLIAM (1600–1669). Barrister; prolific writer; presbyterian, Calvinist, royalist; was imprisoned under both Charles I and Oliver Cromwell.

RAINOLDS, JOHN (1549–1607). Scholar; president of Corpus Christi College, Oxford; participant in the Hampton Court Conference; one of the King James Bible translators.

RAINOLDS, WILLIAM (1544–1594). Roman Catholic clergyman and controversialist; wrote of the problems of Christians under impious rulers.

RAMUS, PETER: PIERRE DE LA RAMÉE (1515–1572). French protestant philosopher; is known for his rejection of Aristotelian philosophy; devised a dialectic logic.

RAVAILLAC, FRANÇOIS (1578–1610). Roman Catholic religious fanatic and visionary, perhaps insane; assassinated Henry IV of France in 1610.

RISHTON, EDWARD (1550–1586). Roman Catholic clergyman; studied at Oxford and Douai; was banished from England in 1581.

ROBINSON, HENRY (fl. 1620). Knight and sheriff of Northamptonshire.

ROBINSON, JOHN (ca. 1576–1625). Clergyman, controversialist; left the Church of England and formed a congregation in Holland; planned the eventually successful migration to New England, but remained in Leiden.

ROCHEL. LA ROCHELLE. The leading city of the French protestants (Huguenots).

ROGERS, RICHARD (ca. 1550–1618). Nonconformist; opposed John Whitgift and supported Thomas Cartwright.

ROGERS, THOMAS (d. 1616). Chaplain to Richard Bancroft; wrote a two-volume exposition of the Thirty-nine Articles.

ROLLOCK, ROBERT (ca. 1555–1599). Professor of theology in Edinburgh; supported King James.

ROSS, ALEXANDER (1591–1654). Scottish clergyman and religious writer; served as one of the chaplains of Charles I.

ROSSAEUS. Pseudonym used by Thomas More in 1523 and by William Rainolds in 1592; *see* RAINOLDS, WILLIAM, and MORE, THOMAS.

RUFFINUS, TYRANNIUS (343–410). Presbyter and scholar; was a friend of Jerome, but broke with him by defending ideas of Origen.

SABBATARIANS. Christians who hold to a very strict, ascetic observance of the sabbath day, or Sunday.

SAINT DAVID'S IN WALES, BISHOP OF. *See* MIDDLETON, MARMADUKE.

SANCTA CLARA, FRANCISCUS A. Pseudonym of CHRISTOPHER DAVENPORT.

SANDERS (or SANDER), NICHOLAS (*ca.* 1530–1581). Roman Catholic controversialist and historian; taught at Louvain.

SAY. WILLIAM FIENNES, FIRST VISCOUNT SAY AND SELE (1582–1662). Courtier; in the Westminster Assembly; peacemaker in 1647; known as "Old Subtlety."

SCOTUS. JOHANNES SCOTUS DUNS (*ca.* 1265–1308). Scholastic philosopher, logician, and metaphysician; known as "Doctor Subtilis."

SENSYNE. Since then.

SERENIUS GRANIANUS (*ca.* 100). Imperial legate in Syria under Hadrian; sympathetic to Christians.

SIDONIUS. GAIUS SOLLIUS APOLLINARIS (*ca.* 430–*ca.* 487). Bishop of Clermont; Roman official; writer of letters and poems on religious and political topics.

SIMON MAGUS. Magician appearing in Acts, chapter 8, verses 9 through 24; also mentioned in postbiblical writings as a heretic; source of the word *simony.*

SMITH, HENRY (*ca.* 1550–1591). Preacher noted for eloquence; moderate nonconformist once suspended for failure to conform.

SOLYMAN (*ca.* 1496–1566). Turkish sultan, called "the Magnificent"; extended Turkish rule in the Balkans; respected for his abilities as a soldier, a statesman, and patron of arts and sciences.

SOME, ROBERT (1542–1609). Doctor of divinity; master of Peterhouse; wrote against Martin Marprelate.

SPARROW, ANTHONY (1612–1685). Anglican clergyman; royalist.

SPRINT, JOHN (*ca.* 1555–1590). Theologian; doctor of divinity; dean of Bristol from 1574.

SPRINT, JOHN (d. 1623). Son of Dr. John Sprint, dean of Bristol; conformed to the Anglican establishment; wrote under the name Cassander Anglicanus.

STEPHANUS. Pseudonym used by HUBERT LANGUET.

STEPHANUS, ROBERT. *See* ESTIENNE, ROBERT (1503–1559), and ESTIENNE, ROBERT (1530–1570).

STRAFFORD. THOMAS WENTWORTH, FIRST EARL OF STRAFFORD (1593–1641). Strong opponent of nonconformists in religion; became the chief advisor to Charles I; was indicted for treason by the parliamentary party and was executed.

STRAW, JACK (d. 1381). Peasant rebel; follower of Wat Tyler.

SUCKLING, JOHN (1609–1642). English poet, courtier, soldier; staunch royalist; known for dressing his company of soldiers in ornate uniforms.

SURPLICE. Ecclesiastical vestment; originally used in France and England in the eleventh century; use became controversial after the Reformation and almost a symbol of loyalty to the Anglican church under Archbishop Laud.

SUTCLIFFE, MATTHEW (*ca.* 1550–1629). Dean of Exeter from 1588; prominent in writing against the Roman Catholics.

SYNCLER, FRANCIS. Probably an Anglicization of FRANCISCUS A SANCTA CLARA, a pseudonym of CHRISTOPHER DAVENPORT.

TATIANS. Followers of Tatian, an early Syrian Christian (fl. 150–165); were known for asceticism and rejection of Hellenism.

TERTULLIAN. QUINTUS SEPTIMIUS FLORENS TERTULLIANUS (*ca.* 160–*ca.* 230). Church father; early theologian; became a Montanist.

THEODOSIUS I (*ca.* 346–395). Roman emperor; was baptized in 380; was censured by Ambrose for cruelty in a military action.

THOMAS AQUINAS (1225–1274). Dominican theologian; voluminous writer; tried to synthesize Christian theology in *Summa Theologiae* and other works.

THOMASON, GEORGE (d. 1666). London bookseller; amassed and dated a large collection of books and pamphlets published after 1640.

THORNBY. JOHN THORNBOROUGH (1551–1641). Became bishop of Limerick in 1593, of Bristol in 1603, and of Worcester in 1617.

THROCKMORTON (also THROKMORTON and THROGMORTON), JOB (1545–1601). Associate of John Penry; Marprelate author; was indicted for sedition but acquitted.

TOMBES, JOHN (*ca.* 1603–1676). Presbyterian in church government; generally moderate but ardent in opposition to infant baptism.

TRUNCHMAN. Variant of *truchman* (an interpreter).

TYLER, WAT (d. 1381). Leader of a peasant revolt in Kent.

VALENTINUS (early second century). Gnostic heretic; taught in Rome; very influential.

VINDICIAE CONTRA TYRANNOS (1580). Classic antimonarchical protestant work; is attributed most commonly to Hubert Languet; is also attributed to Philippe de Mornay, Theodore Beza, and François Hotman.

VIRETUS. PIERRE VIRET (1511–1571). Protestant reformer; friend and correspondent of John Calvin; renowned preacher.

WALDEGRAVE, ROBERT (1554–1604). Until 1588, London printer of antiepiscopal works; was briefly imprisoned; later was a printer in La Rochelle and from 1590 was the royal printer in Edinburgh.

WATTS, WILLIAM (1590–1649). Doctor of divinity; translated Augustine; chaplain to Prince Rupert.

WESTMINSTER. *See* GOODMAN, GABRIEL.

WHATELY, WILLIAM (1583–1639). Popular minister of Banbury; popular writer; moderate reformer.

WHITAKER, WILLIAM (1548–1595). Master of Saint John's, Cambridge; was noted for learning and tolerance of nonconformists.

WHITGIFT, JOHN (*ca.* 1530–1604). Archbishop of Canterbury after 1583; enforced conformity to Anglican ritual.

WHITTINGHAM, WILLIAM (1524–1579). Marian exile; staunch Calvinist; leading translator of the Geneva Bible.

ZACHARY (d. 752). Pope for ten years; approved Pépin's accession to the throne of France; was canonized.

Index

Index

Daly, Robert, 4*n*
Daneau, Lambert, 257, 259, 262, 267–68
Davenport, Christopher, 122, 157
Davies, Horton, 11
Defoe, Daniel, 7
Dent, Arthur, 115
Dering, Edward, 10*n*
Diogenes, 155
Dod, John, 166, 324, 328
Doleman, Nicholas, 259, 270
Donatists, 71, 110, 115–16, 225, 233, 241, 247, 250
Downe, Bishop of. *See* Leslie, Henry
Downham, George, 112
Dryden, Erasmus, 113
Du Jon, François, 257, 261–62, 289
Dusinberre, Juliet, 12

Earle, John, 207, 278–80
Ebion, 71
Ebionites, 71, 247, 249
Edward I, 256
Edward VI, 339–40
Elizabeth, Queen of Bohemia, 297
Elizabeth I, 7, 8, 14, 16, 34, 43, 64, 68–77, 231, 238, 239, 328
Elyot, Thomas, 51
Emerson, Everett, 14, 24–25
Enthusiasts, 247, 249
Ephori, 262, 265
Epimenides, 240
Epiphanius, 233, 249
Eusden, John Dykstra, 9, 9*n*
Eusebius of Caesarea, 116
Eusebius Phyladelphus (pseud.). *See* Barnaud, Nicholas
Exact Description of a Roundhead, An, 194–201, 203

Factious sermonists, 285, 291, 296
Family of Love, 13, 14, 18, 23, 138, 216, 219, 285–86, 292–93, 296, 332
Farel, Guillaume, 265, 295
Fawkes, Guy, 132
Felltham, Owen, 281–83
Fenner, Dudley, 230, 269
Feuardent, François, 259, 270
Fevardentius. *See* Feuardent, François
Fickler, Johann Baptist, 259, 270

Ficklerus. *See* Fickler, Johann Baptist
Field, John, 34
Fiennes, William. *See* Say, William Fiennes, First Viscount Say and Sele
Florinians, 247, 249
Frederick V, 98, 101–102
Frederick Barbarossa, 243–44
Fulgentius, 256
Fulham, John of. *See* Aylmer, John
Fulke, William, 34, 77
Fuller, Thomas, 22–23, 25, 27, 298, 337

Gardiner, Stephen, 62
Garnett, Henry, 132
Gataker, Thomas, 9*n*, 78
Gee, Henry, 16
George, Charles, 4–5, 4*n*, 8
George, Katherine, 4–5, 4*n*, 8
Geree, John, 117, 207–12
Gilby, Anthony, 230
Gloucester, John of. *See* Bullingham, John
Goodman, Christopher, 259, 266
Goodman, Gabriel, 43, 61, 230
Gouge, William, 9*n*
Goulart, Simon, 269
Gracchus, 134
Greaves, Richard L., 22*n*
Green, J. R., 4
Gregory VII, Pope, 260, 263
Gregory the Great, 256
Greville, Robert, Second Baron Brook, 127, 135, 166
Grigge, Elizabeth, 51
Grindal, Edmund, 8–9, 14, 24, 73, 290
Gunpowder Plot, 23, 255

Hacket, William, 155, 239
Hackwell, George. *See* Hakewill, George
Hadrian, Emperor, 170
Hakewill, George, 111, 116
Hall, Basil, 2, 4, 5, 6, 18, 24–25
Hall, Joseph, 78
Haller, William, 7
Hamilton, Alastair, 13
Harding, Thomas, 244, 259, 260
Hardy, William John, 16
Harkwit. *See* Hakewill, George
Harvey, Gabriel, 3
Hastings, Francis, 77

365

Index